Don
you still lead from
leading —
your Best!

—[illegible signature]

| Praise for *The Best in Us* |

"This is not a book you read once and take away a few key points and then fit in a few small changes as you continue on with your busy life. It's an owner's manual that should be consulted often, if for no other reason than to constantly remind you that you are a leader, not a passenger or a guest, that you have the power to drive your own life, inspire others, and find fulfillment in what you do each and every day."

—PHIL KUMNICK,
Head of Global Acquirer Processing, Visa, Inc.

"*The Best in Us* is a breakthrough book that shows leaders how to build companies by believing in themselves and their people . . . [It] claims that the greatest treasure within organizations is the potential within its people . . . People can be inspired to tap into their very best, and when this happens, magic happens. The paradox is that when people give their all, profits soar—beyond anyone's wildest dreams."

—RYAN C. MACK,
Financial Empowerment Advisor;
President, Optimum Capital Management;
Author, *Living in the Village;* TV Analyst—CNN, CNBC, BET

"*The Best in Us* is a creative and imaginative guide to a better understanding of the crucial potentials of leadership studies."

—JAMES MAC GREGOR BURNS,
Pulitzer–Prize-winning author of *Roosevelt: Soldier of Freedom, 1940–1945* and the seminal book, *Leadership*; Woodrow Wilson Professor of Government Emeritus, Williams College; Distinguished Leadership Scholar, James MacGregor Burns Academy of Leadership, University of Maryland

"If there is a grand unification theory for modern leadership, Cleve Stevens has just delivered it. In the four days it took me to read *The Best in Us* cover to cover I felt remade, rewired, renewed, and reinvigorated . . . A must read for entrepreneurs, founders, and corporate and community leaders."

—DR. SAFWAN SHAH,
University of California Berkeley, Haas School of Business;
Entrepreneur, Venture Finance Expert,
and Founder, Infonox, Inc.

"*The Best in Us* is a systematic and thoughtful approach toward a new model of leadership that has the power to make a fundamental change for both an individual leader and those they lead. Cleve skillfully combines history, mythology, psychology, current events, and modern leadership thinking to engage the reader in a process whereby they may re-consider their own leadership values."

—DR. ROBERT KOVACH,
Director, Cisco Center for Collaborative Leadership,
Cisco Systems, Inc.

"As a business and political entrepreneur, I believe in putting people first for best results. Dr. Cleve Stevens is up to something important for our common future." —JEFFREY B. PETERS,
Founder/President, The US-Mexican Development Corporation;
Co-Founder, We The People

THE BEST IN US

People, Profit, and the Remaking of Modern Leadership

Cleve W. Stevens, PhD

FIRST EDITION

Library of Congress Cataloging-in-Publication Data

Stevens, Cleve W.
The best in us : people, profit, and the remaking of modern leadership / Cleve W. Stevens.
p. cm.
Includes bibliographical references and index.
ISBN 978-0-8253-0684-6 (alk. paper)
1. Leadership. 2. Executive ability. I. Title.
HD57.7.S737 2012
658.4'092--dc23
2012002392

For inquiries about volume orders, please contact:
Beaufort Books
27 West 20th Street, Suite 1102
New York, NY 10011
sales@beaufortbooks.com

Published in the United States by Beaufort Books
www.beaufortbooks.com

Distributed by Midpoint Trade Books
www.midpointtrade.com

Printed in the United States of America

Interior design by Neuwirth & Associates, Inc.
Cover design by Michael Fusco Design

For La Verne Stevens, my intellectual and moral hero, as well as my mother. Her effortless beauty, her towering intellect, and her disarming sense of humor were exceeded only by her fearless, ever-present love—for her family, for life, and for "the least of these." It is her indomitable, loving spirit that informs every word on every page that follows.

And for Bill Stevens, my irrepressible, indefatigable, charismatic father. His enthusiasm for life, his love of laughter, and his passion for people (all people) have shaped my deepest understanding of what it means to live, to love, and to serve. Ultimately, though, it is his profound appreciation for excellence and his life-long drive to realize greatness, nothing less than the extraordinary, that is the very exemplar of the transformative approach to living and leading.

CONTENTS

A NOTE TO THE READER

Throughout this book I share cases of particular individuals (or groups of individuals) to illustrate my larger points. Except for Cox Arizona and Steve Rizley in chapter 22, regardless of the individuals' openness, I have modified some of the facts about their lives in order to protect their privacy. In some instances I changed only their names; in others I also changed their geographic locations and/or other circumstantial facts. My intention, among other things, is to shield them without detracting from the importance of their stories. Finally, in some cases I have employed a good deal of poetic license in order to create composites. That is, I have combined two or more people into one exemplar, primarily for the sake of clarity—to better illustrate an important point, and for the sake of brevity and narrative flow.

In every instance, the experience, the story pattern (often a virtually archetypal pattern), the understanding, the insight, the belief structure, and/or the results are true. They are a function of what has been reported to or shared with me, or they are a function of what I have observed or understood by virtue of firsthand experience. One of the gifts of engaging with the work of transformative leadership for more than two decades, interacting (in many instances at deeply personal levels) with thousands of people all over the globe, is that I have been afforded a vast pool of vivid, real experiences from which to better understand and explain the call and journey of transformation.

ACKNOWLEDGMENTS

This project has been nearly six years in the making and would not have been possible without the thoughtfulness of so many transformative thinkers along the way, people who by virtue of their deep understanding of the human experience have generously (and patiently) afforded me the personal development necessary for a book such as this. At the University of Southern California, colleagues and mentors like John B. Orr with his commitment to the "poor bastards" (all of us) and his pragmatic passion for transformative social leadership; John P. Crossley Jr. with his love for the English language, for the true and the good (and the occasional, well-placed irreverent joke); President Steven B. Sample, the very embodiment of intentional, results-based leadership; the ever-young Robert Turrill, true organizational thinker and ally; and surely Warren G. Bennis, the exemplar of humane, progressive leadership thought, who gave me the opportunity (as well as the support) to redesign and lead our successful two year "experiment" with the Presidential Fellows program—a graduate fellowship program in leadership, our transformative version of which proved to be the prototype for the transformative model in business. And though we met on only one occasion, I am deeply indebted to the transforming leadership thought, the intellectual and moral courage of James MacGregor Burns.

And there are so many others. Doug Perasso and Amelia Rosenberg, who over the course of nearly four years painstakingly trained me in the rationale and nuances of the transformational method in individual development. Don and Lee Hawthorne (my "second parents"), who helped me to see, among other things, the importance of taming the "wild stallion." Kenneth N. Siegel, an intelligent and elegant organizational consultant who introduced me to a smart framework for approaching the organization. My gifted, dedicated publicist, Mike Schwager, whose commitment to the transformative possibility and to this project knows no bounds—and which has paved the way for the book at nearly every turn. My savvy editor, Pam Suwinsky, whose truth telling (and sense of humor) in so many ways made the book possible. Eric Kampmann and Margot Atwell of Beaufort Books, who had the honesty and insight to acknowledge our precarious leadership and organizational predicament and the imagination to see how *The Best in Us* might indeed speak to that need. Kevin Moran, Ivan Johnson, John Kaites, and Bob Philbin—clients, friends, and fellow travelers who offered generous, insightful, honest feedback throughout the process. R. Fox Vernon, colleague, friend, and deep thinker, for reading the manuscript and offering thoughtful philosophical and psychological feedback. Patricia Lynn Reilly, colleague (accomplished writer, editor, and transformative leader) and dear friend who supported me and the project from the beginning. And above all Bill and LaVerne Stevens (my father and mother) and DeLayna Stevens (sister, friend, and most trusted counsel), the very models of steadfast, honest, inspired love: If there are moments in the book when wisdom, beauty, and goodness shine through, they are the ones to thank—it is their hand, their touch that you feel.

Finally, to all of you who have freely permitted my use of your stories, I owe the greatest debt of gratitude. And to all of you who have courageously taken up the call of transformation and in so doing have taught me its power and its promise, I say thank you—you have profoundly contributed to my own ever-unfolding transformation. More important, you represent the noble vanguard, the cutting edge who will lead humankind's next great evolutionary leap. I urge you to be true to your destiny. There is more at stake than we can possibly realize.

Compared to what we ought to be, we are half awake.

—William James

INTRODUCTION

THE MODERN MESS AND WHY IT CALLS FOR *THE BEST IN US*

As I write these words, the evening news is on a muted television across from me in my home. Flashing silently before me are violent images of dying children in the Sudan, wounded soldiers near Kabul, and finally a group of homeless men on the streets of Baltimore. At the same time, just to the left of the television, my balcony doors are opened onto a picture-perfect Southern California summer sunset—silhouetted palm trees against a pinkish-orange sky and the rhythmic sound of waves crashing in the background—now set side by side with these gruesome Middle Eastern images of death and destruction and images of unforgiving poverty in inner-city America. It's a tragic and horrifically real contrast, regardless of how *sur*real it may seem.

And it's a contrast that cries out for the practical proposition of transformation. Our old ways of thinking appear powerless before the seemingly implacable nightmares we face as a society: a worldwide economic meltdown and its painful, slow-burning "recovery," a disappearing middle class, the reality of potentially catastrophic climate change, old and new wars raging in the Middle East. Whether nightmares of our own making or not, they are nightmares nonetheless, *our* nightmares. And they demand a new and better way of understanding and thinking, of being and doing. Continuing to do what we have been doing is not working. Indeed, to continue in the same manner and expect a different and better outcome, as the saying goes, amounts to insanity. The ethic of integrative transformation would seem to raise its unassuming hand and say, "You just might want to consider me." This book represents that raised hand.

A NEED FOR RADICAL HONESTY

In the pages that follow I present a distinct, far-reaching approach to leadership called transforming integrative leadership, or simply *transformative leadership* (TL), as a response to this continuing "insanity." As I later make clear, the transformative leadership approach is distinct from and has emerged out of two previous traditions: transforming leadership and transformational leadership. (The terms "transforming leadership" and especially "transformational leadership" of late have been used a bit promiscuously—overused and surely *mis*applied—but properly understood refer to specific, well-considered schools of thought.) *Transformative leadership* builds upon and respectfully goes beyond them. It's an approach that requires a fundamental rethinking of how we understand leadership and the organization *and* how we live our lives. But to begin that rethinking process, and to do so from a TL perspective, we must first be willing to step into a state of mind that amounts to a radical kind of honesty.

The human capacity for denial is pervasive (we all do it), and though there are ways in which this tendency may serve us, denial of where we are as leaders of the social order is not one of them. It's a hard habit to break. But break it we must. We must become relentlessly honest with ourselves, honest as to how we are faring as individual leaders, as teams of leaders, as a whole culture of leaders. And we must be honest about what we are generating with this leadership in our organizations, because today more than ever before those organizations, business organizations in particular, make up the centerpiece of the larger organism that is society. That is, business, in effect, runs the world. Whether we like it or not, business is the single most influential institution in modern society. There are few serious social observers who would contest this fact. If we are to create a better world, therefore, we must create better business organizations and better business people. Period. And to do that we must begin by telling the truth.

Something Is Rotten Indeed

When Shakespeare's Hamlet recognizes the corruption in the Danish royal house, he is unapologetic in acknowledging it. "Something is rotten in the state of Denmark," he famously declares. The transformative leadership ethic demands that same degree of blunt honesty. What that unapologetic honesty reveals, however, is so disturbing that most of us would prefer not to consider it at all. It's that denial thing, and the denial seems to be the response of a good many of our political, organizational, and, certainly, financial leaders as they blithely ignore the continuing tragedy of the recent economic collapse—after all, if they get their bonuses, it can't be all that bad, now can it? Unfortunately, though, ignoring a danger doesn't make it go away. Reality is just not that forgiving. Gravity is gravity.

We must face up, and when we do, what we see is that much of our business dealings, our financial dealings in particular, have been corrupted,[1] and in some instances have become thoroughly rotten, so rotten that we cannot hope that a few meager reforms (reregulation) are going to rid us of that rot.[2]

Consider the once-venerable financial house of Goldman Sachs & Co., which chose to plead out to the tune of more than half a billion dollars rather than risk the possibility of being found guilty of the charges of civil fraud in a court of law.[3] After Goldman Sachs was charged by the SEC, MIT economist Simon Johnson said, "The current management of Goldman . . . have destroyed the value of an illustrious franchise. Goldman used to stand for something that customers felt they could trust; now it is just a sophisticated way of ripping them off."[4]

But the recent disturbing revelations of malfeasance are not the real problem, transformative leadership would argue. They are the symptom, the inevitable consequence of a wrongheaded understanding of what it means to lead an organization, particularly a business organization. This corruption, TL says, is the unavoidable result of the ascendant business and business leadership rationale, a mind-set that over the past forty to fifty years has become increasingly strident and self-assured, indeed certain that it is the *only* basis for business leadership. That rationale claims that *extrinsic rewards and results*—monetary rewards in particular—are the sole reason for the organization's existence, and the people are, de facto, merely the means to that end. It doesn't matter if that extrinsic result is profit, market share, new products, or even helping the have-nots of the world. (That an organization may be committed to doing good in the world does not mean that its leadership methods are necessarily enlightened; it doesn't mean that doing good within the organization is ever even considered.)

To put matters bluntly, when we begin to buy into an ethic that declares shareholder value as the only value, we have set ourselves on a course, as we are now seeing, that ultimately and inevitably leads to bust. From the transformative point of view, the issue is one of pragmatism—every bit as much an issue of what works and does not work as it is an issue of what is good, true, and right. And in that pragmatic light what is clear is that the profit principle as the exclusive rationale for doing business seems *not* to work, at least not anymore, surely not in the way we're applying it.

The angry protests across the political spectrum are clearly warranted. Most of us understand that the pain and suffering we've created demand a voice. But the simplistic explanations of the right (bloated government is to blame) and the left (the greed of Wall Street is to blame) miss the larger point.

And mainstream Western business just continues on in its denial of the simple, obvious fact that what we're doing ain't working. Because it is unable to imagine an alternative, it just keeps dancing, faster and faster, assuring us the music isn't going to stop. It wants to believe that what the world recently witnessed—the near-*total* collapse of the world financial system—and what we are still experiencing—a daunting, at best, path to recovery—is but the extreme end of the normal business cycle, greatly influenced by a few powerful "bad apples" and a healthy dose of "irrational exuberance." It wants to believe that with a few tweaks here, a few adjustments there, everything will be all right.

But most of us know better. In our heart of hearts we know that something is rotten with the royal house of Western business, and by extension something is wrong with how we think about leading the organization. Moreover, those who are students of history also know that there is nothing certain about the future of Western democracy and nothing guaranteed about Western capitalism. We are still engaged in what is best described as a political and economic experiment: democratic capitalism. The experiment has been remarkably successful but of late has revealed some weaknesses, some dangerous blind spots. These revelations demand that we step back and consider, really think, about what we are doing and why we are doing it. It demands that we honestly and openly consider the way in which democratic capitalism should and must look if it is to survive going forward.

Profits: The By-Product and Hallmark of Excellence

The considerable problems we face are not insoluble, not if we have enough integrity to face up to them, to honestly see what is happening right in front of us and why. Today, in the second decade of the twenty-first century, a seismic shift of global proportions is happening. It would seem we've reached an inflection point. Standing in that crucial place of decision we are presented with several options. One—we can avert our eyes, look away, and pretend that there is nothing wrong, just hoping for a sunnier tomorrow. Two—we can argue that all we need to do is more of the same but to do it better this time, to do it more "ethically" (more and better rules, perhaps?). Or, three—we can set our tendency for denial aside and honestly accept the fact that the world has changed; we can accept the fact that what may have worked in 1975 no longer applies in the second decade of the twenty-first century. In other words, like grown-ups, we can face up to what is.

In a recent speech at Mansion House in London, Stephen Green, then chairman of HSBC, one the world's largest financial institutions, put matters rather bluntly. In a direct challenge to the twentieth-century laissez-faire philosophy of Milton Friedman, he said, "*Of course* you need a profit, but it is a by-product, a hallmark of success. It is not the be all and end all. It is not the raison d'être of business." Then, flying directly in the face of Wall Street's most essential business imperative, he asked, "What is the purpose of business? Friedman says the social responsibility of business is to make a profit, but that will no longer do."[5] Indeed, as our economic malaise continues, the fact that this twentieth-century perspective will no longer do seems increasingly apparent. And keep in mind that these are not the words of some on-the-periphery, left-wing politician but those of a champion of free-market capitalism and now Britain's conservative minister of trade.

But still, the ordinary leader of little imagination resists: "Profit as a by-product? Are you kidding me?! And this, you say, is capitalism? Really?"

You bet, the transformative leader responds. It may in fact be capitalism at its very finest.

Even so, if you listen closely you can hear the gnashing of teeth, the wails and rants echoing through the canyons of Wall Street: "Sounds like socialism to me, by God. Sounds like the end of all that we love and hold dear, damn it. This could mean war!"

But these old boys are unwittingly seeing through a prism of irrational fear, one built in the 1970s and '80s—with all that those filters would infer from world affairs, including the Cold War and the looming threat to the West that the Soviet Union once represented.

What they fear is a false threat that clouds their more rational faculties. The simple truth is that the transformative model *loves* profit, but not as an end in and of itself. The TL approach loves profit in the manner that Britain's minister of trade has it, as a natural by-product of success, as a hallmark of excellence, and, in the TL world, as an irrefutable measure of how well we are leading, developing, and growing our people.

And here's the disarming part, the part that simply does not compute for the profit-as-the-singular-purpose-of-business mentality: The principle of profit-as-a-natural-by-product-of-excellence, indeed the principle that sees profit as a result of smartly growing our people, "out-profits" the profit principle. The mind-set that says profit is a by-product of pursuing something better, something richer, something higher, out-produces the mind-set that says business is primarily or exclusively for increasing shareholder value. When fully implemented, particularly in the transformative model, this business philosophy is a *better* creator of wealth than the pure profit principle. It is capitalism cubed, as it were.

This is the would-be preposterous proposition—it would be preposterous *if* it were not so, if it were not the empirical reality that it is. But it *is* so, and here it is: In the transformative model (1) the leader necessarily gets to feel good about himself, and (2) at the same time he is turning a tremendous profit.

First, he gets to feel good about who he is and what he is up to as a leader, because he is doing good, truly doing good every day of his leadership life. And remember, this does not mean that he is walking around passing out pizza and Coke with a goofy grin on his face; it means he is demanding, pushing, teaching, expecting ever-increasing achievement and providing, when needed, the swift kick in the butt—accountability goes up, not down, in this growth model. He understands that what he is getting done (growing his followers) is of significance, far greater significance than merely producing a profit. His leadership has a meaning and depth that would be impossible in an exclusively transactional, profit-principle model.

But the cool, perhaps unexpected, part is the second point of the empirical reality: Doing good goes hand in glove with making bank. As he does good he also *does well.* That is, he produces better financial returns on his leadership investment than he ever could have done otherwise. Put more simply, he makes more money by doing good, and thus he has greater financial reward for himself, for his people, and of course for his shareholders. It bears repeating: He does well by doing good.

BUT IT TAKES SOME GUTS

Lest it appear that the TL approach is a thornless bed of roses, let me be clear: While this model is proven (it works), it is *not* easy to implement. In fact, it is possibly the single most challenging approach to leadership that exists. It produces the greatest results, promises the most far-reaching rewards because, in no small measure, it demands the greatest commitment from the senior leader and the senior leadership. It requires that we step onto a path that, in the early stages especially, is fraught with uncertainty, has numerous potholes to navigate, and even has the occasional land mine to be carefully avoided. For this reason, among others, it is not for everyone. Because of the inherent difficulty in leading at the transformative, integrating level, a quality of greatness must be summoned—a quality, I believe, that we all have in us, but that only a select few have the courage and love to call forth.

Greatness in leadership, any kind of leadership, but especially transformative leadership, requires first and foremost a greatness of spirit. At its root what that means is there's an emergent toughness, a toughness that issues from a passion for the leadership game itself—for the process, for the challenging journey, for the struggle.

In the words of the legendary college basketball coach John Wooden, "competitive greatness [is] a real love for the hard battle, knowing it offers the opportunity to be at your best when your best is required." The great competitors, he says, "have shared a joy derived from the struggle itself—the journey, the contest." This joy cannot be found in anything less than the mighty challenge, a challenge that requires nothing less than our full person. Only in this "supreme effort," Wooden says, "is there an opportunity to summon your best, a personal greatness that cannot be diminished, dismissed, or derided" by anyone or anything, not even "the final score or bottom line."[6]

Perhaps ironically, the transformative leader—the one who falls in love with the enormity of the challenge, with his own sharpening and growth journey, with the immense and sometimes explosive process of developing his people, the leader who is not focused on the final score or bottom line—is usually the one who wins and wins at the deepest, broadest, and highest levels, which includes the bottom and top line, or in Wooden's case ten NCAA championships in twelve years. This is the leader who realizes the vision, the often outrageous vision. This is the leader and the leadership that society, business, and the organization in general most need today. If we but have the courage to see.

WHO IT'S FOR

The Best in Us is directed at two overlapping audiences. First, it's for those people who lead others—in business, nonprofits, volunteer agencies, government, or other capacities—who want to do so at an entirely more powerful level, with a far greater impact on the people they lead, on the organizations they lead, and on the results generated by both. It's for those people who intuitively understand that their leadership could have more meaning and purpose. In this regard it is especially for leaders who understand the urgency of the moment, this moment so pregnant with both danger and possibility. Leaders who recognize but are undaunted by the enormous challenge and opportunity we face as a society, as a civilization even; leaders who are realizing that more of the same (just done a bit better) is not the solution needed in the brave new world of the twenty-first century. It's for leaders, or would-be leaders, then, who hunger for an approach to leading that has more teeth and fewer gimmicks, one that is worthy of and demands their very best, and simultaneously promises exceptional results at all levels.

Second, this book is for the leaders who know they could lead their *lives* more effectively as well, far beyond their roles as leaders—those who may have figured out that how they lead others is a direct reflection of how they show up in the rest of their lives. Though the book is directed at leaders, then, part II of the book will be of value to anyone who would like to see greater levels of excellence in their lives in general: greater meaning, greater joy, greater love, and a greater sense of power and personal effectiveness. It's for those leaders (and individuals) who would like to *live* life rather than merely survive it (and then die having never lived at all). It's for people who know the quality of their lives can be greater than it currently is. People who know it and want it.

THE BEST IN US IN OUTLINE

Part I (chapters 1—3) describes the basics of the transformative model, differentiating it from the dominant approach to leadership, the transactional model. It lays out, in broad terms, the kind of growth this model demands of the leader and why—characterizing transformation as a movement, or fundamental shift, from one mind-set to another: from a mind-set that at best "manages" life or *reacts* to what life sends its way, to a mind-set of "leading" life, of intentionally and consciously *causing* life (and leadership) to happen. In chapters 2 and 3 we then consider the often radical nature of what the transformative leader seeks to get done with her people, her organization, and the results they produce.

But to create the kind of bold, brave, imaginative leadership that we need today, we must avoid racing too quickly into the "doingness" of leadership. We must first deal with the leader (the person) and his growth before we deal with his leadership (the method). To that end, part II of the book (chapters 4 through 17), articulates the nature of the leader's personal transformation. In addition to laying the foundation for a radical take on organizational leadership in part III, part II clearly explains and guides the reader through the explicit steps of leadership development via self-expansion and personal growth—what for many amounts to radical personal growth.

Part III (chapters 17 through 25) builds on this growth foundation and presents an unapologetically radical take on organizational leadership, *real* leadership. It's at this point that we take on the doingness of the transformative model, explicitly articulating what the leader and the organization must do to embrace the extraordinary promise of the moment. Part III amounts to an admittedly strong commentary on the conventional approach to leadership that seems to have run its course, one that may have been sufficient in the Industrial Age, perhaps in the early and mid-twentieth century, but is ill suited for the age of instant information, social media, hypernetworking, and democratic openness. The third section of the book offers an antidote, a bold antidote, to the economic and social malaise we now face as a result of, at least in part, that old transactional way of leading.

In the epilogue, *Is it Too Much to Ask?,* we come full circle, considering once more the big picture—where we are as organizational leaders (and as a society) and why it is we must lead nothing less than transformation, within the organization and beyond.

Finally, for those leaders and organizations ready to get the fundamental transformative shift underway, the appendix, *From Transactional to Transformative: Getting It All Started*, lays out the immediate and necessary actions to be taken, discussing in some detail specific essential steps required as leaders and as a leadership body (team).

AN INVITATION TO SOMETHING RICHER

What's in front of you, then, is an invitation to begin leading, actually *leading* a life of greater meaning, greater power, and greater joy as you simultaneously elevate how you lead others, how you lead and transform the organization, and how you inevitably affect society. *The Best in Us* invites you to radically enhance and expand your range as a leader, as well as the range and vibrancy of the organization you may lead. It is also a challenge to reconsider the very nature and intent of organizational life in business and beyond.

For those of you, then, who would like to actually live life, to *lead* life, indeed, above all, to powerfully lead others from a braver, bolder understanding, the gauntlet is being thrown down. To pick it up demands a level of integrity and imagination we all want, I believe, but that few people and few leaders have the courage and desire to fully embrace. Perhaps the only question is, *Are you one of the few?* If the answer is "Yes" or even "Maybe," I invite you to join me on this odyssey compelled by our transformative moment.

THE BEST IN US

People, Profit, and the Remaking of Modern Leadership

When Nothing Else Will Do: Transformation, Leadership, and Achieving the Extraordinary

CHAPTER 1

WHY TRANSFORMATION MATTERS AND A BIG DISTINCTION

> In the kind of world we have today, a transformation of humanity might well be our only hope for survival.
>
> **—Stanislav Grof**

To *transform* something means to change it, but not in a modest manner, as in "to modify." Rather, to transform something means to change it in a radical way, as in "from the roots up," as the original Latin, *radicalis*, suggests. Transformation literally refers to the process of rising above or transcending something such that it no longer is the same thing it was prior to the act of transcendence; there is something fundamentally, in most cases permanently, different about the thing once transformation has occurred. In the case of leadership and personal transformation, one of the primary differences we see is a difference in power.

After more than two decades of working with leaders, organizations, university students, and the general public—in the Far East, Europe, and North America—it has become unmistakably clear to me that it is power that we are all after, the power to create and have lives of joy, meaning, and purpose. *Power* as opposed to *force*. Even if we are only vaguely aware of it, beyond the simple struggle to survive, what we are all after is power. Not the power to dominate others but the power to live life fully, to intentionally cause, and to influence others, free of the fears that run most people's lives most of the time.

And just to the side of power, tugging at our sleeves is this gentle, persistent thing we call transformation. This nudge of transformation is a primary reason so many seek psychotherapy; it is a fundamental reason why many who are religious or spiritual seek the touch of the divine; it's one of the reasons the wealthy (perhaps with less satisfaction) are so often driven after ever more wealth; and it's a primary reason for our culture's misguided obsession with celebrity. Within every one of us there is an instinct to believe that our lives could be more satisfying, more meaningful, or just plain better. It seems inseparable from our deepest self-understandings. And if we are true leaders of people (or aspire to be) it is that inner voice, the whisper of transformation, that reminds us that there is so much more we can still be and become, do and achieve, through our leadership.

It is there in all of us, that transformative whisper, even if we are unaware of its gentle urging, drowned out as it often is by the relentless distractions and demands of modern life. And that's one of life's great tragedies: In the race to survive, to simply make it across the finish line in order to run another day, we lose sight of life's promise, life's possibility, and surely *our* possibility as leaders. In the fierce, angry din of contemporary existence, that gentle whisper seems to have been all but extinguished.

But the voice is still there. Even if in a muted form, it remains an innate piece of what it means to be human—and to be a leader of other humans. The great thinkers have always known this truth. As far back as ancient Greece, people recognized that all living things seek the actualization of their potential. It's in our very bones, built into the nature of life itself. Inherent within the tiny acorn is the form of the mighty oak, Plato and Aristotle tell us. It doesn't need to be told or taught what to do. It is in the nature of the acorn, in its essential form, to grow toward and call forth its oakness.

And like the acorn and the oak, it is natural for us to want to realize our still-hidden potential as leaders and people. I would go so far as to say it is a basic human need that *must* be satisfied if we are to have fulfilling, meaningful, and ultimately happy lives. It is this natural urge for the fulfillment of potential, the urging of transformation, that is at the root of all human progress and is the core of our development and growth, as leaders and as individuals. And it is the very heart of perhaps the single most powerful expression of leadership, transformative leadership.

THE PROBLEM

The unfortunate truth, however, is that most of us have driven this innate longing deep beneath the surface of our conscious minds. For in the face of life's slings and arrows, in view of the seemingly endless string of ups and downs that normal living brings, to continue holding on to these hopes and dreams of who we might become and what we might achieve is to beat on against the relentless current, which only invites the pain of further disappointment. If for a time we hold fast to these deepest longings and youthful dreams, we find ourselves staring into a gaping psychological abyss, a promised but fading future that seems to defy realization: There it is, that still-unrealized dream staring back at us, even taunting us if we look at it too long. So we turn away. We choose not to think about it, and over time it fades further and further and further from our consciousness.

In younger, less jaded days we may have dreamt of exploring exotic, faraway lands and cultures, or of achieving profound things for the good of humanity, or of being an important artist, a brilliant engineer, a great novelist, or, yes, even that innovative, dynamic business or political leader—the kind who inspires people, changes organizations and lives, and leaves a meaningful mark on the world.

But "grown-ups" and friends scoffed when we revealed our bold dreams. Or we were confronted by our personal limitations, perceived or real, and the understandable discouragement that failure brings. It may have been a failed (and embarrassing) leadership effort. Or it may have had nothing to do with leadership as such: a failed career or business, a failed academic effort, a failed relationship—or a series of them. And authority figures, real or in our heads, told us in response to all of these stumbles to "grow up and get a real life." We heard it, or said it to ourselves, again and again and again and again.

The Silent Capitulation

Today, faced with these disappointments and our own fierce inner critics, and faced, perhaps, with a lack of external support, most of us quietly, almost entirely unaware we're doing so, concede defeat. We give in and lower our sights, learn to "live within our means," become more "reasonable" about our life aspirations and our expectations of what life (and thus our leadership) might hold for us. And a part of us dies.

On the surface we don't notice it; our bodies seem to be functioning more or less as normal, and we may mask our defeat beneath the banal drumbeat of clever conformity, celebrity worship, or basic consumerism—or voyeurism, or spectatorism, or any other number of *-isms*. But the dis-integrating process and, in a sense, the dying of our spirits has begun. We do what we must to survive in a challenging, often confusing world, but disintegration is underway.

Unfortunately, this state of survival and doctored-over resignation is the mental and emotional ocean in which most of us swim, even if we're unaware of it. They are the waters of diminished hope and "wisely" lowered expectations. They are the psychological and emotional conditions we have reluctantly, unconsciously accepted in exchange for a sense of security and a flavorless stability. It may not be exciting, it may not bring us joy, but it is safe, or at least we *feel* a bit more safe, possibly even secure.

And, of course, since how we lead is but an extension of who we are, the great capitulation inevitably shows up in our leadership as well. It shows up in what we seek to achieve and in what we actually accomplish with our bland approach to leading.

Having quietly given in, we soldier on with the almost unnoticeable, slightly slumped shoulders that resignation and conformity bring. Is it any wonder that the tabloid culture of the twenty-first century flourishes as it does? We are reduced to vicariously living through the exploits of godlike Hollywood stars and athletes, or we're reduced to taking mean-spirited pleasure in seeing them brought to earth with the rest of us mortals.

The vast majority of the human population in the industrialized West is engaged in some version of this ongoing act of capitulation, this letting go of our deepest, perhaps even heroic, desires exchanged for a more "reasonable" approach to life, whether we are leaders, would-be leaders, or members of the general population. We may ease the pain and sadness of having dispersed our power and dispensed with our dreams by calling it "realism" or even referring to it as "growing up." But that does not for one moment change the truth. At some point along the way many of us (probably most of us) have quit on ourselves, on our dreams, and by extension, surely on our leadership promise. The best we might offer the world (and ourselves) remains buried deep within—buried and all but forgotten. It is not a pleasant thing to hear, not something we want to admit, but until we face the reality of our resignation there is nothing we can do about it.

THE AUDACIOUS ANSWER

The challenge of the transformative ethic and transformative leadership in particular is to have the courage, indeed, the audacity, to shake ourselves from our torpor. It's a challenge to risk some discomfort for the possibility of summoning latent promise. It is to risk the chance we may be seen as foolish, perhaps overly idealistic, for the possibility that our lives and our leadership might count for something meaningful. It is to risk the chance of failure for the possibility of realizing greatness, even true transformation—the transformation of our lives, our leadership, and surely the people we lead.

When Henry David Thoreau introduces us to his experience at Walden Pond, he says that it represented his determination to transcend the numbing experience of the "mass of men," leading "lives of quiet desperation," a description of humanity every bit as applicable today as it was then. For the simple fact is that most people are run by a low-grade anxiety, an anxiety that we have become so accustomed to, so familiar with that we don't even know it's there much of the time.

But it's there all right, running us this way and that, keeping us in a mind-set that is so often one of mere survival. But lizards and cockroaches survive! Rocks and trees survive, for heaven's sake. As human beings, creatures of complex consciousness, beings with the capacity for love and courage, for creativity, for growth and expansion, we have the capacity to *live*. To really live life. In Thoreau's words, we have the ability to suck the "very marrow from life," to *lead* it rather than *survive* it for a time, only then to die. The sad fact is, however, the vast majority of human beings walking the planet *do* only survive life for a time, and then they die, never having lived life at all.

Transformative leadership, therefore, assumes a powerful, perhaps reawakened, passion for life and from that a passion for truly leading others and *living* life—beyond the resignation that mere existence brings. It demands a willingness to remember or uncover, to commit to and live from, our hearts' deepest desires, a willingness to summon the best we still have within us and thereby learn to lead from our souls' most compelling sense of meaning and purpose. It's a call to an intentional, focused, vivid approach to leading and living that is, to say the least, uncommon in today's instantaneous, scattered, and temporary society.

THE BIG DISTINCTION: LEADING VS. MANAGING

The model for leading and leadership growth described in these pages takes a decidedly aggressive and optimistic position regarding the possibility of personal and organizational change. And by *change*, again, let me be clear. I am not talking about a minor tweak or slight adjustment in attitude, a simple rearranging of the living room furniture. I am suggesting a complete reconsideration of what it means to lead people and the organization at a level that produces nothing less than extraordinary results. I'm talking about what it means to be a vital human being engaged with other human beings, engaged with and *by* the transformative possibility such that heretofore unimagined levels of performance and excellence become the accepted norm. But to better understand the book's method and how we'll get to those outcomes, we employ an important distinction.

The majority of human beings *manage* their lives. Most of us, in fact, do not *lead* our lives. And by the same token, most people who are formally designated as leaders, whether in business, politics, education, or anything else, do far more managing than they do leading. Unfortunately the designation *leader* more times than not is a misnomer. And the difference in these two modes of being—managing versus leading—could not be greater. As it turns out, that difference also serves to distinguish between merely getting by, trying to handle life, reacting to it, surviving it, on the one hand, and living life with intention, clarity, power, and joy, on the other. The distinction between managing and leading clarifies the nature and meaning of transformation.

To *manage* something means to maintain it, literally to handle it—the word comes from the Latin *manus*, meaning "hand." To manage well means to respond well to what comes at you, to adjust and adapt as life unfolds. To manage well, therefore, means to react with effectiveness. The problem with management as a life skill, however, is that the manager is more or less always on the defensive, always in various stages of reacting. Most of us approach nearly the entirety of our lives from this management sensibility, though we probably haven't thought of it in these terms. We may be quick or slow in how we react, we may manage with greater or lesser degrees of anticipation, but we still live our lives from a largely reactive place.

To *lead* a life, on the other hand, means to initiate and create life. It is fundamentally a proactive approach to life, from the Anglo-Saxon *lidhan*, meaning "to go" or "to glide on." To lead, in effect, means to intentionally step out ahead, to go forth and cause desired outcomes, and to do so out of our capacity for choice and action. It is *pro*actively to step into, or "to go" into the experience of living. It is not a hope to merely handle or manage what life brings but rather a determination to generate what might be possible, in effect to be on the offensive. Thus it demands imagination and desire despite, not because of, the circumstances of life. To lead, therefore, also necessarily means to embrace life with a greater openness to risk and uncertainty, knowing well that such openness to risk, along with its inherent dangers, affords a greater potential for reward, accomplishment, and satisfaction.

One, *managing*, seeks to maintain, while the other, *leading*, seeks to create; one is reactive, the other is proactive; one desires security, the other desires actualization; one is tactical, the other is strategic; one wants control, the other wants release and liberation; one is expressly cautious, the other is bold; one is suspicious, the other is open; one is focused down, the other is focused out, et cetera, et cetera. Table 1.1 draws out the differences in a more vivid way.

[TABLE 1.1] MANAGING	VERSUS LEADING
Manage: From the Latin *manus,* "hand." Originally to *manage* meant to train a horse in its paces. It came to be applied more broadly meaning to handle (*manus*), to wield, or to control. *Webster's* says, among other things, it is "to get (a person) to do what one wishes, especially by skill, tact, flattery, etc.; to make docile or submissive to control," and "to handle, use (money, supplies, etc.) carefully."	**Lead:** From the Anglo-Saxon, *laedon*, "to lead," from *lidhan*, "to go, glide on." Implicit (or explicit) in virtually all definitions of the verb *to lead* is the suggestion of forward or proactive movement, and in the original there is an implied fluidness of movement (*glide on*). *Webster's* says, among other things, to lead is "to precede; to introduce by going first," and "to induce; to prevail upon; to influence."
Reactive: Anticipates what comes from "over there"; maintains what already is; capitulates to what has been.	**Creative:** Generates what comes from "in here"; expands what already is; actualizes what must and is yet to be.
Victim/Optional: Perceives one's life as driven by external forces; sees outcomes as determined by precedent.	**Responsible/Possible:** Perceives self as cause; sees outcomes as liberated by the reach of imagination.
Automatic: Unconscious, is taken.	**Intentional:** Conscious, chooses.
Fear-based: Distrusts, is suspicious of self, others, and life; seeks to diminish "opponents"; anxious, impatient, and doubtful.	**Love-based:** Trusts self, others, and life; seeks to elevate colleagues; calm, clear, and confident.
Exerts force: Seeks control; craves security; fortifies boundaries; view is singular and down.	**Actualizes power:** Seeks release; looks for adventure; breaks boundaries; view is comprehensive and out.
Operates as guest: Assumes it belongs to "them" and asks, "What can I get for me?"	**Operates as host:** Assumes it is "ours" and asks, "How can I contribute?"

Managing and leading, then, represent two fundamentally distinct approaches to life. And this distinction represents the springboard from which we initiate the transformative leadership journey, as well as the frame of reference to which we periodically return throughout the process, in both parts II and III of this book.

A Common Organizational Confusion

When we apply this distinction to the organizational world, what we see is not especially pretty. The simple truth is that what we call "leadership" more times than not is merely management by another name. I don't want to diminish the importance and difficulty of effective organizational management. Rather, I draw an important line of demarcation between what are clearly distinct organizational functions, between the function of leading and that of managing, regardless of the type of organization. Organizational leadership and organizational management are different organizational functions. Indeed, it is the conflation of leadership and management that is at the root of many an organization's most serious problems.

Labeling oneself a leader, attending a leadership conference, or reading the latest leadership book does not a leader make. Much like Shakespeare's rose, a manager by any other name is still a manager. To truly lead others is to step into an entirely different way of thinking, being, and doing. It is a heady domain that many fancy for themselves but few have the will, imagination, and courage to occupy. The recent elevation of leadership as a focus of attention and study in our universities and business schools has, to a degree at least, rendered leadership itself feckless. Everyone is a leader and no one is. Before leadership became so sexy, when the emphasis was more on management, leaders may have been few and far between, but at least we knew one when we saw one.

Furthermore, most of what we call leadership is of a *transactional* or *exchange-based* nature. You give me your loyalty and follow my organizational dictates, and I'll give you a good-paying job; or you give me your vote, and I'll implement policies that serve your interests. It's a quid pro quo, an exchange of mutual self-interest. All of which is fine, as far as it goes. But in today's world this approach simply does not go far enough.

This transactional approach to leadership is almost always concerned with the maintenance of the current order of things. It is, I contend, this very way of thinking about organizational leadership, and business leadership in particular, that informed the "leaders" who drove us headlong into the Great Recession of 2008 and continues to weigh us down as we fight our way out of its excruciating aftermath. It is the transactional ethic that permitted and permits, that is the foundation for, the breathtaking corruption pervasive in the current world of international finance, business generally, and politics.

Only The Extraordinary Will Do

Think about this for a moment. Most people who are labeled successes in our culture are people who have learned to do the ordinary well, perhaps *very* well. But it's still just the ordinary, the ordinary magnified. I'm talking about most successful doctors and lawyers. I'm talking about the majority of successful business leaders. I'm talking about the vast majority of successful politicians, presidents, and prime ministers. And surely most film stars, rock stars, and professional athletes. These are all people who have learned to do the ordinary quite well, to excel within the conventional framework of success. And to that I say, "Bravo!" and "Nice job." It is not easily done. Not many achieve it.

But to that I also say, "Big deal." Nicely done, to be sure, but there is nothing extraordinary about the vast majority of these folks and their accomplishments. Doing the ordinary well is kind of like learning the mechanics of a complex machine, the machine of society and the ascending social order, say, and then conforming effectively to this mechanical world and its mechanistic laws. It takes noteworthy willpower, certainly, and in some instances, above-average smarts, but it takes little imagination. It's all been done before. Nothing new there, nothing fresh or expansive, nothing that truly moves the individual or humanity to a bigger and better place.

The truth is, from the transformative point of view, from the leading rather than managing point of view, it's relatively boring. Doing the ordinary very well is successful mediocrity. It's of little interest to the transformative soul, to individuals who would lead their lives and truly lead others.

Indeed, a life well lived is about authoring one's own life, and not in a vacuum. That is, it's about writing one's unique story within the larger human narrative, within the greater web of human relatedness out of which we come, to which and for which we are responsible. Consider the implications of an individual life that is a courageous response to the call of transformation. Simply put, it is almost inevitably a life of leadership. When we recognize and respond to this call, we are naturally pushing out beyond the borders of what we have previously imagined and beyond the limits of what others have thought and done. We are living a life of thoughtful passion, a life of imagination and intentionality second to none, by definition. As a result, other people want to "play" with us, they want to follow us, they want to be around us, they even want to be like us. To say as much is not arrogance. It's merely an articulation of what is so, and there is no stopping it.

From the daring and bravery of an Amelia Earhart to the searing intelligence and provocative questioning of a Margaret Mead. From the audacious political vision and intentionality of a Mohandas Gandhi to the tireless moral courage of a Martin Luther King Jr. From the entrepreneurial bravado and boundless imagination of a Richard Branson to the brilliant swagger and drive to "put a dent in the universe" of a Steve Jobs. Each of these people could not help but follow the call to realize the extraordinary. And each is a person who could not help but be followed by others.

And, of course, there are others still, people who may or may not be famous (yet), but they are people who have gone even further to become true and complete transformative leaders—some of whom you will meet in the pages that follow. They are people who stood for something and had their stands alter reality. They answered the transformative call and, as a result, they achieved the extraordinary.

SUMMARY

There is an ethic, a mind-set for embracing life and leading others, that emerges as a natural response to the deeper urgings of life itself. It is called the transformative ethic, and it can be applied to the leader and the organization to better create excellence and success, and to the individual to better live life. It audaciously says that there is *so* much more available to us as leaders and as individuals than most of us currently know, than most of us have been willing to imagine. We have only to listen to that gentle whisper that still calls to us from within.

The world is in the continuing throes of crisis, and it awaits the courageous few who will creatively step up and fill the void being left by a worn-out understanding of leadership. For those still invested in (trapped by) the status quo, the best that can be imagined is a short-sighted will to continue propping up the tired, old edifice of business as usual. A new coat of paint here, a fresh infusion of cash there, and *voila!* The old is new again.

But it's not. And we all know it. The simple fact remains that these old ways of thinking and leading are a crumbling ruin; they represent a smoldering, wheezing era dangerously past its prime. The time is ripe, it seems, for a better and braver way of understanding our experience together—in the organization and in society. The time is right for leadership that is inspired by life itself, by life's innate drive for more meaning, more power, more beauty, and more joy, indeed for a way of leading inspired by the possibility of transformation.

CHAPTER 2

AN ENTIRELY DIFFERENT GAME: The Emergence (and Basics) of Transformative Leadership

> The leader's fundamental act is to induce people to be aware or conscious of what they feel—to feel their true needs so strongly, to define their values so meaningfully, that they can be moved to purposeful action.
>
> —**James MacGregor Burns**

The supposition of *The Best in Us* is simple and unapologetic. We are at a critical juncture in our evolution as a species and as a civilization, and our very survival requires a new way of thinking about how we interact as human beings and, therefore, a new way of understanding what we mean by leadership and the purpose of the organization. That new way of thinking is supplied, at least in part, by transformative leadership. It's a method that challenges the dominant, transactional mind-set, which in business declares profit (or shareholder value) as the only real value, the only basis for the business organization.

The transformative method contends that there are two additional values or objectives that are preeminent. The first is the growth and development of the people, and the second is the achievement of excellence at all levels as the result of this development. To achieve these objectives, a third element must be present: The leader must be committed to his or her own growth, both as a leader and as a human being. Finally, profit, or more generally, objective results, are understood as the quantifiable measure of the leader's effectiveness in the growth of the people and his or her own growth as a leader. Profit is extremely important in the transformative approach, but not as an end in itself. Rather, it is the byproduct of, and tool for measuring, the two higher ends.

The four key elements of transformative leadership are:

- A commitment to the growth of the people as a primary end
- A commitment to the realization of excellence via the people's growth
- A commitment by the organization's leaders to develop themselves, both as people and as leaders
- The use of hard results (profits and beyond) as the measure of the leaders' success as leaders—in growing themselves, producing excellence, and, above all, in developing the organization's people

From the outset it should be clear that the leader's commitment to the people within the model does not imply the soft and squishy, every-child-gets-a-toy nonsense that some might imagine. To the contrary, it is based in a "tough-love" kind of leadership strength, which says my job as a leader is to expect (demand even) growth and achievement from all employees, and therefore, the realization of excellence in all facets of organizational life—which further means that the organization becomes a vehicle for the education that leads to this growth and excellence and the resulting measurable levels of achievement. Thus, the leader becomes what great leaders have always been: a teacher who is concerned with the whole person of the employees, not just their numbers.

Thus, accountability at all levels goes up, not down. Leadership engagement, from the field level all the way up to the boardroom, goes up, not down. Expectation goes up, not down. Morale—passion, commitment, and joy—necessarily and as a consequence goes up, not down. And productivity, quantifiable results, go up ("and to the right"), not down.

But before we address the model of transformative leadership, it will be helpful to briefly place it within its larger historical context, distinguishing it from the conventional, transactional approach to leadership.

THE TRANSFORMATIVE LEADER IN A TRANSACTIONAL WORLD

The leader who brings about transformation is not unique to the twenty-first century. Throughout much of recorded history there have been moments when this type of leader has emerged and left an indelible mark on the culture from which he or she comes: Socrates, Plato, Francis of Assisi, Erasmus, Marie "Madame" Curie, Albert Schweitzer, Mohandas K. Gandhi, Martin Luther King Jr., Nelson Mandela, and Aung San Suu Kyi, to name a few. But leaders like these have been few and far between. And still, as human culture has evolved, as we have become more complex and more sophisticated—socially, scientifically, technologically, politically, organizationally, intellectually, and psychologically—so have certain aspects of our understanding of the art and skill of leading. As a consequence of this increased complexity, we have seen an increase in the incidence of transformation-oriented leadership in all walks of life, including business—companies like Southwest Airlines in the United States or retailer John Lewis in the United Kingdom, for instance. Nevertheless, today transforming leadership remains the exception, not the rule.

The first serious consideration of the transforming approach gained traction in the late 1970s and early '80s, expressed most vividly by Pulitzer Prize–winning historian James MacGregor Burns. In his seminal 1978 book, *Leadership,*[1] he draws out the distinction between what he sees as the two fundamental types of leaders. On the one hand we have the conventional, ordinary leader, whom he labels the "transactional leader." This leadership type constitutes the vast majority of all leaders, today and throughout recorded history. The transactional leader is not good or bad, right or wrong, as such. He can go either way. Rather, he merely represents the common or dominant approach to leadership. On the other hand we have the atypical leader, the exceptional or "extraordinary leader," whom Burns labels the "transforming leader," who seeks the growth and well-being of her followers as a primary objective. Though she is rare, her ranks today are growing.

It's the Norm: The Transaction Is Everything

The pivot point of the leader–follower relationship in transactional leadership is the *exchange* or transaction that takes place between leader and follower. In this approach the reason for the leader–follower relationship is mutual self-interest. The leader gets something of value from the follower, and the follower gets something of value from the leader. This exchange or transaction is the primary, usually the exclusive, reason for the relationship. The challenge, as leadership scholar Thomas Wren says, is that transactional leadership "is not an enduring, or particularly uplifting, relationship."[2] Without the transaction, in fact, the leader–follower relationship dissolves. The leader has no followers and vice versa. The transaction is everything.

For instance, in the professional world, the leader has money or capital, or represents those who do. The follower has talent or time or energy, that is, labor. The leader says, in effect, "I have something you need, money, and you have something I need, labor. So let's make an exchange and serve both of our interests."

In this approach, the leader's concern is with productivity, with the generation of the chosen results, results to be produced by his followers. Nothing wrong with that. By definition, then, this leader is not concerned with the "who" of his follower beyond the results that this "who" can produce for him. Interest in the greater well-being of the follower is always tied directly to productivity. Anything beyond that—interest in the follower's home life, say, or his or her general happiness—is above and beyond the call of leadership duty. Concern for the greater well-being of the workforce may happen, often does, but in the transactional framework, this kind of personal interest is the sign of a boss or a leader who also happens to be a good person. It's a bonus, not a requirement.

We may want our leaders to have interest in us as people, but that is not a part of the transactional leader's job description. Indeed, today we may even expect as much, but it's still not part of the transactional requirement. Generally speaking, when we sign up to work with a company (or a school, or nonprofit, or the military, et cetera), we make a tacit agreement: I'll give you my work and produce results, and you'll give me a paycheck and perhaps some security.

The upshot of this quid pro quo mentality is that the leader and the follower see one another, above all, as the means, the tool or mechanism, for realizing the accepted end. While this may seem a harsh assessment, the fact is that in most professional environments people are seen as objects rather than objectives, as a means to be used rather than as ends to be valued. And as unpleasant as this claim may be, the potential outcome of the transactional arrangement is far more troubling. For if the leader and follower are each perceived, politely or not, as the means to an end, at some point along the way the whole transactional venture can, and often does, devolve into one that is dehumanizing for both parties, leaders and followers. Peter Senge, widely regarded as one of the top leadership and management thinkers in the world, says, "When we're used as an instrument to serve something other than life, we lose our feeling and our capacity to sense. We just go through the motions. This happens to people all the time, for example, in corporations whose purpose is to make money for the sake of making money."[3]

THE TL APPROACH AND ITS PECULIAR CONSEQUENCES

This is the point at which, and the reason why, the transactional and transformative approaches part ways. The transformative leader understands the leader's job to be about growing and developing, awakening and inspiring the people such that not only do they take more effective action as followers (leading to measurably better results) but so that at the end of the day they are more complete, more alive human beings. The transformative leader's job is nothing less and nothing more than her followers—even, perhaps especially, in the business organization. The vision, the strategies and tactics, the policies and procedures of this organization all bend toward that end and not the other way around. As Burns says, "The transforming leader looks for potential motives in followers, seeks to satisfy higher needs and engages the full person of the follower."[4] Our approach, the transformative approach, agrees. The transformative approach builds upon Burns's transforming mind-set—and it goes several steps beyond the approach known as transformational leadership, which was championed, codified, and extensively researched by scholar Bernard Bass and others.[5]

It is this idea of "the full person," as we'll soon see, that is so essential in the transformative context, suggesting the complexity of the human being, for whom only one aspect of his identity is who he is as an employee in the workplace. Yet this type of leadership redounds to the leader's benefit as well. When transformative leadership is present, people "engage with others in such a way that leaders and followers raise one another to higher levels of motivation and morality."[6] The leader is inspired, encouraged, and elevated by his followers. Everyone's game is enhanced. Everyone's range, whether as leader or effective employee, is expanded. Both leader and follower are served, both are far more productive, and as a result, both are more engaged with the organization and with life itself.

The Result's the Thing

This all may seem like heady, perhaps overly idealistic stuff, especially for business as we know it. But before we dismiss it as impractical, there's one important thing to keep in mind. In terms of producing robust, clearly measurable, "soft" as well as "hard" results, transformative leadership *works*. In the right leadership hands, in fact, it is unrivalled. Indeed, when fully implemented within an organization (whether business, educational, nonprofit, military, or governmental) and when all other things are equal, transformative leadership has the curious tendency to *run circles around the more common transactional approaches to leadership, particularly in terms of customer satisfaction, employee satisfaction, and in the top and bottom lines.*[7]

Understanding the reason for this success does not require an advanced degree in organizational behavior. It's quite intuitive, actually. If an organization's people are (1) rigorously challenged, called upon to become bigger, stronger, smarter, more productive; (2) systematically and systemically supported in playing this "bigger game"; (3) making, and are aware of making, a substantive contribution to their colleagues and the larger corporate enterprise; (4) genuinely appreciated and cared for and aware of it; and (5) invested in a greater vision that they see as fundamentally meaningful, then it is not surprising that they are so productive.

Transformative leadership encompasses all five of these areas. People invested in an organization animated by such a transformative culture typically go home at night feeling good about themselves and as a result are likely to be better parents, better spouses, better friends and neighbors, and better adult children to their parents. They are also more likely to come back to work the following morning more committed, more creative, more loyal, and more willing to go the extra mile without being asked. It just makes sense.

Is it any wonder, then, that the transformative model outstrips even the best-executed expressions of the transactional approach? When we slow down for a moment and think about it, it's not even remotely counterintuitive. When we wisely and relentlessly invest in our chief resource—people—when we systematically challenge, push, grow, demand from, listen to, expect of, inspire and are inspired by, hold to account, and generally elevate our people (and ourselves), extraordinary results will follow. *They always do.* And the leaders themselves become better, smarter, more powerful human beings and surely better business and organizational players. They must, even if only to stay one step ahead of the development of their people, who are rapidly picking up the rear and nipping at their heels.

The most exciting and perhaps daunting aspect of this model of leadership, however, is that it all begins with you, the leader (or would-be leader). It begins with a willingness to take yourself on as a leader and human being. But before we turn to that transformative growth process, there are a couple of other matters that need addressing, the first of which, the TL do-functions, we look at now.

WHAT A TRANSFORMATIVE LEADER DOES

Though we'll be taking up the nature of the transformative organization and the transformative leader in considerable depth in part III of this book, to complete the larger picture of transformative leadership we need to briefly look at several "do-functions," some of the specific actions of the transformative approach.

On the surface, some of the actions appear to be the same as the actions of a transactional leader. In fact, in several instances they are the same. What distinguishes the transformative leader is his come-from, the deeper rationale for his actions, all of his actions. That rationale is simple: to do only that which grows his followers and himself and, as a result, produces ever-increasing levels of excellence throughout the organization. There are, however, specific actions the transformative leader takes that are not typically found in the transactional organization.

Commits to, Acts upon Own Growth

First, the transformative leader makes an unswerving commitment to take herself on. That is, even if she is already an accomplished leader, she is unabashed and open about the fact that she has not got this whole leadership and life thing all figured out. And since she knows that becoming a better leader necessarily entails becoming a better human being, *she has made an unqualified commitment to expanding her range and depth as a human being and as a leader.* This commitment leads to clear, decisive action around gaining support in her growth—whether it's hiring a transformation-based executive coach; actively and systematically seeking feedback from peers and her direct and indirect reports; and/or intentionally surrounding herself with people equally committed to realizing their promise, people unafraid to confront her about her blind spots. She is also in the process of taking herself on regarding her general health, diet, and fitness. Above all, she has the guts to do (and therefore does) the deep, introspective, developmental work with herself (see chapters 4–12) that will enable the full expression of her power as a leader and as an individual.

Systematically Creates a Growth-Centric, Achievement-Oriented Culture

Second, understanding that one of the organization's two primary objectives is the development of its people, the transformative leader institutes ongoing growth opportunities within the organization, oriented toward both deep inner-personal work (emotional and intellectual) and professional development, both of which are typically done in the context of an intensive team process. He ties both types of developmental work to explicit excellence and achievement goals (organizational and personal) for which each individual leader/employee formally and regularly accounts (monthly, quarterly, or annually).

He understands that the achievement of the goals are the *measure* of the primary objective, not the objective itself. Nevertheless, success is understood as the realization of the goal (not merely trying) and is expected, and understood as the norm. Indeed, the greater the investment of the organization in the growth, development, and well-being of the people, the greater the demand for excellence and achievement.

Finally, the transformative leader (as well as the leaders who report to him, those who report to them, and so on) systematically and authentically recognizes and celebrates the growth and accomplishments (professional and personal) of his employees. Indeed, he takes great pleasure in their individual successes. But we must be clear at this point, this is not rah-rah fluff where everyone gets a prize. It is acknowledgement based on measurable, *real* accomplishment, accomplishment that is a result of the developmental culture that the leader has instituted. The context of celebration based on achievement that exists is powerful precisely because it is authentic.

Expands Standards for Selection

Third, in selecting those whom and with whom she will lead, the transformative leader employs a more extensive set of standards than conventional leadership typically allows, what she calls "standards plus." All the basic essentials involved in hiring a stellar employee—talent, intelligence, experience, a strong relationship with results, accomplishment, vision, et cetera—are a given. To these she adds the transformative elements: a clearly expressed commitment to excellence and growth and the possibility of such (personally and professionally); an articulated commitment to people—a gut understanding that people are what matters; an openness in sharing herself with others—who she really is, what matters to her, why she's a leader, et cetera; a willingness to demand and expect growth and excellence from those being led; a vivid drive to achieve the extraordinary; and so on. The irony about this "standards plus" list is that it actually makes the selecting process—hiring, promoting, and firing—easier, not harder.

One of the first things a leader who seeks to become a transformative leader does, then, is begin a process of evaluating her current set of direct reports. This does not mean she quickly begins getting rid of those on her team who do not immediately measure up to the transformative standard (though in some cases, of course, that may ultimately become necessary). Rather, in the process of evaluating her reports she also begins introducing them to the new standards and expectations (and she simultaneously begins challenging and supporting them in the process of rising up to these greater expectations—primarily in the transformative team process, following).

Creates, Operates Out of a Real and Transformative Vision

The fourth and fifth actions, the creation and implementation of a vision and a team, respectively, at a superficial level might appear similar to the actions of a conventional leader, but that is only at a superficial level. Upon closer inspection what we see is that both of these functions are infused with a whole new and different level of complexity, meaning, and power.

The fourth action is the creation of a living vision. Unlike most transactional leaders who assume that a string of financial and, let's say, market-share goals are an organizational vision, the transformative leader works to create a picture that really is a picture—a vivid, detailed image—of a future that is yet to be, a picture rich in meaning, a picture of the possible that must and will be achieved. Working with his direct reports and others he crafts a compelling mosaic that includes exceptional financial achievement as a natural byproduct of an ever-evolving commitment to excellence and unrivaled achievement, but while including these relatively conventional objectives it also transcends them.

That is, the vision includes an employee base where people are encouraged and afforded the chance to grow themselves, where they love their work and the workplace (even if their work is making simple widgets), and where, as a result, they have a markedly positive effect on their families and friends. It includes a description of the powerful and beneficial effect the organization has on the local community, the business community, and in the organization's given industry. Moreover, the vision paints this picture of the possible in such a manner that it becomes an incomparable source of inspiration and the basis for the entire organization's commitment to excellence—as TL has it, it inspires employees to be, act, and achieve in ways that otherwise would be inconceivable. Finally, this transformative vision becomes the filter through which all significant decisions must and do pass, facilitating and improving the decision-making process.

Creates a Radically Different Kind of Senior Team

Fifth, the transformative leader initiates an unapologetically honest, integrative team-forming process based on the understanding that authentic, powerful teamness at the senior level (later to be replicated down through the rest of the organization) is the only foundation for successfully achieving the four actions above and the only basis for creating a truly powerful, transformative organization of excellence. This team process is described in detail in chapter 23, but for now suffice it to say it is built on the assumption that the team serves as one of the key means for each team member's growth and development, personally and as a leader.

What's more, as the leader initiates the transformative team process he is clear about the fact that he will be fully engaged in the same growth process as his reports and, thus, will likely employ an outside expert's help (or at the very least a *genuinely* empowered internal OD leader's) to guide the forming (or re-forming) team to the highest standards of transformative team excellence—which for each leader includes, among other things, a fierce commitment to the success of the other team members and of the team itself, a commitment to risk-taking and openness with one another, a commitment to brutal but caring honesty, and a commitment to the soon-to-be-completed organizational vision.

SUMMARY

Given the fact that what used to work in leadership (business and otherwise) no longer does the job, and given the fact that we live in a fundamentally different world than that of 1965, transformative leadership offers a simple but markedly distinct alternative to the old, transactional approach. The development of people and the generation of unqualified excellence are the two preeminent values that impel this approach, an approach that turns out to be the highest expression of pragmatism—for those with the eyes to see, the ears to hear, and the brains to think clearly. Profits matter, but not as the singular end-game that they represent in the transactional world. Profits matter as the inevitable by-product and, most important, as the measure of the organizational leader's success in achieving the two higher values.

There are specifically unique actions taken by the transformative leader, but it is what informs this leader's actions, the deeper, abiding rationale for his actions, that above all else makes this kind of leader unique: that unswerving commitment to the people's growth and the full expression of excellence across the entire organization. It is, among other things, this call to excellence that informs the transformative leader's drive to achieve the extraordinary—in the lives of his people and in the results they produce.

Indeed, the last thing that we must address before we dive into the leader's transformative process is what we mean by "extraordinary." There is a reason the extraordinary is both compelling and daunting. In chapter 3 we address the nature, the why and wherefore, of what it means to achieve the extraordinary within the transformative context.

CHAPTER 3

DISPATCHES FROM THE GATES OF HELL: Disclosing New Worlds (and Upending Old Ones)

> Remembering that I'll be dead soon is the most important tool I've ever encountered to help me make the big choices in life. Because almost everything—all external expectations, all pride, all fear of embarrassment or failure—these things just fall away in the face of death, leaving only what is truly important. Remembering that you are going to die is the best way I know to avoid the trap of thinking you have something to lose. You are already naked. There is no reason not to follow your heart.
>
> **—Steve Jobs**

My eighty-seven-year-old father is a World War II veteran. A few years ago we spent two weeks traveling together, just him and me, retracing some of his experiences from the war as we visited England, Wales, and France. Over the course of that invaluable time together he regaled me with story after story of his life-changing sojourn in the European theatre of war. Perhaps the most poignant story of them all is one that represented the beginning of his two-year journey. With several thousand other young men (he was eighteen at the time), he set sail on the *Queen Mary*, newly converted into a cramped troop carrier, from New York City.

"As we left the harbor and headed out to sea," he said, "I found a porthole I could see the Statue of Liberty from. I'm not sure how noisy it was or wasn't, but my memory is it was silent—that's the way it was in my head, anyway. I was oblivious to anything outside of my thoughts." He paused often as he told of this brief moment, caught up in the vividness of the recollection. "I stood there for I don't know how long," he continued. "It may have been only twenty or thirty minutes, but it seemed like a lifetime. I watched as the Statue of Liberty just got smaller and smaller and smaller and then finally completely disappeared over the horizon. As it shrunk, the pit in my stomach grew. It got bigger and bigger. It was almost paralyzing—I was just a kid, and I knew I was doing the right thing, but I also knew there was a real good chance I was sailing into my death. We all knew it." He paused again with that faraway look in his eyes, that look that says he's fully engaged in the experience all over again. At that moment we were driving our rental car across the French countryside. Our destination that day was the beaches of Normandy.

In the next moment as we drove along, my father chuckled. "Then it hit me," he said. "The Nazis were only going to kill me once! They weren't gonna get me twice. If I died, I died. Nothing I could do about it. And until they did, *if* they did, I was gonna live. Live like there would be no tomorrow—there might not be. 'So live, damn it, live.' And I did. It may be one of the reasons I'm alive today. Who knows? But I know this: I stared death in the face and said, 'Big deal, so what.' And that pit of fear began to shrink away just as the Statue of Liberty had."

There was as much wonder as there was pride in his voice at that moment, as if he understood that it was at that precise moment that the eighteen-year-old kid had grown up, become an adult. In the very moment he had embraced death, he had found life.

LEADING THE EXTRAORDINARY IN AN ORDINARY WORLD

Because Thoreau is right that "the mass of men lead lives of quiet desperation," it's also true that most of us, most of the time, play a small game in life. We don't really live life; we merely exist. We get by. We survive. We play it safe. But why? What are we afraid of? The short answer is that we're afraid of nothing less than death. It's a fear that today, in one sense at least, is entirely irrational—failing or being rejected by a friend or lover, a colleague or a boss, for instance, does not mean death by exclusion from the tribe, as it did 50,000 years ago. And yet this primitive fear, deeply embedded in the limbic system of our brains, constricts our imaginations, cripples our capacity to create richer, more meaningful lives, and so we play the game of life with little life at all. And death has won.

The only way to defeat the grip of death, as suggested by the Steve Jobs quote at the beginning of the chapter, is to stare death in the face, like my father did as he left New York Harbor. The only way to overcome the deeply embedded, usually unconscious fear of death is to look it in the eyes, to stare into the abyss and accept death's reality—and the fact that it could come for us at any moment. Oddly perhaps, by consciously, intentionally accepting our own eventual death we are freed to live, to live *now*, fully alive in this moment.

To some, I suppose, this may sound poetic, quaint even. But quaint it ain't. Powerful it is, powerful because of its liberating effect. Consider this fear of death—a fear that dramatically limits our power and freedom even though it is largely unconscious—from another perspective that further demonstrates the fear's irrationality. Simply enough, to fear death is an act of utter futility, because there's no escape from it. "No one gets out alive" from this thing called life. Thus, when we honestly, quietly gaze into fear's eyes, when we realize that it's "only gonna kill me once!" we are liberated—the irrationality of the fear is seen in all of its glory. In a state of sober acceptance we are liberated to lead, liberated to risk, and finally liberated to play big.

In fact, a willingness to stare death down by being willing to risk is essential to leading large. So at this early stage of the game, let's be clear: If you are unwilling to risk big, then you're unwilling to lead big. And remember, playing big is one of the non-negotiable demands of transformative leadership. It is the call to be extraordinary, to cause and lead others in causing the extraordinary, which is never small. Not ever. Therefore, the last issue we must examine, before considering the individual growth process of TL, is what it means to cause the extraordinary from the transformative point of view.

IN THE GRIP OF THE WORLD OF AGREEMENT

It seems everyone these days wants to emulate Apple. Long before Steve Jobs's recent death drew even greater attention to the company he created, Apple was seen as just about the "coolest company anywhere," as *Fast Company* recently noted. *Fortune* magazine named it the most admired company in America in 2008 and the most admired company in the world in 2008, 2009, and 2010. In May 2011, Apple was named the "world's most valuable brand," knocking Google from its lofty perch. "Everyone wants to be like Steve Jobs and his powerhouse company," says business journalist Farhad Manjoo, but "it's not as easy as it looks."[1]

Indeed not. It's not easy because most business and organizational leaders are unwilling to do many of the things that Jobs saw as essential, and one thing in particular stands out. Manjoo, again: "How does one become the 'Apple of [insert industry here]'?" he asks. It's abundantly clear. "The answer centers around discipline, focus, long-term thinking, and," he says, "*a willingness to flout the rules that govern everybody else's business*"[2] (italics mine). This last tendency seems to suggest Jobs's legendary rebel streak, summed up best, perhaps, by his line, "It's better to be a pirate than join the Navy." Such a mind-set may have landed him in hot water on occasion, but it also opened the door for his capacity and desire to violate the accepted wisdom, known in the transformative model as the "world of agreement."

It was Jobs's willingness to see the world as an array of bold possibilities that set him apart, informed his genius. In acknowledging those who, like him, fearlessly think from the nether reaches of the unreasonable, Jobs once said:

> Here's to the crazy ones, the misfits, the rebels, the troublemakers, the round pegs in the square holes . . . the ones who see things differently—they're not fond of rules. . . . You can quote them, disagree with them, glorify or vilify them, but the one thing you can't do is ignore them because they change things. . . . They push the human race forward, and while some may see them as the

crazy ones, we see genius, because the ones who are crazy enough to think that they can change the world, are the ones who do.[3]

This is Jobs in a nutshell. And these "crazy ones" who "see things differently" are the ones he wanted near him, because they're the ones who are best able to recognize and defy the accepted wisdom, to defy the world of agreement. It was Jobs's, and therefore Apple's, passion for breaking out of the grip of the accepted wisdom that has allowed the Cupertino, California company "that reinvented the personal computer, transformed the music business and created the world's most popular tablet"[4] to distance itself from other would-be leaders of the future.

And what is the world of agreement?

As transformative leadership sees it, it is the largely unexamined, unrecognized even, set of standards and rules that make up key elements of our culture and our individual lives. These standards and rules tell us what is good and bad, what is acceptable and what is not, and perhaps most important, what is doable and what isn't. The world of agreement is a collection of beliefs that we have adopted, usually without being aware that they even exist, let alone that we've adopted them. It's not merely the status quo. Rather, it is an unconscious, internalized status quo, one that we have accepted as immutable, eternal truth.

For instance, though there is no explicit law against spitting (unless you live in Singapore, apparently), in North America and Europe spitting in public is frowned upon, and most of us, most of the time, comply with this agreement. For instance, it would not serve you at all if at a dinner party of well-mannered people you loudly cleared your throat—or "hocked up a louggie," as my seventh grade buddies and I liked to say—leaned back in your chair to open the dining room window behind you, and then spit out into the garden. In reality, you have done nothing particularly unsanitary, especially if you close your mouth as you "hock it up" and wipe your lips properly after you spit. And it's unlikely that you've harmed the hibiscus—they're a hardy breed, I'm told. So in reality it should be "no harm, no foul," right?

Wrong. No matter how much you may protest, you have violated accepted standards for appropriate public behavior, the rules of proper etiquette, especially when dining with the Montagues. This unwritten rule is a world-of-agreement belief that's held, in effect, as truth, as reflecting appropriate (and sanitary) behavior when in polite company. Yet regardless of how some may argue that such behavior is *inherently* repugnant, that simply is not so. This belief (and the rule) is entirely a social construct. That is, the rule as well as our response to the rule's violation are a function of convention, a function of what we have made up as a society.

Why are diamonds so expensive? Is it because they are so rare? Is it because they are so objectively beautiful? No and no. It's because DeBeers said so. Yep, they and their diamond-selling pals said that this rock is worth, say, ten grand, and that rock is worth twenty, and that one over there fifty, and so on. Then as a collective of consumers we say, "Okay, if you say so," and then operate as if it *is* so. But it is so only because we've given our assent, only because we've all agreed and complied with that unproven and unexamined "wisdom."

The only inherent value of a diamond, of course, is its capacity to cut glass. Admittedly some diamonds truly are beautiful, but that is not why the market will bear what the market will bear.

The same thing applies to currency, whether the dollar, the pound, the yen, the euro, or a string of seashells on some faraway island. None of these has any inherent value, though we operate, necessarily, *as if* they do. They only have value insofar as we have agreed to it. Indeed, the hold of the world of agreement is the single most important thing that makes the world of finance work as it does, when it does. Because we all say, "Okay, we'll accept that." We just do it and get on with it. There's no good in quibbling.

The Pivotal Points

There are three important points to keep in mind in understanding the world of agreement. First, *We usually ain't aware of it*: The grip of the world of agreement takes place automatically and largely out of conscious view. We walk through our lives mostly oblivious to the rules and accepted limitations that shape much of our lives and most of society.

Second, *It ain't inherently so*: We operate as if, and in some instances consciously think, that these socially constructed norms are the truth. We act as if it's the very nature of the beast, that "it's just the way it is," rather than recognizing what is actually the case: They are socially constructed beliefs about what is so.

Rocks *are* innately hard, yes. Certainly water *is* innately wet. These are not socially constructed beliefs. They are so, inherently so. But those things that make up the world of agreement *aren't* inherently so, and in some cases are not true at all. In 1890, for instance, the rather austere argument against human flight was that God did not intend for us to fly, "else we'd have wings, by Jove!" If you were a good, God-fearing soul, the logic of the assertion was difficult to refute. It was accepted as innately so by most, but that did not make it so—as the Wright brothers and others demonstrated, and as we now demonstrate thousands of times a day. The Wright brothers violated and transcended the prevailing world of agreement, proving "it ain't necessarily so."

The third thing to keep in mind is, *It's massively reinforced*: The pervasive influence of the world of agreement resides in the fact that it's accepted and reinforced *by the majority*. The vast majority of human beings cannot be bothered with questioning the accepted wisdom. They're too busy surviving—fighting to get by. Thus, they lend their collective assent to a socially constructed belief and in so doing make it difficult for others to assert anything to the contrary. The collective, tacit assent of the "masses of men," over time turns into the fortified belief that becomes a part of the world of agreement. Over the course of the unfolding years it becomes an unexamined "of course," with the force of the great, unthinking majority holding it firmly in place, in effect daring anyone to challenge it.

However, that a belief is accepted as true by the general population does not make it good or true or right, nor does it make it bad or false or wrong. It just makes it popularly accepted as so, and, thus, difficult to resist. Further, the fact that a belief has become embedded in the collective cultural mind-set and pushed out of our immediate conscious awareness makes it difficult to recognize or identify as a mere social construction that may or may not be true.

Just seeing the world of agreement as such in our day-to-day affairs is a considerable feat for most of us. To violate and transcend the accepted wisdom, as the Apples of the world continuously do, is even more difficult, but it is precisely what transformative organizations do.

IT'S NOT BAD OR WRONG, BUT WE GOTTA SEE IT

The importance of understanding the existence of this limiting, invisible reality cannot be overstated. Indeed, every great leader has understood the importance of rising above these unexamined conventions, rising above the accepted limits of what could and should be done. And I do mean *every* great leader. From Thomas Jefferson, Benjamin Franklin, and John Adams in the political world, to Max Planck, Erwin Schrödinger, Albert Einstein, and Niels Bohr in physics, to Martha Graham in dance, Pablo Picasso in the visual arts, Igor Stravinsky in music, and Frank Lloyd Wright in architecture, to Bill Gates, Steve Jobs, Warren Buffet, Larry Page, and Sergey Brin in business, to Oprah Winfrey and Mark Zuckerberg in the media—all of these people said "No" to the false constrictions of the world of agreement. Every last one of these leaders refused to be constrained by the socially constructed limits of their cultures and in effect said, "Those may be your limits, but they sure as hell aren't mine." Their effectiveness as leaders issued in a large measure from their ability to see beyond the world of agreement, to answer to an entirely different awareness of what was and is possible.

Moreover, because the accepted conventions have come to represent what is comfortable, familiar, and safe, each of these leaders has had to learn to deal with resistance to their radical new ideas, resistance from the ordinary players in society, the unwitting defenders of the world as it is. Indeed, often the resistance is systematically organized and in some instances borders on the violent. To make this point to my clients, I often pose a little riddle: "How do you tell a true leader from a wannabe leader?" The answer? "The true leader is the one with arrows sticking out of his ass." Thus, the transformative leader is one who has wisely surrounded himself with a good, strong support team, if only to help remove those arrows, apply the healing salve, and thus help keep the leader on track in surmounting the world of agreement.

If we remember that the call of the transformative leader is a call to *cause the extraordinary*, to make a significant impact on the human circumstance—or in Jobs's now-famous words, "to put a dent in the universe"—then it's easy to see the importance of recognizing the world of agreement as it plays out in the everyday world of social interaction. It is one of *the* essential qualities that makes the transformative leader transforming: her commitment to rising above this world of unexamined beliefs.

More explicitly, the transformative leader is called upon to do two specific things in the face of the accepted wisdom that she recognizes as false: to *violate* it and then to *transcend* it. One naturally follows the other, but they are distinct actions, requiring distinct skills and mind-sets, generating noticeably different though complementary outcomes.

AT THE GATES OF HELL: VIOLATING THE WORLD OF AGREEMENT

When I consider the phrase "violating the world of agreement" or "breaking the grip of the accepted wisdom," I'm reminded of August Rodin's magnificent, eighteen-foot sculpture entitled *The Gates of Hell*, inspired by Dante's masterwork, *The Inferno*. Rodin's masterpiece is a vivid depiction of the entrance to the feared realm of "eternal damnation," a rendering that is both beautiful and horrific, at once violent and serene. We see the mayhem of writhing, agonizing souls with outstretched limbs, desperately reaching up for a salvation that's never to come; then there is the sublime serenity of *The Thinker* perched at the top of the work, calmly presiding over it all, silently contemplating for all eternity. Its exquisite detail and vitality are as inspired as its theme of torment and eternal misery is disturbing.

Okay, resistance to change is one thing, but why would such strong, even violent images come to mind? Simply because when we decide to violate—that is, overtly challenge—the world of agreement we must be prepared for what will almost inevitably follow. And typically what follows is not pretty. Though the extraordinary result we seek to create is likely intended for the good of all, and violence is sure to be the furthest thing from our minds, what we are doing will be experienced by many as an act of violence, violence to the accepted and protected norms of the culture. When we propose a new and better possibility, we threaten many people's places in the world, or so it will seem to them. Many will think, in some cases rightly so, that their standing and stature in the already established order is being called into question.

Rising above the accepted norm is usually disturbing to a large percentage of those affected. Even those who may benefit from the new direction (or the new policy or the proposed new world) are often fiercely resistant. What is perhaps most surprising to many leaders of bold, significant change is that sometimes even those who have requested the change (like the board of directors) are resistant! On the surface all of this would seem to make little sense, but looking a bit deeper and considering our unconscious, often irrational nature (to be taken up at length a bit later), we can understand the reasons.

The fact is, saying things are going to change triggers fear. Even if we couch it in the respectful language of "It worked for us yesterday but won't work for us tomorrow," the often-vehement, frequently irrational resistance is still likely to emerge. The experience some people will have is that of being made wrong, or worse, being made obsolete. It's a response that is generated by the fear of losing out, of being left out, and of being left behind: "Where will I fit in? Will I have the same status I now hold? Will I have a place in this new world at all? Will they surpass what we achieved and thus make our achievements seem less important?" All of these questions and others reflect anxieties residing just beneath the surface, many of which, remember, are entirely irrational. But they are real fears nonetheless, masked in all manner of resistance, anger, hostility, and resentment: "What a ridiculous idea, what a preposterous plan!" or, "Why wasn't I consulted?" or, "It's not possible. You're outta yer mind," or more covertly, "I'm actually fine with it, but I don't think it will fly—people aren't gonna like it, not in this company. Nope, don't think it'll get off the ground."

The resistance may be overt—"You're nuts!"—or slightly masked—"*I'm* fine with it, but . . . "—but if the vision of the new and possible truly rises above the accepted wisdom, rest assured, *some* people, *somewhere*, will take exception, probably passionate exception, to the proposition. And, in one sense at least, that's the good news, for when that happens (and the arrows and bullets are flying) it surely means we have violated (or are violating) the world of agreement: *We have created a whole new, radical conversation about what is possible.* Upheaval will have been created—we are standing before the gates of Hell—and that's just the beginning.

BUT HELL HATH NOT PREVAILED: TRANSCENDING THE WORLD OF AGREEMENT

Yet stirring up the pot, though perhaps uncomfortable, is the easy part. And it's not the objective, not the end point we're after. If we were to stop here, it would amount to throwing gas on a fire and idly watching it become a conflagration. The objective is to rise above what came before so that we might then disclose a new possibility and create a new and different world of understanding, a better world of action and results. This is where the need for courage enters the picture, where fortitude, strength of conviction, imagination, and staying power all become essential. Courage, as we will later discuss in detail, is not the absence of fear but rather the capacity to have fear and still move toward the desired end with your wits about you. And it is at this point in the leadership game that many would-be leaders understandably faint and lose heart—when those arrows, bullets, rocks, and darts begin to hit their mark, it can be painful, to say the least.

But this is also where the true leaders of transformation are made. For it is often at this point, as the heat rises, as the accusations of craziness and foolishness reach a crescendo, that we realize that all the noise and antagonism we have stirred up may reflect the fact that we're doing something right. It may tell us we are revealing a better world, proposing a better set of possibilities for the team, for the organization, for society.

Of course, resistance does not itself assure that the new proposition is good and right. The resistance might be because the bold new idea is a bad one. Given this possibility, the transformative leader, in the face of the upset that the proposal has generated, stops and listens and then carefully reflects on what he or she has heard. If upon this further reflection, however, the proposal continues to appear right and good, then the leader's resolve becomes stronger. The fact that some others don't see it or don't seem to want it is not a bad thing, the leader now realizes with even greater clarity, nor does it make these doubters wrong or bad.

Resistance, more times than not, is to be expected. And it's one of the reasons leaders are required in the first place! Our job is to surmount the resistance and anxiety that inevitably follows the introduction of the boldly new and different; our job is to lead and enroll the fearful resisters (*fearful,* not wrong or bad) into the new proposition. Indeed, if we are truly becoming transformative leaders, as the cacophony of fearful resistance reaches its peak, we remember that this is the "fun part," the part where we separate the children from the adults. We remember Wooden's words, that we derive joy from the struggle itself, from being sharpened, made stronger, becoming more engaged, more alive by the very fight for what is possible. Most important, we remember the importance of what we are doing, the beauty, power, and goodness of the vision that we have become increasingly committed to realizing. The upset that has been sparked forces us to reconnect with the deeper reason and the deeper wisdom that informed the proposed change in the first place.

And in that moment, *that moment*, the battle is won. There comes a flash of clarity, a split second of quiet, a becalmed knowing that seems to cause everything around us to slow way down, an instant that seems to last an eternity. In this moment, we now *know*. We know beyond any shadow of a doubt that we *won't* back down, that we *will*, somehow, some way, make it. We understand that we *must* and we *shall*. We may not know the precise means or mechanism for its achievement, but the outcome *will* be realized: We will have it turn out—come hell or high water.

And then, as we persist, slowly but surely we notice the conversations around us beginning to shift, to subtly but fundamentally change. The heat begins to let up, and a cool breeze begins to gently blow. The rattling din now seems a soothing hum, and in the stillness that follows we understand what is happening: We are *transcending* the accepted wisdom. We have broken its grip, and a whole new possibility is being born; a new world is, in fact, being disclosed. The iPod, in effect, is born, and how we listen to music will never be the same.

1774 as the Beginnings of Violation; 1776 as the Beginnings of Transcendence

Let's consider the ideas of violation and transcendence within the historical context of the American Revolution. The two years preceding the declaration of independence from Great Britain was a time of rancorous division between the colonial leaders—the colonies that were to become a union were anything but united. On one side of the debate were the colonists who believed rebellion to be unwise at best, idiotic and suicidal at worst. On the other side were those who saw a magnificent possibility at best and a noble failure "even unto death" at worst. Either way, both sides fully recognized that rebellion and the attempt to create a nation of people who governed themselves was an unmistakable violation of the conventional understanding (the world of agreement) of the time.

There were two underlying conventional beliefs that seemed most in need of violation and transcendence. First, was the belief that government without a monarch as the supreme authority was impractical, yea, a foolhardy pipe dream. The notion of self-rule, of some sort of a democratic republic, was deemed by most objective observers as preposterous. Indeed, virtually all recorded history up to that point in time would attest to the reasonable nature of this argument.

Second, was the conventional wisdom that held that the mighty British Empire would have little trouble slapping down the impudent, rag-tag collection of militias (primarily consisting of still-unorganized, largely illiterate farmers) that would become the rebellion's army. As is typically the case, reason seemed to be on the side of the accepted wisdom.

And the violation of these conventional understandings was indeed violent. First, in the contention among the colonists themselves, the rhetoric was often violent. High emotion—fear, anger, outrage, despair—greeted the proposed rebellion. Second, this rhetorical violation was followed by concrete violation and material violence: the bloody war that ensued from the declared independence.

Yet the transcendence of the accepted wisdom, the disclosure of a new world with a new set of standards and possibilities, began to happen only upon the war's cessation, as the officially recognized government of the United States of America took shape in the real world as a measurable fact, not simply an idea. Only then could it be said that the world of agreement had been transcended, that a new world had been disclosed and its creation begun.

Transcendence is present when fresh new possibilities are disclosed and become unfolding realities, *ever*-unfolding realities, when a new and different context has been, and *continues* to be, manifest—as when George Washington freely hands over power to Adams or when the union is knit back together after the Civil War or when a constitutional crisis is averted after Watergate. Transcendence has occurred when new expectations have been, are being, embraced and when, as a consequence, new and better results are being produced, and consistently so. Furthermore, those new results that demonstrate the transcendence are manifest both as a difference in degree—a dramatic drop in the crime rate, say, or a notable rise in revenue and margin—and as a difference in kind—entirely new and different things to be measured, observed, and experienced, like employee happiness, leadership growth, and organizational impact in the world.

When all is said and done, then, the transformative leader has a remarkable charge. She must be willing to take herself on and take her people on, and *then* she must be willing to stand for something and have that stand alter reality—she must bravely violate and transcend the world of agreement, her personal world of agreement as well as that of the organizational world in which she leads. The faint-hearted need not apply. It is a task only for those who would embrace adulthood, for those who would choose to achieve the great deed. And it is only for those who would stare death in the face and defiantly say, "So what?"

A CLARIFYING NOTE: WE ARE THE MEASURE

Lest some become daunted by the bigness of our examples in addressing the extraordinary, a qualification is in order: The transformative leader is not expected to be the next Richard Branson or Steve Jobs, not necessarily anyway. That's not the point. Indeed, being able to violate the world of agreement, to transcend the conventional wisdom does not require that we change *the* world, certainly not on such a scale (though we may surprise ourselves when we truly open up to the possible).

What it requires is a radical willingness to change *our* world, in *our* organizations, in *our* ways of leading and living—however grand or modest our circumstance. It requires creating that which is extraordinary within the context and in the lives of those we lead and in the results we and they produce. And it requires a willingness to be as big, as wise, as powerful, as caring, as creative and productive as we still have it in us to be. In other words, it requires that we summon the best we have within us. *We* are the scale against which we are to measure ourselves. Realizing *our* potential—the talent and promise, hidden and seen, that we possess impacting the world into which we have been "thrown" as leaders and individuals—is alone what matters. Beyond that, let's just say, it's gravy.

A TRANSFORMATIVE LEADER'S PRAYER

You're gonna die. So am I. No cure for death as yet. The transformative leader does not scoff at such a suggestion, doesn't think a statement of death's inevitability is obvious. He knows that, in fact, it is *not* obvious; he understands that most people live in denial of its reality. But not him. He periodically stands at the edge of the abyss and calmly peers into its infinite void. As he gazes into the rich, eternal layers of darkness he welcomes the fact that "the abyss also gaze[s] back into" him, as Friedrich Nietzsche[5] puts it, and in so doing he accepts the reality of his eventual demise—could be tomorrow, could be fifty years from now. But it's real. Gonna happen.

Thus accepting the inexhaustible mystery of death, he is struck by the even greater mystery of life. That there is *something*—the universe, creation, life, even a grain of sand on the beach—*rather than nothing* astonishes him, bends his finite mind, stirs his yearning soul. That he is alive, now, here, that he has power and will, intellect and imagination, the capacity for courage, the bent for love—all of these things are things he considers with frequency, because these remind him, in the face of death's reality, to live, to really live. They remind him to not be run by smallness, by the fears that run the "mass of men." He calmly realizes the power that is available when he is willing to see and surrender to the reality of what is, as he is willing to care, to stand, to give, to cause. Indeed, to cause nothing less than the extraordinary.

Suddenly he is overcome with a profound sense of gratitude for the brilliant challenge that is before him, the dangerous adventure of bringing into existence things that never before existed. Like goodness. The opportunity to be about, to lead others in, goodness, perhaps even to greatness. He is grateful. Humbled. Awake. Alive. . . . And then deep, rich, cool, dark silence.

A few moments more and he quietly steps back from the abyss, restored by its cool, fertile air, renewed as he recalls the sacred privilege of his leadership, refreshed by the prospect of being sharpened by the vital struggle, the struggle with his colleagues, for his colleagues, the struggle with his competition, even *for* his competition, the struggle for his people, for his industry, his struggle to serve something larger than himself. As he now makes his way back to the world of people and organizations, he realizes that in the context of integrating growth and self-expansion, in the context of leading to the extraordinary, this struggle is no struggle at all. It's a practice of increasing ease, simply the process by which he is made into a greater human being and leader of life, a greater leader of men and women, the kind of leader who causes others, his followers in particular, to know the power of connection and union as they make their collective and individual dents in the universe.

He remembers what most of us spend most of our lives trying to forget: that he, like everyone, as Jobs observes, is "already naked." And thus he also remembers, "There's no reason not to follow [his] heart." And he, *he* . . . he has a heart for the extraordinary, the beautiful, the good. Nothing less will do.

SUMMARY

The call of the transformative ethic is a call to transcend the ordinary, and in the domain of leadership that means three simple things: We must be able to identify the world of agreement as it plays out around us; we must have the courage to confront and violate it; and we must have the staying power to transcend it and disclose new and better worlds of organizational possibility and success, of organizational goodness and life. And while that may sound lofty, it is a most practical application of power and purpose.

With this rather brief depiction of the transformative leader, what she does, and the nature of what she accomplishes, we now turn to how she shapes herself into this kind of leader. In part II we address, in living color, the specific steps to be taken to develop ourselves more fully as leaders committed to life and its ever-emerging promise.

A Leader's Transformative Quest:

Summoning the Best We Have Within

CHAPTER 4

GETTING THE PICTURE:
A View from the Top

> Do not go where the path may lead, go instead where there is no path and leave a trail.
>
> **—Ralph Waldo Emerson**

When I was a boy, family friends owned a modest, two-story log cabin in an idyllic pine forest several miles west of Yellowstone National Park. Frequently during the summers we used the rustic getaway for family vacations, vacations that remain unsurpassed in my memory for sheer adventure, beauty, and wonder.

The first time I saw the small cabin was itself a moment of wonder. I was no older than five. It was near midnight in the midst of a torrential downpour as we slowly searched for the cabin in our red Rambler station wagon on an unpaved, muddy road. My father had stopped the car at a fork in the forest road when suddenly it struck: the loudest clap of thunder I had ever heard; it caused my sisters and me to scream at the top of our lungs, rattling the windows and my parents' ears. But in the next instant I was struck dumb by what I witnessed. The pitch-black night, for a split second, was perfectly and brilliantly illuminated by a flash of what my mother later called "sheet lightning." And there before us sat the little cabin in its humble, dry safety. The explosion of light was the most amazing thing I had ever seen. One second everything was blanketed in impenetrable, rain-soaked darkness, complete uncertainty; in the next second, perfect, stark clarity—everything revealed. By the time the darkness returned in the next moment, the vivid image of the wooded cabin had been forever and in detail etched on my mind.

For some, the whisper of the transformative possibility is not a whisper at all, but rather a vivid moment of clarity—with the jaw-dropping power of thunder and lightning. It may be only an instantaneous flash wherein the figurative darkness is briefly replaced by a vision of delicious possibility only to return to vague uncertainty. But the image remains, indelibly imprinted on the mind's eye. And the image? It's of a better life, with greater happiness and power and more meaningful success. It's of a leadership of such impact and substance that at the end of a full life, as death approaches, we're able to peacefully say to ourselves, "Well done. I used my time on this mortal plane effectively. I summoned the best of my promise and had greatest impact possible. Well done, indeed."

Even if our leadership (and our lives) seem to be clicking right along, that undeniable moment of clarity may flash before our eyes: There may be still greater possibilities, greater achievements, greater meaning and fulfillment available to us. But how do we turn the inner urge toward the bigger, better, and best into a reality? How do we learn to lead our lives and not simply manage them? How do we learn to lead others at more brave and effective levels? The short answer is that it all begins with a picture, a vivid picture of what does not yet exist but is nonetheless possible. It doesn't matter whether that picture appears in a flash or, more typically, emerges over the course of time.

Our initial step on the transformative path is to address the nature and importance of this picture. But to do that properly we must first make note of the reality that the picture is intended to supplant.

MORE THAN A TWEAK

For the majority of people walking the planet, life amounts to a series of passing moments of relief in between longer moments of struggle and stress. Think about it. For most leaders, and most people in general (even those we deem highly "successful"), life is a series of emotional and mental wrestling matches—with this person or that, with this problem or that, with this old anxiety or that—punctuated (we hope) with brief moments of respite, only to start all over again the following day. So what the hell are we fighting for? Slightly longer moments of relief in between the struggle and stress? That's all?

The transformative leader understands that this will not do. A simple change in degree (like those longer moments of relief) will not be sufficient. A mere tweak won't cut it. A change in *kind* is the order of the day. We're talking about a fundamental change in the quality of our leadership and our lives. But such a fundamental shift can only be found as we awaken a long-dormant aspect of ourselves, one that reflects, as Pulitzer Prize–winning scholar Ernest Becker says, our "private inner being, the great mystery"[1] that we feel at the heart of who we truly are. This private inner being, this great mystery at our essence, represents nothing less than the best that we have to offer the world, each other, and ourselves. To experience that greater life, indeed to summon that leadership greatness, we must learn to call forth those better selves. We must learn to live from that essence. And that brings us right back to the picture.

It's All in a Picture: The Minds of Revolutionaries

To better grasp the centrality of a picture or vision, once more we briefly consider the unlikely emergence of the United States of America. And it *was* unlikely. Indeed, for the independent nation to become a reality the revolutionary leaders had to overcome the longest of odds. Not just by defeating the world's only super power but by creating a system of government based on self-rule that has now lasted roughly two-and-a-half centuries and has inspired democracy around the world. Moreover, to suggest that the odds against their enterprise were long is to significantly understate, like suggesting that climbing Mt. Everest alone, in a blizzard, with a broken leg, would be a bit of a challenge. It was preposterous. Insane. The furthest thing from reasonable. The fact is, the reasonable thing for the colonial leaders to do was *not* to follow the idealistic vision of these fomenters of rebellion (Adams, Franklin, Jefferson, and company). The reasonable thing to do was to negotiate with the crown, work out a deal, placate, mollify, and otherwise cajole the king in order to gain some small benefit for the good of the colonies.

Yet the commitment of the founders was to something greater; their commitment was to achieving something quite extraordinary, and they did so. Against all odds. But how?

Rest assured, it wasn't simply the hatred that some held for their English overlords. While hatred can fuel resistance and even revenge, it cannot fuel the creation of something that is lasting and demonstrably good. So how did they create something so unlikely from nothing?

The short answer is they had an emerging and compelling dream. They had a vision, a vivid and growing picture in their minds of a world that *could* be, one that was not based on the past and certainly not on the present. Moreover, that it was an *emerging* vision means it didn't come to them whole cloth. It grew over time in their collective imagination. It was this vision that informed everything about the American Revolution. And it did guide and shape *everything*. It was their source of inspiration and their source of creativity. It informed their strategy and their tactics, and it was the basis for and sustenance of their courage and will to fight on in the face of ever-increasing adversity.

But what was it? It was a clear, detailed, textured, ever-growing picture of the possible—of something that by definition did not yet exist and had never before existed—of what could be, what might be: a society in which people were free to decide their own fates and govern themselves (even if indirectly), empowered to rise or fall of their own accord. It was on this vision that the founders forged their unswerving commitment ("unto death," if need be) and out of which they shaped their passion and constancy. It was this vision that summoned their integrity, inspired their strength to stand against the odds, and ignited their boldness to think the unthinkable.

Without this vision of the possible, the Revolutionary War might well have happened (despotic rule tends to generate violent resistance), but the success of the revolution would have been more than doubtful and the creation of the first modern democracy virtually impossible. Yes, it took grit and strategy, tactics and endless bravery, the aid of the French, and of course, money. But it was all nourished by this picture that existed entirely in the founders' imaginations, this picture of what could be, what might be, what they believed should be, and what they came to know *must* be—in spite of what the rest of the world might have said about the viability of their enterprise (and, for the record, most of the rest of the world thought they were out of their minds). Over time, for each of the leaders of the revolution, the emerging vision became more complex, not less; more personal, not less; and more vivid and compelling, not less.

And what was it that was behind the unfolding dream, behind the vision itself? Nothing less than the urge of radical possibility, an urge that transformed angry rebels into visionary leaders, transformed irregular bands of undisciplined militias into a united, irresistible force, and transformed thirteen divided colonies into the first and most successful modern democracy, with all of its warts, problems, and proclivities for the grand mistake. It was the urge for a better, truer, more meaningful and complete life—the same urge that informs transformative leadership—that was the fire and the fuel of the dream that rudely rattled the world.

WHY WE GET STUCK

Yet when we consider our organizations, our leadership, and our lives, the change we want seems to happen at a snail's pace, if it happens at all. Life is pretty much the same as it ever was. But we know that this static description of reality is not accurate. We know that change is the "one constant in the universe." Everything is change—and *everything* includes you and me and the world we live in. We and it are always either in a process of growth or decay. Stability is the illusion, not change.

Okay, so why, then, is it so hard to change our lives (and our leadership impact), change our companies, change this old messed-up world of ours? Here's the in-a-nutshell answer: Reality is not the problem. Reality in fact is imminently malleable. As hard as this may be to believe, it's waiting to be changed. The problem is that we keep on keepin' on, without ever realizing that we're doing it. That is, we keep reenvisioning the same world, the same life, the same reality, the same organization, the same relationships, the same *problems* again and again and again and again and again. Even if we are envisioning our leadership (or aspects of our lives) from the point of view that says "I don't like this," or "I hate that," or "When is this ever going to change?" we're still unwittingly seeing and *reinforcing* the very circumstance we find objectionable.

And it's as if life says, "Well, okay. Since you keep asking for it, here ya go," and plop, right in our laps drops the same stuff one more time—and we never quite figure out that we've "asked" for it with our unwitting expectations, our repetitive focus on and complaints about the problem. And here's the kicker: There is never a time when we are not driven by some sort of vision, never a time when we don't have a sense (usually an inarticulate sense) of what the future will be. We're not aware that we're creating (and recreating) out of a picture—it happens automatically, just beneath the surface of our awareness, but it happens nonetheless.

So it's not that things stay the same as much as it is that we recreate the same things, again and again, without recognizing we're doing anything at all. In so doing *we* are perpetuating the world (and our worlds) as it was (as they were), as it is, and as it shall be—until, that is, we change the damn picture. *We* are the culprits, not life, not reality. Our repetitive, largely subconscious, visioning of the old is to blame. *That* is what makes life the "same as it ever was," what makes things change very slowly, if ever.

Our best hope, then, is in our capacity to begin seeing a *different* picture—of ourselves, our lives, our leadership, our organizations, and our world. Period. If we want to change things, the creation of a new, compelling picture of what could be is not an option. It's mandatory. It's not an accident, after all, that the civil rights movement in the United States was so interwoven with Martin Luther King Jr.'s "I Have a Dream" speech. And while creating and living from a new picture is not necessarily easy, it *is* doable. It's been happening since human beings first showed up.

A COMPELLING PICTURE

Now then, back to the original question: *How do we develop a more far-reaching, effective, meaningful leadership? How do we get to that bigger, richer, deeper life?* It is found within this capacity to see, to imagine, to evoke and envision that greater capacity for leadership, that greater quality of life that most of us have stored away, locked deep within our psyches. It is the capacity to bring that picture up and out into the light of day that is key. It's this willingness to reimagine or to create anew the vibrant picture of the possible that is at the very heart of the transformative process—for the individual and for the organization. And like the need for love and the desire for happiness, that vision is there in all of us, if only in a still-undeveloped form.

Over the years we have trampled all over it, kicked dirt in its face, in our efforts to heed the demands of "realism," and over time it has been deeply buried and perhaps completely forgotten. But it's there. Rest assured, it *is* there. It must be summoned and developed in vivid detail. It is a picture of who we might become, of what we might do and get done with our leadership and beyond—the success we might have and the life we might yet lead—and I don't care *how* old you are!

It is the lifeblood of transformation—for the leader (the individual) and for the group. It is the preeminent and perhaps most challenging immediate task for the transformative journey we are beginning. Because without an increasingly clear and compelling picture of what we want to be, what we want to do and accomplish with what remains of our lives, without a clear picture of who we might become and what we might get done as leaders, we will not be likely to call forth the courage, imagination, and power necessary to overcome the formidable obstacles that will surely arise in our paths. And they *will* arise. Without a clear picture of what we would get done as leaders, with others and with the organization, those largely subterranean "personal issues" that have always kept us from successfully responding to our deeper possibilities will again prevail.

Despite the effectiveness of the growth and leadership methods described in the chapters to follow, despite the tried and true techniques for manifesting the possible, *if there is not a sense of why, a growing understanding of who and what might be created, that is, if there isn't a* vision, *then the transformative fire will not have sufficient fuel to see the transformation through to the end.* And the fuel, the very nearly infinite fuel, is that well-honed, ever-more-vivid dream, that image and story of what you want in your life, in your leadership, and in the lives of the people you love and lead. The importance of establishing this picture could not be greater. It is both an act of creating and uncovering—or in some instances simply admitting—what you aspire to be, to do, and to have.

Finally, we must understand that this whole vision thing requires a good dose of courage. There are reasons that long ago we let go of those desires, those hopes and dreams, reasons that remain largely out of view of our conscious explanations, out of view of what have become our rationalizations. For reasons that will later become clear, overcoming those largely unconscious rationales requires moral fiber of a kind that can only be called courageous. Thus, for many, just creating the vision, let alone achieving it, will require a true commitment to the life and leadership that you deeply desire.

The "Who We Really Are" Thing

It has been suggested that the great problem of the late twentieth and early twenty-first centuries is the problem of authenticity. That is, with such an abundance of options available to us, we are not sure who we are and what we should do with our individual as well as our collective lives. The great Swiss psychoanalyst Carl Jung puts the dilemma in stark relief. "In the final analysis," he says, "we count for something only because of the essential we embody and if we do not embody that, life is wasted."[2] His terse finality should give us pause. To embody something means to be a living, physical manifestation of an idea, principle, or quality, to in fact be the personification of a trait or attitude or feeling. The only life that is not wasted, according to Jung, is a life in which the individual first, sees what her unique essence is and second, lives it out fully. Even with a generous interpretation of what Jung means, by his standard the vast majority of human beings (at least in the wealthy industrialized countries of the world) seem to be in the process of wasting their lives.

While that may go a bit too far, there surely is some truth in it, a lot of truth. Let's assume for the moment, then, that Jung *is* correct: To live a life that counts for something, and by extension to be a leader who counts for something, we must embody what we are in our unique essence—anything less is failure. The only way to live a life worth living, then, the only way to make it to the end of our lives and know that we took full advantage of the incomparable gift of life, is to get down to the unvarnished truth of who we are at our core, at our deepest and highest. To see it fully and to demand of ourselves that we live up to this essentialness in the fullness of the life we are given.

Let's consider our dilemma from a slightly different perspective, again through the wise eyes of Ernest Becker. He says plainly:

> [there is but one] real problem of life, the only worthwhile preoccupation of mankind: What is one's true talent, his secret gift, his authentic vocation? In what way is one truly unique and how can he express this uniqueness, give it form, dedicate it to something beyond himself? How can the person take his private inner being, the great mystery that he feels at the heart of himself, his emotions, his yearnings and use them to live more distinctly, to enrich both himself and humankind with the peculiar quality of his talent?[3]

The secret to living a life of meaning, a life of distinctness, a life of power is found in getting at the heart of who we are and living that out completely.

What is surprising about this seemingly idealistic idea of this "private inner being," and these curious "yearnings" is that they turn out to be entirely practical. Once we uncover and face up to these deeper desires (what Joseph Campbell calls our "bliss"), we realize they usually are not far-fetched, out-of-this-world summits that we must conquer, or over-the-top forms of self-expression. More times than not, they turn out to be economically and emotionally of this world and far more readily realized than we may have feared. This inner mystery is not all that mystifying. Summoning our leadership (and personal) best, becoming what we still have it in us to be, even achieving what we understand as the extraordinary, requires a get-it-done attitude and a measurable level of effectiveness, and it generates a real-world, sustainable quality of happiness. And finally, it enriches not just our lives but the lives of those around us and surely the lives of those we lead.

The "What We Want" Thing

The personal vision process is an exercise in turning an abstraction (an idea, a feeling, a desire) into something concrete. What is true about most great leaders in history and virtually all powerful people in general is that they have known what they wanted and have been unafraid to go get it. They were, they are, *clear*. Evidence consistently and increasingly suggests that the greatest obstacle in expanding our quality of life, in enhancing our leadership and changing our organizations, in transforming our world, in fact, is insufficient clarity about the desired outcome. We fail at manifesting the new and different in our leadership and our lives because we have not generated the courage and discipline to *imagine it*—the person, the life, the leadership success, the better world—in vivid detail and to then lead lives informed by that vision. The secret to powerful manifestation—of the life you desire, the leadership success you seek, the corporation and the world you long to see—is clarity. *Clarity*. Clarity in riveting, colorful, textured, thrilling detail. Clarity and ever-increasing clarity. Am I making myself clear?

The first step in the TL process is identifying (uncovering and creating) the better vision of you: who you can be, how you can lead, and what you can achieve. Your immediate challenge is to take an opening stab at what's possible, an opening shot at uncovering the vision that seeks to emerge from your inner, perhaps truer self. The best way to do that is to go through the process that follows: Exercise 4.1 "A Thought Experiment Einstein Would Appreciate."

I strongly encourage you to complete the challenging work of the exercise, all three steps—give it everything you've got. The impact of the rest of the book will be far greater if you have made this opening foray into shaping your vision before reading on.

EXERCISE 4.1 A THOUGHT EXPERIMENT EINSTEIN WOULD APPRECIATE

Albert Einstein was well known for turning reality on its ear, famous for having said things like, "Imagination is more important than knowledge," and, "Intuition is more important than IQ." What is beyond question is that one of the greatest scientific minds in human history understood the extraordinary importance of imagining things that did not yet exist in our three-dimensional world. He once said that he never discovered anything with his rational mind and claimed that he discovered his theory of general relativity by riding "a beam of light" (in his imagination, of course). Intuition and imagination were not the products of childish reverie. Rather they were conduits for a deeper and broader understanding of reality—of both what is and what could be.

As a theoretical physicist he employed what are called "thought experiments." So did (and do) many other leading thinkers. "Thought experiments," says the *Stanford Encyclopedia of Philosophy*, "are devices of the imagination used to investigate the nature of things."[4] They are speculative responses to questions or situations explored in the mind and then usually put down on paper (or explored in the mind *as* they are put down on paper).

In the Einsteinian thought experiment, imagination is central. If the very thought of considering yourself or your life in this way makes your skin crawl, I suggest, well, that you get over it. This is important stuff. It's only the rest of your life that's at stake! Your self-understanding determines every single aspect of your life, and this process is central to deepening and expanding that understanding.

Instructions

Assume that for the next few minutes you've been granted the extraordinary power to reinvent yourself—who you are (your dominant ways of being), your ways of relating to others, even your talents and skills as a leader, as a spouse or lover, as a friend, as a colleague, as a boss, and so on—and to reinvent your life—what you do and accomplish, where and how you live, how you are regarded by others in your world. Remember, this is not about being reasonable. If John Adams had been reasonable the revolution wouldn't have happened.

Overview: Imagine your best self and your perfect life fully (prompts 1 and 2 below) and write it down. This is riding the beam of light, getting beyond the boundaries within which you've lived. Then respond to prompt 3: How would you need to live your life differently than you are now to be this person and to have what this person has?

I recommend that you use a notebook or journal to do all the work proposed in this book, preferably one that is exclusively dedicated to the process of your personal and leadership growth (you'll return to this work often, so loose papers are not advised). Further, I strongly encourage you *not* to do this on a computer. Write it out, longhand. Brain scans demonstrate that writing by hand engages more regions of the brain than typing. We want to bring as much of ourselves to the equation as possible.

Three Action Steps: In writing, respond in imaginative detail (Put your back into it!) to the following three prompts:

1. Describe in specifics your ideal self. Describe the character traits or qualities you see as most essential to this perfect you—things like confidence, calmness, passion, courage, integrity, honesty, purposefulness, self-respect, compassion, generosity, joy, sense of humor, capacity for vision, capacity to inspire, presence, intentionality, and power. Describe how you feel about yourself as this ideal you. Describe how others, generally speaking, look upon you. How do they regard you as a man or woman in the world? Also describe yourself physically—your fitness and overall health and your appearance. Do this in as much elaborative detail as you can muster. Remember, this is your ideal self, your perfect self. Unleash your imagination. Get beyond your normal comfort zone and ride that beam of light.

2. Then, describe in detail your ideal life, the exterior circumstances of your life. Where do you live, with whom, and in what kind of a home? What is your chief way of spending your time, what is your vocation, your career? If you already lead others or aspire to, how so? What is the nature of the impact you have as a leader? What is your status in this perfect life? How are you recognized by others (professionally and personally) in this world? What is your relationship to wealth and prosperity—how much money, friends, free time, property, leisure, and travel do you have/do? Who are your primary relationships with and what is the quality of these relationships? Again, remember, this is about letting your imagination run wild. Playing it safe, being reasonable will not work. Stretch yourself here. It is not about what you think might be available to you, but what you *want*. Give yourself permission to want what you really want. Throw caution to the wind, at least for the purposes of this exercise.

3. After fully completing 1 and 2, respond to these speculative questions: Given this ideal world (who you are and what your life looks like in its most perfect expression), how must you live your life differently? How must you regard, understand, esteem yourself? How must you approach others (the "most and the least of these")? How must you approach and think about your professional relationships and your friendships? Do you need to be more selective or more inclusive? How must you regard yourself as a player in your profession, your business, your industry, the world? How must you approach your primary relationships (spouse or partner, children, family, closest friends)? How must you honor your deepest commitments? How must you nurture your creativity? How must you take care of yourself? How must you push and demand from yourself? How must you assert yourself and take risks?

SUMMARY

The possibility that our leadership and our lives could be more powerful and rewarding may reveal itself in a thrilling flash or may become clear over the unfolding course of time; it might show up as the result of a painful personal crisis, or it may emerge out of a nagging sense that there simply must be more to life than we currently know and experience. However it is manifest, deep within all of us there is this desire for a richer, more fulfilling life, and in most of us there's a recognition that our leadership impact can be far greater than it already is. Though the urge toward greater life and more meaningful leadership influence is often suppressed beneath the pressures to conform or merely survive, it remains present in every one of us.

Transforming our lives, our leadership, and our world is possible through a step-by-step protocol. The first step is to begin to see, to imagine, what might yet be—as leaders and as individuals. Only as we begin to glimpse who we can still become, what we can yet achieve, and how we may potentially affect the lives of others are we able to summon the necessary courage to get beyond our self-imposed false limitations. In chapter 5 we consider the three foundational principles that must be understood and acted upon to get past these unnecessary limitations and affect the lasting changes that our emerging personal visions require.

CHAPTER 5

THE TRANSFORMING TRIAD:
A Metaphor with Three Legs

> This mountain of release is such that the
> ascent's most painful at the start, below;
> the more you rise, the milder it will be.
> And when the slope feels gentle to the point that
> climbing up sheer rock is effortless
> as though you were gliding downstream in a boat,
> then you will have arrived where this path ends.
>
> **—Dante, *The Divine Comedy***

To *transform* something means to change it in a radical rather than a modest way. It means to fundamentally alter what that something is at a basic level. It means to call forth its most essential qualities, qualities that heretofore may have been latent or dormant or only present in potential. Transformation as movement away from managing one's life and toward leading it necessarily speaks to an awakening of new degrees and qualities of power—power that is available to every human being who is willing to take the necessary action.

And yet, the pursuit of a better life more times than not leaves us in a state of frustration. We get a glimpse of what is possible, what might be and become of our leadership and our lives, but when we reach out to grab it, the possibility seems to vanish. The power and beauty that might await almost seems like a tease. But it's not. What it *is* is demanding. Achieving it is simple but not easy. In fact, it's work—hard work. And most people are unwilling to pay that price. They might take a stab at it, but when the reward is not instantaneous they throw their hands up in frustration and return to the ordinary "same as it ever was."

There is no shortcut, no magic pill, no three-day workshop that is going to permanently expand our range and depth as men and women. The rewards of bravely answering the transformative call are real, but its dictates and requirements are tall. Transformation is not for the faint of heart.

So let's be clear about the demands of transformation as leaders and as individuals. What is required is courage, love, imagination, and above all, commitment. We must have the *courage* to withstand the taunts that will emerge from the mediocrity that surrounds us—both from within (our doubts about our ability and worth) and outside of us (others who will be uncomfortable with and resistant to our desire for excellence). We must *love* ourselves and others enough to accept the fact that we and they deserve the goodness that will be a consequence of our pursuit of the extraordinary. We must be willing to do the brave work of *imagining* what does not yet exist but is, nevertheless, available if we will but see and fastidiously hold to it. And, finally, we must summon the fierce *commitment* to embark on this journey and remain steadfast to the end. It's a lifelong process—and it ends only upon our deaths.

Did I mention that? That we never arrive, that we must embrace the fact that transformation is a lifelong journey? It is. The good news is that the glorious rewards—the beauty, the accomplishment, the abundance, the joy—happen all along the way. And after a while we begin to enjoy the process. Indeed, as we learn to enjoy the process, the process itself becomes rewarding.

But the best news of all, perhaps, is that transformation happens by following clearly understandable and doable steps, built upon immutable principles.

THREE KEYS TO TRANSFORMATION

The first key to transformation is *responsibility and changing our minds*; the second is *intention and possibility*; and the third is *contribution*.

1. *Responsibility* is the recognition and embrace of our nature as an agent of cause. We must accept the fact that as adults we have caused and continue to cause our lives to be as they are. *Changing our minds* refers to the act of literally and permanently changing how our brains function as a means of liberating our latent talents, our deepest passions, our ability to care, and our capacity for consistent success as leaders and beyond.

2. *Intention* may be the single most important character trait in the entire pantheon of leadership and life-effectiveness virtues, especially in creating sustainable success. It is not a wish, a hope, or a desire. Rather, it is a state of mind that reflects the highest quality of commitment a leader can attain. *Possibility* is the domain from which all true intention and creativity emerge. Unlike an option, which by definition is limited by historical precedent, a possibility is unlimited and represents the point of origin for acts of authentic leadership.

3. As high-minded as *contribution* to others might seem, it is at the same time fundamentally practical. When we grasp the power and importance of genuine contribution, we also grasp the remarkable fact that as we get ourselves out of the way and see "the other," we simultaneously liberate our talents and capacities. If there is such a thing as a secret to life, genuine contribution is it. Life just works when we get this mystifying truth (though "getting it" is more easily said than done).

We use the metaphor of a stool with three legs, as depicted in Figure 5.1, to represent the three principles of transformation.

The Floor Beneath the Stool

There is one more element to our metaphor that needs to be addressed: the floor on which the three-legged stool rests. The floor beneath the stool is the ground of being of the transformational process. It informs all aspects of the stool—all three legs and the seat. We are the floor, you and I. More specifically, the mind-set that we bring to the process is the floor. The nature of that mind-set will determine the success or failure of our endeavor. And, of course, just any mind-set won't do.

Figure 5.1 The Three-Legged Stool of Transformation

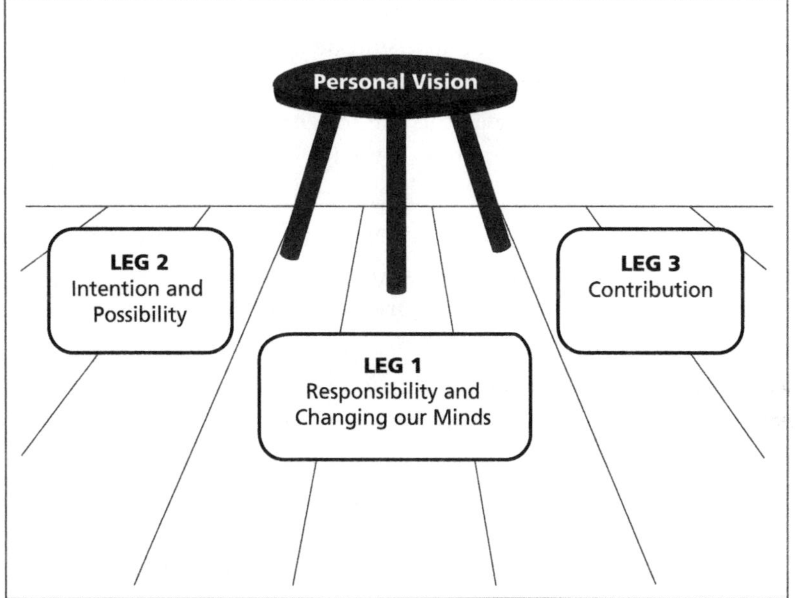

The stool's seat represents our personal vision, such as the one you began developing in Exercise 4.1. That personal vision is supported by the three legs of individual transformation. The first leg of the stool is responsibility and changing our minds; the second leg is intention and possibility; the third leg is contribution.

We must approach the transforming process with three fundamental mental and emotional qualities: openness, thoughtfulness, and the heart to see things through. *Openness* simply means a willingness to try this process on, a willingness to suspend prejudice (pre-judgment) long enough to give all aspects of the transformative process full and fair consideration. It also means that you must be open to the possibilities that exist for you and your life—you must be willing to give those possibilities their due, even possibilities you may not have yet imagined.

Thoughtfulness means a willingness to think hard about the concepts being presented and about yourself. As a society we tend to be intellectually lazy. As we soon will see, much of what we call "thinking" is little more than automatic, preprogrammed patterns of reaction. We don't think as much as we react and then call it thought. Real thinking is not easy. But this process requires it. It demands that we carefully consider, that we do the difficult work of honest, careful, deliberate thinking.

Finally, to approach this process with *heart* means to summon the passion and the will, the love and dedication, to see it through to the end. In a culture that says, "If I want it, I must have it, and have it *now*," staying power, the will to see a promise through to its completion, is not a virtue that is much fostered. Yet we have that capacity, and the transforming journey requires it in full measure.

The floor on which the transforming stool stands, then, is a mind-set that displays all three of these sensibilities. As we move into the substance of part II, I urge you to periodically check in with yourself to ensure that you are operating from all three qualities as they are specifically called for. The more you remember to embrace this mind-set, the more readily you will make this process a success.

So, do the work. And remember it's your life that is at stake here; half-assin' it won't do.

Besides, what have you got to lose? A few wasted nights in front of the TV? Come on! To paraphrase the wonderfully irreverent Monty Python, we come into this old world with nothin', and we go out of it with nothin'. So what have we lost? Nothin'! Do the doggone work, and do it with conviction.

SUMMARY

The future is not necessarily determined by the past. How it's always been is not how it always must be. As human beings we have two remarkable faculties: the capacity to imagine what does not yet exist and the ability to bring that imagined thing into existence, whether it's a whole new world or a qualitatively different individual life. If we have the courage, we have the capacity for transformation.

But if we are to radically change ourselves in any domain—if we are to learn to lead rather than merely manage our lives, and if we are to learn to *powerfully* lead others—we must accept transformation's unbending ways. Transformation's arresting poetry is matched only by the logic of its geometry, which demands that we first recognize the transforming stool with three legs: Leg 1, *responsibility and changing our minds;* Leg 2, *intention and possibility;* and Leg 3, *contribution*. Transformation makes one other thing unmistakably clear: We are to begin at the beginning, and so, to Leg 1 we now turn.

LEG 1:

Responsibility and Changing Our Minds

Leg 1 of the three-legged stool of transformation is the most complex of the legs. It is made up of two larger actions: first, acknowledging the nature of the human mind and understanding the nature of true responsibility, and second, out of that understanding, taking the necessary action to permanently change our thinking. We break these two actions down further into four basic steps: acknowledgment, responsibility, recognition, and changing our minds, illustrated in Figure L.1.

Figure L.1 Leg 1 of the Transformational Stool: Responsibility and Changing Our Minds

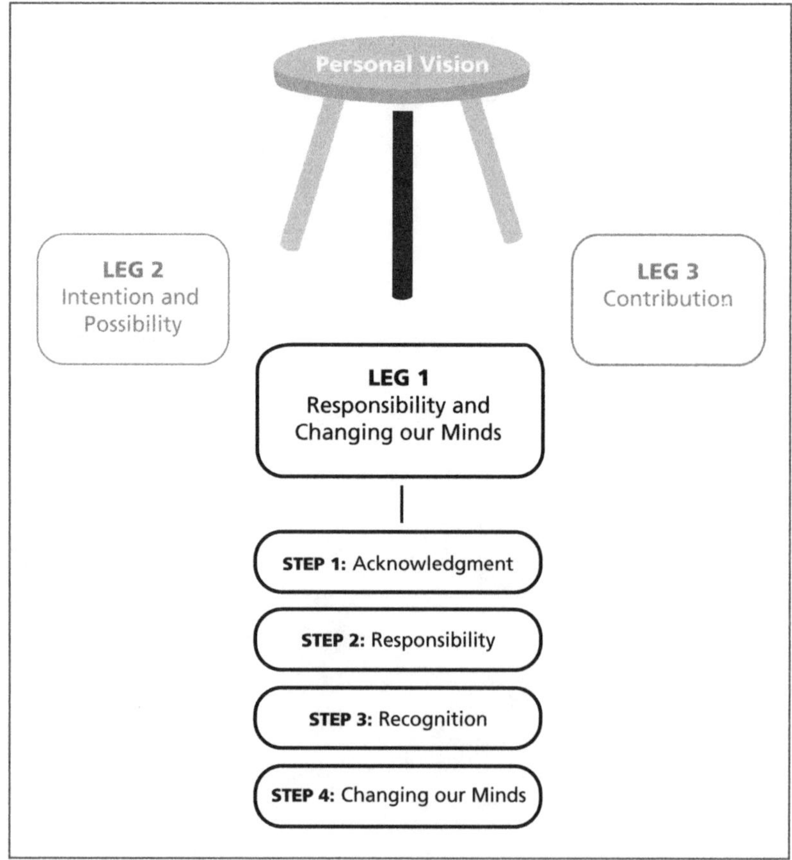

Acknowledging the Nature of the Mind and "Getting" Real Responsibility

To lead our lives and to lead others at new levels of effectiveness and power, we must first understand as deeply as possible and acknowledge the nature of the human mind (primarily that we are not as conscious as we assume), and we must grasp the essential qualities of authentic individual responsibility. This is an audacious task, no doubt; philosophers and psychologists have been wrestling with these issues for centuries. Still, to achieve the extraordinary, no small measure of audacity is required.

Taking Action to Change Our Minds

But intellectual assent is not enough. To generate the growth and change we seek, we must *act*, taking advantage of that understanding. We must recognize the simple fact that as individuals each one of us has a unique set of filtering beliefs that operate largely out of view of our conscious understanding, hindering our personal and leadership effectiveness. Identifying these limiting, typically false, beliefs allows us to begin the process of replacing them with more powerful and accurate understandings.

In chapter 6 we address step 1, acknowledgment of the reality and extent of our unconscious mental tendencies. Chapters 7 and 8 address step 2, true responsibility. Chapters 9 and 10 address step 3, recognition of our false, limiting beliefs; and chapters 11 and 12 address step 4, changing the architecture of our minds by changing the biology and functioning of our brains.

CHAPTER 6

ACKNOWLEDGMENT: Facing Up to Our Unconscious Condition

> Consciousness is like the child who "plays" a video game at an arcade without putting any money into it. He moves the control, unaware that he is seeing a demonstration program that is independent of his actions. The child (consciousness) believes he is controlling the action, while in fact the software in the machine (nonconsciousness) is completely in control.
>
> **—Timothy D. Wilson**

The first step in the TL growth process requires that we face up to the disquieting fact that we as human beings are not the conscious, rational beings we think we are. In fact, the majority of our cognitive activity, our thinking, occurs at an automatic *un*conscious level. Thus, in effect, we must become conscious of the fact that we are largely unconscious beings, driven by our unconscious impulses, attitudes, and perceptions. As cutting-edge research suggests, we are largely unconscious creatures more or less pretending to be conscious. The truth of this matter and its vast consequences are lost on most of us. But the facts are the facts, and the first step in transformation is awakening to, honestly facing into—acknowledging—the far-reaching implications of our fundamental lack of consciousness.

It is not pleasant to hear, but most us live our lives in a kind of "autopilot" mode—an almost dazed state of repetition, of automatic action and reaction, all the while thinking we are operating

Figure 6.1 Acknowledgment

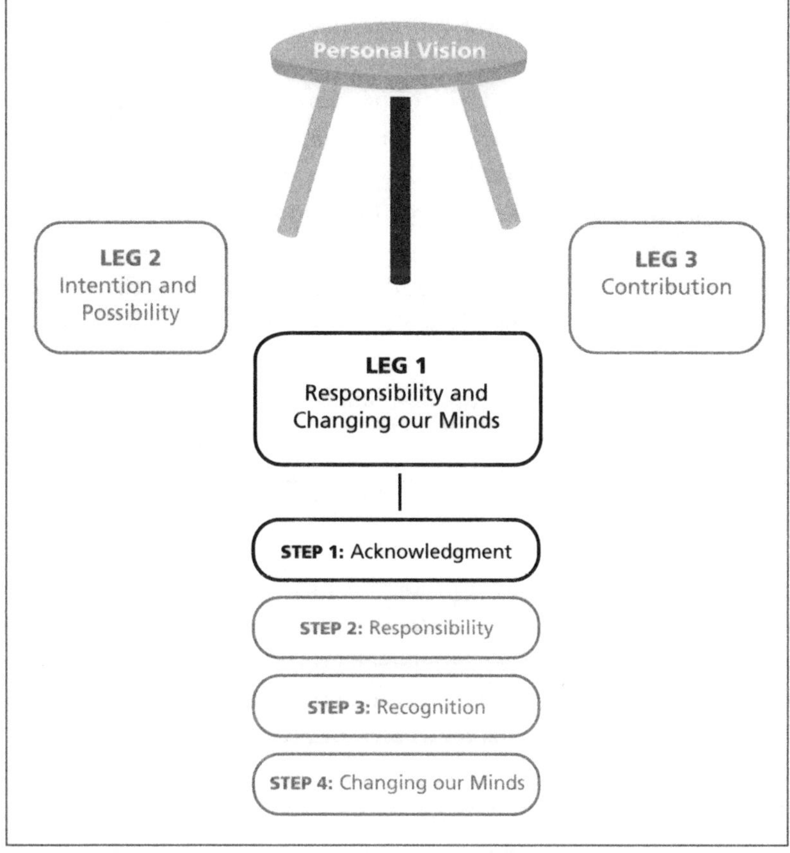

from a conscious state of mind. That doesn't sound like you, you say? Well, stay tuned; you may be surprised.

For decades, psychology has asserted the reality of our unconscious ways, and breakthroughs in the late twentieth and early twenty-first centuries in our understanding of how the brain works are confirming many of these psychological assertions. And here is what the foremost leaders in the study of the mind have to say: No matter how you slice it, we are not the rational, consciously thinking creatures that we have fancied ourselves to be. As University of Virginia research psychologist Timothy Wilson puts it, we are, to some degree at least, strangers to ourselves.[1] Philosopher René Descartes's famous dictum *cogito ergo sum*, "I think, therefore I am," is only true within a carefully qualified context. Most of the time we *don't* think. Most of the time we merely react and tell ourselves that it's thinking. In essence, we fool ourselves.

Many of the reasons we do what we do and say what we say are *not* for the reasons we think—not for the reasons we tell ourselves and others. The majority of our daily "thinking" and decision making occurs automatically at this unconscious level.[2] If this fact is not at least a little a bit disturbing, you may be missing the point. And this unconscious decision-making mind of ours is like a preprogrammed computer that "thinks," in part, based on embedded beliefs, impressionistic understandings, and judgments that each of us made up or downloaded long ago and far away, mostly as very young children. Let me say that again so you don't miss it: The majority of our thinking (our decision-making) happens unconsciously; and much of that "thinking" is based on our preprogrammed filtering system that emerged out of our experiences of ourselves and the world, good and bad, *as young children.*

This psychological reality has vast consequences. Much of what we call *rationality* is actually a process of rational*izing* (a kind of lying about) what our unconscious minds have already decided for us, long before it ever reaches the conscious level of awareness. Our unconscious minds decide for their own reasons, and our conscious minds explain it in a way that makes us comfortable with the decision.

For instance, I may tell myself that the reason I decided not to go for that big promotion I previously wanted was because of the time it would take away from my family or my social life. At a deeper level the truth may be something quite different. At this deeper level, the real reason may be that I fear I don't deserve the success it represents, or I may doubt my ability to handle the job, or I may fear I won't get it and will thus look bad (like a failure) to my colleagues. But this less-than-appealing truth is not what I admit to myself, not what I am willing to accept with my conscious mind. So I rationalize and do so at an instantaneous, automatic level without even realizing I am doing so. I do it unconsciously.

Not a particularly pleasing thought, if we get its import. And its import? We're not the ones doing much of our thinking, our unconscious is; we're not the ones in charge of how we feel much of the time, our unconscious is; we're not the ones dictating much of our behaviors on a day-to-day basis, our . . . well, you get the point.

And so, yes, the truth about and implications of our unconscious condition are vast and a bit troubling. So we resist. We deny the implications. We would simply prefer to look the other way, which is exactly what we do.

THE DENIAL THAT WE DO

This denial is understandable. First, simply enough, we don't *want* to believe it. We just don't want to surrender to the fact that so much of what we do and feel is beyond the control of our conscious minds. It's unsettling to think that we are not the masters of our own destinies, that we are not the autonomous creatures we would like to believe we are. Second, it is counterintuitive. Every day while we are awake it *feels* as though it is our conscious minds making our decisions. It *seems* like what we do, we do for the reasons we tell ourselves. It seems that way, and it feels so much better to believe that it *is* that way, even though it's not.

The third reason we choose to deny, despite the evidence to the contrary, is the most interesting and most human of all. Much like our intellectual ancestors, we are inclined to resist the new and different. And the more radical and counterintuitive the idea, the greater our resistance. This tendency is not good or bad. It's just what human beings do. It's natural.

The Earth Is Flat, Doggone It!

It wasn't until nearly two centuries after it was first proven by Nicolaus Copernicus in the sixteenth century that a significant chunk of people living in the Western world began to accept the notion that the Earth is not the center of the universe, that it is round and moving rather than flat and stationary. After all, the mere suggestion that we are on a spinning ball that is flying through space was entirely contrary to instinct and appearances—that is, it was counterintuitive.

It was simply foolish to think that we are on a ball. *Why, pray tell, did it look so flat?* That it is spinning. *Why wasn't everything being knocked about?* That it is hurtling at astonishing speeds through space. *What?! Foolishness, absolute foolishness!* And absolutely true. A few centuries ago we *knew* the Earth was flat. We didn't *believe* it. We *knew* it. What we know today is that what we *thought* we knew a few hundred years ago was wrong. That something is counterintuitive does not make it right or wrong, but it does make it easier to deny.

Of Snowballs and Icebergs: Today's Counterintuitive Hurdle

Today, as we stand in the early years of the twenty-first century, we are in the throes of another radical shift in our understanding of the human circumstance. Much as we turned our understanding of the physical universe on its ear four or five hundred years ago, we are now rethinking our understanding of the human mind and thus the human experience. And as with all significant change, our natural reaction is resistance—or flat-out denial. It's counterintuitive, and it doesn't necessarily feel good. So we go along our merry way, whistling past the graveyard, pretending to be far, far more conscious than in truth we are.

Resist though we may, the reality of our unconscious nature remains. "According to the modern perspective," Professor Wilson tells us, "Freud's view of the unconscious was far too limited. When he said . . . consciousness is the tip of the mental iceberg, he was short of the mark by quite a bit—it may be more the size of a snowball on top of that iceberg."[3] It is a reality, counterintuitive or not, that we must come to terms with.

For a moment consider what this all suggests. Major aspects of our leadership and our living in general are not governed by our "awake" minds. They are driven by that enigmatic, subterranean region of fears, hopes, memories, and beliefs beneath the surface of our conscious thought. We may think we are thinking, but much of the time we are merely reacting. And vast portions of this hidden domain that determines our instantaneous reactions are made up of beliefs, judgments, hopes, attitudes, fears, feelings, and still-vague, impressionistic perceptions that were largely "downloaded" while we were very young. And this would explain (though not explain away) much of the idiocy we see on display with many of our public figures—political and business leaders for instance—not to mention our own, sometimes puzzling, foolishness. But how does this all happen and what, if anything, can we do about it?

THE DICEY-NESS OF DEVELOPMENT

During our first seven to eight years of life, by virtue of normal neurobiological development, our brains are learning to do some amazing things. But they are not yet able to do some other things—like make subtle, critical distinctions about who we are, who other people are, and how the world is. During these years we largely accept as true what we are told. In effect, we download information, much like that computer, uncritically logging information in as it's presented to us, or as we *think* it's being presented to us. Developmentally our brains are such that it's impossible to do much more than absorb, so *absorb* is precisely what our highly impressionable minds do.

During this critical developmental period, we pay special heed to what primary adult figures imply, or directly tell us, is true. As young children we see our parents as gods of a sort. They don't speak the truth. They *are* the truth. If they say it or do it, imply it or display it, it is so. No argument. And it's duly registered. Thus, if they communicate that we are clever or smart and do this on a recurring basis, odds are we are going to assume that "yes, I must be smart." This communication from the god-figures can be direct statements to or about us, or it can be subtle and indirect, as in tone of voice, facial expressions, or behaviors that indirectly suggest meaning. How they treat us is as important as what they say to us.

So, if the god or goddess regularly suggests or overtly states that we are dumb, or less intelligent than, say, an older sibling, it is likely that a specific belief will begin to form. For good measure, let's say that the older sibling in question, who to us is a sort of demigod, happily reinforces the notion of our inferiority at every opportunity. Regardless of how high our IQ may be, it is likely that we will decide that "I am dumb," or at least "less smart than others," and then log it away.

Our Memory Banks

Regardless of their accuracy, these impressionistic beliefs, positive or negative, are downloaded into the memory bank that will eventually come to make up large portions of our unconscious filtering system.

It does not matter how utterly absurd the constructed belief may later turn out to be when we see it through the eyes of our conscious mind: The small percentage of our mind that is conscious will not overpower the large percentage that is unconscious.[4] It's not a fair fight, even as adults, as we will see.

The belief that "I'm not all that smart," over the unfolding years of your early life becomes a part of your psychic backdrop; it slowly fades deep into the background of your mind. At the surface, conscious level it is gone. Indeed, you have done your best to completely forget about it, to push it down and away. It's a painful, unpleasant thought, after all. Who wants something like that floating around at the surface? But rest assured it is still there, and it is holding a vaunted place of power in the pantheon of your beliefs about yourself.

The years roll by, and today, with your conscious rational mind, you know that you are bright—you have an "ego wall" in your office full of diplomas and awards attesting to your mental prowess. However, this ego wall itself is an unconscious compensation, a testament to the not-so-deeply buried belief or fear about your true intellect. Your demonstrated intellectual power notwithstanding, this hidden fear still directs large aspects of your leadership and your life. It may touch every area of your life—without you ever consciously seeing it. I don't care if you have an IQ of 150 and a master's degree in cultural anthropology from Cambridge. This false belief, this childhood lie ("I'm not that smart") still runs and impairs major portions of who you are and how you show up in life.

Its manifestation is probably subtle and all the more insidious because of that subtlety. Beyond the ego wall, the false belief may show up in a creeping anxiety that you'll be found out, that one day, sooner or later, they will discover you have simply fooled 'em, all of 'em. Or, if the lie is buried even deeper, it may show up in scorn for those who seem less intelligent, in a contempt for and condescension to those who are not blessed with your intellectual gifts. The mere association with these "lesser lights" can make your skin crawl. Because deep beneath the surface of your awareness, despite all the evidence to the contrary, you fear *you* may be a bit dim. Fear you might be *like* them. Thus being near them is irritating, like having a rock in your shoe.

If you're like most of us, the manifestation of this type of false belief is seen in that you simply don't go after some of the things you want—and then you rationalize that you really didn't want them anyway. Thus without you ever knowing it, you concede and the unconscious lie wins. Game, set, and match. And all of it—the overcompensation, or knee-jerk, visceral contempt, or quitting before you even begin—is a function of what you made up, or downloaded about yourself, at the hands of your fiercely critical father or your indifferent mother, or your scornful sister, or your dismissive grandfather, and on and on. All of it is the result of the stuff you arrived at, lo, those many years ago, before your brain's development would allow you to distinguish between someone's opinion and the truth.

THE CASE OF THE BABY SHOES

On one occasion a client of mine was puzzling over the fact that a single childhood experience seemed to have such a lasting impact on her unconscious self-beliefs. "When I was in second grade," she said, "I had a weird little thing that happened to me, though it didn't seem little at the time, and it still haunts me today. I'm reasonably sure it is the source of some of my limiting beliefs," she told me during a workshop with her colleagues.

At the age of three she had been diagnosed with flat feet. "From that time on," she said, "I had to wear corrective shoes. Okay, I lived with it; didn't have much choice. But on the first day of school, in the second grade, a kid who was two years older than me pointed out that my corrective saddle shoes looked like 'baby shoes.' He said I was wearing *baby* shoes!" she exclaimed. "I was humiliated. Horrified. I sobbed all the way home. It was horrible. And as silly as it seems today, the pain of that event still is there. Could that be at the heart of a fear [one she had recently uncovered] that I am a misfit, that I don't belong, that I'm less significant than other people or something?"

Well, sort of but not exactly. It is more likely that this singular shaming experience was something of a tipping point—the point at which her growing catalog of self-doubts reached critical mass. The fact that at the age of three she had to wear corrective shoes may have indicated to her rapidly forming mind that she was somehow *in*correct. Those corrective shoes, as suggested by her intense embarrassment, even shame, told her that there was something strange or wrong with her, at the very least something wrong with her feet. It was something that made her different from the other "normal" kids.

At this point in my explanation she gasped and said, "Oh my God, that's it." She paused for a moment, apparently in deep reflection, then she continued. "For as long as I can remember, further back than the 'baby shoes' thing, I can remember feeling like I wasn't normal, like I was, pardon my language, fucked up, like I just didn't and wouldn't ever quite fit in. That event in the second grade only reinforced, or cemented or whatever, that fear."

And she was right. Given the fundamental human need to be loved and to fit in, a small child's awareness of the fact that she has "abnormal" feet can become a big deal. It was big enough of a deal that she had to have expensive, specially made shoes to correct and compensate for the rather minor disorder. Depending on other incidental circumstances, like how the condition of her feet was subtly or not-so-subtly regarded and handled by her parents or by siblings or other key figures, it could contribute to feelings or fears of being odd, being an outsider, or somehow "fucked up," as she put it.

Moreover, there may have been other chronic minor events or circumstances that fed her still-forming self-doubts. If she had been poor or from the "wrong side of the tracks," say, or if she had come from an immigrant or minority family, all of these circumstances could have further contributed to feelings of being an outsider. And then this single, rather cruel event at the hands of an older child proved it. This embarrassing, single event caused all the fears that may have been building for three or four years to be confirmed as the truth. By being humiliated in front of other kids, being told that she was a *baby*, of all things, the fears and chronic self-doubts were vividly crystallized. As a result this memory, with all of its childhood trauma, lingers not as the cause but as a symbol of her deeper unconscious belief, as a bitter and painful reminder of her deeper feelings about being unacceptable.

THE REAL REASONS WE DO WHAT WE DO

There are many and varied conditions or experiences, some dramatic and some chronically ordinary, out of which we construct, automatically and without exception, the subterranean psychological backdrops that will more or less determine major aspects of our adult lives. That both the construction of the beliefs as children and their recurring manifestation as adults happens without us consciously realizing it does not change the reality of their existence one iota.

So in general terms, if as children we believe we are worthy of love at this unconscious level, as adults we are likely to create loving relationships. If as children we develop the hidden belief that we don't deserve to give and receive love, as adults we are likely to keep people at an emotional distance, particularly in matters of intimacy. It is far too dangerous, our hidden fear tells us, to let people in, for they may then discover our "brokenness," our "unloveableness." With our conscious, rational minds we may see how ridiculous the false belief is, but that in no way diminishes its power, because its power and influence does not happen at this conscious level. More times than not, however, we don't realize the belief is there at all. Rather, we rationalize our loneliness away by saying things like, "I just prefer to be alone," or "Books are smarter company," or "Dogs are more reliable." And then dismiss the whole situation.

If we downloaded the belief that life is good and the world is a reasonably warm and safe place, as adults we are likely to look upon life as a possibility, perhaps even as an ever-unfolding adventure, as something that is to be embraced with zest and hopefulness. If, though, our early experiences of the world and the people who make it up are dark, forbidding, dangerous, or disappointing, we will likely construct unconscious beliefs that reflect as much: As adults we are likely to be suspicious of people's motives, leery of new possibilities, and inclined to expect things not to turn out as we would wish. Not because of how the world actually is, not because of how other people actually are, but because of our unconscious programming. These programmed patterns of thought then cause us to create the proverbial self-fulfilling prophecies that only further reinforce the invisible belief system.

And here's the larger point: Much, arguably most, of the time these beliefs are the *real* reasons we do what we do, in spite of what we may tell ourselves at the surface level.

To fully realize our promise and potential, to approach becoming our authentic selves, and to truly become more effective leaders, we must come to grips with the consequences of those early years: the beliefs we formed then that truly drive much, probably most, of our behaviors today.

Consider the Implications: Riots of Irrationality

Again, step back for a moment and digest what all of this means. If these assertions are true, much of your daily decisions are in effect being made by the mind of an eight-year-old child: you. The filters, good and bad, that we set in place long ago run major aspects of our lives. Consider what this portends just in your professional life, when your childhood programming unexpectedly erupts and mucks things up.

Imagine: Your boss comes to you to discuss the merits of a proposal you have recently made. During the course of your conversation you sense something is amiss; you feel it in the pit of your stomach. At first you ignore this semi-conscious disturbance. With your conscious mind, for the time being at least, you're calmly going along with the flow of the discussion. But your boss has a cool, distant way of speaking that has always seemed vaguely familiar, always made you a bit uncomfortable.

Your subconscious mind is now beginning to race: "There! There it is. She's doing it again; she's looking at me with that condescending smile, *that* smile." It's ever so subtle, but it's one that your unconscious mind immediately "recognizes." In a split second, it thinks, "I know that look; I know that dangerous aloofness." It reminds you, it's almost identical to the expression your big brother regularly used to make—some thirty years ago!—just before he contemptuously bashed you in the face with a basketball.

While your conscious, rational mind is oblivious to all of this extracurricular anxiety (still only vaguely aware of a creeping, anxious pit in your stomach), your unconscious mind now kicks into overdrive. It does not stop and make the distinction, "This is your boss, *not* your brother," or, "Her smile may actually be sincere." It simply plows ahead: "Danger! You are about to be attacked; this person does not have your best interest at heart; this person is about to harm you. Don't trust her. You've seen this all before: you know what is coming. *Be careful!*"

And all of this from a simple facial expression from your boss? You bet.

Now, you may not bolt from the room or lunge at your boss before she "attacks" you, but you slip into automatic, defensive posturing, the expression on your face changes from hopeful to suspicious, even defensive, and the tone of your voice has changed a bit. And your boss notices. It all strikes her as a bit weird, in fact, as strangely incongruous and surely inappropriate. Now she grows uncomfortable.

"Is something wrong?" she asks you, her furrowed brow suggesting her irritation. "I said I think your suggestion has promise," she continues. "Have you been listening to me? Have you heard what I've been saying? I think this is *good*. But you look almost . . . angry."

With a slightly annoyed, almost patronizing look on her face she asks, "Are you all right?"

You nod sheepishly, and as she walks away you think you notice her slightly shaking her head. Suddenly, for a brief moment, you realize the inappropriateness of your reaction, and you now feel foolish. "Why the hell did I do that?" you wonder.

But before you can answer your own momentarily sane question, your feelings of anxiousness now surge with a vengeance. Your imagination begins to run wild, and your emotions really start to go haywire. Alas, the unconscious filtering system, now writ large in the guise of rationality, is reaching a crescendo: "What is she up to?" you think suspiciously. "What was her *real* reason for talking to me? What was it I sensed in her cold tone of voice? I could see it in her eyes. Something is just not right. I just know it."

That sinking feeling in your gut is getting worse. Your mind is alternating between (1) kicking yourself for responding inappropriately and (2) being certain that your boss has some dark agenda with you, knowing (yikes!) that your strong reaction was founded. "I bet I'm gonna get fired. She's setting me up. She knows my proposal will fail, and it's her way of getting me out of here. Damn. That's it. Damn. I knew this gig wasn't going to last."

This "thinking," remember, is being fueled by what is happening at an unconscious or, at best, semi-conscious level. All you're aware of is the sinking feeling in your stomach and the mounting tension in your back. For entirely irrational, unfounded, and unconscious reasons you are heading into an emotional tailspin that may take you hours or even days to get out of.

THE GOOD NEWS—AND THERE IS GOOD NEWS

There is hope. If we can see that consciousness as we typically understand it is an illusion, we can begin a journey that can take us beyond this sort of innocent idiocy—and beyond other much more subtle and common ways in which the unconscious mind limits our effectiveness in life. Yet, as long as we labor under the illusion of full consciousness, we remain vulnerable to the limiting control of the subconscious domain. And let's be very clear once more: consciousness, at least as most of us think about it, *is* an illusion. [5]

The good news, perhaps ironically, is that the moment we surrender to the fact of our unconsciousness, the possibility of operating from new levels of consciousness start to arise, and entirely new possibilities emerge along with it. Most important, as we begin to see these deeply embedded patterns we can also begin literally changing how our brains are wired, allowing for alignment between our conscious and unconscious selves, enabling us to unleash unrealized or only partially expressed talents, and allowing us to express authentic power. And *that* is truly good news.

SUMMARY

The first step of Leg 1, acknowledgment, is a kind of surrender. Surrender here does not mean to give up or give in, does not mean to admit defeat. Surrender is a willingness to give up futile resistance to what is so. It is to accept reality for what it is. The first step in the process of personal leadership transformation is to surrender to the simple fact that you and I and every other person walking the planet are far less conscious, and far more *un*conscious, than we would like to believe. It is to acknowledge and accept the fact that to improve our effectiveness in life and leadership, we must first accept the nature of mind, the reality of our unconscious tendencies. It is then, and only then, that we can begin the process of permanently changing our minds for the better. Counterintuitive though it may be, we must acknowledge the true nature of the mind, the true nature of *our* minds.

With this awareness squarely in front of us, we can now turn our attention to Step 2 of Leg 1—the act of coming to terms with the often ignored and misunderstood principle of responsibility. Without a vivid grasp of what it means to be the agent of cause in our lives and in the lives of others (which is the heart of responsibility), learning to lead our lives and to better lead others remains but an empty wish. In chapter 7, we take on the real meaning of responsibility.

CHAPTER 7

RESPONSIBILITY: Embracing Our Causality

God has entrusted me with myself.

—Epictetus

The global insurance company Liberty Mutual recently ran a commercial on American television called "Responsibility. What's Your Policy?" In the advertisement, video clips portraying acts of human compassion are skillfully linked together while a piece of moving music plays gently in the background: A woman in a coffee shop prevents a man's cup of coffee from falling off of the table; later someone else inspired by this act of kindness helps a stranger up from a sidewalk tumble; witnessing this act of generosity, someone else then holds an elevator door for another person, and so on. At the end of the spot a narrator's voice says, "When it's people doing the right thing, they call it being responsible. When it's an insurance company, they call it Liberty Mutual. Responsibility. What's your policy?"

It's a beautifully done piece of ad work that in the space of sixty seconds shows the chain effect that one person's act of caring can have on so many other people. The only problem is that the ad gets the description of the narrative all wrong. What the commercial portrays isn't responsibility at all. What it portrays is people doing the right thing, or people committing random acts of kindness. We could refer to this type of behavior as "being adult," or "acting with compassion," or "being conscientious"; we might understand it as being morally upstanding, decent, or good, but it is not responsibility in the most essential sense of the word.

Responsibility, as this TV commercial demonstrates, is an often misunderstood, or only partially understood, word. It is often exclusively used in the assignment of blame, as in, "Who's responsible for this mess?" It is commonly understood as accountability, which is only one aspect of true responsibility. It is frequently disingenuously used to demonstrate maturity or gravitas, for instance, when someone, often with a deep and self-important voice, declares, "I take responsibility" for this or that situation. It is commonly used as a weapon of guilt to enforce control by parents, teachers, and other authority figures. But it is rarely understood in its most essential and important sense, and even more rarely is it lived out.

Beyond any doubt, however, the linchpin of transformation is the full embrace of the principle of true responsibility. Without it the wheels of growth fly off the axel and the journey comes to a screeching, jarring halt. Or more times than not, without it the process of transformative growth never gets going. Without a fundamental understanding of responsibility in its truest sense, the possibility for authentic and lasting change is in fact nonexistent. Yet when we do have a clear grasp of true responsibility and when we live from it, we have a legitimate shot at becoming our most powerful selves. We then have the chance of becoming extraordinarily effective leaders.

And we have the capacity to successfully answer the call of transformation, for true responsibility is that act of owning our lives. It frees us to act upon our lives and the endless array of possibilities that a life well led affords. Responsibility, therefore, is the essential step 2 of the first leg of the process of personal and leadership transformation.

AGENCY AND POWER

Responsibility means that I am the *causal agent* in my life. In other words, it recognizes that *I*, the individual, am the principal agent who causes or generates the things and circumstances that appear

Figure 7.1 Step 2: Responsibility

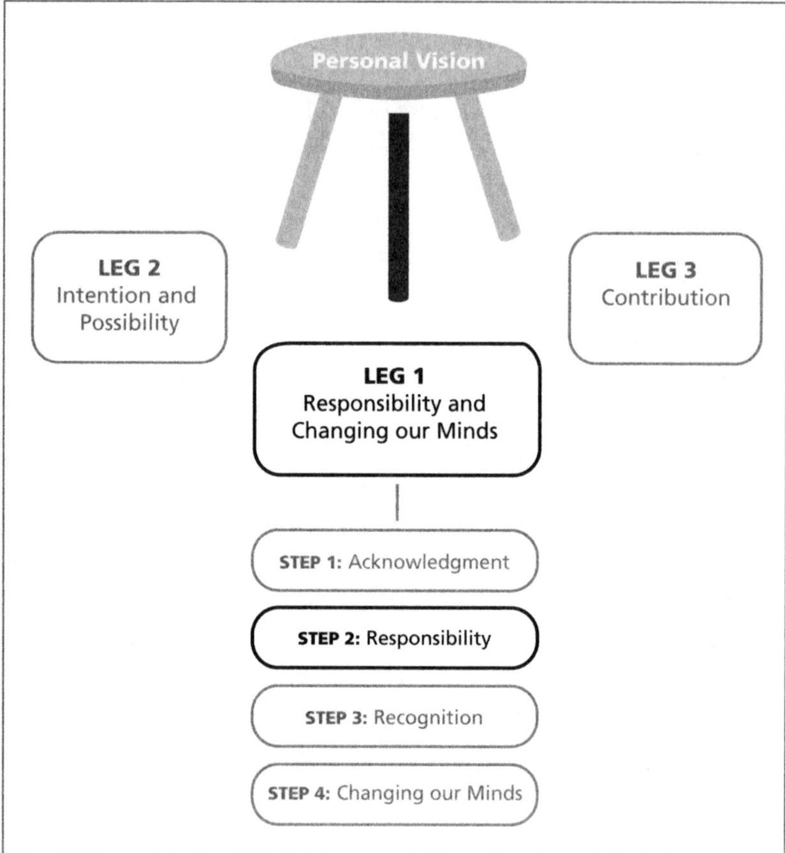

in my life. When I grasp responsibility in its full and truest sense, I operate as if my life is as it is be*cause* I have caused it to be that way. In this sense, responsibility is saying that I accept the fact that it is *my* life, that I am generating the results therein, which include how I am affecting others and the world around me. Ultimately it is making a simple factual assessment of what exists from a cause-and-effect perspective: What is present in *my* world, generally speaking, is there because I have somehow caused it to be present. I am the agent of cause, for good or ill, in my life. Period.

A Caveat

Before we go any further, however, let's clear something up. This is not to say that other people or things may not have also contributed to my circumstances; they surely have. Nor is it saying that I have caused every single detail of my life. I have not. For instance, I am not somehow responsible for being born into a loving home of wealth and opportunity or for being born into a home of abject poverty and despair.

It is saying that at some point early in our lives we become the primary agents of cause in our lives. *We* are causal and therefore truly responsible for the lives we have generated and will yet generate. From the transformative perspective, this is a reality that is not up for debate any more than the theory of gravity is up for debate. My feelings about the matter of responsibility simply do not have any bearing on its factual reality. I may kick and scream till the cows come home, but I am still the primary cause of what is present in my life.

A Promise of Power

True responsibility is non-negotiable within the context of authentic, lasting change simply because absent true responsibility, intentional change is not possible. The moment I truly understand responsibility and do so free of guilt or blame, I simultaneously step into the possibility of power. The moment I quit resisting this law of life and see it as an objective description of reality, power becomes a possibility.

Consider for a moment the implications of this last statement, perhaps the single most important statement in the entire book: Until I come to terms with my essential causality—the fact that I am the one who has generated and who will generate my life conditions and qualities, its successes and failures—I am largely incapable of realizing fulfillment and effectiveness, as a leader and as a person.

If you are able to truly get your head around this one simple understanding, that *you* are cause, I can assure you your life will be forever different. But grasping this simple fact, beyond mere intellectual assent, is not as easy as it seems. So let's consider more fully what we mean by "true responsibility."

WHAT RESPONSIBILITY IS

The word *responsible* comes to us from the Latin word *respondere*, which means "to answer, offer in return." It has two features: answering for something and offering up something "in return" for, or as a reply to, that answer. The first feature, answering for something, means accepting ownership for that something and then assessing how effective we are in owning it. If it's my behavior that's in question, then it's *my* behavior, no one else's. I own the behavior and the results that are produced by it—they're my results. *Answering* for it, then, means determining how effective my behavior is based on those results.

The second feature, *offering in return* or responding to that assessment, means I make things right by taking some sort of action (offering up something) in response to my assessment: I fix what I have caused, or change it, or build upon it, or cause something entirely new, or simply accept that it is fine and leave it alone. So, to be responsible is, first, to own and assess (answer for) and second, to respond to that assessment with action (offer in return). Note that both features are proactive. Simple enough.

The problem we run into, in Anglo-American culture especially, is that we seem to focus automatically on the first piece, and do that rather narrowly, often to the complete exclusion of the second piece. Most of us think that all responsibility amounts to is accountability (answering for); and in being true to our puritanical heritage, what we usually mean by accountability is little more than blame or guilt.

But when we look at the root meaning of the word, this guilt-riddled understanding seems entirely unwarranted. Remember, responsibility means to own and honestly assess what we have caused and then to cause anew, to fix, create, expand, and so on.

Responsibility, therefore, is a judgment-free realization (no Puritans allowed!) that as human beings we are fundamentally agents of cause. That is, we are causal and perpetually so. In other words, as individuals we are a force of life, infused through and through by and with life energy:

1. We have and are made up of vital energy.
2. We think, consciously and unconsciously.

3. We "be" and do as a result of this energy and this thinking.
4. As a result of this thinking, being, and doing we create/attract/allow/cause certain realities around us.
5. These realities we've caused around us constitute the conditions and circumstances that make up our individual lives, that in fact, *are* our lives. And we are always doing this creating/causing thing. Subtle though it may be at times, we never stop doing it. Never. Responsibility, therefore, is a pragmatic realization of the simple cause-and-effect nature of reality.

If as an adult with normal cognitive abilities I look up and see that the conditions of my life are a certain way, the only powerful and honest way to respond, according to the principle of real responsibility, is to begin investigating how I, the cause, have made the conditions of my life as they are. My intent is to make this assessment *without judgment or emotion*, using my powers of observation and using cause-and-effect reasoning. Though basic, it is not simple because we are not as rational and conscious as we would like to believe, remember. Nevertheless this basic understanding of our agency in life is something that powerful and effective leaders and individuals have always understood, whether or not they have done much explicit thinking about it.

WHAT RESPONSIBILITY IS NOT

Let's unmask a couple of misleading colloquialisms. First, we are not talking about "personal responsibility," simply because there is no other kind; there is no such thing as *impersonal* responsibility. Thus, "personal responsibility" is redundant. Almost without exception, when someone speaks of personal responsibility he or she is making a moral judgment and usually directing it at someone else, typically suggesting how that person *should* act in order to be a better person. Or the speaker is attempting to draw a distinction between "me" and those in my tribe, the good ones, and "them," those in that tribe over there, the bad ones: "I and people like me take responsibility, personal responsibility, for our lives. We are better than those lazy turds over there." Such a use of the word *responsibility* typically misrepresents the causal nature of reality to which responsibility always points. Responsibility is always personal, always social, always inextricably attached to me and the reality that I touch and create with my existence all the time.

Second, we are not talking about "taking responsibility." You cannot *take* responsibility when you already *are* responsible, when you already are the cause. You are, or you are not; it's binary. Therefore, there is nothing to take. The person who understands his or her causal nature also understands that to suggest we can take responsibility implies that there are also moments when we can somehow stop being responsible, which is like saying we can turn our causality on or off as we choose. We can never stop being responsible for our lives any more than we can somehow start being responsible. When someone claims or "takes" responsibility for a matter it is likely that that person doesn't fully grasp the true nature of responsibility. In fact, as often as not, when a person says, "I take responsibility," he or she is either posturing in order to appear more "grown up" or is saying with faux nobility, "Blame me," making him- or herself into a martyr. In neither case is true responsibility in effect.

OPERATING *AS IF*

The way to operate responsibly is to operate *as if* I am the cause of all that is in my life. The *as if* qualifier suggests that I am aware that there are many things over which I have little or no control, but I choose not to spend excessive time separating out those things I control from those I don't. Since I understand my fundamental causality, I am going to simply assume that I cause most things around me and go from there. And I do this because when I operate *as if* I have caused it all, without blame or guilt, I put myself in a position of power that allows me to change it, correct it, or do whatever I need to do with or for it. I don't get stuck in the fruitless and powerless muck of assigning blame by pointing the finger at someone else. I simply get busy making things work, either by rationally assessing how I have caused, contributed to, or allowed it to be and then jumping on a solution, or without even bothering to assess, I simply figure out a way to make it better. Operating from "I am cause" gives me power; operating from "someone else is to blame" renders me helpless.

The *as if* is important for one other reason. It reminds us that embracing our causality does not mean that we are responsible for many of the circumstances of our early lives—the circumstances and experiences that led us to create the unconscious filtering systems that still run major aspects of our lives today. Responsibility does not suppose that we somehow magically selected our parents, our race, our gender, our geographical location, our historical period, and so on, which is what would have to be the case if we were to suggest that everything, from the moment of birth to the moment of death, is what we have caused. It should go without saying that much of what happens in our lives, certainly in our early years, is the product of happy or unhappy accident. Of course, these circumstances shape us into the people who then become cause through our unconscious programming and our conscious choices of the further circumstances in our lives, but the fact remains we are not the cause of everything in our lives.

For example, I did not choose to be born to Bill and LaVerne Stevens, a preacher and a teacher, respectively, who with their middle-class work ethic esteemed education as the surest way of achieving a life worth living. I did not cause this; it was a function of fortune—from my vantage point, good fortune. Nor did I choose to be born white and male in a society that continues, by and large, to be run by white males, even with all of our pluralistic advances over the past several decades, including the election of the first African American president of the United States. As a result of being a white man who looks a certain way, holds himself a certain way, dresses a certain way, speaks a certain way, all of which are largely accidents of birth, doors open to me that to others might remain closed. And I am happy and grateful for my good fortune. If I spoke with a different inflection, were brown rather than white, female rather than male, gay rather than straight, I would face a set of challenges that as it is I simply do not face.

Nevertheless, as an adult I am still the ultimate causal agent in my life. Me and no one else. As a result of the choices I make on a daily basis, most of which are a function of my automatic, unconscious worldview, beliefs, and ways of thinking, I generate my life. Consciously and even more so unconsciously, based on my beliefs about myself, my beliefs about the world, my beliefs about others, I determine how I express my life energy and how people respond to me. Based on how I regard and esteem myself, again mostly unconsciously, to a great extent I determine how others regard and esteem me. Sometimes it is subtle, very subtle indeed, but it is a fact, simple cause and effect; it's simple and undeniable.

We choose not only what we seek to achieve in life but also the degree to which the strength of our commitment overcomes the circumstances that may operate against us. The quality of our chosen commitment to a given outcome, whether to a relationship, to financial achievement, to leadership and organizational success, or to social change, always is more significant than the eminent circumstances and conditions that may surround the commitment. And the quality of our commitment is a function of our desire—how badly we want something—combined with our willingness to embrace our true causality—our capacity to cause the desired outcome.

The truth is that we are always at cause, always; we are always generating, though it might not at first glance be apparent. And we are the only ones who can cause our lives to have meaning and power, the only ones who can cause our lives to be different and better. Period.

If I had been born a black woman, a Hispanic man, an Asian lesbian, or a child of a drug-addicted inner-city parent, I would still be causal. Of course, as a black woman born and raised in Boston, for instance, I would not have generated my blackness or my gender or the racism and sexism of Massachusetts—or London or Dubai. These conditions may well have worked against me in painful ways. But I didn't cause this circumstantial, accident-of-birth reality.

Yet despite the circumstances of my birth, I still generate, always and forever. Because I think, because I "be" and do in certain ways, because I receive and express energy, attitudes, judgments, and perceptions, and because I take actions, I am always at cause. And the sooner I come to terms with my causality, my power by virtue of my mind-set, my commitment and my resulting actions, the sooner I can begin to overcome the racism, sexism, classism, and homophobia I must overcome in order to live the life that is possible for me. Moreover, the sooner I come to terms with my own causality, the sooner I can become pivotal in changing some of the social and economic inequities that continue to plague humankind.

So let's be clear: This understanding of real responsibility is not to be misunderstood as license for a simplistic pull-yourself-up-by-your-bootstraps philosophy that might justify turning a blind eye to the suffering and misfortune of others. Ironically, perhaps, the more fully those of us in the wealthy West embrace authentic responsibility and experience the power of transformation, the more we come to terms with the degree to which "I am cause" is balanced with unearned good fortune, with accident of birth, or even with grace. The more we fully own our lives as *our* lives, the more we realize our responsibility to our primary relationships, to our communities, to our society, to humankind, and to the world itself, all of which we increasingly claim as *our own.*

Still, I respectfully assert without equivocation this fact: As it stands today in the West, the single greatest limiting element in life is not race, sex, sexual orientation, health, lack of wealth, lack of higher education, physical impairment, or even the damaging residual effects of patently bad parenting. It is a lack of willingness to embrace real responsibility, an unwillingness to surrender to our true capacity for cause, to embrace authentic ownership of our own lives, and thus to move ourselves from here, where we are now, to over there, where we want to be.

When I operate *as if* I am the cause of all that is present in my life, I gain at least an even chance of having my life turn out as I would like. Until I do that, however, the best I can do is whine, feel sorry for myself, point the finger of blame outward, and hope I will be rescued by someone or something—all of which are the antithesis of power.

POWERLESSNESS AND VICTIMHOOD

The considerable inequities of life notwithstanding, until we understand that by virtue of our unconscious and conscious minds we generate the conditions and circumstances of our lives, we remain confined within the various manifestations of "victimhood." Under the normal conditions of life, victimhood is a psychologically distorted state. Victimhood is a mind-set in which we are seduced by a largely unacknowledged fear that "I'm not enough," that "I don't have what it takes." It's a powerless mind-set that believes our problems are caused by something outside of us, which means the solutions to those problems are outside of us as well. When we perceive the world through this distorted lens we are further constrained by the belief that happiness in life is therefore contingent on something over which we have little control, whether that's a person, an institution, society, or even fate.

All of us, no doubt, have a bit of the victim within, and we pay the consequent price of powerlessness when that victim is set loose to prowl in our imaginations and in our lives. Indeed, on occasion we all may slip into the indulgent mind-set of feeling like a victim, but beyond that normal if fruitless tendency there is a type of person who has become what we might call the "committed victim," a person who is virtually committed to having life not work.

The committed victim has a vivid pedigree, a nearly universal set of behaviors, and thus is not difficult to spot. The usual hallmark of such victimness is an abiding degree of anger, sometimes low grade and sometimes glaring, that suggests a generalized sense of weakness, if not complete powerlessness, before the vagaries of life. This anger or frustration usually remains at an unconscious or semiconscious level almost entirely, but when it emerges into full view it usually sounds like this: My life is unfulfilled because "they" or "that" or "those things" are preventing it—the church, the government, the corporation, my husband or wife, my parents or friends or children, racism, sexism, ageism, reverse discrimination, the union, the "man," the system, the economy, my sister, my brother, Uncle Harry, et cetera, et cetera.

What is always beneath the whine is a fundamental lack of belief in our own capacity to cause the desired outcomes in our lives, a lack of self-confidence. The good news is that these hidden fears about our insufficiency are usually wrong, despite how pervasive and strong the beliefs may be. The better news is that when we recognize what is really at work in our need to blame something or someone, we can begin to address the real issue, which in one way or another always has to do with how we understand ourselves at the deepest level, particularly in terms of confidence, competence, and worth. But it must begin with the radical realization that we are the fundamental cause, like it or not, in our lives. In effect, power, true power, begins when we are able to say to ourselves with conviction, "I am it."

SUMMARY

In the transformative model, responsibility is understood as accepting the causal nature of our existence as human beings. It says, I am the primary cause of the realities in my life. Responsibility has nothing to do with blame or guilt and everything to do with coming from a unique and powerful perspective that operates as if "my life is as it is because I have caused it to be that way, consciously or otherwise." The only real alternative to authentic responsibility is in playing the role, to one degree or another, of the victim. When we operate from "I am it," or "If it's to be, it's up to me," we have at least a 50/50 chance of having things turn out in our lives and in our leadership. When we operate as a victim, we are bereft of the power required to have life work as we would like it to work.

True power in leading lives of meaning and joy, and of affecting the lives of others, indeed the possibility of becoming truly powerful leaders, therefore, only exists when we come to grips with our fundamental, unavoidable causality. In chapter 8 we consider a vivid example of the life-changing power of embracing and living from real responsibility.

CHAPTER 8

RESPONSIBILITY IN ACTION:
The Case of Charlie Costas

> Take your life in your own hands and what happens?
> A terrible thing: no one to blame.
>
> **—Erica Jong**

> We cannot solve a problem by saying "It's not my problem." We cannot solve a problem by hoping someone else will solve it for us. I can solve a problem only when I say "This is *my* problem and it's up to me to solve it."
>
> **—M. Scott Peck**

True responsibility represents an awakened sense not only of no longer having anyone to blame but also of no longer *needing* anyone to blame. At its heart is an emerging quality of self-confidence and personal strength, an understanding that "I am it" and "I can handle it," as the example we are about to visit demonstrates.

THE CASE OF CHARLIE COSTAS

Charlie is forty-four years old. He is married with two kids and teaches at a small liberal arts college outside of Portland, Oregon. His wife, Larissa, is an executive for a software company in nearby

Beaverton. Charlie is a charismatic, witty, deeply committed professor of English who for more than six years could not find a full-time tenure-track teaching job in the discipline he loved, English literature, though he held a PhD in comparative literature from a small university in the Midwest. During his six-plus-year hunt for a university position, he taught English and history at a local parochial high school. But he simply could not land a tenure-track teaching job anywhere in the country, despite the fact that he applied every year to nearly every position that came available.

Charlie's self-effacing manner, dedicated teaching style, and generous attitude to both his students and his colleagues on the parochial school faculty earned him favorable evaluations from students and ringing endorsements from fellow teachers and administrators. Also to his credit, he had four years of university teaching experience at his alma mater subsequent to earning his doctorate and had published several papers in academic journals (and numerous poems in two different literary magazines). Yet Charlie could not get the desired job. Anywhere. Larissa was confident that by virtue of her own stellar credentials and management success she would be able to relocate nearly anywhere Charlie found a job, so from her point of view that was not a limitation. The problem, it seemed, was Charlie.

As he entered the seventh year of his fruitless search, Charlie was at the end of a rapidly fraying rope. According to Larissa, however, those who were paying the biggest price for Charlie's failing job search and his consequent growing self-contempt were their two daughters, Justine, age nine, and Claire, seven, from whom their father was increasingly distant. The other price being paid was in Charlie and Larissa's relationship of nearly twelve years, which was rapidly approaching a point of no return. As Charlie would later put it, "When you are filled with scorn for yourself, it's hard to love anyone else."

Charlie, it seems, was the quintessential victim. Though he had always been supportive of Larissa's career and had truly enjoyed her success, he was increasingly convinced that it was women in the workplace who were the source of his troubles. Add to that a dash here and there of "ambitious minority folk" and what you have, Charlie believed, was a real nightmare for the suburban white guy. Charlie was convinced that he was the victim of a case of unqualified reverse discrimination. And there you have it, "a white guy in

Anglo-America being punished for being a white guy in decreasingly Anglo-America," as he bitterly put it.

At more than one dinner party, after a couple of glasses of wine Charlie would let loose, much to Larissa's embarrassment. "They may *say* it's because my doctorate is not in English lit," he complained, emboldened by his cabernet, "but everyone knows the truth. I'm not saying women and minorities are not smart or talented, but they are not any better than me. Hell, who's a better teacher, at any level, than me? But they get special treatment, *pri-vel-eged* treatment, and the jobs. And at whose expense? The hard-working, white male stiff, that's who. Level the playing field, my ass." Few people who knew Charlie would think of him as a "working stiff," but the self-reference was telling.

On one such evening, upon returning home, Larissa spoke her mind to Charlie in no uncertain terms. As Charlie would later say, it turned out to be his "blessed wake-up call."

"She let me have it, and as she unloaded I began to sober up pretty quickly, literally and figuratively." The confrontation amounted to Charlie being shaken from what he would later see as his years-long torpor. The biggest thing she pointed out was that he was being a "whining baby, a wimp," as he recalled. "And then she hit me over the head with a rhetorical rolling pin: 'You're playing the role of a goddamn victim! Poor, poor, pitiful Charlie. What a shrinking violet Charlie is. Pathetic! What do you think that teaches the girls? How to feel sorry for yourself? Jeepers, look at Dad! Boy, it sure makes *this wife* proud. When are you gonna quit wallowing in your misery and making everyone else miserable? We're sick of it, Charlie. Grow up. Just go out and get another goddamn PhD, the right one this time from the right university and get the damn adult job.' She unloaded on me and good."

The confrontation was like a bucket of ice water in Charlie's face. He had always prided himself on his willingness to "take" responsibility, to live from a place of "personal responsibility," but he knew she was right. He was playing the victim in the biggest way. As much as he may have wanted to fight back and defend himself, he couldn't. She was dead on, and he knew it. Charlie seized the opening that Larissa's unvarnished honesty created and began a process of rethinking who he was and what he was up to with his teaching career and with his life in general.

On the surface Charlie first recognized his hypocrisy with his daughters. "I have always told them 'Life isn't fair; you gotta get tough, get up and do it.' Meaning, it doesn't matter what life gives you, you play your hand and make it work. It's not what you have that matters," he said. "It's what you *make* of what you have that matters." What this meant for Charlie was that his complaints about unfair treatment were but a smokescreen, one that "allowed me to avoid playing my hand and making it work."

"It's not that there wasn't some form of reverse discrimination going on. There was, I'm sure. But be that as it may, whatever was going on was more or less irrelevant to me, Charlie Costas." What mattered was Charlie's response.

Rather than rising to the occasion and using his considerable intellect to get what he was after, it was much easier to blame the system and thereby escape responsibility. Rather than owning the circumstances of his life and intentionally doing what he must to generate the outcome he desired (that is, *leading* his life), he had chosen to fearfully react to his life (attempt to *manage* his life). It was far easier to point the finger out there, periodically bemoaning his woeful and unjust predicament.

At a deeper level, what became clear to Charlie was the fact that beneath his need to blame the system was a fundamental, largely unconscious fear that he didn't have what it would take to get another PhD, this time in English literature and, more important, from a top- tier university. The real issue, as is often the case for those who would just as soon escape responsibility, was one of fundamental self-confidence and self-worth. Do I have the ability to achieve what I truly desire? Do I deserve the stature and satisfaction that I associate with its realization? And as is the case with most of us, Charlie's inhibiting fears did not operate at a conscious, rational, overt level. These were fears that Charlie kept neatly hidden from himself, hidden beneath his bitter bravado.

In fact, initially Charlie would flat-out dismiss any suggestion that he didn't believe in his own capacity. "I'm Charlie Costas, for god's sake. I don't lack the ability or faith in that ability," he would say with bluster, but also with a good dose of sincerity. The self-doubts were deeply buried, unconscious, and his normal need to feel good about himself caused him to ignore these quietly gurgling fears. Remember, unconscious beliefs are easy to ignore or deny. Indeed, they do their darnedest to remain unseen. And like most of us, Charlie had been denying these beliefs most of his life.

His conscious mind, on the other hand, simply had to look at the rational evidence all around him—his published papers, his degrees, his evaluations, et cetera—to convince himself that he did not doubt his abilities. And the fact that Charlie *was* highly intelligent gave him every reason to deny the existence of the irrational self-doubts about his mental prowess. "It would be absurd for me to think that I'm not smart enough to get the doctorate from a first tier institution," he once said in protest. And he was right. It *was* absurd. It was also a fact that the absurd beliefs were there and operative, running his professional life all the same—and increasingly affecting nearly all aspects of his family life. Until he uncovered and addressed these absurd, irrational beliefs he was doomed to remain stuck in the foolish and fruitless loop of the victim, bitterly lashing out at those who "victimized" him, all the while watching his relationship with his wife and his daughters deteriorate and his career go nowhere.

As Charlie began to confront the deeper fears, to address them head-on, a new sense of self and a renewed sense of competence began to emerge. Charlie began to snap out of the victim's daze into which he had fallen, to accept ownership of his situation, and finally to achieve a solution.

Within a few short years Charlie had completed his PhD in English literature at one of the nation's top research universities and had accepted a tenure-track position at a small private college where he teaches today. By consciously addressing his false beliefs and powerfully surrendering to his own causality, by embracing the reality of real responsibility, Charlie had crossed over from managing to leading his professional life. Of course, it did not come without a price: He had to courageously confront and overcome his deeply buried fears about himself, and he had to relinquish his longtime companion, blame. But in doing so he not only opened the door for career success but also allowed himself to renew and reinvigorate his relationships with his wife and his daughters.

Charlie's Discrete Actions

Charlie Costas made a fundamental change in his understanding of himself and how he relates to the world. In breaking down Charlie's process we can see at least four distinct elements at play. First, Charlie *noticed*. He noticed that he had been perceiving himself as powerless before the larger educational system, before the competition, before the vagaries of life. He had in fact placed himself, unwittingly of course, in the role of the victim. And the telltale sign was his low-grade anger that periodically emerged, or erupted, under different circumstances.

Second, he began to *uncover what was beneath* his need to play the victim. As painful as it was to admit to himself, at the deepest level he did not have sufficient confidence in his ability to cause the outcome that he desired. No one chooses to play the role of victim without good reason, and the reason, nine times out of ten, is a fundamental lack of faith in one's ability to achieve the desired objective. In Charlie's case it was a lingering doubt that he had the intellectual acumen required for a PhD from a top-ranked school where he would be standing side by side with some of the top intellects in the world. Because of his childhood programming, he was being run by a fear that he was "clever and quick but not really intelligent," as irrational, indeed absurd, as that belief was.

Third, in uncovering and addressing the irrational belief he *shifted his way of thinking and being*. As Charlie began to see what was going on at a deeper level he was able, with discipline and rigor, to alter his conscious and unconscious thinking. Thus he was able to summon a different, more rational way of being: legitimate self-confidence.

Finally, out of this shift in his awareness and above all else this shift in his belief about himself, Charlie began to *take action*, action that now seemed a no-brainer, action that led to the necessary degree from the right university and his new job, a job and career that were worthy of Charlie Costas. The actions that Charlie took, however, were not simply the result of forcing a change in his behavior. Rather, they were an organic and systematic response to a change in his thinking, in his self-understanding, at the deepest level.

But let's be clear about one thing: Charlie was well aware that in embracing true responsibility there were still no guarantees. He knew well that he still might fail. But at least now he had a legitimate chance at success, and out of that understanding Charlie made it happen.

THE GAUNTLET

Of course, victimhood has its rewards. Or else, like Charlie, we wouldn't be so well versed in its many and varied expressions. Indeed, as long as we continue to play the blame game, as long as we continue to operate at affect of life, governed by the circumstances of life, we don't have to do anything about making our own lives and organizations work, enhancing our leadership, or making this messy and chaotic world any better.

With impunity we can toss our hands in the air and simply say, "See! See what I mean?! I told you. That's just the way it is." Or take your pick: "You don't know my husband," "You haven't met my business partner or you'd understand," "It's this economy—it sucks," "The leadership here is utterly clueless," "My boss/wife/partner/son is a complete idiot," "Republicans are heartless pricks," "Democrats are bleeding-heart fools," "Independents are gutless fence-sitters," "This world is just plain screwed up and always will be," "You don't understand how screwed up my childhood was," "Ya play the hand you were dealt and mine was crap," "You ever been around my dad for more than five minutes?" and on and on and on. Our rationalized laziness abides and abides and abides and then we die. Yuck!

Yet for those who have the integrity and the heart, the true power to change our lives, to improve our organizations, and perhaps even to transform our world awaits our intentional embrace of responsibility. And let me be very clear about this: Until we are willing to embrace the fact that responsibility *is* what is so, we will not be able to *lead* our lives, and we won't be able to transform ourselves into the sort of leaders we have the potential for being. Until we accept our causal nature the best we can hope for are reactive attempts to manage our lives. Until we take up the mantle of our authentic moral agency, accepting our power to consciously generate, we will never lead others, truly lead them, with anything approaching consistent and lasting success.

And so we have reached another "gauntlet moment," for the gauntlet of individual agency is being thrown before you. Accept that you are indeed the cause of your life as it is and as it will be . . . or go home. What happens from this point forward is for grown-ups only. No victims, no whiners, no children posing as adults allowed.

RESPONSIBILITY ASSESSMENT

Since we all have a tendency from time to time to slip into the role of victim, learning to notice that tendency and then effectively and quickly recalibrating ourselves is essential—if, that is, we intend to pick up that gauntlet.

The pivotal element in the assessment process is first accepting that the results around us are *our* results, results that we, not someone else, have caused. Second, we must observe and discern the ways of being and/or the behaviors that are producing the result—for Charlie it was excessive caution (and denial) and an unwillingness to risk, to put himself out there and get the necessary credentials from the right institution. Third, we must identify the self-perceptions that inform or lead to the behavior. Charlie identified a belief that he was clever but not intelligent. Uncovering the irrational belief allows us to take the fourth step: to address the false belief and shift the ineffective way of being or ineffective behavior. This last step allows us to begin the process of changing our minds, specifically our self-understanding—a process to be addressed in detail in the chapters that follow. It also frees us up to take wiser, more decisive actions that will then lead to the desired results.

Yet for this whole responsibility assessment thing to work, we must not be tripped up by the normal tendency to beat ourselves up, to indulge in blame and guilt, which is always a danger when we're not getting the result we want. Responsibility does not allow for self-abuse—victimizing ourselves. There is no time for it. The only purpose beating ourselves up serves is to preclude our ability to see what we must see in order to change the behaviors and actions that are keeping us from achieving the desired results. We must learn to gently, honestly discover the causal behavior, uncover the root cause (the underlying belief), and with a forgiving spirit, proactively shift and move forward. Responsibility is only responsibility when, free of self-antagonism, we are able to coolly and honestly assess and fix, when we are able to get busy and consciously make things happen. Guilt and blame have nothing to do with it.

SUMMARY

Responsibility is a state of mind that recognizes the causal nature of all human beings. It is based on reason, logic, and the deductive ability to rationally assess evidence as it unfolds around us. Free of emotion, it asks a simple question: *What is the cause of this situation, this circumstance, this result?* To be responsible means to soberly assess what is before us, to coolly examine the situation and determine one's causality, if any. To ask the question "What is it about me that caused this?" is not to look for a way to make ourselves wrong or to do pseudo-penance for feelings of guilt (which is usually a substitute for fixing the problem we now face). Rather, to be responsible is to act with an almost surgical degree of precision in getting at the way of being and/or doing that may have caused the situation and to then alter that way of being/doing in order to produce the desired outcome.

Perhaps the greatest gift that comes with the embrace of true responsibility is nothing less than the power to change our minds, the power to not simply alter our behavior in the moment but to literally and permanently alter the way our minds work. Responsibility opens that door, but to walk through it and into a more compelling and worthy life, to be able to step up into a dramatically enhanced leadership capacity, something else is needed. We must learn how to recognize and neutralize the limiting beliefs we observe in the process of assessing our causality. It is this essential skill of recognition that we take on in full measure in chapter 9.

CHAPTER 9

RECOGNITION: Seeing Our Personal Paradigms

> Until you make the unconscious conscious, it will direct your life and you will call it fate.
>
> **—C. G. Jung**

> We are not who we think we are. We narrate our lives, shading every last detail, and even changing the script retrospectively, depending on the event, most of the time subconsciously. The storyteller never stops, except perhaps during deep sleep.
>
> **—Benedict Carey (on the findings of neuroscientist Michael Gazzaniga)**

In the 1960s the scholar Thomas Kuhn shook up the world of science and in the process popularized the term *paradigm*.[1] He pointed out that scientists are not the objective, above-the-fray rationalists we so often make them out to be. They are human. They have blind spots. In fact, they are biased by what he called "scientific paradigms." What Kuhn meant by *paradigm* was an agreed-upon set of beliefs, theories, and interpretations of reality. These perceptions and ways of understanding information frame, color, and filter how the scientific community sees the world, interprets data, and recognizes facts.

Here's the tricky part: Aspects of the paradigm, over time, slip from the conscious view of the person who holds the particular interpretive framework. This increasingly invisible set of judgments can be so strong, in fact, that it will cause a sort of intellectual blindness, preventing the scientific observer from otherwise seeing facts and data that may exist directly in front of her.

The point here is not that scientists are consciously pigheaded. It's not that they are willfully turning away from facts that they can plainly see but may not like. Rather, because of the mitigating or filtering effect of their particular worldviews, because of their paradigms, they simply cannot see the new, and in some cases not-so-new, facts even though they may hover directly before their eyes.

But what's this got to do with leading life and leading others? The short answer is that we—you and I, and every other person on the planet—all have our own paradigms. The difference for us is that our personal paradigms are almost *entirely* out of our conscious view. Another difference is that each individual's paradigm is unique to that individual. What's more, our personal paradigms are even more blinding than Kuhn's scientific paradigms. In fact, because of their relatively invisible, often pervasive nature, our personal paradigms can be very nearly crippling. Until we identify the makeup of our own paradigmatic beliefs, it is difficult, if not impossible, to fully respond to the promise of transformation.

The good news, and it is *really* good news, is that recognition is possible. Without the capacity for recognition we would be, in a sense, doomed to continue producing more or less the same results we've always produced. We're not doomed *because* of our capacity for recognition.

IN THE CONTEXT OF THE STOOL

Having completed the acknowledgment (chapter 6) and the responsibility (chapters 7–8) steps of Leg 1 of the three-legged, transformative stool, we move on to Step 3, *recognition* (see Figure 9.1). Recognition involves doing the work of uncovering our personal paradigms, uncovering and thus understanding our unconscious programming, the subterranean beliefs, perceptions, and judgments that drive so much of our behavior—without us ever knowing. Many of these beliefs are patently false and unnecessarily limiting. They

Figure 9.1 Step 3: Recognition

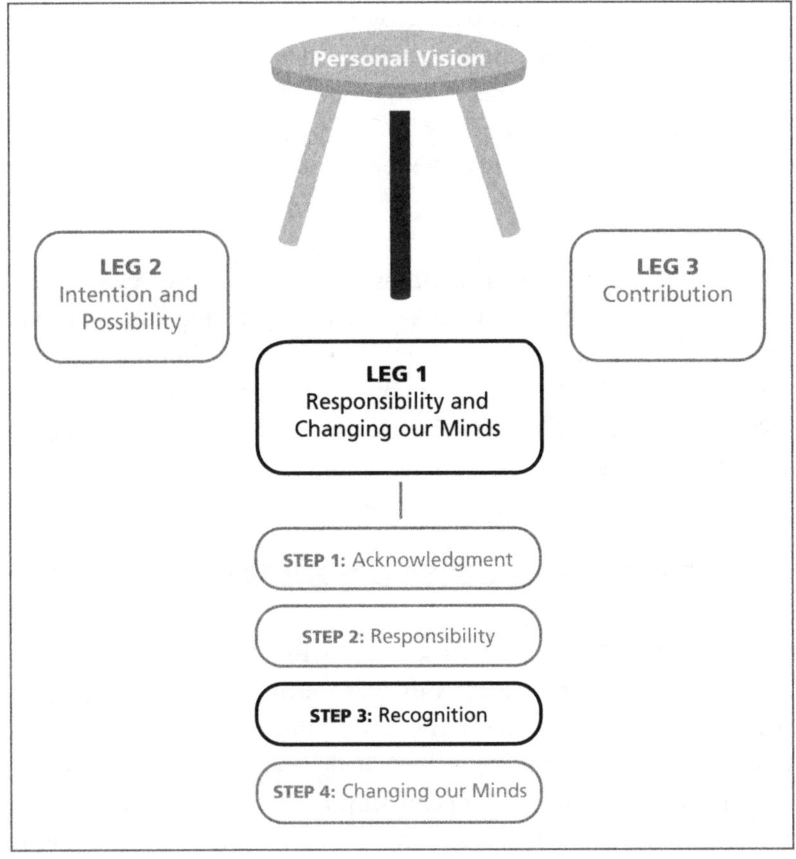

are the barriers that must be overcome if we are to realize authentic power and fulfillment. *If they remain unaddressed, lasting change of any significance cannot and will not happen.* Period. Indeed, these unaddressed beliefs are the reason most self-help books do not and cannot work.

Our paradigms are made up of a collection of vivid beliefs and strong but often shapeless perceptions that remain almost entirely out of sight, carefully hidden beneath the surface of our conscious mental lives. It is their seeming "nonexistence," their degree of obscurity, that gives them their power to blind and constrict us.

Though every individual paradigm is unique, there are universal themes that characterize the content of most. They include understandings about, among other things:

- our fundamental worth or value
- our attractiveness and desirability
- our loveableness and capacity to love
- our competence, intelligence, and/or talent
- our goodness or badness
- the trustworthiness of others
- the goodness and safety or badness and danger of life and the world

Nevertheless, because each individual has a unique genetic disposition and has had distinct experiences growing up, there are infinite variations on these themes, and thus an infinite number of personal beliefs that make up our individual paradigms. A specific case will help to clarify the nature and influence of these programmed beliefs.

THE CASE OF MELISSA MERRIMAN

Melissa "Mel" Merriman was known as the "Steel Icicle." Coming from some of her colleagues this was meant as a compliment, reflecting Melissa's strong backbone and willingness to make tough, incisive decisions; for others it was an insult, suggesting her ruthlessness and apparent complete lack of empathy. For her part, she rather liked the nickname. She was a forty-nine-year-old CFO of a $2.4 billion services company headquartered in the Midwest. She lived in a major metropolitan area with her second husband, an accomplished, rather stoic corporate executive. She had no children. While Melissa's professional life was one of considerable achievement, it was her chronic loneliness that drove her to begin a transforming journey.

Melissa, by any standard of measure, was closely guarded emotionally, even suspicious, in her demeanor. To say the least, she was emotionally shut down. And she realized that this transformative work she was being exposed to by her company might be an opportunity to get past some of her increasing feelings of isolation.

Through a series of bitter personal crises, she had been forced to be honest with herself about the emptiness she felt at work and the "sterility" of her personal life. She had long been aware of being alienated from her colleagues and her employees, but lately she seemed to notice it almost daily. And her lack of intimate friendships was becoming an issue she could no longer ignore. Her relationship with her husband was the only thing approaching intimacy in her life, and even that was becoming less intimate with every passing day. The biting pain of her loneliness had become so pronounced that it now outweighed her considerable fear, the "terror, actually," of opening herself up to others and doing the hard work of facing up to herself at the deepest levels.

Her courage won the day. As she reluctantly but persistently put herself into transforming, integrative work, she gradually began to drop her psychic and emotional armor and to open up. Over time the emotional floodgates burst, and out flowed a warmth and longing, indeed a depth of humanity that was astonishing, even inspiring. Beneath the cold efficient façade of a brilliant businesswoman and financial warrior was a profound, almost desperate need to make contact with other human beings, a need she could no longer ignore.

Melissa had been raised in upper-middle-class suburbia, in a home her parents could barely afford—her father was determined to do almost anything in order to avoid being a part of the "ordinary masses of the middle classes." She was the only child of a "sweet yet repressed" and largely passive mother and an alcoholic, occasionally violent father. When he was sober her father was not mean; he was even kind, doting on her mother, and every now and again doting on Melissa. The problem developmentally for her was that in her early years it seemed she rarely saw her father when he was sober.

Her parents had met as undergraduates in the school of journalism at a prestigious university in the Northeast. Her father had had grand ambitions of becoming a world-class broadcast journalist; her mother had dreams of one day writing for the *New York Times*. But when they got pregnant with Melissa in their junior year, they dropped out of college and began the task of creating a family and a home. While Melissa's mother was reasonably satisfied with becoming a homemaker, her father had a tough time swallowing what seemed to be his new fate. As time progressed, his dissatisfaction only grew. He hated his up-and-down corporate sales job; indeed, he hated himself for being in this position. After all, he believed he was meant to be traveling the world and breaking important news stories that would affect world affairs, not pleading with people to buy his widget.

Eventually the sense of loss became too strong, and Melissa's father began a pattern that would last for more than two decades. To drown his contempt for his lot in life, every evening before arriving home he would stop at the local bar and sufficiently numb himself with alcohol. What Melissa wanted and needed from her father, what every child wants and needs, was attention, affection, tenderness, and affirmation. But when her father stumbled in through the front door what Melissa often got was a swift kick and usually a hefty dose of verbal abuse.

"You're the reason I'm in this miserable job, selling my soul every day," he would blare. "You're the little shit that has ruined my life. Get the hell outta my presence before I wring your worthless neck." He blamed Melissa for the unhappy turn his adult life had taken, and when he was drunk he was determined to take his misplaced anger out on her. Meanwhile, her mother was almost as frightened of the raging drunk as Melissa was. Rather than protect Melissa, rather than seeking to undo the damage being done, she sought simply to mollify the violent breadwinner, to somehow keep his fury from spinning completely out of control.

Over time Melissa grew to distrust, fear, and even hate her father. What she didn't realize at the time was that she was also growing to distrust people in general and to see herself as essentially unlovable, judgments that would gradually retreat from her conscious mind and take up residence as major players in her unconscious psychological landscape.

As three-, four-, or five-year-old children we don't have the cognitive capacity to reasonably assess situations like this one—even as adults we may lack as much. We don't have the ability to calmly say to ourselves, "This behavior [of our parents, siblings, authority figures] has little or nothing to do with me." It's entirely beyond our mental and emotional development to analyze the matter.

Remember, as young children we simply and naturally absorb and react, we download the communications we receive, explicit and implicit, as truth. When Melissa's father would violently lash out at her, she would naturally think something to the effect of "I did something wrong or he'd love me, not hate me," and she would instantly internalize the feelings, fears, and doubts about herself that would start to emerge. Remember, as children, for good or ill, our parents are like gods to us. They don't just speak the truth; they *are* the truth.

Over time, at a very deep level Melissa began to assume that there was something wrong with *her*, that "I'm messed up," that "I am unlovable," or *bad* or *worthless* or simply *wrong*, perhaps *wrong to the bone*. "As Dad says," gradually she would decide, "*I* am the problem. I *am* a worthless shit. I must be—I sure *feel* that way." And why would she think or feel otherwise? After all, her father was one of the two towering figures of authority in her life, *the* truth, as it were. And her mother, paralyzed by fear herself, was reduced to standing idly by, only later to silently, tearfully collect Melissa after he finished each tirade. As she would tell Melissa much later in life, watching this violence and abuse sickened her, but she felt completely powerless before her husband's rage.

And so began the construction of Mel's personal, unconscious, existential belief system. Slowly, through the unfolding of her childhood, based on further external reinforcement and her own self-fulfilling prophecies, she solidified her collection of stark assessments about herself and about what she perceived as a dangerous, largely loveless world. As she grew up these perceptions about herself—"I'm not loveable," "I'm bad," "I make people unhappy if they are too close" and about life—"The world is a dangerous and cold place," "People can't be trusted," "Dropping your guard means danger" became a constant companion, became the figurative waters in which she swam.

As she grew into adolescence these beliefs and judgments receded into her psychic background, but they were always there. They had become invisible, pushed from conscious view, but they remained the existential, unconscious psychological echo chamber in which Melissa lived, driving virtually all of her relationships, including above all else the one with herself, thus directly or indirectly driving how she approached most of her life and how she would organize her future.

The good news for Melissa was that she also had some positive, accurate self-understandings, not the least of which were "I'm rather intelligent" and "I'm quite good with numbers." These beliefs were fueled by a healthy dose of ambition, perhaps one of the good things she received from her father. As an adult she achieved a good deal of success. She graduated from a prestigious California university, received an MBA from an equally prestigious business school, and she rapidly moved up the ranks in the business world, becoming the first female senior executive and first female CFO of her company.

But she was still stifled by her paradigmatic beliefs about herself and others. While by virtue of her brilliant mind she had effectively compensated for some of her beliefs, even as compensation these beliefs ran major aspects of her life.

Given the fact that so much of our thinking and our interpretations of life occur at an automatic, unconscious level, it matters little that we are shrewd, intelligent, singularly focused, or whatever. The fact remains that until we uncover and confront the beliefs we made up about the world and ourselves, probably at a very young age, those beliefs still determine us. It is little wonder that Melissa would want to protect herself, shield herself from the vulnerabilities of human interaction.

To the child of an aggressively dominant, unreliable, hostile, and violent parent, people are not to be trusted, regardless of what that child might later say to herself consciously as an adult. The world of human beings is dangerous and fraught with peril, an entirely unforgiving place, so it is wise to be on one's guard. Always. Second, and perhaps even more important for someone whose invisible, unconscious filtering beliefs include "I am a worthless shit" and "In relationships I am a source of pain and problems," letting people in, allowing people to see who she really is, who at this unconscious level she fears she might be, would be doubly perilous. For not only are people untrustworthy, but "once inside my walls of emotional fortification they may discover that I am not at all like the façade I present to the world: I am not just a competent, intelligent contributor; not at all. I am also a worthless shit and a problem, not a solution, and once they see this about me, I may be attacked or surely rejected once again. Why in heaven's name would I allow for that?," or so Melissa fears (through the eyes of a five-year-old girl) at an instantaneous, automatic, unconscious level. And remember, *unconscious* means that as an adult she doesn't realize that these core, fundamental beliefs are active, deciding for her, driving her behavior, and in effect determining her state of mind.

So, even though with her rational mind she knows she is competent, intelligent, and a worthy contributor, with her irrational mind, her unconscious mind, she fears the worst. There is little question which side will win out. The odds are clearly stacked in the favor of the irrational set of beliefs that have been operative since childhood.

Thus, regardless of how much Melissa may achieve in the world, until she uncovers and changes her program-fueled inner world, she is doomed to reproduce more or less the same results, again and again. Regardless. Unconscious compensation is what most of us spend most of our lives doing—seeking to prove, for instance, that we are better than others, because at a deep, deep level we fear we are less than others, inadequate or wanting. But compensation, regardless how brilliantly done, never satiates our paradigmatic monsters. Compensation, in fact, only seems to make them stronger. In fighting to disprove the fear, we are, in reality, giving the limiting perceptions energy, the fuel they need to survive and strengthen their hold on us.

Our own childhood experiences may not have been as dramatic or as extreme as Melissa's. Still, the fact remains that our early experiences in life, subtle or stark, dramatic or bland, have led to the creation of our unconscious life filters, through which we translate and interpret life. Though we cannot directly see them, though we rarely realize they are there, we cannot escape them.

It may be helpful to think of these belief systems as interpretive lenses, almost like contact lenses attached snugly and invisibly to our eyes. They are lenses we have worn for so long and become so familiar and comfortable with that we have forgotten about them, have little or no idea they even exist. In fact, there is a good chance that we never knew they existed to begin with. If our lenses have a yellow tint to them, no matter how many people tell us the sky is blue, our experience tells us the sky is green. Only as we realize that we're wearing the lenses and then take them off can we see the true color of sky.

IT'S WHAT WE MAKE UP THAT MATTERS

There is one final distinction that must be made before we address the process of discovering our lies. As adults, these deeply buried but ever-so-active undercover perceptions manifest themselves in our primary relationships, in feelings of victimization or of power, in the degree of success we achieve in our careers, in the amount of money we make in our lifetimes, in the love we experience in our daily lives, in the happiness and meaning we experience, and so on. But it is not the childhood *events* that are at issue. That's done, those events are over with, and nothing can be done about their historical reality. They are de facto abstractions that today mean absolutely nothing. All they are are "stories." What are at issue are the *beliefs* that we constructed as a *result* of those events.

It is crucial that this distinction be clear as we move forward: *The beliefs we unknowingly created as a result of our historical experiences, not the histories themselves, are what matter.* Those false beliefs have been fixed in our unconscious minds, deeply imbedded in our brains. They (not our history! not our story!) are the primary elements that limit us in being and becoming the people we have it in us to be.

In fact, beyond the catharsis and emotional completion that may sometimes accompany the process of revisiting our pasts, the *only reason* for digging up the old, putrid dirt is to better uncover the lies that still exist today. Using the transformative method, you shouldn't care one iota about your past, your history, or your story beyond their capacity to illuminate your current limiting beliefs.

SUMMARY

Left unexamined and unaltered, your paradigmatic beliefs, not the historical events that generated them, will surreptitiously dog you and run major aspects of your life, probably for the rest of your life. And this process will continue to happen automatically and instantaneously without you ever noticing it. Only as we become conscious of what has seemingly forever been unconscious is there hope for the type of expansive growth that the word *transformation* suggests.

How, then, do we go about this task of uncovering our lies, this task that seems so daunting? How do we uncover these false self-understandings so as to change them? The answer to that question is the heart of the step of recognition, and to that answer we now turn in chapter 10.

CHAPTER 10

RECOGNITION: Nailing Our Limiting Beliefs

> The range of what we think and do is limited by what we fail to notice. And because we fail to notice that we fail to notice there is little we can do to change until we notice how failing to notice shapes our thoughts and deeds.
>
> **—Daniel Goleman**

Today, in the early twenty-first century, we are just now beginning to comprehend the layers of nuance in how we think, understand, experience, and know. What we do know, however, can be life changing if we are willing to apply it and do the hard work. And what we do know is that we can both identify and liberate ourselves from the misunderstandings that constitute many of the beliefs in our personal paradigms. As we noted in chapter 9 with Melissa Merriman, these deeply buried, irrational (inaccurate) thought patterns can impair even the most intellectually gifted individual. But we can and must see—and then get past—these constricting misperceptions.

THEY ARE RESISTANT BUGGERS

The obvious challenge in uncovering and recognizing our unconscious beliefs is that they are *un*conscious. At first blush, then, it would appear we're setting out on a fool's errand—if they're unconscious, how are we supposed to see them with our conscious mind? But that's only at first blush. As we begin to take specific, thoughtful, and committed action, our unconscious mind's resistance to being found out begins to break down. It begins, over time, to give up the ghost. It's *as if* when the unconscious mind sees that we are committed to recognizing our unconscious patterns, it slowly begins to relent.

But be assured, our unconscious beliefs are likely to resist. *We* resist at an unconscious level, even though our conscious mind is saying "Go for it." In fact, it may seem as though these beliefs, these lies, are separate little entities that have taken up residence in our heads and are determined at all costs *not* to be discovered. Like any living entity, the chief mandate of the embedded belief is to survive, and being discovered can mean its eventual death, or at the very least the belief's diminished power to control aspects of our lives. Of course, the truth is, the paradigmatic beliefs are not separate entities living within us; they just feel that way sometimes.

And be forewarned: your unconscious mind will do anything and everything to prevent you from getting to this work. So as we begin laying out the method (and the exercises) for discovery, don't waste time just thinking about it. Do the recommended work. Make a commitment and get going. Now. Don't put it off. Use that portion of your mind that is conscious to stand up and dig in. Determine to be self-determining and get busy.

WATCHING THE DETECTIVE

Given the unconscious mind's tendency to resist discovery, it will be helpful to think of yourself as a psychological sleuth. That is, we'll be going through a five-step writing process that is a kind of detective work, based on simple deductive reasoning. Each step is called a *thought action*, a focused *thinking* process, thinking on paper, as it were. I warn you from the outset: For many people this is not easy work. It takes guts and tenacity. And it takes some time. But if you keep in mind that it's your life and the quality of your leadership that are at stake, you should be able to summon the courage, the will, and the imagination to see it through. And there's a good chance you'll even enjoy the process; many people do. After all, it's all about you.

The five actions that follow take an organic course. Thought Action 1 focuses on your early life. Thought Action 2 addresses your history as an adult. Thought Action 3 looks at your current life circumstances. Thought Action 4 reviews what you've just written, seen through the prism of transformative principles. And thought Action 5 is an assessment and speculation as to what the information tells you about your personal paradigm. There are no shortcuts to this process—a shortcut here amounts to cutting yourself off at the knees. So get to it, all of it, and stay with it. You and those you love and lead deserve as much.

A Long, Hard Look

A good private eye gathers as many facts as possible and based on those facts makes logical inferences (deductive reasoning) that might lead to solving the case at hand. So like a detective, first you'll make some observations about yourself and your life. You'll be going on a fact-finding mission about you. To do that you'll need to figuratively step out of your life to notice things you may have only vaguely seen or things you have never before noticed. It requires that you take a good, long, hard, honest look at your life conditions as they are today, all the things you have generated in your life that you love, that you hate, and that you're indifferent to. It requires that you examine your life conditions as they were in the recent past and the not-so-recent past. And it requires that you remember your life as it was, as far as you are able to recall, as a child growing up. And remember, as we delve into the past, this process is not concerned one whit about the past itself. Your past is dead and gone. Our concern is with what you may have *made up* out of that past, what you unconsciously still believe about yourself, about others, and about the world *because* of those past experiences.

A word of advice as you proceed: we are often inclined to clean things up a bit when we remember our pasts; we're inclined to make things a bit better than they may have been. It's especially a temptation for those who did not have major dramatic or traumatic events growing up. We must be committed to resisting the ever-so-human tendency to deny, to pretend that things are or were better than they are or were. We must be willing to drop our carefully crafted defenses and public personas and honestly look at what we may have been denying for decades.

Later, after you have gathered a sufficient array of facts and personal data, you will begin the process of making inferences, deducing what some of your unconscious beliefs *might* be. For those of you who think you already know or have a sense about what some of your beliefs are, it is essential that you do the detective work nonetheless; you'll be surprised at what you uncover in this process, but you gotta do the work.

There are two further things that you'll need to keep in mind throughout this process. Since the investigation we are beginning is deductive in nature, by definition you'll be doing a considerable amount of speculation. You will strive to logically piece things together, but you'll never have all of the pieces. So based on the limited information that you will be able to gather, you are going to have to make some logical *guesses*. First, bear in mind that *the initial stages of uncovering are simply guesswork*. You are striving for some degree of impartiality about yourself, attempting to step back and become an honest observer in order to make some smart guesses. The key here is to remember that at this point in the process it's *only* informed guesswork. That's all. You are not seeking here to arrive at certainty. Just smart guesswork.

The second thing to remember is that this first pass at self-recognition is speculative; *you don't need to be right*. It's okay to speculate that there are certain beliefs that may later turn out to not be there at all. Initially you may be slightly or even completely inaccurate about what you come up with. That's all right. Do not expect to get it right the first time out. Self-righteously demanding that "I've got to figure all of these things out and right now! Got to uncover everything now!" is not going to work. That kind of forced determination usually causes constriction, the exact opposite of what is needed.

What is needed is openness and willingness. So relax. Decide to be patient. This type of introspective digging takes time, and over time, if you remain committed to becoming what you still have it in you to become, the beliefs will reveal themselves. I assure you. The important thing is to get over the need for instant perfection and certainty. Suspend the need to understand it all right now. Just do the work and trust the process. As long as you are persistent and patient, the truth will win the day. It always does for those who persist.

Thought Action 1: Writing Your Early Story

The first thought action that you will undertake is to write out your childhood story, from the time you were born up to your early adolescence, age thirteen, fourteen, or fifteen. And notice I said "write." It won't work for you to merely recall these things in your head. You must write these things down.

For many people dredging up the past is the last thing they want to do. I understand. But it's necessary. And remember, though you'll be looking at your past, your history is not what we're concerned with. The past contains the evidence that helps you determine your beliefs. Investigating the past is not the only vehicle for uncovering those beliefs, but for most people it is by far the best and the most direct. So, difficult though it may be, do it.

I recommend that you do all of your writing and thinking for this process in the same notebook or journal you used for Exercise 4.1 in chapter 4 (the journal dedicated to your transformative journey), and I suggest that you keep this notebook or journal private. It's no one else's business.

So, addressing the ten questions below, go back as far as you can remember and describe the early years of your life in narrative form as if you were telling someone who didn't know you. Just let it pour out, and start at the beginning. For example:

> I was born on October 8, 1966, in Vancouver, Washington, to John and Mary Wilson. For the first eleven years of my life we lived just outside of the city limits in a blue-collar, working-class neighborhood. I was the third of six children in a deeply religious, Roman Catholic family. My father was a union welder for Descidgio Corporation; he worked six days a week, left the house every day at 5 a.m., and returned at 6:15 on the spot every evening. He would collapse into his easy chair with a Miller beer in one hand and a cigarette in the other, and by 8:30, after three or four beers, he was passed out. My mom was a stay-at-home mom for the first eight years of my life. She was devoutly Catholic, very kind and hard-working, but very frustrated with her life of raising six kids. She was also always angry at my dad for a huge number of things. . . .

The questions you are to address in writing your story are as follows—and please address all ten areas listed; this process and these questions are tried and true:

1. Where were you born and where did you live during your early years?
2. What did your parents or the people who raised you do for a living? How did they relate to each other, to others within and outside of the family? And above all, how did they relate to you?
3. Did you have siblings? If so, where were you in the birth order, how did they relate to each other, and specifically how did they relate to you (and vice versa)?
4. Did you have many friends growing up? Were there times when you had friends and times when you didn't? What kind of memories do you have of other children during these early years? List both happy and sad memories.
5. What big memories, positive and negative, stand out for you as a child? Are there experiences that serve as markers in your past, pivotal points that may have had a lasting influence? Give yourself permission to speculate about what events mattered, large and small. If you have a memory of it, there's a good chance it was important (even if seemingly minor) in ways you may not have yet realized.
6. What were some of the chronic, mundane, recurring events that you remember from your early life? What were the seemingly uneventful life circumstances that may have shaped your view of yourself and your view of the world?
7. What were the things that brought you happiness and joy?
8. What were the things that brought you sadness and pain?
9. What were your hopes and dreams as a kid? What did you fantasize about, dream of, and hope that you or your life might become one day?
10. What were your doubts and fears? What were the things that filled you with anxiety, the things that may have made you feel uncertain? Regardless of how silly they may seem today, write them down. Write them down! All of them.

The more brutally honest you are in this process of writing and remembering, the more revealing the process will be. As you write, you may well be surprised by some of the things that emerge from your pen. There is something visceral and even liberating about the process of putting pen to paper, something that the technological wonders of the laptop, desktop, or iPad just cannot match.

Allow the process of writing to have a life of its own, and create the time and space to ensure that you are not interrupted by family or friends. It is of utmost importance that you have an extended period of uninterrupted time, forty-five minutes to one hour minimum; two hours or more is ideal. Most people can scarcely imagine this much uninterrupted time alone. But get over it and do it. It's your life we're dealing with here. What is at stake is far greater than most people will allow themselves to imagine. If you are unable or more accurately, unwilling to create an hour of time for yourself because you are too busy taking care of other things and other people, the odds are you're accustomed to playing the role of victim or martyr. Don't go there. It has no virtue. None. Sorry.

Thought Action 2: Your Recent and Not-So-Recent Past

Having written your early history, you'll now move on to your adult life, beginning with your experiences as a young adult, moving up to your most recent past. As you do this historical survey, do not get bogged down with every last detail. Rather, consider the salient features of your "grown-up" or growing-up past. What moments stand out as particularly joyful, sad, or frustrating—or all three? The moments of greatest accomplishment or failure, or both? Of satisfaction or disappointment? Or perhaps those extended moments when nothing was outstanding, those periods during which everything just seemed blah and uneventful, neither sad nor happy, just status quo, ordinary, somewhat empty? Of course, for some people, these uneventful times were pleasant times. If so, write about that, but do your best to remember what you truly experienced at the time, not what you might like to remember.

What were your life conditions? What were the results you created in your life during these periods of time? Remember, at this point you are simply gathering the data. You are playing the role of *Dragnet*'s Joe Friday: "Just the facts, ma'am." That's all we're after here; just the facts. (For those too young to get this reference, Google it.) That means you are *not* analyzing or interpreting the facts. The temptation is to slip into assessment. Don't do that. Assessment will come later. For now, just collect the historical data: where you were living, what you were doing professionally, what was going on personally, who was in your life (describe the significant relationships in all the gory details), to what extent you were happy, sad, bored, successful, financially flush, destitute, et cetera.

You are to revisit up to but not including the present time. In your journal or notebook you will want to write no less than two to three pages. If you want to write more, that's fine. Some people double up on this. There is, after all, a lot of life to consider. Regardless, just put pen to paper and get busy.

Thought Action 3: Your Current State

Focus your attention, your detective's eye for important details, on your current life circumstances. Where are you today in your life? The facts. Write them down. Being fully objective is impossible, but do your best to see the facts and avoid *assessment.*

Where do you live and what are you living in, that is, your home or living quarters? Who are the people currently in your life (regardless of how you feel about them), including family (spouse and children, as well as parents, siblings, in-laws, et cetera), friends, enemies, bosses, employees, significant other, and so on? How satisfying, or not, are those relationships? Consider especially those relationships you deem as meaningful. What is the nature of your leadership and professional life (include a brief description of your industry or profession), whom you lead and are led by, the extent to which you are fulfilled or not, and your sense of accomplishment in your chosen leadership and life endeavor? Is it really your "life endeavor"—what you want to be doing with your finite life energy? What is your economic or financial condition? Do you live from paycheck to paycheck? Do you live in a state of perpetual worry about money? Do you make more money than you'll ever be able to spend? How wise are you with your money in terms of planning and investments? Is your financial future secure?

What do you do for pleasure or recreation, including hobbies and interests? What are the challenges you face in your life, particularly with other people, family, money, your love life, your emotional state, and your career or profession? Are you where you expected or hoped to be in your life when you reached this age or juncture in time? If not, why not? This last question can lead into a lot of opinion, so be careful here. Do your best to remain as factual as possible. You're still in the fact-finding stage.

Finally, after you have answered these factual questions, consider and answer these questions of ultimate concern: What is of greatest importance to you today in your life? That is, what do you care about at the deepest, most compelling level? And then, How well do the current facts of your life seem to match up with your answer to this question of ultimate concern?

What you are attempting to do here can be difficult because you are currently swimming in the very pool you are attempting to describe. So do your best to momentarily climb out of the figurative waters of your life in order to better observe and describe them. As you address the final questions, do your best to honestly ascertain your *experience* of your life conditions. To what extent do you experience happiness or joy, satisfaction or contentment? Sadness, pain, and disappointment? Fulfillment and, perhaps above all, meaning? These are among the big questions of life, questions we may want to turn away from, fearing the answers that may emerge. So the courage that self-honesty requires is called for. It is the quality of your life and the impact of your leadership that are at stake, nothing less.

Once more, you should expect to write a minimum of two to three pages in your notebook or journal, and allow for sufficient time and solitude.

For some of you, I suspect, life on autopilot is pretty good. If so, the odds are you've been doing the ordinary well, perhaps very well. But the odds are also that your possibility, your greatest potential, still remains largely untapped. The degree of leadership impact, the quality of the life you might create, and the good you might do, in all likelihood, far exceed what you've allowed yourself to imagine. If you're still reading this book, there's a better than good chance you have a desire to become the leader and person you still have it in you to be, and you know you're not there yet. So do the work.

Thought Action 4: Reviewing What You've Got and Looking for Patterns

Having gathered the data, the next step has two distinct parts that must be done in order. First, carefully view Figure 10.1, The

Figure 10.1 The Anatomy of Transformation (Facing Up To What Is)

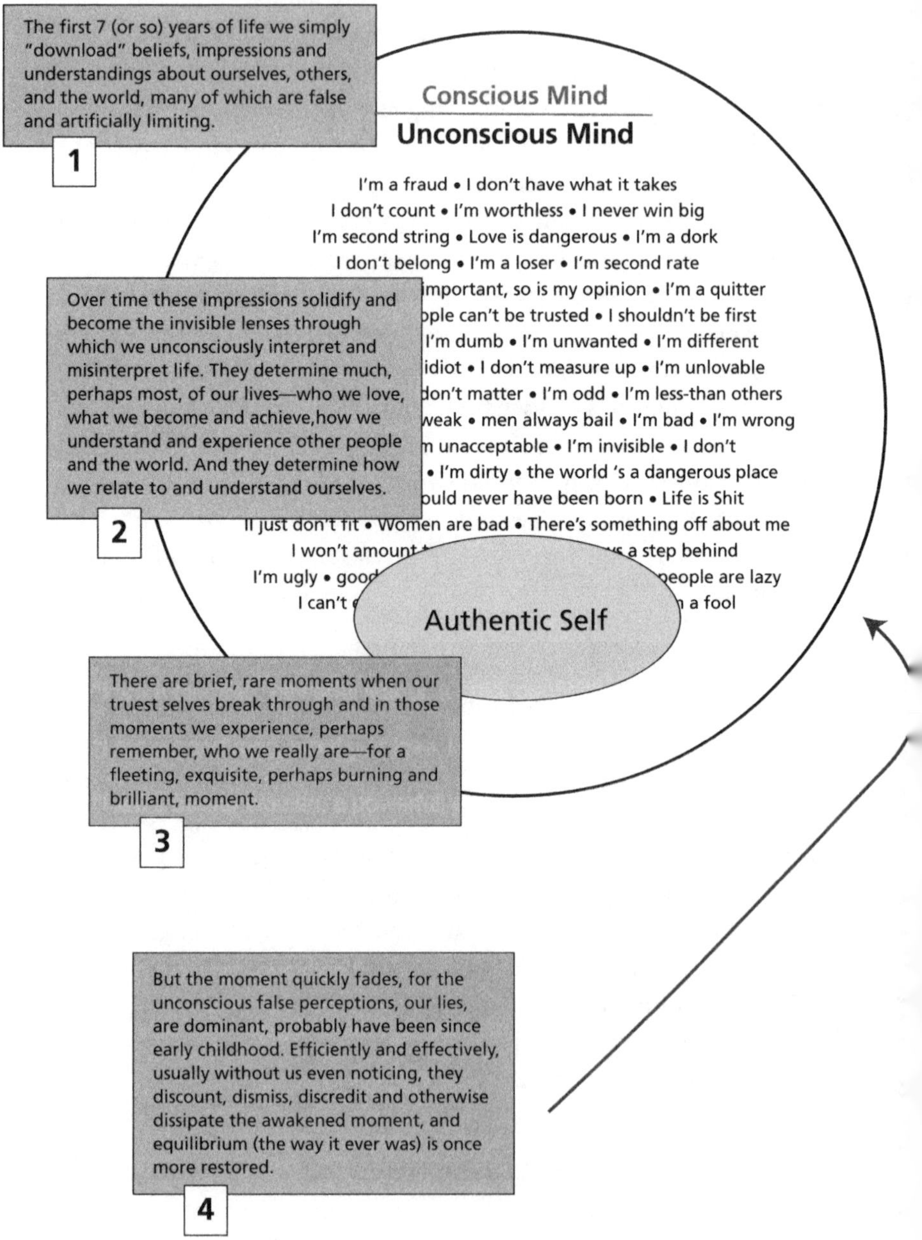

Anatomy of Transformation. This briefly sketches the process by which we construct our unconscious understandings of ourselves and the world, giving us a snapshot of how we create our personal paradigms and the types of beliefs they contain. Bear in mind that the list of unconscious beliefs in the circle is not exhaustive. There are infinite variations on those themes.

Second, with Figure 10.1 in mind, read what you have written about your life—all three pieces of your story: your childhood history, your adult history, and your current circumstances. Read every word, and read carefully—do not skim it or read it quickly. And don't assume you remember what you've written. You may be surprised at what came out of your pen. Remember, there are no shortcuts in this process.

As you revisit your life, periodically stop along the way and consider the *patterns* you are noticing. Write down your observations as they pop into your mind. What are the most poignant and stirring aspects of your childhood? What do you notice about your primary relationships with your parents or parent figures, other adults, siblings, and friends? What feelings, good and bad, and what fears emerge as you reread your text? What kinds of things were you told (with or without words) about you, about other people, about specific types of people, about the world?

Patterns become important as you move into your adult history. Begin looking for patterns of behavior and recurring tendencies in all aspects of your life: in your relationships (friendships and the types of personalities you attract as friends and in key intimate relationships), in educational experiences and achievement, in work or career experience and professional accomplishment, in your leadership success or failure, in financial circumstances, in the rewards and recognition you receive or fail to receive, in the overall results you've created, and in your general life success and happiness.

After you have spent some extended time noticing and writing down some of these emerging patterns, you can move on to the fifth and final deductive thought action.

Thought Action 5: Assessment and Speculation

The final thought action is the process of *assessing* the patterns, the recurring behaviors, and results you are noticing. Out of that assessment you'll begin making educated guesses regarding your primary beliefs. For example, a single woman who repeatedly attracts a certain type of man into her life as a love interest may have an underlying perception about who she is—a belief about what she deserves, what she is capable of, how she is to be in the world, and the like—that will profoundly influence her choices and the nature of her love life. She may declare that her choices in men are just a matter of taste. While there is likely to be an element of truth in her assertion, beneath the surface there is more going on. Her operative unconscious beliefs inform, direct, perhaps even determine her "taste."

There are three things to keep in mind as you venture into assessment and speculation. First, there are no accidents in the domain of results; that is, the only powerful and responsible way to operate in life is from the perspective "I am cause, and therefore somehow I have caused this." Second, remember, we rarely do what we do or decide what we decide entirely for the reasons we tell ourselves. Third, the results we have generated in our lives are virtually always a function, to one degree or another, of our underlying beliefs, seen or unseen, about ourselves, about others, and about the world.

With these three notions in mind, begin your deductive work. The deductive process can either work backward from recent history or forward from childhood history.

Working Backward (Backward Deduction), Action 5

Backward deduction (working backward) starts from the list of relatively recent recurring behaviors, patterns, and results you've noticed and then speculates as to the underlying beliefs that may inform or cause the behaviors, patterns, and results. For instance, John Averageman may find a pattern of underachievement in his life, in his leadership impact, in the quality of his friendships, in the level of his financial success, and in the stature of the job he holds. It may have shown up in his degree of success socially and athletically in high school and at the university. Based on these patterns, he speculates that there may be two beliefs at work. One, "I'm second rate or second string always," and, two, rather bluntly, "I am a loser." These are both hard for John to swallow, hard to accept as something he might unwittingly believe about himself—they are entirely contrary to the image he diligently tries to present to the world and to himself. But based purely on deductive reasoning, based on the evidence he has gathered, he conjectures that there may be a kernel of truth to them.

Let's consider how his reasoning process has worked. First, neither of the proposed beliefs is a belief that John feels or believes at a conscious level. In other words, if you asked him straight up, "Do you think of yourself as a loser or as second rate?" he would answer, in total honesty, "Absolutely not." But he realizes his focus here is to be on the unconscious and that unconscious perceptions can be (often are) completely divorced from reality and from what we tell ourselves at a conscious level. Thus he suspends his visceral, defensive reaction to thinking of himself as a loser and simply considers the facts.

At the most basic level, his reasoning might go something like this:

> Fact one: I never come in first place. In high school, I was the second-string quarterback all four years and the starting tight end three. But I wanted to be the starting quarterback, nothing more, nothing less, and based on what everyone, including both of my coaches, told me, I had significantly better talent than the guy who started ahead of me. However I may want to spin this thing, I lost that race.
>
> Fact two: in other matters like my career and the amount of money I earn, I always tend to be smack-dab in the middle of the pack. I never excel. I want to excel, to succeed, to win. But I don't. Based on what I really want in life, what I say I want in life, these results—the not excelling, not succeeding, not flat-out winning—all amount to a kind of failure. I wonder if it might not be that deep down, in spite of what I tell myself, I *really* believe I'm a loser, an "also ran," or second rate, someone who deep down thinks he shouldn't win, maybe thinks he doesn't deserve it.

John is not suggesting that these events in his high school and adult life caused the belief that he's second rate. Rather, he is saying that this deep, subconscious belief may have caused these chronic results in his life—if, that is, it does turn out on further thought and investigation that his speculation is correct. For now, he reminds himself, this is all just logical guesswork. One further point on the implications of John's reasoned conjecture: while the events in John's adult life are not the original source of his beliefs, they do serve to reinforce those beliefs. Though it is likely that the operative beliefs were put in place while he was a child, the chronic events nevertheless serve as further supporting evidence, evidence that his unconscious mind has continued to gather over the years to support and strengthen its belief in John's "loserness" or his secondary value. The perceptions and beliefs are never static. They always are seeking to take over more terrain in our minds, to strengthen themselves.

Working Forward (Forward Deduction), Action 5

Forward deductive speculation is as simple as backward deduction and perhaps a bit more obvious. Beginning with our childhood history, we consider the salient formative experiences, the pivotal formative relationships, and all other manner of events we may have experienced, and we then ask a specific question.

First let's consider how the reasoning might unfold: "I regularly experienced this from Mom and that from Dad, which was similar to what I experienced from my big sister and in my relationship with Uncle Harry, and then there was that brutally painful event in first grade at the hands of that fourth grade 'gang' of hoodlums." With this prominent data before us, we ask the simple question, "Given all of this, what might a normal four- or five-year-old child decide about herself? What might she decide about the world and life and others?"

As you begin the process of assessment and speculation, I recommend that you create a narrative report. Cynthia's assessment and speculation (narrative report) are presented in Box 10.1. Note the way Cynthia systematically approaches it. She has taken her history and current life circumstances and from her assessment of these two elements constructed a possible framework (list of beliefs) for understanding her unconscious filtering system, her personal paradigm. By combining her observations about (1) her current life circumstance, (2) her recent past circumstances and the patterns she notes in examining both, and then considering (3) all of this in the context of her childhood, she logically, and spontaneously in one instance, arrives at four possible limiting beliefs.

Box 10.1 Cynthia's First Pass on Cynthia

(Note: She has chosen to write in the third person, which is an option for you as well.)

• Facts •

1. Recently Cynthia has been reasonably happy, depending on how that is defined. Her current professional life is going pretty well; she's a senior director at Machitupp and Associates Property Management; she's been at Machitupp nearly four years now. She continues to produce results that give her a sense of job security, but her production could be better, could always be better; her boss and superiors like her, think she's smart but believe that she could do better work in developing her people. Her people (direct reports) say that she knows the business well, she's tough but fair most of the time, she can be a bit dictatorial at times, she often seems too "wrapped up in her own stuff and indifferent to theirs" (this comment stings Cynthia), and she often seems anxious about how the big boss sees her. She describes herself today as a well-put-together woman, attractive, nice figure (in good shape, works hard at it), and (with the good fortune of having good genes) looks younger than she is.

2. She is divorced (still a bit bitter over that, she admits); has a 13-year-old son, Joshua (whom she raises alone by her choice—ex-husband is still in Colorado, she and her son in California). She's in a six-month-old relationship with Scotty, but she doesn't see a future. Like so many men she has had in her life, he's a wimp (though her ex-husband was the opposite of that, a self-described "part-time petty tyrant").

3. Four years ago Cynthia felt stuck in her job—had reached the level of associate director but could not seem to move any further up the corporate ladder. She had been accused by colleagues and one of her superiors of being "cold and self-absorbed" (which at the time she thought was rubbish, and she wondered aloud what that had to do with producing results, but now she is reconsidering both responses). After she realized that unprofessional pettiness and who-knows-what-else would prevent her from any further professional movement, she left and went to Machitupp.

(continued on next page)

(continued from previous page)

4. Seven years ago she divorced her husband on the grounds that he was distant, emotionally and sexually aloof, and, she strongly suspected but without hard evidence, unfaithful. He was a very angry man; it was bottled up most of the time, but it came out every once in a while in tirades when the pressures of being a financial analyst got to him. She is not sure how or why she ever fell in love with him; she's not actually sure that "in love" could ever have described her feelings for him.

• Relevant Childhood Fact •

Cynthia's mother was a strong, stoic Midwestern Lutheran. She was not affectionate; she thinks her mother honestly thought affection was a sin, but Cynthia says (or used to say) that she always knew that she was loved. As she thinks about it now, she is not so sure that as a child she knew that she was loved. She never experienced much or any affection or affirmation from her mother. She realizes that now. And her father, a good man, was always on the road with work. Cynthia's mother always pushed her to excel, and she did excel at school, at piano (she studied to be a concert pianist for nearly ten years), at soccer, at virtually everything she tried. She knew that her mother was proud of her, but even her successes produced little affection, little warmth. Her mother kept Cynthia busy with mostly individualistic, high-minded tasks. It is just recently that Cynthia is realizing this emotional distance may have had more impact than she had previously understood. Today she and her mother are "pretty good friends"; they talk a couple of times a week. Cynthia says her mother is far more affectionate with Cynthia's son than she ever was with Cynthia. This hurts a bit for her to realize. She is thrilled to see her son getting affection, but seeing it brings home what she didn't get.

• Detective's Preliminary Deduction •

Based on the real-world evidence gleaned from Cynthia's recent and extensive writing and thinking about her adult life and her childhood; based on the results of her adult life, currently and in her recent past; and based on her newly awakened sense of the relevance of her relationship with her mother; she is beginning to believe the following:

I am kind of an angry person, I think. I'm actually very surprised to say this, to see this. I'm just now recognizing it, at the age of 41. Actually, I'm very angry; beneath my "got it together" presentation, I'm angry and I'm lonely; goodness, I think I have always been lonely, even during the supposedly happy time of my marriage I think I was lonely. Back to the anger bit, the person I'm angry with, and intolerant of, is me. I can understand the intolerance, that is what I saw modeled growing up, but I don't yet get why I am so angry with myself. And I take this anger out on Joshua, which makes me feel like crap, really, really crummy. And, of course, I take it out on myself.

• Cynthia's Conclusion •

There are four false beliefs or lies that I think I may have attached myself to or created as a child.

1. There is not a lot of love in this world, so don't expect too much; it's rather cold out there.

2. I am undeserving of warmth and love and recognition.

3. I will never measure up, no matter how hard I try; what I do will never be quite sufficient; I will never be quite sufficient.

These first three make sense to me but I'm still not sure about the wording. The last one, below, though, is a direct hit. It hit me very hard and it saddened me as I heard it:

4. *I am odd.* I have a vivid memory of being about 8 or 9, my mother driving me to piano lessons, and feeling like I wanted to cry, but holding it in, always holding it in. I wanted to cry because I couldn't do what other girls did and didn't even know what that was, and I remember thinking, "It's because I'm odd." It was so vivid, so clear. It was as if someone had said it out loud to me. This memory sickens me (until

(continued on next page)

(continued from previous page)

yesterday I had completely forgotten it). My mother's closest thing to a term of endearment was to refer to me as her "odd little duck." The "reason" I had so few friends, that I had to practice piano rather than talk about boys was because I was odd. That is how I understood my lonely little world back then. Wow, that is so vivid. I feel it right now. It's alive in my stomach right now. I was odd, I am odd. That's the belief. The BIG one. Heck, I didn't even know that I was pretty until my sophomore year in college when my roommate got drunk and confessed that she hated me, was horribly jealous of me because I was so beautiful. I was astonished, because "I'm odd." How is it possible that I am "beautiful"? I think that this one, number 4, and number 2 (undeserving of warmth and love) explain much of my loneliness. Maybe some of my anger too.

On the first three beliefs Cynthia has done good detective work, making reasonable and smart guesses based on the results of her life and her experiences growing up. She is using deductive reasoning. On the fourth belief she experiences what might be called an "insight breakthrough"—she wasn't thinking as much as she was receiving: Her unconscious just gave it up, so to speak. "It just came to me," she later says. This sort of unforced insight is always a function of surrendering to the process, of truly becoming committed to your life and its still unrealized promise and doing the work.

Your final step in this initial effort to uncover your paradigm, then, is to take what you have done and put it all together in a format similar to what Cynthia has done. In your journal, based on the work you've done, begin your own assessment and speculation. Once again, do not leave it to mere thinking. Write it out. It's your life we're dealing with here. You, as well as the lives you will positively touch as a result of moving yourself forward, are worth the time and effort. So think and think hard.

SUMMARY

As daunting as it may initially seem, uncovering the limiting beliefs that comprise our personal paradigm is doable. We can become conscious of our unconscious perceptions and judgments. Until we do that, however, the dramatic growth, the leadership and personal development promised by the transformative method is not possible. The good news is that there are specific actions that we can take, thought actions, that when combined with good, sound reasoning can lead to breakthroughs.

Once we have arrived at some sense of what our dominant, limiting beliefs may be the real fun can begin. Though they are powerful, these beliefs are not *all*-powerful. Our brains and minds are imminently changeable if we know what we're dealing with—the specific, limiting perceptions—and if we're willing to do the work. We can change our minds and do it permanently. That is what the next stop on our journey is all about.

CHAPTER 11

CHANGING OUR MINDS TO CHANGE OUR BRAINS: The Beginnings of a Practice

> The idea that the brain can change its own structure and function through thought and activity is, I believe, the most important alteration in our view of the brain since we first sketched out its basic anatomy and the workings of its basic component, the neuron.
>
> **—Norman Doidge**

Recognition, the act of uncovering our previously hidden, limiting false beliefs, is essential to transformative journey, but it is not an end in and of itself. Discovery, in fact, is only the beginning of the compelling ascent. The biggest challenges and the biggest rewards are still ahead of us. That's because identifying the unconscious self-misunderstandings does not suddenly cause them to go away. After all, these beliefs have been there, in most cases, for decades. They represent well-honed patterns of subliminal thought that die hard.

We discover our unconscious beliefs in Step 3 of Leg 1 of the transformational stool so that we can undo these beliefs and create new and more accurate understandings of ourselves and of the world. So that we can create more effective ways of being and doing in life. So that we can rewire the faulty wiring and establish new, trued-up, and powerful thought patterns.

All of those "so that's" point us to Step 4: *changing our minds* (see Figure 11.1). Step 4 is a call to thoughtful, disciplined action. It is a call to use our conscious capacity (our minds) in an intentional way to change our biology (our brains) and, in the process, to change our psychology (expressed in our ways of being). It is a call to step out beyond the familiar comfort of our pasts. And it is to boldly summon untapped, or infrequently tapped, abilities of imagination and accomplishment, abilities of compassion and courage, abilities that cause us to move from a reactive mind-set of *managing* life to a proactive mind-set that *leads* life.

Figure 11.1 Step 4: Changing Our Minds

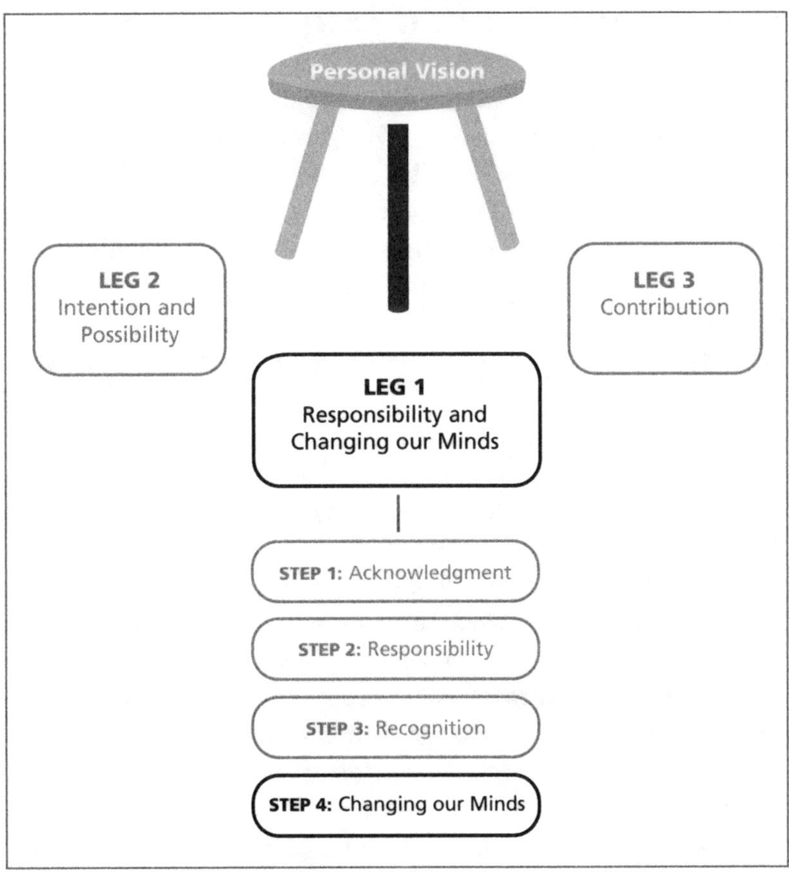

And that, in the final analysis, is what we are after in our response to the impulse of transformation: making a fundamental and lasting shift from merely reacting to what life throws our way to proactively leading others (and our lives) from a place of purpose and power. Thus, in Step 4 we are called upon to intentionally create new, more accurate beliefs at the deepest levels of the mind, literally changing the biological architecture of our brains, to replace our "lies"—our unconscious, inaccurate beliefs—with truths. And we're called to simultaneously live from more authentic, more robust ways of being, and finally, to take the necessary action (bold, courageous, creative action) that will reinforce our new mind-sets and produce measurably better results, results that we love, both personally and organizationally.

TRAIN YOUR MIND, CHANGE YOUR BRAIN

In the book *Train Your Mind, Change Your Brain: How a New Science Reveals Our Extraordinary Potential to Transform Ourselves*, award-winning science writer Sharon Begley points out that for decades the "textbook wisdom held that the adult brain is hardwired, fixed in form and function, so that by the time we reach adulthood, we are pretty much stuck with what we have."[1] But today we know that, like the historic certainty that the Earth was flat, this too is false. The human brain in fact is *plastic*, meaning it is moldable, changeable, capable of being transformed. And today, in the second decade of the twenty-first century, it is no longer a matter of speculation. It's a matter of scientific fact. The answer to the question "Can we intentionally change our brains and therefore our minds?" Begley declares, is an emphatic *yes*.

The research is so compelling that a new scientific discipline has emerged from it: the science of neuroplasticity, the focused study of the brain's ability to change itself. The *Encyclopedia Britannica* defines *neuroplasticity* as "the capacity of neurons and neural networks in the brain to change their connections and behavior in response to new information, sensory stimulation, development, damage, or dysfunction."

We know today that the adult brain can be rewired. It has the ability to grow new neurons and permanently rearrange the existing synaptic networks. In Begley's words, it can "change the circuitry that weaves neurons into the networks that allow us to remember, feel, suffer, think, imagine, and dream."[2] Most important from a transformative perspective, the brain's plastic quality allows us to intentionally change the circuitry that is central to becoming the leaders, indeed the women and men we would like to be, that in some deeper sense we already are. It allows us to become the leaders that we know we must become.

But to do that we must come to grips with the power we wield by virtue of our capacity to think. Begley writes, "The [mental] actions we take can literally expand or contract different regions of the brain, pour more juice into quiet circuits, and damp down activity in buzzing ones. . . . That is, the brain can change as a result of the thoughts we have thought."[3] Transformation is no longer addressed exclusively in psychological and spiritual camps; now the hard sciences, full throttle, are almost daily uncovering empirical evidence that support its possibility, in fact, its reality. The only question, then, is how we effectively apply these radical new insights.

For the answer to that question we turn to two leading neuroscientists, Michael Merzenich and R.C. deCharms. The short answer they give is that we apply these scientific breakthroughs simply by learning to focus and pay attention. The simple act of choosing what we attend to leads to the results we produce in our lives. *What* we pay attention to is the pivot point here. The fundamental act of paying attention to the *right* things with *sufficient intensity and consistency* can lead to transformation. When all is said and done, we are left, they say, "with a clear physiological fact. . . . Moment by moment we choose and sculpt how our ever-changing minds will work, we choose who we will be the next moment in a very real sense, and these choices are left embossed in physical form on our material selves."[4]

We are the sculptors of our brains and not merely in some abstract or metaphorical sense. We sculpt our gray matter, in fact and in deed. By way of extension, then, we also shape our minds and always have. From a transformative point of view, then, we *re*shape our minds by the quality and power of our attention, by choosing to focus our attention in specific areas, on specific thoughts, and with specific degrees of intensity, consistency, and focus.

It is how we *focus and direct* our capacity for attention that matters. That's it. In a sense, that's all there is to it. But we must not be seduced by the apparent simplicity of the formula. The specific type of attending and focusing that brings about intentional change in our minds requires focus and discipline. Changing our minds is achievable, but it takes a true and unshakable dedication to who we can be and what we can achieve. It takes grit and guts, imagination and a powerful, disciplined commitment.

Furthermore, it takes a healthy dose of unlearning—we must unlearn old understandings to make room for new ones. "The science of unlearning is a very new one," prominent research scientist Norman Doidge says. "Because plasticity is competitive, when a person develops a neural network, it becomes efficient and self-sustaining and, like a bad habit, hard to unlearn."[5] But unlearn it we must. We've been laying down these metaphoric grooves in our brains for decades, and thus they've become "self-sustaining." That is, the lies reinforce themselves at every chance, solidifying their place in our largely unseen psychological landscape. Over time they've become strong, in some cases nearly indestructible, a force to be reckoned with. So we must approach the process of undoing and unlearning them systematically, as we simultaneously establish more accurate and liberating understandings of self, life, leadership, and others.

It Takes Practice: Making It Happen

Understanding that we can literally change our brains by attending to targeted patterns of thought is one thing. Doing it is quite another. The fact is that we have multiple reasons for resisting this kind of disciplined thinking, not the least of which is our innate laziness. Add to that, as we've already noted, the fact that our old thought patterns resist being rooted out at almost any cost. And finally, most of these false, limiting beliefs have been active for so long they've become old, familiar friends, even if they are the sort of friends who cause us misery. It is little wonder, then, that *thinking* about changing our thought patterns is very different than actually *making* the change and having it stick.

So let's be clear about all of this: Changing our minds through the power of attention requires a healthy dose of *intention*. Nothing less than a fierce and clear-headed commitment will be sufficient. And one of the best means of evoking that commitment and of doing the work of focused, brain-changing thought is an application known as a *responsibility ritual* or *responsibility practice*.

First, we must come to terms with the very notion of a daily practice, something that is foreign to most people living in the West. The best spiritual methodologies (Eastern and Western) and some of the most progressive scientific psycho-therapeutic approaches have long advocated what is called a "daily practice." What that generally means is the creation and implementation of a discipline that is done every day, a discipline of calming and focusing the mind and connecting, so to speak, with our better, more authentic selves. In the process of quieting and concentrating our thinking, we allow ourselves to consciously *choose* the thoughts we will think, specific thoughts that will help us reshape our minds and thereby enhance our effectiveness and power. In the words of Merzenich and deCharms, we are choosing "the details that we will pay attention to."[6] In a ritual process we "pay attention" on a rigorous yet calm, repetitive yet engaged basis. As simple as it may sound, for those who are willing to stick with it, it represents the beginnings of true and lasting transformation.

The process is termed a ritual not because it has any explicit religious intent. Rather, the word *ritual* is used because something we perform with repetitive dedication is something we deem important. A ritual is something that reminds us of, returns our minds to, that which holds special meaning and value. It is a *responsibility* ritual because the act of consciously choosing to focus our minds and direct our thoughts represents a full embrace of personal causality and a full embrace of what it means to *lead* rather than manage our lives. Remember, responsibility is surrendering to the fact that we have been and always will be the cause in our lives, like it or not. Becoming intentional about that causal capacity is at the heart of the ritual process.

The responsibility ritual consists of three non-negotiable elements: a personal purpose statement, a truths-and-lies process, and a personal truth statement (or statements). Additional elements (the nice-to-haves) include music that enhances focus and stirs the spirit; meditation or contemplative prayer, which among other things creates calmness and clarity; and visualization, a practice that serves a variety of purposes. All three can greatly enhance the power and impact of the ritual practice, depending on the practitioner's needs and preferences.

The Ritual's Rationale: Changing Our Relationship With the Self

When we change our minds, as we mean it here, we are changing how we relate to and understand ourselves at the deepest level. This focus on the self is not an act of narcissism but rather an act of liberation from the fears and insecurities that lead to narcissistic behavior. How we view ourselves at these deep-seated levels directly affects, even determines, every other relationship we have as leaders (with our colleagues and followers) and in our personal lives. It is central in determining our relationship with leadership success, with money, with accomplishment, and in the end, with happiness and fulfillment. As we learn to more effectively honor, respect, and love ourselves we become less self-absorbed, not more; we become more free to see beyond ourselves, not less; and we become free to actually see and connect with others at more meaningful and powerful levels. Thus, we learn to express our leadership in less self-conscious, far more effective and meaningful ways.

The Need for Meaning and the First Component

Consider this most basic question: "Why are we here?" It's one of the big, eternal, often perplexing questions of life, the sort of question that philosophers and ordinary thoughtful people alike have pondered from time immemorial. Why do we exist and what is the meaning of life, if any? If we are reasonably healthy, nominally thoughtful people, it's a question at one time or another we've asked in a more personal way: "Why am *I* here?" Is there a larger reason that would make sense out of all the disparate pieces of our sometimes-jangled lives, of the seeming chaos of existence?

It's a question that speaks to our essential need for meaning. Indeed, this need for meaning is one of *the* fundamental higher human needs. Because, at heart, we are fundamentally meaning-seeking creatures. Many millennia ago, when we were still wandering about in hunter-gatherer tribes, because of our need for meaning, when lighting would strike and thunder would clap we would immediately assign it divine significance: God is angry, say, or the gods are at war. Today, from our modern perch, we may look back on our primitive forbearers with smug superiority, but such condescension seems a bit unwarranted. In modern times we *still* do this dubious meaning assignment thing. Drive down the street of any major city in the world and sooner or later you are sure to come upon that flashing neon sign declaring PALM READINGS, $40, or the like. Soothsayers and mediums of all descriptions have never done better business than they do today. After all, if someone can tell us our future, it means we have a destiny, and if we have a destiny we have meaning.

Though today we may be less inclined to assign significance where there is none, as human beings we all still have the need for meaning. And if that need goes unmet, you cannot be, you will not be, a fully functioning, fully happy, fully healthy woman or man—and yes, having meaning in your life even has a direct effect on your physical health. The need for meaning seems built into our very DNA and built into our highest perceptions of self. The expression of it is going to be different for each of us, *but* finding it is not as difficult as it may seem. In fact, at some level you probably already know what it is you're "meant" to do with the gift of your life, as you'll soon see.

The first step in creating a daily practice that is to change your mind in a lasting way is to establish a meaningful context and a powerful rationale for making that change in the first place. In other words, the first step is to create a personal purpose statement, as described in Exercise 11.1. A personal purpose statement is a short, powerful declaration of who you are and what you are up to with your life.

Bear in mind that creating a declaration like this is usually a work in progress. You're dealing with nothing less than the bigness, the fullness, the promise and potential of your life. It may take some time to get it so that it works just right. Thus, over time you will likely revise and refine it. But don't wait for perfection; as the prompts that follow request, simply put pen to paper and allow it to unfold. Over time, as you create and carry out a daily practice and other actions to be recommended it will become more and more clear. For now, just jump in and once you have something down, start using it immediately.

EXERCISE 11.1. CREATING A PERSONAL PURPOSE STATEMENT

1. ***Consider Joy.*** Begin by asking yourself some fundamental questions about your deeper, perhaps forgotten, passions. In the words of Joseph Campbell, we ask, "What is our *bliss*?" What are those things in life that light us up, that have lit us up in the past? What are the things in recent or distant memory that brought us deep, abiding joy? I don't necessarily mean temporary titillation or those fleeting flashes of happiness or fun, though those can sometimes point to our bliss.

What I mean is that experience that struck a resonant chord of vitality and purpose, of deeply felt pleasure, of profound, possibly quiet, happiness, of deep, seemingly intrinsic, satisfaction. We can also think of it as those experiences that have moved, encouraged, especially inspired us. Those things that caused us to feel more like ourselves; those things that caused us to feel more connected to life, to others, perhaps even to Truth and Beauty, even a sense of the Infinite, perhaps especially a sense of the Infinite. Think long and hard on these moments of deep bliss, for perhaps, therein lies your meaning.

2. ***Consider Your Dreams.*** Another way of getting at our purpose in life is to remember some of our dreams as children. What were the aspects of these musings that were, perhaps still are, most meaningful? What do they suggest about your urge for expressing yourself in life? If you dreamt of being an architect, say, the deeper meaning may be found in the need to create things, possibly things that are both functional and beautiful. It may have nothing to do with actually being an architect as such. For someone who dreamt of being a firefighter, the deeper meaning might be in assisting those who are vulnerable in the face of life's twists and turns; it may have little to do with bravely dashing into a burning building.

For someone who dreamt of being a CEO or a politician, the deeper meaning might have to do with effecting great accomplishments for humankind or for a large organization; or it might be about organizing and leading groups of people, large or small, in a purposeful way, in a way that they achieve and become what they otherwise would not. Whatever your childhood dreams may have been, take these once-wished-for realities seriously. Look for what might be the larger or deeper longing within, for the truth contained within the desire, for it is there that your deeper meaning might be found.

3. *Free write.* Set aside no less than an hour, and in your journal do some writing (do this before actually formulating the statement). First, write about those things that have given you the greatest degree of satisfaction, pleasure, and joy (Prompt 1); write a page or two. Then do some writing on your dreams as a child, regardless how fantastic or even silly they may seem today (Prompt 2); write another page or two if you can. Don't try to get it right, and don't think about it too logically. Just write and let it flow out. A free writing process is meant to be a stream-of-consciousness process. So turn your imagination loose and enjoy.

4. *Draft.* Once you've begun reconnecting with those deeper moments of joy and desire, clarify and specify it in the initial drafts of a purpose statement. Bear in mind that a purpose statement is not meant to be a suggestion or wish. It is a strong assertion of *what is*, a declaration in fact. Thus, it starts off in a certain, declarative voice. "My reason for being alive is . . . ," or "My purpose in life is . . . ," or "The reason I am on the planet is . . . ," or "I was born to . . . ," and so on. There is nothing wishy-washy or conditional about it. So, no "One day I hope to," no "I think I like . . . ," or even "I feel really good when . . . " There is nothing hopeful, wistful, or wanting, nothing uncertain in it at all. It is a bold, demonstrative statement of what actually *is* at the deepest level, an assertion of the truth about who you are and what you are up to with your life at the most meaningful level. Its intent is to remind you of your truest, best self, to inspire you to reconnect with that better self. It is meant to reignite a passion for who you are, who you yet can be, and what you can yet get done with your leadership and your life. No small deal, to be sure.

Box 11.1 presents several examples of purpose statements. Read each one. They may trigger some further ideas about your own purpose statement.

Box 11.1 Examples of Personal Purpose Statements

"My reason for being alive is to learn to care and contribute in such a way that my life positively affects my husband, my children, and all of those I regularly touch. My reason for waking up each day is to become the kind of leader who positively impacts the lives of those who follow me. My reason for living is to make life into an adventure, an adventure of growth, passion, love, and ultimately one of powerful change."

"My reason for being here is to win, to create excellence, and to powerfully shape for the good the lives of those I lead, to lead the business I am entrusted with to a whole new level of success and understanding of what is possible in the [__________] industry, and with utmost integrity to even change [that industry] and how it is understood."

"My purpose in life is to express power and beauty—through my painting, through my business dealings, through my interactions with all my employees. My purpose is to allow the genius within, the remarkable gifts as an artist and as a leader, to come through in such a way that when I die I'll know that the world is better off because I lived. My purpose in life is to be the man I know I am capable of being—powerful, committed, loving, and calm. This is why I am alive."

"I am alive so that I can experience the adventure and love of a life well lived, a life lived to the fullest. That is my purpose. I am alive so that I can become the woman I must be, the woman I have it within me to be—calm, clear, and strong, a woman who respects herself at every turn. I am here to become this woman. That is my purpose."

"I am alive so that I can make a difference in the lives of those in the NGO world—with both those we seek to serve and those who are doing the serving, my employees. And I am alive to have fun! I am alive to truly be alive. That is my purpose."

"I was created to serve God and all of God's children, to connect with God's love, to experience it and be an expression of it. I was put on earth to realize, to develop and grow, the many gifts and talents I've been given, to become the man I have the potential to be. This is my purpose and destiny."

"My purpose in life is to create success, real power, and *unqualified, categorical abundance in all areas of my life*, to thus enjoy life completely. And I'm here to use that success, power, and abundance to generate joy and meaning in the lives of others. That's it for me, who I am and what I am about, at my very essence, my core."

"I am here to learn to live life at ever-increasing levels of clarity and power. I'm here to make [the company I work for] function at a more enlightened level of leadership and effectiveness, producing awesome results because of its commitment to results and to the well-being of people. I am here to become a *truly* powerful leader, one who helps improve the way business is done in North America and Europe. This is my purpose and my commitment."

SUMMARY

As powerful as the identification of our deep-seated, previously hidden beliefs may feel, these insights are not ends in themselves. Identifying them does not make them go away. Identifying them is essential but also only the beginning of the transformative process. We must learn to *think* and *be* differently. We must learn to understand ourselves differently and to do so at the deepest levels of the mind. The good news is that we can do just that; we can retrain our brains and in so doing permanently change our minds. The latest breakthroughs in neuroscience confirm that the architecture of the brain is plastic, that it can be molded and, in effect, reshaped so that it serves us in better, far more effective ways. Though not easily done, it *can* and is being done!

The daily practice of the responsibility ritual is a proven means for beginning that reshaping process. The ritual's first component is based on our innate need for meaning: the creation of a personal purpose statement. As we more completely engage with our essential purpose we derive the necessary courage to take on the other two aspects of the ritual process, the truths-and-lies technique and the personal truth statement, both of which are addressed in chapter 12.

If you have not yet done the purpose statement work, you'll be best served by doing it now, before you turn to the next chapter. In that chapter we significantly up the ante (and the payout) in the process of changing our minds.

CHAPTER 12

CHANGING OUR BRAINS TO CHANGE OUR MINDS: Rewiring Our Circuits

> For it is now clear that the attentional state of the brain produces physical change in its structure and future functioning. The seemingly simple act of "paying attention" produces real and powerful changes in the brain.
>
> **—Jeffrey M. Schwartz, M.D.**

The idea that we are the ones who shape our lives takes on a whole new level of meaning when we consider the reality of the brain's plasticity, when we realize that not only can we mold our minds but that we are, in effect, always molding our minds with the focus and quality of our attention. The only real question, then, is "To what are we attending?" To be able to answer that question with greater certainty and to assure that we are taking full advantage of our brains' capacity to be molded, we now address the two remaining essential elements of the responsibility ritual: the truths-and-lies technique and the truth statement process.

THE TRUTHS-AND-LIES TECHNIQUE

One of the pleasant surprises in my work with leaders has been the discovery of a technique I've called "truths-and-lies." It's deceptively simple, but it's as powerful as it is modest. It's designed to do two things: First, to make us more vividly aware of and thereby weaken the hold of our pivotal limiting beliefs—to expose the extent of their impact and their fraudulent nature; second, and most important, it is intended to help us see and, by virtue of focused attention, extend the amount of time we spend operating from the truths that counter those lies, truths about who we are and what we are able to achieve. In biological terms, it's designed to help us rewire the brain's circuitry to better reflect what is so.

Two ideas form the foundation for the technique. The first idea informs our acknowledging the lie: The more we can recognize the presence and inhibiting influence of the false beliefs we harbor, the more we can neutralize their power today, in this moment. By regularly seeing them for what they are, *lies*, beliefs entirely without merit, we begin to mitigate their impact on us. The second idea informs the act of asserting the truth: By regularly and frequently articulating what is true—the direct opposite of the lie—the more readily we can cause that truth to form the basis for how we live, how we lead our lives, and how we lead others. In so doing we are beginning to rewire essential neural networks. This technique, like the personal purpose statement in chapter 11, is a structured method for "paying attention."

But first, an important caveat. Recall the fact that these false limiting beliefs seem to "want" to do anything to remain out of sight. In fact, at a subconscious level what's really going on is that we just prefer to remain oblivious to their existence. It's just too painful to think that we do not believe we deserve acceptance or love or power or success or happiness or meaning. It doesn't make any sense to our adult minds, and it surely does not comport with our ego needs, with the images and personae we present to the world.

And what do I mean by "personae"? They're the autopilot (automatic, instantaneous, knee-jerk) façades we use to comfort (feel okay about) ourselves and present ourselves to (gain acceptance from) the world. They're the self-images that are unacknowledged compensations for the beliefs or fears we harbor just below the surface of our awareness. We use them to assure ourselves that everything is all right, that *we're* all right. And we instinctively and fiercely defend them. Indeed, since our unconscious false beliefs often don't match up with these well-crafted self-images, we resist the very suggestion that the false beliefs exist in the first place. We deny: "There is no way I believe I'm unlovable," "It's silly to think I might believe that I don't belong or fit in," "How could I possibly believe at some deep, dark level that I'm not intelligent? Look at my degrees, my awards."

Because of our attachment to the image, it can be difficult, even painful, to admit that the constricting lies exist. In other words, we are inclined to lie to ourselves about the existence of the lies. We may contend that the lies don't exist at all, or more likely, we will acknowledge their existence in theory but will be "unable" to identify our own lies. In effect, once again, we find ourselves whistling past the graveyard, pretending we're not afraid and hoping that this pretense will keep the ghouls and goblins from getting us.

The problem is, of course, these ghouls and goblins (the false perceptions and beliefs) *are* there, and pretending they're not there by defending our petty self-images only gives them more power. The ability to permanently change our minds and more fully liberate our talents comes only after we concede that they exist and specifically identify them. Despite our natural tendencies toward self-deception, we must be honest enough with ourselves to raise the existence of these falsehoods to our conscious awareness. As Jung says, we must make the unconscious conscious. We must recognize that the false self-perceptions are there and have been there, and more important, we must get our minds around the fact that they *are* falsehoods, absolutely wrong. And we must then create or strengthen the belief that is true such that the truth becomes one of our fundamental grounds of being.

Through the daily act of calmly recognizing the lie *as* a lie and then strongly asserting and focusing our attention on the truth, we enable ourselves to make a fundamental and potentially permanent shift. We are able to shift our ways of being from ones based on lies and weakness to ones founded in rational truth and authentic strength. The more frequently and more consistently we practice this targeted cognitive exercise, and the more focused and attentive we are as we do so, the more readily we will shift our self-understanding at the most essential level. To put it another way, the more we acknowledge the preposterousness of the lie and then consciously step into, embrace, and live from the truth, the more the truth becomes a part of our essential way of being.

But to do this requires discipline—it takes practice, consistency, and endless repetition. Remember, we have lived with these lies (and we've unwittingly reinforced them again and again) for twenty, forty, in some cases sixty years or more. They don't give up the ghost easily, so we must be prepared to stay with the daily practice, which is why it is called a *daily practice* to begin with. And central to that practice is this truths-and-lies technique.

Precise Thinking and Limited Brain Space

One of the reasons the truths-and-lies process is effective is its ever-increasing precision. It requires a laser-like focus on the targeted belief because the networks of lies we are dismantling are not generic, one-size-fits-all belief systems. They are as unique to us individually as our fingerprints.

No doubt, there are overarching universal themes central to our most basic needs: themes around our lovability, worthiness, belongingness, capability, intelligence, attractiveness, strength, and power; themes regarding the goodness or badness of life, the trustworthiness of others, the degree to which we deserve prosperity and success, and the extent to which we can and should impact others. But the pivotal variations on these themes are specific to each individual, and understanding them with precision makes *all* the difference. Indeed, the more vividly we identify the lies, the more clearly and consciously we recognize their effect on us, the more we can reduce their power over us in the moment.

There's another reason, a biological reason, that makes precision important: We have limited brain space. Even though we all have roughly a hundred billion neurons (or brain cells) that make up the gray matter in our craniums, the brain allots limited space for specific types of thinking—only so much, let's say, for thoughts about hammers, saws, and other tools and only so much, say, for matters of love, or food, or hockey, and so on.[1] Thus, we must neutralize the false, limiting understandings so that the neurons and neural networks that had been used for the lies (about our intelligence, for instance) can now be used to serve the truth of who we are (intellectually) and who we might yet become.

According to Doidge, "When we learn something new neurons fire together and wire together, and a chemical process occurs at the neuronal level . . . [that] strengthens the connections between neurons." But first the unlearning and weakening of these old networks must take place. "If we only strengthened connections," he says, "our neuronal networks would get saturated. Evidence suggests that unlearning existing memories is necessary to make room for new memories in our networks."[2] We cannot simply create new thought patterns from whole cloth, hoping to place these new beliefs beside or on top of the old false ones.

Hitting the Critical Points

There is yet another important reason for seeking precision in the truths-and-lies process. It emerges out of something called *critical point analysis*. Derived from physics, critical point analysis says that every highly complex system has a specific, critical point at which "the smallest input will result in the greatest change."[3] By locating and, in effect, applying pressure at the critical point, we can significantly alter the entire system with relatively little effort. In effect, the slightest tweak at the precise, critical point will bring a giant to his knees. It's not much of a stretch to apply this principle to the mind—a complex emotional and intellectual (psychological) system—and to the brain—a complex neurological (biological) system.

The critical point for each of us (as human beings and as leaders) is *our relationship with ourselves*. Leadership, after all, *is* relationship. Recall that every other relationship we have is a direct reflection of this primary relationship. Everything we accomplish or fail to accomplish directly reflects the relationship we have with ourselves—this complex configuration of impressions and beliefs about self, the world, and how we relate to and fit in with the world.

My largely unconscious understanding of me, your largely unconscious understanding of you—the extent to which we unconsciously deem ourselves worthy of goodness, love, happiness, power, and success, the extent to which we hold ourselves as capable of accomplishment at the highest level—is what determines who we are, what we achieve, all that we have, and all that we experience in our personal and surely in our leadership lives.

Changing our minds and, thus, our leadership impact therefore means locating and altering the critical points in our self-understanding. Indeed, neutralizing the critical-point falsehoods (the really *big* lies), and simultaneously strengthening the critical point truths, are perhaps the most important aspects of changing our minds.

What this all means, again, is simple: We must identify and confront our limiting false beliefs (shrink the neurological networks given to the lies); simultaneously we must develop and strengthen the critical truths about who we are (enlarge and fortify the neural networks that support our authentic power, talent, and goodness). This act of undoing the lie and strengthening the truth becomes a centerpiece in our personal and leadership transformation. By hitting these critical points in our relationship with ourselves, the change we cause touches *every* area of our lives. Changing our minds, then, is undoing the lies and establishing the truths.

The Technique

The truths-and-lies technique is a simple, systematic method for focusing our attention and consciously choosing to *think* targeted thoughts. It's an exercise in disciplined thought, a simple cause-and-effect formula that when consistently followed leads to direct, noticeable, intended consequences. The process is explained in Exercise 12.1, and examples of truths-and-lies statements are presented Box 12.1.

EXERCISE 12.1 THE TRUTHS-AND-LIES TECHNIQUE

The technique is a process of asserting (usually out loud) a series of point and counterpoint declarations. The lie (L) is asserted once. The truth (T) is asserted at least three times. For instance: (L) "It is a lie to believe I am a misfit, a loser. That is a lie." (T) "The truth is I belong; I deserve to be accepted, welcomed into the center of the social circle as I am. That is the truth."

1. ***The Lie.*** In this process of stating the lie we are observing the lie *as* a lie. We are, in effect, stepping back from ourselves and noticing first, that we have believed this falsehood and second, that it is false—that it *is* a lie, that we have been innocently misinformed to have believed

it lo these many years. Thus we begin each lie statement by saying, "It is a lie ... " and concluding with "That is a lie," or "a horrible lie" or even "a preposterous lie." The more intellectual and emotional energy we bring to the awareness, the better. Another lie statement might go like this: "It is a lie to think that I'm supposed to struggle financially, to believe that good people don't care about money, don't have it. That is an idiotic, dangerous lie."

2. *The Truth.* After we've spent a few moments recognizing the lie *as* a lie, we then declare out loud the counterpoint truth that corrects the lie. And again, the more focused energy, the more passion, the more unswerving intellectual clarity and force of personality we bring to bear, the better. Though it may feel awkward (it often does, at first), we assert the truth with authority.

At this early point in the process how we *feel* about a truth is immaterial. What matters is how we logically understand the issue with our rational, conscious mind and out of that then consciously choosing to think and declare the logical truth. If we have in fact identified a critical point lie-truth dyad, odds are that asserting the truth will feel uncomfortable. And there's a better-than-even chance that the discomfort we feel is a function of the pervasive strength of the lie, the false impression. Assert the truth at least three times (the more the better) with focused passion and clarity.

The truth statement that would countermand the lie above might go like this: "The truth is money in the hands of good people (like me) is a good thing. Money is wonderful. I am worthy of it and I am receptive to bringing it into my life now ... lots of it. The more wealth I have, the more good I can do. That is the truth."

Each lie-truth dyad will take only a few seconds, no more than a minute. Given this brevity, we must force ourselves to truly think about it as we're doing it. Giving in to the tendency to slip into rote repetition weakens the formative power of the process. Think. It only amounts to a few brief moments out of our day. Demanding focused awareness during these moments makes all the difference.

Box 12.1 Examples of Truths-and-Lies Statements

"It is a lie that I am not lovable, that there is something broken, wrong, bad and fundamentally unlovable about who I am. That is a really fucked up, dirty rotten lie. Wrong, absolutely wrong." (The obscenity in this lie assertion helped the individual who used it to better express clarity and passion in undoing the lie. These lies aren't kind with us; no need for us to be kind with them. It's what works for you in undoing them that matters.) The lie is stated, and seen, as a lie, one time.

"The Truth is I am a good man, a lovable, warm, caring man, worthy of love and acceptance as I am. I am attracting love, rich, flowing love, into my life right now. I welcome it. I deserve it. Now. This is the truth." The truth is stated emphatically at least three times.

"It's a lie to believe that I am not as smart as those around me. A lie to believe that I have just been lucky, that I somehow in all my dumbness just outsmarted the system. That is a really screwed-up lie."

"The truth is, I am brilliant. The incontrovertible evidence is everywhere I look, and it all points out the simple truth: I'm extremely intelligent, yes, brilliant! I really am. I can hold my own with any executive in the industry. Fact. I am deeply intelligent. That is the truth."

"It is a lie to believe that deep down I am really weak, more or less powerless before the big strong people that seem to be all around me. This is a stinkin' lie. Complete B.S."

"The truth is I am strong. I am a woman of resilience, fortitude, and power. I am a woman of courage and insight. I am a powerful woman. This is the absolute truth."

THE PERSONAL TRUTH STATEMENT

The greater our focused attention and the greater our constancy in applying that attention, the greater our capacity to change our brains, to rewire our neuronal networks, or in the language of Merzenich and deCharms, to resculpt our minds. Thus in addition to the truths-and-lies process the transformative approach to leadership development encourages us to create and regularly articulate what we call a "personal truth statement" (or statement*s* as the case may be). The truth statement is nothing more than a further step in intentional, repetitive focused attention, based primarily on the truth side of the lie-truth dyad. The basics of the personal truth statement are presented in Exercise 12.2, and several examples appear in Box 12.2.

Boxes 12.3 and 12.4 provide examples of complete rituals that combine the three non-negotiable elements (a personal purpose statement, a truths-and-lies technique, and a personal truth statement) with the nice-to-have elements of music, meditation or contemplative prayer, and visualization.

EXERCISE 12.2 CREATING A PERSONAL TRUTH STATEMENT

1. Drawing from our one or two most essential lie-truth dyads, we take the truth side of the dyad and make it as simple and direct as possible, being careful to not reduce its fundamental power in any way. In so doing we are making the truth more easily remembered, articulated, and embraced. I say "embraced" because the truth statement is intended to become something that we figuratively shift or step into, something we embody, a state of mind we authentically adopt in a moment's notice. In other words, it's intended to trigger a change in our way of being. Thus, it often begins with or includes the words "I am" (a form of the verb "to be"): *I am a bold, confident man*, for instance, or *I am an open, powerful woman*. Finally, in your truth statement, refer to yourself as a "man" or "woman," which suggests life, warmth, and humanity. Do not refer to yourself as a "person" or "individual," which are bloodless, sterile abstractions.

2. Using the truth statement involves asserting and being the statement as frequently as possible through the day, whether we assert it out loud or quietly to ourselves, remembering the objective is to shift our way of being, actually *being* different—being confident, being focused, being grounded, being sober-minded, being brave, being powerful, being open, being caring and on and on—as a simple matter of conscious choice. It is repetitive, focused attention stated, thought about, lived from, *five, ten, twenty, a hundred times a day.* (Remember, repetition is the thing here: repetitive, deeply focused, thoughtful shifts in our ways of being.) It is a conscious choice, returning us to a state of mind, a way of thinking and being about ourselves that allows us to live more authentically, to engage with others and life more fully. Thus, we determine our experience and our focus.

As Merzenich and deCharms remind us, we "choose what we will experience, then we choose the details we will pay attention to."[3] And it works the other way, as well: By choosing what we pay attention to, we alter what we experience and how we experience it. It's powerful, brain-changing stuff.

Box 12.2 Examples of Personal Truth Statements

"I am a talented, powerful leader, a bold, confident man."

"I am a good man, worthy of love. I am lovable."

"I am a strong woman, a powerful, enlightened, caring leader."

"Money is wonderful. I am worthy of wealth in overflowing abundance."

"I am a powerful woman."

"I am a courageous man."

"I have deep, insightful intelligence. I am vividly intelligent."

"I am a grounded, sober-minded, focused woman."

"I am a relentless, focused man, a man of singular, unswerving purpose."

"I am a supremely confident woman. I know who I am."

"Trust is good. I am an open, honest, trusting man."

Box 12.3 Ritual Example 1

Time required: about 10 minutes

I begin my practice by slowing myself down a bit, usually by listening to a piece by Vivaldi, Mozart, or Copeland. (about 2 minutes)

I do a brief meditation, simply focusing on my breathing, allowing my mind to slow down further. (about 3 minutes)

I then, with conviction, loudly state my personal truth statement and be it, two or three times. (about 30 seconds)

I then read and think about my personal purpose statement, carefully remembering what each line means and why it matters to me, why it is essential to who I really am and who I am becoming. (about 60 seconds)

I then do my truths-and-lies process (I have two lie-truth dyads) with passion and a good deal of volume. (about 2 minutes)

Finally, I assert and be my personal truth statement twice more. (about 30 seconds)

When I'm done I usually take about 2 minutes more to set up my day, thinking about what I'm going to do and how (and who!) I'm going to be. I usually visualize myself being that man. The whole process usually takes around 10 minutes, sometimes a little less, sometimes a little more. Typically I'm very focused and clear by the time I'm done.

Box 12.4 Ritual Example 2

Time required: about 4 minutes

After I shower in the morning, I sit down at my desk and take myself through my responsibility ritual. I begin with the truths-and-lies (I have three of 'em), confronting the lies, which heretofore have run so much of my life, and loudly declaring the truths and the facts about my gifts, my abilities, and my commitments in life. It's kick-ass stuff for me. Really lines me up. This takes me about two minutes.

(continued on next page)

(continued from previous page)

Item 2 is my purpose statement, and it really is, really has become, my reason. I say it once, very slowly, thinking about each word. I actually, in the moment, be and feel myself as the man that the purpose statement describes. It fills me with urgency. Every time I say it (I take it with me to work on a laminated 3×5 card and read it at least once more during the work day), it feels like I'm pounding a stake into the ground—here I stand, I can do no other, like that. It takes a little less than a minute, given the slow, methodical way in which I do it. It's powerful. Sometimes it really fills me up, strong stuff.

The last thing I do is declare my truth statement, at least 4 or 5 times. Takes about a minute.

I do a slightly compressed version of this same thing just before I go to bed, almost every night.

MELISSA, CONTINUED

Let's pick up where we left off with Melissa "Mel" Merriman in chapter 9. As Melissa continued her work, she implemented a daily practice. As with everything else that Melissa had done in her life, she approached her practice with unqualified commitment. She employed all six of the items noted—personal purpose statement, truths-and-lies process, truth statement, music, meditation, and visualization. And she did so rigorously, often twice a day. In fact, she didn't miss a single day for more than two years. She took her process of transforming integration seriously, to say the least.

Melissa began to surrender to the reality of her deep-seated subtle angers and doubts and to recognize the cold, self-protective ways in which they were manifest in her life. In doing so she began to identify the pervasive fear-based beliefs that were the foundation of the anger. And "something magnificent," as one of her colleagues put it, began to happen. By allowing herself to consciously recognize the unconscious waters in which she had always been swimming, and by bravely descending into the darkest depths of her personal paradigm, she began seeing and understanding her lies fully and on their own terms. This was not pleasant and not easy, but as she courageously stood before her self-created, unconscious monsters and demons she understood two distinct and ultimately liberating things.

First, she realized how pervasive her unconscious, false beliefs were, including beliefs like "I'm a shit," "I don't deserve unconditional love," "Passionate men are *violent* men," and "The world is a loveless and unforgiving place." And she began to realize how, *entirely unbeknownst to her*, the beliefs had been influencing, even driving, major aspects of her life. It is important to remember that while she may have come off as cool and aloof, she was also seen as "brilliant," "incisive," "gutsy," and "frightfully witty," and as someone who was together professionally and who didn't need or want anyone. Thus, like most of us, she had become highly skillful in hiding her deepest fears and self-doubts, *especially from herself*.

The importance of this last observation cannot be overstated, because the simple fact is that most of us, like Melissa, have done such a good job of presenting our public personae to the world that we have bought the pretense ourselves—we've sold ourselves on the cover-up, without ever knowing it's a cover-up. And we must be willing to do as Melissa did and blow the cover right off the pretense.

The second thing Melissa realized at a most profound level was that her limiting beliefs were in fact false, mere fictions that she had understandably but inaccurately fashioned as a young girl. She recognized in no uncertain terms that these paradigmatic beliefs were in fact *lies*, a "crock of crap, nothing less, nothing more," as she put it, and entirely disconnected from reality. They were wrong. Powerful, yes—but absolutely false, a misrepresentation of the world, of other people, and most important of herself *to* herself.

Upon Melissa's understanding these two facts, that "something magnificent" slowly began to emerge. But first, it seems, her body had to signify its fundamental rejection of the lies under which she had labored all those years. In the midst of a group workshop, during a probing, somewhat emotional process, I noticed that Melissa was beginning to look a bit pale; before I could ask her if she was all right, she stood up and raced from the room, down the hall, and into the bathroom in order, it turns out, to vomit. Her body, mind, and spirit were saying that she could no longer allow these toxic lies to determine her life.

Fortunately, literal regurgitation is not a mandatory piece of the transformative process; however, for Melissa this unexpected act of biological rejection served as a watermark, signifying a release of the old and, above all, a commitment to the new—reconstructing her self-understanding in a way that would allow her to connect with herself and others—in effect, to join the human race.

As a result of Melissa's powerful insight, two things began to happen. First, she became acutely aware of how much she cared about others. "It was as if I saw people as, you know, *people* for the first time," she later recounted. "My colleagues and employees who had earlier seemed as threats now appeared as decent folk who needed me as an ally. It's not that I had ever consciously thought of them as threats—I could never have admitted that anyone threatened *me*, for Pete's sake. But when I unexpectedly began to see them as decent, kind, and safe, it was as if someone switched on the light and I saw how I *had* been seeing people . . . ,"—as threats. By realizing, truly getting, that she was not "a little shit," not "the problem" but in fact truly a solution, truly deserving of love and acceptance, the people who were around her seemed to be magically "transformed."

"It was as if suddenly I had a whole new understanding of why I was alive," she explained. "My job as CFO was not simply to slay the quarterly financial dragons and to protect myself with wealth and inviolable material success. My job—I hardly can think of it as a job at this moment—became a sort of calling. I was now to use my skills to help create an organization of excellence and integrity that served our employees and customers like no other. It sounds a bit pretentious, maybe, but my job—as a CFO no less—was to create beauty in a place where our people could flourish." Excellence, integrity, service, and success all seemed to coalesce, and in a flash. "I just *knew*," she went on, "I didn't have to think, I didn't have to analyze or scrutinize, I just knew. It was done." Seemingly in an instant of knowing, Melissa Merriman had stepped out of a world of management and into a world of leadership, leading her life and leading others, "in a flash," as she put it.

But Not Really in a Flash

This account is not intended to suggest that Melissa was suddenly "transformed." Transformation is a process, often a tedious process, one that spans a lifetime, and this was her beginning. And begin she did. Over the coming months as Melissa's journey continued to unfold, the second big thing began happening for her: The walls of self-protection began to gradually come down. Slowly but surely, over time, a warmth was emerging, with fits and starts, but consistently emerging nonetheless. She began to display a quality of kindness and caring that no one in her professional world had ever before even imagined she might possess. And far from limiting her professional effectiveness, this emerging generosity only enhanced her "capacity to influence, to create, to lead" at an entirely different and bigger level.

As she began to consciously, intentionally, and systematically create new beliefs about herself and about others, slowly a different person seemed to show up. "Mel," the domineering, defiant, and forceful corporate warlord, began to allow "Melissa," the powerful yet warm, strong yet gentle, financial leader to emerge. In the process, virtually all of her relationships, including her relationship with her husband, began changing for the better.

And keep in mind, her productivity as CFO did not decrease with this newfound level of warmth and openness; rather, it improved and markedly so. To give but one example, her ability to effectively hold people accountable "soared off the charts." Instead of dictating through fear and almost gleefully dishing out punishment "when necessary," she began to *persuade* people, even inspire them. "To my amazement people actually now want to keep their word to me. They don't want to let me down!" To have her direct reports *want* to do well for her, their boss, was a revelation for Melissa. It seems their affection, appreciation, and respect for her rose in direct proportion to her increase in openness and caring. She was still as tough and demanding as she had ever been, but now it seemed to come from a different place altogether and to surely render a different and better result.

As compelling as Melissa's story is, there are two important points to keep in mind. The first is that these changes emerged over time; they did not happen overnight. The powerful insights, the psychological and physiological reactions that she experienced did not signal a fait accompli—her moments of jarring self-insight were not a done deal by any stretch of the imagination. Rather they signaled the beginning of a growth process that unfolded over the course of more than two years and still carries on today. The second point is that the work she began was, first and foremost, a disciplined daily practice in the form of a responsibility practice. And she did her practice religiously.

SUMMARY

Insight may feel great, but it's not enough. Working with the brain's plasticity we must, with focused attention, begin the disciplined work of changing our minds by altering the neural networks that constitute our most deeply embedded and affecting beliefs. The breakthroughs in neurobiology confirm the fact that we can, with sufficient dedication and precise targeting, resculpt our minds by consciously choosing how and to what we pay attention. To that end, two of the most powerful tools at our disposal are the truths-and-lies technique and the personal truth statement. Combined with a personal purpose statement and employed with constancy, transformation—that is, real, lasting, meaningful change—can begin to take place.

Thus we conclude the discussion of Leg 1, *responsibility and changing our minds*. As we examine the second and third legs of the transformational stool, we will continue to draw upon the foundational understandings of Leg 1, particularly as they relate to the powerful principles of intention in chapter 13. Given that the experience of our transformative promise compels us to thoughtful self-expansion, to becoming what we have it in us to be, the embrace of intention and possibility, Leg 2, is nothing less than stepping into a bigger, braver, more powerful game, a game we are called to win.

LEG 2:

Intention and Possibility

If responsibility is the linchpin that secures the wheels of the transformative process, then intention is the engine that propels the process to fruition. As such, intention moves us from the reactive state of managing to the proactive state of leading, from the automatic and suspicious to the conscious and trusting, from being confined by what has been to being set free by what still might be.

Possibility is infinite, limitless, constricted only, if at all, by the range of human imagination. Every significant advance in human history, whether by happy accident or by design, has come as a consequence of possibility breaking in upon human consciousness. Possibility is the reason Albert Einstein could say that "imagination is more important than knowledge," and that he had "no special talents, I'm just passionately curious,"[1] passionately open to possibility. To live from or operate within the domain of possibility is to be nourished by the fertile soil of the imagination, the place from which all forward movement and all creativity emerges. Thus we can say with considerable certainty that *to lead, which necessarily assumes creation, requires that we learn the language of possibility*; to truly embrace the power to cause, the power of intentionality, as any powerful leader must, we must simultaneously become familiar with what it means to create and "hold a possibility."

We continue our journey of transformation, then, by moving to the second leg of the three-legged stool (see Figure L.2). Chapter 13 deals with intention and chapter 14 with possibility. By understanding the transforming process articulated in Leg 1 and beginning the hard work of becoming our truest and best selves, we prepare ourselves for the next phase of leadership and personal expansion. We prepare ourselves for a whole new level of demand and adventure. As we follow the path upward it narrows some, but the views are increasingly breathtaking—at once dizzying and emboldening. So, on to the next level of the ascent, Leg 2, we go.

• • •

Figure L.2 Leg 2: Intention and Possibility

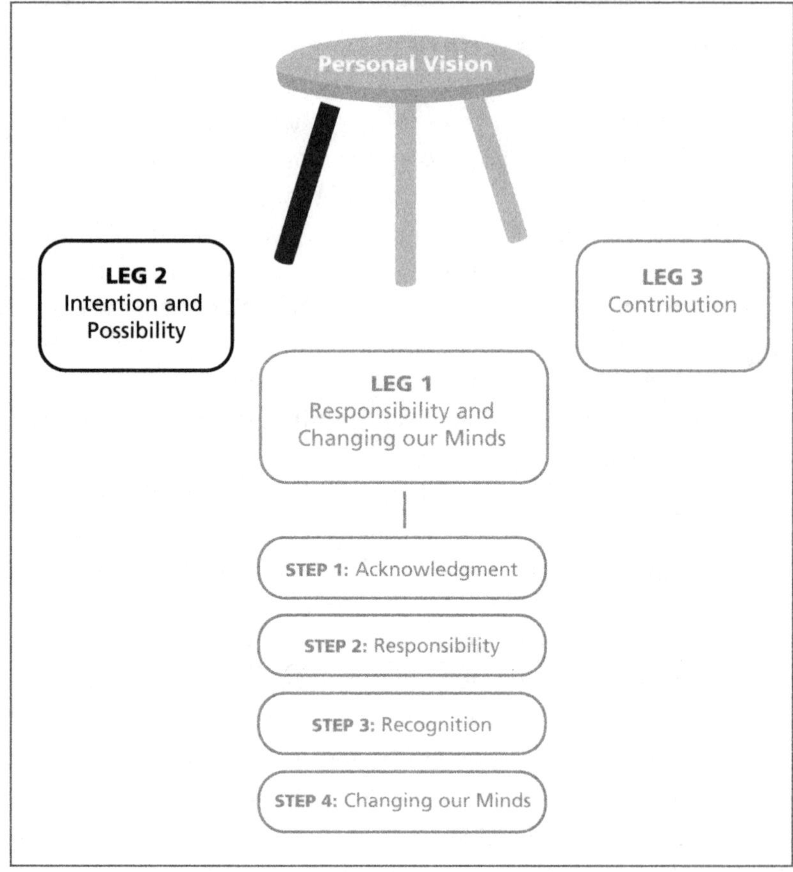

CHAPTER 13

INTENTION: The Heart of Power

The universe does not exist "out there," independent of us. We are inescapably involved in bringing about that which appears to be happening. We are not only observers. We are participators. In some strange sense, this is a participatory universe.

—**John Archibald Wheeler**

It has been said that authentic intention is at the heart of all creativity that endures, that intention is the only thing that brings about lasting change in the world and, by extension, lasting change in our lives. Intention, true intention, then, is central to fulfilling the destiny that emerges before us when we faithfully heed the call of transformation. For the transformative destination is nothing if as it calls us to personal change it does not also call us to lead lasting change in our world—in our organizations and in our society.

So what, then, is true intention? Intention is an unequivocal commitment to a wisely chosen outcome that leads to (even causes) the realization of the chosen outcome. The meaning of *intention* that I'm suggesting is not the one that is typically meant when the word is used in everyday speech. More times than not, *intention* refers to a wish, a hope, or a desire. It usually points to what we *want* or *would like* to see happen, as in the well-worn cliché, "The road to hell is paved with good intentions." Intention in this common usage means something to the effect of "good will," "wishes," or "well-meaning desires," desires that have little effect on outcome.

Simply wanting something does not necessarily lead to having it. Wanting and having are two entirely different things. The one—wishing, hoping, and wanting—never guarantees the other—achieving or having. Wishing for something, even if we wish really, really hard, has little bearing on whether or not it comes to pass. A want or a wish is not an intention, even if in our clichés and colloquialisms we might interchange the two.

As we learned in the section on responsibility, we are unavoidably and always agents of cause. We are perpetual creators. And as quantum mechanics makes clear, there is no such thing as objective observation or neutral, passive noticing. The mere act of observation unavoidably changes that which is being observed. Simply *being*, without any overt action, has cause-and-effect consequences. Fact. And the best, perhaps only, way to consciously harness our perpetual causality is via the conscientious embrace of intentionality.

In the transformative understanding, intention is a *quality of commitment*, the purest expression of commitment that an individual can have. It is not going too far to say that intention in a sense is *the* thing, in and of itself, that causes the desired outcome to be realized. It is both the intelligence and the energy of causality at the most profound level. And from a true leadership perspective, it is the single most important quality, characteristic, or state of mind, we can have, particularly when it comes to generating desired results of any kind.

Intention is a state of mind that declares without equivocation that a particular outcome "must be." There is no alternative that is acceptable. Nothing but this outcome will do, and it *shall* be . . . because I will cause it to be. Period. And when this state of mind is achieved, a broad array of circumstances and conditions, both in and around the "intender," begin to change at obvious and not so obvious levels.

WHAT INTENTIONALITY IS NOT

Intentionality is not to be confused with willfulness. Though often mistaken as the same thing, they are two entirely different realities that issue from diametrically opposed motivations and result in vastly different outcomes. Willfulness is a mind-set that is properly associated with force and is fear based. There is a clutching, relentless, almost angry and "dogged" quality informing willfulness, all of which usually issue from a type of anxiety. With tightened fists and clenched teeth, the willful actor will declare, "I will get this done no matter what. No matter what!"

Thus, willfulness usually has little regard for how it will adversely affect others. Often this disregard for others is not conscious, in which case the willful actor simply has not taken others into consideration. Yet, whether conscious or not, a defining characteristic of willfulness is that it leaves bodies in its wake. In its ferocious, willful struggle to achieve the outcome at any cost, casualties abound. The achievement comes at a heavy price to the player as well as to multiple innocent bystanders who happened to get caught up in the unexpected wake. Willfulness, even if the goal is accomplished, leaves the residue of destruction in its path. The collateral damage may not appear immediately, but the logical causal nature of life guarantees that over time the harmful consequences will materialize.

The most obvious example of willfulness run amok would be the global economic catastrophe that culminated in 2008. The further we get from the initial wreckage the more clearly we can see that the business and financial leaders who caused it were operating from a purely willful mentality. Their unbridled greed left no room for considering the impact it would have on the innocent bystanders. As congressional testimony and the economic toll make clear, the focus of these investment bankers and insurance company executives was unmistakably singular: I'll get mine and the rest of you be damned. The "bodies left in their wake" were the millions of people left unemployed, the tens of millions whose savings were destroyed, the hundreds of thousands who lost their homes, and the taxpayers who were left holding the bag for these executives' willful contempt.

WHAT INTENTIONALITY IS

Intention, because it issues from a radically different place than willfulness, has a vastly different manifestation from beginning to end. Intention always emerges out of a place of *power* rather than force. It is love or creativity based, founded in a deep understanding of personal sufficiency and confidence. The mind-set of the intentional actor knows that "who I am is enough, here and now" and that "I have what it takes to have it turn out," and therefore, "I'll have it turn out." When intention is in play there is often a quiet, almost becalmed quality to the intender, for there's a near-certainty that things must and in fact *will* turn out as desired. This certainty is a reflection not so much of faith or belief as it is a reflection of understanding, a knowing perhaps, that issues from an unshakable confidence in the virtue of the chosen outcome and the capacity of the players who have chosen to bring it about. It will happen because they will cause it to happen and do so with relative ease.

In almost every case of true intentionality, there is a sober-minded, unapologetic, and unassuming confidence that leads to what I call the "must-be" mind-set. It is a clarity that says, "After much thoughtful consideration I have decided that this particular outcome simply *must be*"; anything less is unacceptable, indeed, anything less is intolerable. You can almost see it in the intentional actor's eyes: a fierce yet somehow gentle focus, an almost laser-like clarity of direction that is at once stirring *and* settling. Further, the intentional actor always expresses and evokes inspiration, and this inspiration usually happens naturally, with little overt effort at all.

Because intentionality is based in a fundamentally compassionate, self-confident state of mind, a major distinguishing characteristic of intentionality is that, far from leaving behind a trail of destruction, it elevates the accidental tourists caught up in its path; they are invariably better off as a result of merely being exposed to the intention and to those who are the conveyors of the intention. Indeed, much of the power of intentionality comes from the fact that a true intention, almost without exception, has a compelling quality to it. Often, even those who come in casual contact with the intention can readily imagine themselves as a part of the vision or intended outcome. They are drawn to it and often want to participate in the world that it is creating, that it represents.

An Upstart Case in Point: Herb Kelleher and Southwest Airlines

Coincidentally, perhaps, I am writing these words as I fly across the California desert aboard a 737 that belongs to the airline that has long been the envy of the airline industry: Southwest Airlines. They recently posted their thirty-eighth consecutive year of profitability. Most U.S. carriers would be thrilled to claim four or five consecutive years of profitability. It's a staggering accomplishment, one of the many that has left Southwest's competition in the dust, or the clouds, as it were.

The remarkable tale of Southwest Airlines does not need to be retold here. Suffice it to say that when the iconoclastic Herb Kelleher and his partner Rollin King first set out to create a cut-rate airline they knew that a commitment to cheap airfares in itself would probably not be enough to guarantee success. So they set out to make a "special airline," one focused on people, one that would create a totally unique flying experience. Their intention was to democratize air travel via airfares that the "common person" could afford and to generate joy while doing so. And it *was* an intention, one shared by their employees, particularly in the early days.

As Kelleher puts it, "The core of our success . . . [is] the most difficult thing for a competitor to imitate. They can buy all the physical things. The things you can't buy are dedication, devotion, loyalty—the feeling that you are participating in a crusade."[1] The deeper reason for Southwest's success was something their competition could not grasp because the primary mover in that success was something business schools rarely ever address. And that primary mover? It's suggested by Kelleher's choice of words in describing their mission: they were on a "crusade" (from which the dedication, devotion, and loyalty naturally emerged).

A crusade is not something one goes about with mere wishes and wants. A crusade is something one enters with a certainty that success must be realized. It's a life-and-death venture, all for a higher purpose. Failure is not an option for the crusading organization.

Simply put, Kelleher and the people he led were intentional. They had to be in order to overcome the odds stacked against them, including three established airlines that fought with all their legal might to keep the fledgling airline from ever getting off the ground.

As it is with all true intentions, the people associated with the fulfillment of the Southwest intention have been elevated by it, made better as a result of their association with that intention. Everyone who has flown a Southwest flight knows that the pilots and the flight attendants take their work seriously, but they don't take themselves too seriously. As a frequent flyer of Southwest, I admit there have been times when I've been annoyed by the sometimes-over-the-top jocularity of the flight attendants. But more times than not, I am amused and even amazed by how the playfulness of these unconventional air stewards enhance the experience of the passengers, creating laughter, sometimes even sing-alongs, and usually a bounty of smiles.

The employees are typically proud to be part of such a cutting-edge company. And the customers who are cared for by the happy employees don't feel gouged. The uplifting psychological, cultural, and economic footprint of Southwest all attest to the intentional basis of its emergence and continuing success. And remember, intention is love based, while willfulness is always bound in fear, even if that fear is masked as something else. And love unabashedly is a regular theme in all things Southwest.

Ultimately, intention has one final characteristic that is also witnessed within the Southwest universe. Intention has a self-generating energy to it. Rather than perpetually needing to be reinfused with new life by various means, as an ordinary commitment does, a true intention generates vitality in and of itself. It stimulates and draws from heretofore unrecognized sources of passion and power. The intender has a purposeful charisma, a charisma that is generated by the innate vigor of the intention itself. A simple revisitation of the intention, or "crusade," is often all that is needed to renew the spirit, to reinvigorate the resolve of those who are called to action by the intention. In the domain of genuine intentionality, the intention itself becomes the primary source of inspiration, passion, revitalized commitment, courage, confidence, imagination, insight, and curiously enough, wisdom. True intention is and does all that.

The next questions, then, would be "Precisely how do we arrive at this intentional state of mind? How do we attain this mind-set that seems to be the Holy Grail of the transformative leader?" and "What must be present in the intention itself and in the intender herself for intentionality to be manifest?"

President John F. Kennedy and the Moon Shot

History is rife with examples of intentionality, well-documented instances when outcomes that were implausible, even impossible by most standards, were realized. One such instance that still captures the modern imagination is the space race of the 1960s and John F. Kennedy's bold declaration in 1961 that the United States would land a man on the moon and return him home safely before the end of the decade and ahead of the Soviet Union.

The rationale, indeed the deeper motivating passion behind the declaration, was not mere national pride. At the time the United States was at the height of the Cold War, and those of us in the West were in the midst of a moral and political struggle with the Soviet bloc. What was at stake was not only bragging rights for technological superiority. When seen through the existential and psychological prism of the early 1960s, what was at stake was freedom itself. Should we succeed in reaching the moon first, it would not merely be Washington bettering Moscow, it would be the pragmatic, symbolic, and moral evidence pointing to the virtue of freedom and democracy over totalitarianism.

Speaking to a joint session of Congress when he first announced the goal, Kennedy said that we should not underestimate "the impact of this adventure on the minds of men everywhere who are attempting to make a determination of which road [capitalistic democracy or communism] to take."[2] It was framed in and understood to be a matter of pragmatic necessity, moral integrity, and political imperative.

What we often fail to remember when we look back on the whole matter today is just how risky and in fact outrageous the declaration was. First, the Soviet Union was far ahead of the United States in its understanding of rocketry. At the time we had still not achieved what the Soviets had achieved by successfully and safely orbiting the Earth—Alan Shepard's space flight on May 5, 1961, was a much shorter (suborbital) flight than the earlier Soviet success. Second, and more important, the technological understanding was simply not yet available to get us safely to the moon and back in as much perhaps as twenty years, let alone nine years. For many in the scientific community, including some at NASA itself, Kennedy's bold declaration was optimistic at best, dangerous and expensively wasteful at worst. At the time the projected expenditure was as much as $35 billion, astonishing by 1960 standards. It would be the largest single government expenditure during peacetime ever. More reasonable minds opposed and openly questioned not so much the goal, but the relatively short time frame Kennedy had placed on the feat and the additional costs that the time parameters would require.

But Kennedy was resolute, and by the time he spoke at Rice University in Houston several months later, his proposal, despite the numerous skeptics and naysayers, had become an intention. "To be sure," he said, addressing some of his critics, "we are behind [the Soviets], and will be behind for some time in manned flight. But we do not intend to stay behind, and in this decade we shall make up and move ahead." Acknowledging the enormity and difficulty, what many deemed the impossibility, of the task, he declared again and this time with certitude, "But it will get done. And it will be done before the end of this decade."[3]

Of course, we all know what happened on July 20, 1969, but Neil Armstrong's momentous step for humankind would not have been possible, and certainly not in the decade of the '60s, without Kennedy's bold intention. By 1969 Kennedy was long since dead, but his intention lived on and had become the intention of tens of thousands of scientists, technicians, and politicians until it was realized on that historic day. Today the remarkable nature of the intent that led to the moonwalk may seem utterly unremarkable, but that is the distortion that inevitably comes from looking through the lens of what we now know. At the time, Kennedy's intention was little short of fantastic, indeed for some it was little more than science fiction fantasy.

Thus, we can readily imagine how those more reasonable, scientifically minded advisors may have attempted to dissuade the young, ambitious president from foolhardy overreach. And given the real-world facts—some of the basic logic and reason and surely the pragmatic geopolitics—they might well have successfully inveighed against Kennedy's bold vision. For a less intentional man, the powerful dissenting voices of moderation, of reasonableness and discretion, may well have won the day. The dramatic scientific, political, and moral success of July 1969 would not have become reality but for Kennedy's unequivocal commitment and courage, his intention. Intention *is* all that.

THE THREE REQUIREMENTS OF INTENTION

So what then must be present for a desire to become an intention? What are the intellectual and emotional conditions necessary to attain an intentional state of mind?

There are three prerequisites for changing a desire into an intention, for becoming intentional, and they pertain to both the intended outcome and to the person doing the intending. The first is *clarity and passion* around the intended outcome. In other words, we must have a burning desire for its realization. Second, the would-be intention must align with *the larger, most authentic trajectory or direction of our lives*. If it conflicts, even subtly, with who we are and where we are going, it's a nonstarter. Third, intention, unlike willfulness, is not amoral, and thus it must directly or indirectly *contribute to the greater good*, to something larger than our individual interests.[4] Let's consider all three prerequisites in depth.

Clarity and Passion

When something becomes an intention in the truest sense of the word, a shift takes place in the mind, in the beingness, of the person who holds the intention. In effect, the individual becomes lined up at a conscious and an unconscious level. This integrated alignment is experienced to the very core of our being, at what amounts to a mental, emotional, and even cellular level. Mind, body, and soul, as it were, are in sync. Thus, there is a clarity and a knowing, an "of-courseness," to how the person regards herself in relationship to the objective at hand.

In effect, there is a truing-up process that happens: The conscious desire is understood so clearly, embraced so fully, and is of such magnitude that the unconscious elements of resistance (our paradigmatic, false, limiting beliefs) surrender or are overcome; of necessity they must and do line up and have no significant impact. To put the whole matter in imperative form: We must be clear about what we want, and we must want it really, *really* badly.

Alignment with the Trajectory of Our Lives

Every life has a trajectory, the arc that suggests the where and why of who we are and what we are up to with our finite life energy. In order to see this inspired trajectory, the one that speaks to who we are at the deepest level, we must, in effect, stop and step out of our day-to-day affairs, the "rat race" that is driven by our survival instincts. Much as we are challenged to think about our lives in the process of creating a personal purpose statement (chapter 11), we must observe and see our larger, more authentic purpose and thus our life's truest direction.

For a desire to become an intention, the would-be intention must accord with this authentic life trajectory. If, for instance, I am someone who has always derived energy, meaning, and joy from working with children, helping them learn to solve problems and better understand life's bigness and their place in it, then working within the educational system might well be a part of my life trajectory. And this deeper purpose might make it impossible to become intentional about realizing a goal I set for myself in college to become a successful business executive. Because the aspiration represents movement away from my life trajectory, it causes internal conflict, precluding true intention.

Regardless of how much, for whatever reasons, becoming a captain of industry may appeal to me at this moment in time (or back when I was in college), if it fundamentally conflicts with what is true for me at this essential level, it will not become an intention. I can become willful and forceful about it, but not intentional, for I will be unable to get myself lined up body, mind, and soul.

Contribution to a Greater Good

There are two points that we must recognize in order to understand the third requirement for intentionality. The first is that *we are moral beings*. This does not mean we always do the right thing or that functional evil does not exist. We don't, and it does. It simply means (assuming we're not pathological) that we know the difference between right and wrong. Yet, today, as we move further into the twenty-first century, we have come to understand, as never before, the degree to which truth and knowledge are contingent upon the culture, the ethnic group, the society, and the era in which we are born. To a considerable degree, we realize that some truth is relative.

The upside of this awareness is that we are more tolerant and understanding and more concerned with fairness and equality than ever before. More than ever, we realize that our perspective may not be the only perspective of importance, that our point of view is not necessarily the universal point of view. The downside is that it is easy to assume that *every*thing is relative, that there is no such thing as objective truth or goodness or beauty—just "my truth" or "your goodness" or "our (my 'tribe's') beauty." In some quarters, in fact, it has become acceptable only to speak in subjective terms: "This is just true for me; it may not be true for you."

Human beings are nevertheless and undeniably moral animals. Assuming that we are not sociopaths, we all have an irreducible sense of what is good and bad, regardless of whether we attribute this culture- and time-transcending quality of truth to eternal spiritual verities or to evolutionary psychology. Here's the crucial point: To a greater or lesser degree, *we all have an essential need to be in harmony with that deeper moral sense.*

The second point we must grasp is that one of the things that this deeper moral sense points us to is the fact that *we are all connected and thus interdependent*. In our better moments we may experience an awakened sense of knowing or understanding: We all are one, figuratively and in some vague, hard-to-explain sense, literally. As Albert Einstein explains:

> A human being is a part of a whole, called by us "Universe"; a part limited in time and space. He experiences himself, his

> thoughts and feelings as something separated from the rest—a kind of optical delusion of his consciousness. This delusion is a kind of prison for us, restricting us to our personal desires and to affection for a few persons nearest us. Our task must be to free ourselves from this prison.[5]

The delusion that creates the prison is the belief in our separateness; the truth that exists beneath the delusion is our undeniable interconnection. You and I are somehow one, which is why in some sense we really are our brother's and sister's keepers. And we know it.

When we combine these two principles—our need to be in moral harmony and our deeper sense of caring—our third requirement becomes clear. For a desire to become an intention, at the very least it must not conflict with the greater good of humanity and life, or at the very best, it must serve this common weal. If at the deepest level we are moral creatures, then to aspire toward something that directly or indirectly does harm to the greater good puts us in conflict with our truest selves. Even if the conflict is at a deeply buried level, the conflict is real; alignment (of body, mind, and soul), a requirement of true intentionality, is not possible. We are unable to make our conscious desire line up with who we truly are at the most profound level, who we are as moral animals. Authentic intentionality requires such alignment and is not possible without it.

Yet, when what we desire serves the greater good, we are free of this interior conflict. The possibility for alignment thus exists, and the possibility of having our considerable powers of imagination, courage, and commitment unleashed becomes real.

INTENTION VERSUS MECHANISM

When I first address the issue of intention with clients and students, I frequently begin the conversation by displaying a simple equation on a flipchart at the front of the room: INTENTION + MECHANISM = 100% RESULTS. I then ask the participants, who are now in small groups, to arrive as a team at definitions for both *intention* and *mechanism* and then to create group consensus regarding the percentage breakdown between intention and mechanism that will lead to 100% results. In other words, to arrive at perfect results, what percentage of the equation (of our effort) should be assigned to intention and what percentage to mechanism? Is it 50 percent intention (I) and 50 percent mechanism (M) that leads to 100 percent results? Or is it 80 I and 20 M, or 25 I and 75 M, or 90 I and 10M, or 5 I and 95 M, et cetera? There is one right answer, I assure them as they get to work.

Arriving at the definitions usually is not difficult. They typically come up with something like "Intention is a strong desire to have a certain thing happen." Not too bad. And "Mechanism is the means or method used to make the intention happen." Close enough. Where they run into difficulty is in determining the percentage that belongs to intention and the percentage that belongs to mechanism. Some will argue for the safety of a 50/50 split, some contend the weight, 80 or 90 percent, let's say, should be on the side of intention, and others will advocate for mechanism's ascendancy. On rare occasions someone will come up with the right answer, but in almost every case these "lone rangers" who would buck convention are shot down by the more reasonable members of the small group. Thus, the vast majority of the time the answer the groups arrive at is in the range of 80/20, 70/30, or 60/40 in favor of intention. And the correct answer? 100 percent intention, 0 percent mechanism.

Before you hyper-analytical types get carried away in protest, let me explain. Intention, as we have already noted, is the root source of all creation. Everything that exists first begins with an intention. If I make a meal I first have an intention of doing so; if I spend time on a relationship, I first have an intention of doing so; if I get myself physically fit, I first have an intention of doing so. In fact, if I have an intention, any intention, and if it is a strong enough intention, what the transformative leadership approach calls "true intention," I *will* find a way, a mechanism, for making it happen, regardless of the circumstances that may prevail. The reverse is not true. Mechanism of itself can never generate an intention. I may have multiple mechanisms available to me, brilliant and perfectly effective mechanisms, but until I have an intention, nothing, absolutely nothing will get done.

For instance, I may have the intention of eating an omelet. It meets all three of the given prerequisites, and I'm seriously hungry. But when I go into the kitchen, I find I have no utensils in the cupboard and no food in the refrigerator. Obviously, if my intention is real, what I am likely to do is to go to the store and purchase the necessary ingredients and utensils and then return home to make my omelet, or even easier, I'll head to the local café and order one up. The lack of an apparent means, a mechanism, is of no issue if I want an omelet badly enough. Even if I am in some backwater far from the reaches of Western civilization, if I want an omelet badly enough, if I am intentional about my yearning for the meal, I will find a means for having one.

On the other hand, I may have in my kitchen all manner of cookware and utensils and a refrigerator full of the finest ingredients. Or I may have a stack of coupons for free omelets at the finest diner in the world, which happens to be just down the street. But if I lack the "omelet intention," it all is for naught. The omelet won't happen. Mechanism or no, without an intention nothing happens. A mechanism does not an intention make, but an intention always creates a mechanism for its own fulfillment. In fact, built in to every true intention is the mechanism for its fulfillment. When that intention is clear, a mechanism always, and I do mean always, will appear. Or multiple mechanisms will appear, since we may have to try out many before we arrive at the one that works best.

The road to hell is not paved with good intentions. The road to hell is paved with nice hopes, neat ideas, and groovy dreams. Without intention, they are only really swell desires. But when we are clear, unequivocally clear, about an outcome that absolutely *must* be, having the means of getting there is not the issue; the issue is strengthening that clarity and resolve. Indeed, given intention's infinite organizing powers, the issue always remains the intention itself. This is not to suggest that we are to sit back and take it easy once we've become intentional. Far from it—intentionality inspires energetic, courageous, and resolute action, but that action is always initiated upon the crystallization of intent.

To the Moon Once More

When President Kennedy made his bold declaration about the moon landing, the mechanisms for such had not even yet been imagined; the technology was simply not there. In effect there weren't any eggs in the refrigerator—there wasn't even a refrigerator—and there were some who believed we might not even have the hens to lay the eggs. And yet when Kennedy thoughtfully but boldly made his declaration in 1961 he was clear, *and* he had satisfied all three of the requirements for authentic intention.

One, he knew why it was important and was clear that it was a "must be": Democracy might hang in the balance, and the defense of democracy was central to his reason for being a politician, let alone the president of the United States. Thus, it was a burning desire. Two, it clearly fit the trajectory of his life as well as the life of the nation: He was raised to believe that his purpose in life was to lead—not to manage or follow—and this was one of the fundamental acts of leadership during the Cold War. Similarly, in the minds of many of those who founded the United States, America was to be a model for the grand experiment in self-rule and would thus lead others to follow suit; indeed, as far as Kennedy was concerned, to lead in the space race, and thus to lead the way politically, economically, and morally, was nothing less than America's destiny, and his. Three, it seems there was little doubt in Kennedy's mind that going to moon by the end of the 1960s would serve all of humankind. It would not only represent a success for the United States and for democracy and freedom around the globe, but it would also affirm the truth in America's vision for humanity. America's landing a man on the moon and bringing him home safely before 1970 was the greatest of goods for the American population and probably for the entire human race.

His famous declaration was in fact an ode to progress itself. Thus, with no guarantees of any kind and virtually no assurances that it was even possible, Kennedy made his administration's desire into an intention: "It will get done," he said unequivocally. "And it will get done before the end of this decade." Note that he did not say, "We hope" or "We will try." Rather, "It *will* get done." Period. And the rest, as they say . . . well, you know the rest. In the domain of greatness *trying* is not an option; the only option is intention.

SUMMARY

Intention towers above the nice idea or even the passionate longing. The difference between a want, even a fierce want, and an authentic intention is a difference not merely in degree but a difference in kind. If we want something "sort of" and want something else "a whole bunch," the difference is one of degree. It's the difference between being at the low end or the high end on the "want scale": if this scale goes from 1 to 10, then wanting something "sort of" would be a 2 or 3 and wanting something "really badly" would be an 8 or a 9.

Intention is nowhere to be found on such a scale, for it represents something altogether different, something that resides in a completely different domain, entirely removed from mere wants, wishes, and hopes. In fact, when an intention is present, it takes up a unique place of residence in our consciousness. Intuitively, people who operate intentionally know this reality, for when they are being intentional they possess a fundamentally different bearing in life. When we operate from an intentional place, we obtain a calmer, more grounded, centered, sober-minded, and focused way of being.

The challenge for most of us is that we tend to slip into a mechanistic way of being. It is safer and easier to rely on mechanisms. Thus we slip out of the mind-set of leading our lives and leading others and slip into a management mode. We allow the given circumstances, what has come before, and the means available, that is, the mechanism at hand, to determine what we are up to and what we bring into being. But true intention brooks no conditional thinking. Intention is the thing, in and of itself. Period. It is the entirety, 100 percent, in the intention/mechanism equation. Every true intention has within it myriad mechanisms yet to be tapped.

One of the primary reasons for the unique quality of the intentional state of mind and for the extraordinary outcomes it produces is that intention draws upon and is fueled by a specific type of information and intelligence. Hopes, dreams, wishes, and even willfulness come from the domain of options, a mental state that is contingent upon history, on precedent, on what has already been done. Intention draws its imaginative and causal power from and comes out of the domain of possibility. Possibility is the starting point for all new and great achievements, whether in our personal lives or in the social world of leading and influencing others. We venture into this intriguing, seductive, and in some instances, frightening domain, the domain of possibility, in chapter 14.

CHAPTER 14

POSSIBILITY: The Mind of Power

The real voyage of discovery consists not in seeking new landscapes but in having new eyes.

—Marcel Proust

From within its own depths the imagination directly contacts the creative process within nature, realizes the process itself, and brings nature's reality to conscious expression. . . . The human imagination is itself part of the world's intrinsic truth; without it the world is in some sense incomplete.

—Richard Tarnas

The great creators in every age have spoken with deep appreciation, in some cases awe, when discussing the experience of being inspired by a sparkling, new idea. Whether it's a composer or a painter, an architect or an engineer, a business leader, a politician, or an educator, most will say the idea seems to emerge out of nowhere, or they-know-not-where. And the idea seems to have a life of its own, a vitality that awakens something—excitement, hopefulness, openness, curiosity, desire, joy, wonder, awe—that may have long been dormant. In most cases there is an expansiveness, a feeling of limitlessness, perhaps, that accompanies the idea. When you ask someone who has been recently inspired in this way, you often hear the description of something that is very nearly irresistible. It's the beckoning finger that says, "Yoo-hoo. You over there. What you have been looking for is over *here*," even if we weren't consciously looking for anything at all. And that beckoning finger? It's possibility. Possibility, that inexplicable, generative reality that exists in a place all by itself, a place without boundaries.

The opposite of possibility is the much more common basis for choice, the *option.* By definition an option is something that has been previously established by precedent. It has an accepted set of boundaries. It is based on what has come before, based on what has already been imagined and received as reasonable or doable. Therefore, options are available choices that are finite. They are limited, constricted by the conventions of ordinary human awareness and human history. Thus, we say, "your options are A, B, C, or D," for instance.

The peculiar thing about options and how the human mind works is that over time they take root in our unconscious and become fixed as the absolute limits of what is available to us. It's not like we say, "Well I know that there is more out there that might be bigger, perhaps a bit more risky, but I'm gonna take this one here." No, it's more like we say, "This is all there is, end of story," and accept that as that. Consequently, our thinking is artificially constrained on all sides, not by what is truly available, truly achievable, but by what we have unwittingly accepted as available and achievable, by the options that precedent and convention have made concrete. To live and operate from this optional state of mind is to manage, at best. It is not to *lead* life and surely not to lead others, certainly not in a transformative sense.

Transformation is a call to lead well beyond these artificial constraints. It's an awakening, perhaps painful at times, to the fact that we've accepted "This is all there is, end of story" as if it really were the truth. The transformative response to the beckoning finger is a willingness to have the optional illusions shattered, a willingness to recognize that mediocrity and even the ordinary done well are not close to the limit of what is available, nowhere near what may yet be achieved, for those who will heed the call and lead in response to that call. For beyond the shattered illusions of the optional world view is the cool, deep infinite waters of possibility—the wellspring of intention, the basis for all that is transformation, all that is progress, all that is new, fresh, and burgeoning with life.

THE OPTIONAL APPROACH: MANAGING THROUGH LIFE

The sad reality is most people, most of the time, particularly after childhood, spend very little time putting any conscious effort into imagining what might be available in life beyond what social convention tells us is or should be available to us. To put effortful thought into what we might become and what we might create beyond the accepted norm goes against a deeply ingrained need to be accepted into the larger tribe. And it requires a disciplined, imaginative effort. Thus most human beings accept without question what is given as the limit of what is available. It is not smart, it is not an accurate reading of reality, and ultimately it is not very rewarding, but it is understandable.

Let's say you were born into a middle-class family in Tacoma, Washington, where a modest degree of improvement over your parents' socioeconomic standing is expected in education, career success, earning capacity, and so on. You are likely to easily, perhaps even happily, slip into that optional mind-set. Playing your options out, you may decide to attend the local state university, you may marry shortly after college, get a socially acceptable job in marketing—preferably one that has management potential—raise a family, and hope to live, if not happily ever after, at least comfortably ever after.

Or if you are born to a blue-collar family just outside of Milwaukee, Wisconsin, say, raised in a factory town and understand that your options don't include a college education, you would play out your options quite a bit differently. On the Monday following high school graduation you begin your life's work in the plant just down the road. You soon get married, raise a small family, seek to get ahead in the traditional way to the extent that is conceivable and even remotely doable in today's economic conditions.

Unaware as you are that either of these approaches to life may be artificially limited by yourself and by society, you will at best manage your way through life and we will assume, without ever knowing that you are making any assumption at all, that you are doing the best that you can. Indeed, you may be doing the ordinary very well by bringing in, say, a seven-figure income as a Fortune 500 company executive. In fact, that is what good optional living, good life management, leads to: an individual doing a nice job of living an ordinary life, living a well-shined, modestly refined life of optionalism, whether it's bringing home $75,000 a year and living in a tidy tract home or $7.5 million and living in a gated fortress community of custom-built homes with ocean views. In the case of financial opulence, you may have realized a broader array of options, but it's still optionalism and de facto a constricted, managerial approach to life, with the attendant managerial fears and anxieties.

The unconscious optional thing is not a bad thing. It's just not the full *life* thing. It's the survival thing, the existence thing, the just-getting-by thing, even if your optionalism includes a Beverly Hills mansion and a fleet of fine cars. The fact is, optional living and managing life may or may not look successful by established societal standards. What we can be sure of, however, is that it is always a function of the largely unexamined life, a life constrained by our personal paradigms and by the limits of the collective social paradigm, constricted by convention. It's an unwitting acceptance that life is as it is and as it always will be; the best that we can—and should—do is find our place within that established order.

The vast majority of human beings will spend the vast majority of their lives asleep at the wheel in this manner, driving on autopilot with their eyes closed, thinking that they're awake and taking in all there is to see. Most human beings today will live and die without ever knowing that they had a choice to step beyond the confines of optional thinking, without ever knowing that such a thing as optional thinking, their thinking, ever existed. And by the same token, most so-called leaders will go to their leadership graves believing their management of the numbers and their technical skill in doing the ordinary well actually amounted to leadership.

In the larger scheme of things, there's something horribly wrong with this. Because today virtually everything that's an expression of human civilization has been increasingly globalized. That's not an indictment of globalization; it is an indictment of our inability to see and navigate the implications of what we have wrought.

What we have wrought is a world in which the interconnected nature of economics, politics, communication, and technology has tied all our rafts together into one enormous floating metropolis.

Thus, everything—the good and the harmful—is magnified, almost exponentially. And all this good and harm seems to happen in a digital instant. So today, when our business and political leaders are entranced by a fear-based world, one characterized by its optional framework, we are in a far more precarious position than at any other time in human history. The recent global financial collapse, which unfolded and spread throughout the economic world in a matter of days and weeks, serves as but one case in point.

Peace of mind, fulfillment, meaning, joy, and true power are never a function of the option-based life. Never. Not because wealth is bad or good, or poverty is noble or stupid. Not because career success has or lacks virtue but because optionalism is always fear based, artificially constricting, and little more than a misdirecting lie, one that most of us innocently embrace as the truth. Though it is not satisfying, it is much, much easier to walk through life on autopilot. It is easier, that is, until we are willing to step off of the relentless, fear-powered treadmill long enough to notice that the hollow, clanging sound in our heads is the misleading lie of optionalism, the lie declaring that what has come before must determine what comes after. The good news is that there's an alternative.

POSSIBILITY: THE COURAGE TO SEE

The alternative to optionalism is living from, or learning to hold, a possibility. Holding a possibility requires a willingness to step back from the automated rush of daily life, to obtain a degree of critical distance, and then to observe and imagine: *observe* the degree to which we have been captive to optionalism; *imagine* what might be available beyond it; and then have that newly imagined possibility inform our commitments. All three of these actions require no small measure of courage. Courage is the capacity to feel fear—that is, to allow fear to be present rather than repressing it, running from it, or forcefully pushing past it—and in the midst of this fear still go after and create what we desire. Courage therefore *requires* fear and necessarily entails creating a different relationship with fear so that fear doesn't limit us but in fact fuels us.

Observing and imagining require courage because each requires that we step out of the comforts of the conformity to which we have become accustomed. In stepping out of or back from the conventions of the tribe we risk failure and thus rejection. There is one hell of a good reason we are in the tribe to begin with. Even if in our tribal conformity we are miserable, at least we are safe, however we understand "safe." Furthermore, our misery can itself be a kind of comfort; it is a familiar friend—a wretched friend, perhaps, but a friend nonetheless. Letting go of the pathologies of our misery or the numbing quality of our conformity is no small task. It does indeed require courage.

We must be willing to step into foreign territory, uncharted waters, where the outcome of our foray remains undetermined. We may fail or we may succeed; we may get lost and founder or we may reach the promised land. There are no guarantees. Uncertainty abounds. But if we are willing to pay the price of some discomfort, of having fear and still moving forward, then the potential rewards are great. For out of our willingness to observe and then imagine we may learn the language of possibility. That is, we may learn to conceive of new and different outcomes for ourselves and our leadership, for our tribe or organization, perhaps for society and humanity itself. Only thus may we learn to embrace living life as opposed to merely surviving it until we die.

The Courage to Stand: Holding a Possibility

To hold a possibility requires courage at an entirely different level, even beyond that required for observing and imagining, because holding the possibility amounts to creating a mental or psychic space in which the newly imagined possibility is given the opportunity to develop and become manifest. A possibility can only become a reality as we learn to hold it in our mind over time. To live from possibility means to hold, to hang on to and nourish the possibility. This process takes a considerable degree of strength because two forms of resistance invariably inveigh against it.

First and foremost, our own limiting beliefs, our often-poisonous, unconscious (typically inaccurate, flat-out wrong) self-understandings are ferociously activated by the newly imagined possibility, for the realization of this new possibility may represent the death knell for these tried-and-true, well-worn self-beliefs. In effect, the beliefs fight for their lives as if they were separate entities. The new possibility cannot coexist with the deeply seated and contradictory belief, and therefore it must be destroyed.

For example, I may imagine a whole new career path for myself seemingly out of the blue. At the conscious rational level I may be completely inspired by the notion, and in that moment of inspiration it may make brilliant sense. Yet if I am like most people, I will encounter stiff resistance, even violent resistance, at an unconscious level, owing to any number of possible paradigmatic, unconscious beliefs I might have, beliefs that may question my worth, my talent, my knowledge, my intelligence, et cetera. Often the battle will mask itself at the surface level in cool rationality.

But at a deeper level, at the point of origin, what is going on is anything but rational. It's as if a determination has been made by the subterranean beliefs that have been in existence since childhood, a decision, in effect, to protect their place of residence in my unconscious mind. And the determination the threatened beliefs make for me is simple: This new idea will not stand! The net result is that the unconscious mind has sabotaged the new possibility before it ever takes root.

This idea of unconscious self-sabotage is hard for many people to understand and accept, steeped as we are in the false assumption that we are conscious creatures who behave rationally. Steeped in the idea, that is, that we do what we do for the reasons we say we do them. But, remember, we don't. We don't do what we do, certainly not entirely, for the reasons we tell ourselves we do it. Much of the time our explanations are, in fact, *rationalizations* for what our unconscious has already determined for its own reasons. Thus, courage is required to surmount the uprising of these established childhood tyrants. And be assured, they *are* tyrants.

Second, courage is required because convention and a more personalized version of the world of agreement (chapter 3) are sure to weigh in. Other people and the larger social group to which we are attached (and which we may even lead), invariably have an investment in the status quo, *our* status quo. Indeed, often people who claim and sincerely believe themselves to have our best interests at heart are the ones who prove the greatest challenge. A new possibility, especially one that may appear to exclude those in our immediate social sphere, may represent a threat to those we love and to the group with which we identify. The possibility we may now be seeing may represent a threat to their, to its, comfort and even to its safety. And don't forget, these perceptions of being threatened remain largely beneath the surface of *their* awareness and are masked (to them as well as to us!) in various ways. All manner of criticism and judgment, usually in the guise of rational and sophisticated skepticism, even masked as caring, is likely to emerge.

To hold a possibility, then, means to have the strength of character, the clarity of vision, and ultimately the intention to withstand this inevitable onslaught from within and without. Moreover, these two forces work together, almost hand in glove. It becomes a double whammy, a conspiracy of sorts: We are attacked within by our own self-doubt, and we are challenged externally by those who, unaware, feel threatened by the possibility—which only serves to further fuel the internal battle of our self-doubt. Is it any wonder, then, that we would scurry back to the comfort of our personal norm, back to the comfort of the status quo? Clearly then, holding a possibility takes considerable strength and desire.

But when we summon the courage and hold fast to the possibility, the possibility may in fact become a true intention. And when it becomes a true intention a whole new world is about to be disclosed.

Cinematic Lessons in Passion and Possibility

The oddly charming 1998 film *Pleasantville* is a kind of modern day morality play, one that cleverly conveys what happens personally and socially when someone steps from the safe and constricted world of option into the boundless and uncertain domain of possibility. The movie is a fantasy, but its considerable success was due in no small measure to its realistic portrayal of what happens when option is confronted by possibility. In the story, two 1990s teenage siblings are inexplicably transported from their normal, tempestuous life into the "perfect," banal, literally black-and-white world of a 1950s television show called "Pleasantville."

The town of Pleasantville is the archetypal image of America's fanciful nostalgia for 1950s suburbia taken to its logical extreme of empty perfectionism and conformity. The books have no words, the all-white high school basketball team never loses a game, everything happens nicely and without any messy emotions, and no one ever questions why things are the way things are, ever. That is, until the arrival of the new and improved Bud and Mary Sue—the transported '90s teens, David and Jennifer, embody characters that had already existed in Pleasantville. Almost immediately Mary Sue begins to stir things up with her rebellious, hormonal, and angst-riddled teenage turmoil. Out of nowhere, as far as the good folk of Pleasantville are concerned, everything starts to change, radically so, into color. The people and physical reality of Pleasantville that heretofore existed only in black and white now scandalously are beginning to take on the rich and varied hues of Technicolor. And it all happens as Mary Sue and Bud introduce the "dangerous" siren song of possibility.

The transformation of black and white into color is the disruptive metaphor for moving from conformist safety, ultimate optionalism, to the enticing and scary world of passion and possibility. Black, white, and gray represent a set of clearly delimited options. There may be only three of 'em, but we know precisely what they are. Color is infinite in its variations, in its possibilities. The moment any good citizen of Pleasantville becomes open to and is touched by passionate possibility, he or she becomes flushed with vibrant, life-giving color. For these newly transformed people of Pleasantville, it is both startling and liberating. They stand with breathless wonder before the new array of possibilities that now present themselves.

But if the transformed souls of the town are simultaneously thrilled and scared, the other, still black-and-white townsfolk are sent into paroxysms of anxiety. How could this be happening? This is indecent, immoral, and surely *unpleasant*. The mayor and other town leaders react violently and in their unwitting commitment to simple-minded optionalism immediately attempt to quell the revolutionary swell of passion and openness—precisely as our unconscious beliefs will attack the new possibility and seek to keep our untapped potential in check. With the collective force of a meatloaf-loving lynch mob, at all cost they seek to destroy this perceived colorful enemy of the established order. But to no avail. This is Hollywood, after all, and in the end, the promise of the possible, with all of its beauty and its inherent risks, prevails. Unfortunately, most people, and most leaders, don't get to have the Hollywood ending.

We are all Bud and Jennifer, fighting to break out of our own black-and-white worlds, out of our unconsciously optional ways, and we all have within us a semblance of the "good" townsfolk of Pleasantville (our lies) who desperately seek to keep us safely tied to the conventional banality. And, of course, we live in a society that is in some sense unconsciously, fearfully bound to defend the milquetoast comfort of coloring within the lines with only black and gray—again, the world of agreement. Like the people of Pleasantville who have not even imagined color, most of us don't understand that there is a distinction waiting to be made between the optional and the possible, as individuals and as leaders. And so we go through life *fighting for our limitations*, fiercely, unconsciously defending the options that we have unwittingly decided represent the limits of what is available.

Yet possibility exists—in life and in leadership—in bold, brilliant living color. And though we sense it is dangerous and risky, the danger we feel at the prospect of the possible is largely based in irrationality. The flashing lights, the alarms and whistles that may go off in our heads when we step into the uncertain domain of possibility, more times than not, are founded in the foolishness of that oozing, murky world of the unconscious—ours or that of those around us.

For the Few, Possibility Still

Most of us have become so efficient and effective at self-sabotage that in many cases we no longer even entertain the possibility of possibility. In an instant it passes in and out of consciousness, if it is allowed to enter at all, remaining only long enough for us to get a faint whiff, and then it and we move on.

But for those who can still hear the transformative whisper, for those who would learn to *lead* life, and for those who would lead others at an altogether different and higher level, possibility remains. It remains and it demands, "Knock off the self-indulgent dishonesty, dispense with the convenient rationalizations, get rid of the bullshit excuses and stand up like the woman or man that you are, that you have it in you to become." And, "Remember this," it declares, "after all is said and done, life is about overcoming itself, life is about being *and becoming*; you are the acorn that is meant to become the oak. You have it in you, so get busy."

Possibility reminds us that realization of our true form, the manifestation of our true essence is that for which we've been created. To do anything less is not only a failure of nerve and imagination but a failure to realize, to listen to and heed, that to which we are being called, by life and by our deepest and truest selves. Is it going too far, then, to say that *possibility in and of itself becomes nothing less than a moral imperative and thus becomes the heart of true intentionality, the essence of genuine responsibility, the very core of transformation and of leadership itself, leadership in its most powerful and compelling expression*? Possibility says all of that—for those who have the openness to listen, for those who have the courage to hear.

SUMMARY

The more we catch ourselves before falling prey to optional thinking, the more we rise above our *Pleasantville*-esque battles, and the more we change our minds and truly *lead* our lives, the more we are able to enhance, even change the lives of those we lead within the organization. But it doesn't stop there. It never stops there. Even if we wanted it to, it wouldn't. It couldn't. As the lives of key players in organizations begin to change, the organizations themselves begin to change, which influences change in the thinking of leaders in other organizations, which after some additional permutations can even affect the thinking of the leadership within society.

There is something wonderfully unnerving that occurs when intentional people operating from the domain of possibility not only take themselves on but also come together as they do so. Intention and possibility, when expressed by people of united mind and good will, become an irresistible force in ways that defy explanation. They represent a compelling duet in the songbook of the transforming life, indeed one of the essential movements in the concert of transformative leadership, full stop.

But there is an even greater reason for hope as we stare into the face of optional ignorance. That reason is represented by the third leg of the transforming stool, that of contribution. When acted upon, contribution is a principle that liberates us from the fears that unwittingly lead us into the constricting, optional mind-set. And authentic contribution is not merely something we should do because an arbitrary authority said so. It is, rather, one of the true secrets to life. It's the "gas," the "bomb," one of the few things, in and of itself, that gives life its joy. And it is one of the highest expressions of the evolutionary thrust of this transforming force of life. Next stop, then, Leg 3 *contribution*.

LEG 3:

Contribution

With this look at contribution, we address the final leg of the transformative stool. Contribution completes the tripod of bold personal leadership growth (see Figure L.3).

Contribution is not just noble or high minded. Life works when we "get ourselves out of the way" and truly see "the other." Our leadership works when we seek to serve purely for the sake of serving. Life and leadership work when we consciously "disappear" ourselves, so to speak, disappear ourselves out of a commitment to and in the process of serving the greater good. Contribution is smart, for it liberates us from our petty, small-minded selves. Indeed, in the moment of service to and connection with another, our talents and capacities are liberated from the fierce, irrational constraints of our unconscious belief systems, our "stuff." Thus liberated, we experience our truest selves and simultaneously know what it means to be connected with, to be a part of, the larger human circumstance.

In chapters 15 and 16 we consider the interconnected nature of things—of life and the universe as we know it—and how, perhaps ironically, finding our place in the vast configuration of things amounts to losing ourselves, joyfully and powerfully, in the act of contributing to another, as individuals and above all else, as leaders. In doing so we consider another important distinction, that of operating from the point of view of the host rather than that of the guest.

And so now we turn to what many of the greatest minds in history have understood as the secret of life: authentic contribution.

• • •

Figure L.3 Leg 3: Contribution

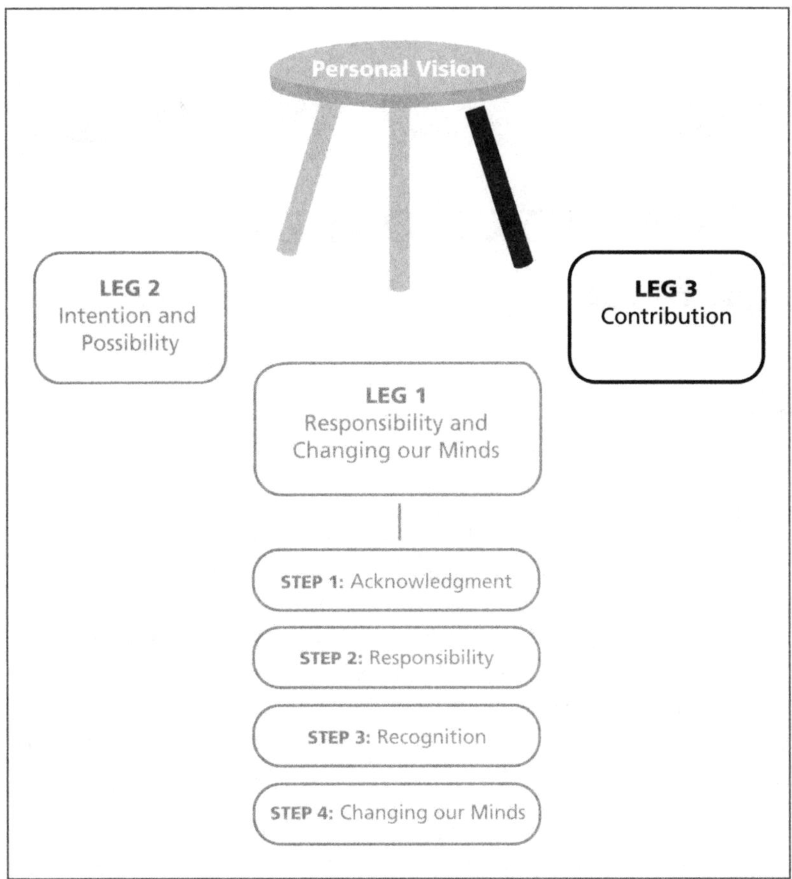

CHAPTER 15

CONTRIBUTION: The Soul of Power

> No man is an island, entire of itself; every man is piece of the continent, a part of the main. If a clod be washed away by the sea, Europe is the less, as well as if a manor of thy friend's or of thine own were. Any man's death diminishes me because I am involved in mankind, and therefore never send to know for whom the bell tolls; it tolls for thee.
>
> **—John Donne, *Meditation XVII***

In medieval Europe, the church or cathedral was the heart of the village, and the ringing of the church bell was a primary form of communication, an announcement marking an important occasion or a piece of important news. As the loud, rhythmic sounds would roll through the town and out into the adjacent farmlands, the villagers and farmers would be alerted that something of importance had happened or was happening.

The normal ringing of the bell, about one ring per second, announced a celebration or a soon-to-begin Mass or worship service. The "chiming" of the bell was a single ring, often used to mark the baptism and naming of a child. But the mournful "tolling" of the bell, ringing only once every four to ten seconds, told of loss, chiefly the loss of life—hence our association of *toll* with death, as in death toll. At the sound of the slow, spaced ringing, villagers or peasants from the nearby countryside would often send someone to the town's center to learn whose funeral was underway.

The epigraph that begins this chapter is taken from a penetrating meditation by John Donne, the seventeenth-century English poet, lawyer, and clergyman. In it he suggests we are wasting time when we "send to know" who has died. As human beings we are all part of a larger whole, all part of a single piece of fabric, the human fabric. We are all interconnected, interdependent, forever intertwined. The death of one person, Donne says, diminishes me, as a piece of earth crumbling to the sea diminishes the continent of Europe. When someone dies, a part of me dies. A part of you, a part of all of us has been lost. So when we hear the death bell ring, he admonishes, we need not ask who has been lost. We all have lost, and so, "It tolls for thee," for you and me.

If this notion of oneness has truth to it, then the ramifications for how we lead our lives and how we lead others are considerable. I may be but a single entity from my subjective vantage point, but this argument tells us that from another perspective I am not singular or separate at all. And quantum physics confirms this disquieting notion: We *are* all connected, all of a single piece in this vast, awe-inspiring *universe*, which literally means "one song." Both figuratively and in a literal, material, sense we are one. Donne happened to be right, more right, perhaps, than he even imagined.

This surprising connectedness that exists at a quantum level is no doubt one of the reasons so many of the great twentieth-century physicists were mystics of a kind. And a central message of all mysticism, scientific or religious, East and West? *All is one.* What I do affects you; what you do affects me. We may not see it. But that does not change the reality of our interdependence any more than our inability to see the Earth's motion makes it stationary.

Thus, it may turn out that giving to and serving others—that is, contribution—is not just a good thing in a moralistic or duty-bound sense. It's not merely some high-minded ideal to which only the best among us should aspire. Rather, it may just be a practical, non-negotiable requirement in creating a life that works, an organization that works, an approach to leadership that works, even a society that works. And (gasp!) maybe it's just good, smart (read: profitable) business. On the other hand, perhaps those who cling to a fear-based, self-absorbed interpretation of life, who would justify their greed and avarice with arguments like "It's a dog-eat-dog world," "It's kill or be killed," and "Charity begins at home," perhaps they are not the clear-eyed realists they suppose themselves to be. Perhaps they are not pragmatists who look at the world honestly. Perhaps they are, if you'll excuse the harshness, just stupid, merely misguided and primitive in how they understand reality. And perhaps because of this misreading of reality they are ill equipped to lead their own lives well, let alone lead others, particularly in an age when life happens and things change in a digitized and hyper-networked fraction of a second.

If William James is correct when he says, "The truth is what works,"[1] and if what we're after is a quality of leadership that works extraordinarily well, then it seems wise to pay heed to the implications of this notion of interconnection, with its practical what-affects-you-affects-me implications, as the transformative method of leadership indeed does.

CONTRIBUTION AND THE FOUR HIGHER NEEDS

The transformative leader understands that all human beings have four essential higher needs, and that experiencing life at its richest, truly *living* life, requires that all four of these needs be satisfied. If we are alive and breathing, regardless of what part of the world we live in or what we do, these four needs are real and are denied only at our peril. Indeed, if it is human beings we are leading and we want those human beings to play at an optimal level—to perform with effectiveness, power, and passion—addressing these four needs to the extent that is possible is the better part of leadership wisdom. And more immediately, if we are to lead a life of physical and emotional health, if we are to lead others and the organization with authentic power and efficacy, the transformative sensibility says we must satisfy all four of these higher needs. When we are operating from contribution, we are addressing all four needs:

1. *The need to love and be loved.* Giving and receiving love is a need, not a luxury, every bit as essential as any other biological need.

2. *The need to grow.* Neutrality or stability (stasis) is a myth; nothing in nature is static; life is eternally dynamic, either growing or in decay. We must grow.
3. *The need to contribute.* It's a law of life: That which does not contribute is eliminated; when we *do* contribute our bigness emerges (and typically so does joy).
4. *The need for meaning.* We are meaning-seeking creatures; we must experience our lives as having purpose, counting for something larger than "me."

Let's consider each of these needs in a bit more depth and how it is that the act of thoughtful contribution satisfies them and sets us up for a more powerful expression of leadership.

The Need to Love and Be Loved

As recent developments in neuroscience, developmental psychology, and general physiology show, consistent expressions of love are not merely "a really good thing when you can get it" but are as essential to full physiological and emotional health as water and air. To love and be loved is a need, pure and simple, a need that goes far beyond our simple emotional well-being. We see this most vividly in love's impact on us in the earliest stages of life. Without it an entire region of the brain, the limbic system—which regulates emotions, the capacity for reading emotions, and the ability to form bonds with others—will fail to develop properly. In fact, many experts today convincingly argue that the love a mother *feels* for her child while the child is still in the womb is crucial to the long-term physical, mental, and emotional health of the child after birth.

Even more intriguing is the importance of the love relationship between parent and child immediately after birth. "The coos and burbles that infants and parents exchange, the cuddling and rocking and joyous peering into each other's faces look innocuous if not inane; one would *not* expect a life-shaping process in the offing," but that is precisely what is going on, say Drs. Thomas Lewis, Fari Amini, and Richard Lannon.[2] The degree to which love is present or absent shapes the physiological structure of the brain. This is not "shaping a life" in the abstract; it's about as actual as we can get: An abundance of love leads to healthy brain development.

Unfortunately the reverse is also true. Paul J. Zak, a pioneer in the new discipline of neuroeconomics, puts the matter in the most blunt terms. He says, "Mammals," that includes you and me "deprived of mother-love (or a suitable substitute), do not develop normal cognitive or social skills, are emotionally stunted, are sick more often and die younger. . . ."[3]

In an even more dramatic demonstration of this need, Lewis and company show that a complete absence of love can lead to the death of an infant. The intimacy that is present between a loving parent and the infant provides a synchronization of the child's "delicate neural rhythms" as they are developing. Thus prolonged separation from the loving source of this synchronization "can be fatal to an immature nervous system, as vital rhythms of heart rate and respiration devolve into chaos."[4] Without the constancy of love, the rhythms of life degenerate into arhythmic confusion and even death.

With these hard, biological facts in full view, then, what most of us have always known intuitively comes into even sharper focus: We are built by and built for love, built to receive it and built to give it away. As Lewis and associates say, "Most of what makes a socially functional human comes from connection, the shaping physiologic force of love."[5] A life without love, it seems, results in a human being without humanity.

But let's take this question of love a step further. If we are reasonably healthy and honest with ourselves, we realize that we all seek love. A life without it in full measure is certainly empty, ultimately bereft of meaning. At the deepest level we all know this. We are intellectually, emotionally, and biologically disposed to seek out love, to experience it, and to give it away.

We cannot achieve even a modest degree of fulfillment without love's two-way expression. When the expression of love is absent, we become, in varying degrees, intellectually and psychologically disabled, emotionally and spiritually crippled. Though we may appear normal, without love we are in the slow process of disintegration. When we are not engaged in the dual process of loving and being loved, we are cut off from a source of nourishment and development every bit as essential to our sustenance as food and water. Under such parched conditions, over long periods of time, our fullness as human beings is diminished, weakened, and reduced to the point that our humanity can be called into question.

Under such conditions, full mental and physical health is nearly impossible.

When love is allowed to flow, however, when we make a conscious choice to risk it, to be open to love and to extend it to others, something far exceeding what we can explain biologically begins to occur. Poets, philosophers, psychologists, and theologians throughout the ages have been awe-struck before its wondrous, transformative powers.

It is, in fact, the constant of love that undergirds existence itself. Though we may be at a loss to explain it, we somehow understand that love is the glue that holds the universe together. Certainly it is the persistent call of love that is at the center of the will to transform our lives, to transform our organizations, and to transform our world. It is the gorgeous, wordless eloquence of love that informs the longing for life and, in a way, *is* life. Indeed, in the words of Joseph Campbell, "The distance of your love is the distance of your life. Love is exactly as strong as life."[6] Love and life itself are inseparable.

And we are by nature, by life itself, called to be a vehicle for love's expression. What you have done "to the least of these . . . you have done also to me," we are told by Jesus in the New Testament. Love must be expressed (and without discrimination) as well as received. It is unavoidably a two-way street. We have a need to give it away every bit as much as we need to receive it. Love can no more be held onto, possessed, than a sparrow can be contained in a shoe box. Under such conditions, both will die. Love demands that it be expressed and expressed fully.

Thus, when we embrace the power to give, when we consciously decide to contribute to the welfare of another, exclusively for the sake of the other, we are making ourselves available for the salient effects of love. In fact, through this act of true giving, contributing to others exclusively with *their* well-being in mind, we unwittingly throw ourselves into the surging, vital, nourishing flow of life itself, a kind of nourishment essential for transformation.

But there's a small catch. In satisfying the need to express love, our focus must be unswerving. To operate from true contribution, we must forget ourselves and truly see the other. Our focus must be on those we would serve. It can never wander onto ourselves, onto how noble or generous we might look to others or onto what we might get as a result of this supposed generosity. Our eyes must be set on their needs, their wants, their hopes and fears, their joy and suffering. In this moment *we* don't matter. Only *they* count. It is when our needs disappear that we are most thoroughly open to the elevating, even transformative power of love. Oddly, perhaps, it's when we don't care what we get that we get the most.

When we give from a desire to contribute rather than to get, we open ourselves to the unavoidably reciprocal flow of love. The reason for that may be due to the way in which selfless giving to someone else affects our own inner demons. In the moment we lose ourselves in the act of caring for and connecting with someone else, we possess incontrovertible evidence that we are good. At a deeper level, we *experience* ourselves as good. Moreover, when we make a deep, non-egocentric connection with another person, not only do we truly see that person in his or her full humanity, we are also seen by that person in ours. And being seen at this level only reinforces the experience of our own goodness.

The self-antagonism that smolders, unseen, within all of us at varying degrees is silenced, and in those pristine moments the transformative arteries are unclogged, releasing a nourishing stream of love—from others, from ourselves, and perhaps, from beyond. In forgetting about ourselves and giving to others we extinguish our deep-seated false beliefs. Thus, by contributing to others, we indirectly foster a different and better relationship with ourselves.

This may sound circular or self-contradictory: We give not to get but know that if we do so we *will* get. It is paradoxical. But here is one of the curious things about the power of love: Even when we enter into it half-heartedly, or with mixed motives, when a true connection is made with the person being served, often we are purified. We lose ourselves. That is, the disappearing of self just happens, effortlessly and automatically. But even when this losing of self-consciousness doesn't happen, good is still occurring, and we know it. Thus, we are affected as we affect.

When we act from contribution, we meet the need to love and be loved, arguably *the* need that trumps all others. It doesn't matter if we give to a stranger on the street, to a lifelong friend, to an estranged family member, to our soul mate, to an employee, or to a boss. What alone matters is that the focus be outward. Then it's contribution. Then the first higher need is being addressed.

The Need to Grow

There are two reasons growth is a need and not just a possibility. First, it's in the very nature of life to seek ever-greater expressions of vitality. Life seeks life. Life seeks expansion and growth. Like the need for love, the need for growth seems written into our DNA.

The second reason growth is a need is that there is only one alternative to it: decay and death. We are either growing or decaying, either expanding and increasing our complexity or disintegrating, falling apart and dying. Stasis, stability, or the maintenance of such exists only in the human imagination. Nowhere in nature do we find such a thing as stability. Even in a balanced ecosystem, there is either expansive, unfolding growth or degeneration, decay, and ultimately death. Thus to forestall decay we must be growing. We *need* to be growing.

The belief that there is a neutral space into which we may one day step—like the safe base in a child's game of tag—where everything stops and all is good, easy, safe, and secure, is a fraud. Retirement is a perfect example of the fraudulent nature of this belief. For many people, it is perceived as the long-awaited, well-earned reward for a life's work well done, perceived as the blissful, safety zone of the golden years. But for most it amounts to a fatal cessation of intellectual and emotional growth. This simple act of taking a "permanent break" from serious self-expansion is one of the reasons the death rate increases so dramatically immediately upon retirement. It's not because the retiree has suddenly and drastically aged overnight. They had been old for quite a while now. Why suddenly, after only two weeks of retirement did they collapse and die?

In retirement the relentless need to stay on top of things is no longer in play. The upside of retirement for most is some degree of diminished stress. The downside is that the need to learn new things, to grow, is also diminished. As a consequence, the natural forces of decay are allowed to accelerate. The disease and illnesses that we had unknowingly held at bay by the drive to keep up with the demands of the job are, in effect, unleashed. Without the purposeful will to remain a valuable participant in the workforce, the second law of thermodynamics, entropy—which says that everything in the universe is falling apart—inevitably kicks it up several notches, often making retirement far less than the satisfying reward we may have imagined.

The simple fact is that most human beings beyond the age of thirty are in the headlong, mostly invisible, throes of decay. Biologically we can only slow this process down some with a commitment to wise nutrition and fitness. But the dying process continues. That's the bad news. The good news is that as human beings we have the possibility to continue our growth intellectually, emotionally, psychologically, and spiritually. In fact, with a commitment to serious lifelong growth and development, today, because of the breakthroughs in nano- and biotechnology, it's within our scope to be more alive, more completely full of life, at seventy or even eighty than we may have been at thirty.

If we are not consciously challenging ourselves to grow, to expand our intellect and our skills and capacities, we cannot be healthy, happy, fulfilled individuals, regardless of our age, health, wealth, or any other external factor. Growth is a need placed on us by nature. If we're not growing, we're dying.

But what does growth have to do with contribution? To answer that question we must first consider an aspect of the human reality that most people are reluctant to acknowledge.

The Fear of Being Not Enough

Every person ever born, to one degree or another, has the fear that *I'm not enough*. As with many of our most "tried-and-true" fears, the fear that we're not enough usually resides just slightly beneath the surface of our consciousness. It's also known as "the imposter syndrome," the fear that we'll be found out as a phony or a fraud who has fooled everyone. It's triggered for each of us by different circumstances, expressed in different ways. And just like we do with most fears, we respond to this fear automatically, instantaneously and unconsciously, such that we don't consciously even register the fear's presence most of the time. We just act instinctively, kick it into overdrive, and power right through with little awareness of the shift in our behavior.

The problem with the automated, "power-right-through" behavior is that in the process we cloak ourselves in inauthentic routines or behind behavioral masks. Beyond the discomfort we may feel, we pay two additional prices. First, we unnecessarily expend enormous amounts of energy keeping the routine or dance going, and second, we limit the expression of our intelligence and natural talents. The result is we're unnaturally fatigued and far less effective in life than we could be. It's a normal behavior. We all do it. And it doesn't serve us.

It works like this. A triggering circumstance or person shows up in our daily life, say, or we're asked to make a presentation to a group of exceptional people, or we have an interaction with a person we find intimidating. The result is that an instantaneous, almost undetectable fear kicks in, and suddenly, automatically, long before our conscious mind has been alerted, we *strike the pose*—typically without ever noticing we're doing it or we've done it. In striking the pose we communicate things we may be entirely unaware of to those around us. Following are a few examples of this not-enough behavior, of the pose, *P*, that we automatically strike, the defensive or protective communication, *C*, we deliver by striking the pose, and the unconscious internal conversation, *IC*, that informs both :

- P: *The emotionless stoic.* C: "I need no one" and/or "Rocks feel no pain." IC: "It's too dangerous to let anyone in because they'll see that I'm unacceptable (or wrong, or undeserving, et cetera) and reject me."
- P: *The invisible man/woman.* C: "Please, please don't notice me." IC: "If I just blend in I'll be safe because that way they won't see that I'm not important."
- P: *The detail freak, hyper-analyst.* C: "I'm a thinker, not a feeler." IC: "My *instinctive* decision making is not to be trusted," and beneath that, "If I'm not perfect I'm worthless."
- P: *The clever jokester.* C: "Notice my wit, not me." IC: "If you notice me you won't like what you see."
- P: *The passionate crusader.* C: "See how morally superior I am." IC: "There's something fundamentally wrong/bad/inferior about me."
- P: *The dangerous threat* or *the slicer-dicer.* C: "Keep your distance or I'll turn my smoldering rage on you." IC: "I'm not acceptable/likeable/loveable, and I must keep them on the defensive, keep them from seeing that fact."
- P: *The cheery, overly nice pleaser.* C: "See my niceness, not me," and/or "Please, *please* like me." IC: "My only value is in pleasing someone else."

- P: *The witty self-deprecator.* C: "See what a down-to-earth, nonthreatening, likable dude I am." IC: "I'm not as important as everyone else or surely not as important as the big people."
- P: *The confused absentee.* C: "If I just space out a bit or go into confusion this will all soon pass." IC: "I don't have what it takes. Hell, I shouldn't even be here."
- P: *The slap-'em-on-the-back life of the party.* C: "I don't have a lot of substance but I'm good to have around." IC: "Gotta keep their eyes on my shiny dancing shoes so they don't see my emptiness and worthlessness."

And so on.

When our not-enough behaviors are activated, what people get is not us, not the real us, anyway. What they get is our routine, our shtick, our number, the one we run automatically in order to keep them from seeing the real us. They get our deflection, our façade, our contrived, self-protection mechanism. They don't see us at all. They see our artful mask. And we've been wearing it for so long, it's such a comfortable fit, we don't realize we've slipped it on—or that it's slipped itself on, it seems.

It takes exceptional courage even to see the mask, to identify the defensive behavior. It takes even more courage to learn how to show up in life without the artifice, without the self-protective device we've so carefully, if unwittingly, refined all these years.

The decision to contribute, to see the other, to connect with and serve, can free us of the mask, the routine, the bullshit behavior. Indeed, when we decide to contribute to the well-being, the growth, and the development of another, something significant begins happening. Our truest, most powerful selves begin to emerge. We begin expanding our range of understanding, our strength of character, our capacity to engage other human beings. In effect, we are expanding our very humanity. Our sense of life, the world, and the people around us is different in this moment of contribution, and a healthier, more accurate reflection of who we are is expressed. In fact, in the process of contributing and connecting, our experience of ourselves is fundamentally different than when we are locked into our isolated, fear-based selves.

And if we live in this space of true contribution often enough, we literally begin to change our brains. We are growing. Thus, when we contribute from a place of authenticity and do so regularly, the people to whom we give benefit and we grow. As one of my clients once wrote after completing a rather risky contribution exercise, "I think it all just kind of clicked for me. When I make that choice to give, even if I'm scared or anxious or whatever, I suddenly see people and the world from a radically different perspective; the weights just seem to drop away. My silly little worries melt away. This may not make any sense," he continued. "I don't understand it, but I feel wiser, more connected. I feel more alive." The truth is it makes all the sense in the world.

The Need to Contribute

Obviously, the need to contribute is satisfied by authentic contribution. But looking a bit deeper, the need to contribute is built on a fundamental law of life: "That which does not contribute is eliminated." When something in nature becomes inefficient or outlives its usefulness, over time it's eliminated. It is a natural outcome of the principle of cause and effect, a notion that has entered common vernacular as the use-it-or-lose-it rule of inevitable consequences. Perhaps the example that hits closest to home for us in the digital age is based on what happens to our bodies as we sit for hours on end in front of our computers or texting or talking on our cell phones.

We all know that muscles that are not used begin to atrophy. Their lack of use tells the body's intelligence system that these muscles in their current size and shape are not required. Thus, nature's bent toward efficiency takes over, directing energy away from these organs and toward muscles and organs of greater immediate importance. The process of elimination has begun. Anyone who has attained a hard-won level of physical fitness knows the frustration that comes from taking a break from the workout regimen. Almost from the moment we interrupt our routine the muscle mass and muscle tone we worked so hard to achieve seem to begin their race to degradation. And if we neglect them long enough, those tight biceps lose their mass and definition and slowly turn to flab.

The muscles are no longer contributing to the body's overall needs, at least not according to the body's survival and efficiency regulators. While we were working out, the muscles were needed to lift the heavy weights. But as the muscle is no longer needed for such heavy lifting, its muscle tissue is eliminated and its size is reduced to the size necessary for modern living, to the size needed for lifting a fork or a mobile phone or for typing on a laptop keyboard. It is a reasonable law of nature: That which does not contribute is eliminated.

And at some level we all know and understand this law. We instinctively understand that those who do not contribute to the tribe are pushed out of the tribe, that is, they are eliminated. Thirty thousand years ago the tribe could not afford to feed those who didn't contribute to its survival. This primitive wiring remains active today, reinforcing what we see in nature and society.

Thus, we all have a need to know that we offer value to those around us, to know that we are making a contribution, though it mostly remains subliminal. If at work, say, we begin to doubt the value of our contribution, we'll also begin to notice a nagging sense of disquiet, the onset of a mild anxiety. Whether the doubt is warranted or not, the anxiety emerges. Because we don't want to be eliminated. It's one of the reasons people need to be recognized for work well done; it assures them they are valuable and quells the largely irrational fear of being eliminated. But if this just-beneath-the-surface unease is allowed to fester and grow, over time it can have a crippling effect on creativity, collaborative capacities, overall effectiveness, and of course even our health; it's one of the causes of that killer known as stress.

When the need to contribute is legitimately satisfied, when we are being challenged to add and are adding noticeable and meaningful value, when we are contributing to the relationship, the family, the team, the cause, the company, and so forth, and we do so regularly, the malaise subsides, usually goes away completely—or never emerges in the first place. Beyond this cessation of angst, however, something else, something quite amazing, begins to happen. Our sense of self, our sense of value and worth, begin to grow. We begin to feel like we belong, like we fit in, like we deserve to be here, not just on the team or in the company but on the planet. It goes that deep. That is, we have a growing sense of what some philosophers refer to as our "existential validity," our fundamental worth as human beings who deserve to be alive, who have an existence (hence "existential") that is warranted. And as our existence is validated at this deep level not only does the anxiousness disappear, but our talents find the fertile soil of trust and a sense of safety that allows them to flourish.

Satisfying the need to contribute calms a normal anxiety and liberates our talents.

The Need for Meaning

Human beings are fundamentally meaning-seeking creatures. Our most essential nature is to search out and find meaning in life, in everyday events and circumstances, in other people, in tragedies and in triumphs. According to renown psychiatrist and holocaust survivor Viktor Frankl, the "striving for meaning in one's life is the primary motivating force in man."[8] Though this need is often suppressed by day-to-day survival demands, it is there, and it is relentless in its requirement for satisfaction. We are naturally disposed to find meaning when we can and to impose it when we're not sure. The vast and bewildering mystery of life demands nothing less.

In other words, we must understand *why*. Why do we exist? Why does anything exist? Is our existence, the universe itself, merely an accident? Or is there a *telos*, an end or goal in life, a reason for it all? Is there something beyond this earthly pale? Or is this it, nothing more? It seems that from the time eons ago when humans first emerged into consciousness, from the time we first developed a sense of a self separate from our surroundings and separate from other people, we've been asking these great questions of meaning. We have also been asking the questions about our personal meaning, as we noted in chapter 11. Why am *I* here? Who am I? What purpose, if any, does my life serve, should my life serve? What am I up to with this riddle called life?

Even if these questions remain unexpressed, we are compelled to seek out and find meaning, to make it up if need be, or die trying. For to live a life without meaning is akin to living a life without love and hope; it is, in effect, to live without anything to justify, or at least make tolerable, the "slings and arrows of outrageous fortune," the "shit" that just "happens," as the bumper-sticker saying goes. And if the worldview that we ultimately arrive at precludes confidence in a greater, inherent end or purpose to life or precludes the possibility that we will ever know this purpose, then at the very least we must arrive at some understanding of our individual value. We must discover a way to show that our individual existence has worth, that we matter as a person, that our time on the planet has had and will continue to possess some significance. Every last one of us *must* have a greater sense of purpose, if, that is, we are to be fully healthy, fully happy, fully functioning human beings.

Indeed, in those moments of genuine validation and purpose, in those moments when we sense our lives have meaning, our energy and our spirits often soar; our talents and faculties come alive, says the Indian sage Patanjali, and we experience a solidity to our existence that otherwise is fleeting.

And here's the point. *When we operate from a mind-set of contribution we experience our lives as meaningful.* In that moment we satisfy our most basic need for meaning or purpose. It does not matter if we believe we have a vivid and specific purpose designed by God, or if we believe we construct our own grand narrative and thus our own unique purpose, or if we remain agnostic about the matter of individual life purpose. In the simple moment that we forget about ourselves and truly see someone else, seeking to serve that person, in that moment we experience meaning. In that moment we know meaning, not in the abstract but real-time, radiant, transcendent meaning. Regardless of what our worldview might tell us. In the moment we make connection with and bring benefit to another life, or some greater cause or organization, our life has a quality and richness to it that feels complete and total. In that moment.

SUMMARY

To make transformation possible in our leadership, in our personal lives, and in our organizations we must grasp and learn to live from all three legs of the transformational stool. Leg 3, *contribution*, satisfies all four of our higher universal needs for love, growth, contribution, and meaning. To live from a place of contribution does not mean we must quit our day jobs and head off to the poverty-stricken quarters of a New Delhi or a Detroit. It means that we must wake up to the opportunities to contribute that are all around us, in our day jobs, in our communities, in our homes, among our families, on the corner, in the grocery store, or standing in line at the cleaners. It may be as simple as helping a confused and frightened senior citizen find her car parked in a sea of cars that all look alike. Or it may be as dramatic as intervening in the life of a neighbor child whom you suspect of being abused by a troubled adult. Or it can mean slowing down long enough to listen to and hear your own child without judgment and expectations. Or maybe it's investing yourself heart and soul in the development of an employee who has the ability but heretofore has lacked the support. And as leaders, the opportunities to contribute daily are almost endless.

On and on it goes. The opportunities to step into the practice of contribution are everywhere, often hidden in plain sight. The good we can do, the contribution we can make, and therefore the meaning, the growth, and the love that we can know is right there in front of us. Right there. Right here. Right now.

The experience of genuine contribution, true giving, is one of the great joys in life. Highly evolved individuals have always known this. It is one of the secrets to making life work. The great thinkers may be right, after all: It may be the secret to life. And it is central to the transformative process.

In chapter 16 we approach the power of contribution from a different angle, considering it in the context of what it means to be an adult. In a world seemingly gone nuts, adults are needed now more than ever. The problem seems to be that most people don't grow up; they simply grow old. We consider how the mind-set of real contribution speaks to this reality and is the much-needed antidote to our current malaise.

CHAPTER 16

IN SEARCH OF ADULTHOOD: Fear and Loathing in Guestville and Playing to Win

"We make a living by what we get, but we make a life by what we give."

—Winston Churchill

No one knows what lies beyond this pale. But if there is anything other than extinction, we can be sure that the best preparation for it, in this brief interval when the bird of time is still on the wing, is to live out our lives and our creativity as fully as we can, experiencing and contributing what we can.

—Rollo May

The call to extraordinary leadership and an expansive life understands that we are social creatures through and through, that our individual growth and our impact as leaders are inseparable from our capacity to authentically connect with others. It further understands that growth means movement from adolescence toward a full embrace of adulthood, that is, we must operate our leadership and our lives from the perspective of the giver, of the grown-up, of the adult. In one moment, then, transformation tells us to be focused on growing and expanding ourselves, and in the next, to forget about ourselves completely and see and serve the other—that to become our truest selves, ironically perhaps, we must learn to *lose* ourselves in contribution to something greater than ourselves. Contribution is the ever-unfolding backdrop, the context that allows for transformation. And it is every bit as essential, as non-negotiable, as either of the other two legs of the stool; it's the final ingredient that allows the fifty-four-year-old adolescent to finally become an adult.

All of which begs a question: What do we mean by the word *adult*? Legally, *adult* denotes a person who has reached the age of majority, in most cases either eighteen or twenty-one. But that's typically not what we mean when we use the word in everyday discourse. When we refer to someone as being adult (or not), usually we're referring to that person's bearing in the world, how she comports herself or conducts herself in life. It's a reference, in most instances, to the person's mental and emotional maturity. A grown-up, the most common synonym for *adult*, is someone who sees the world through discriminating eyes and acts accordingly.

GUESTS VERSUS HOSTS

Perhaps the best way to understand adulthood is through an analogy that contrasts it with adolescence. It's been said that the difference between these two stages of development is the difference between being a guest and being a host.

In the most unvarnished terms, a *guest* at a party expects to be served and unapologetically seeks his own self-interest. It's not that he's crude, rude, or otherwise boorish. His thinking is simply something like "I'm here to enjoy myself" or "I'd like to make a new business contact or otherwise further my stature." His presence at the party is about his pleasure or for his benefit. His mentality is informed by the question, "What's in it for me?" And there is nothing wrong with this sensibility. It is the guest point of view, after all. It's how a guest thinks, what a guest does.

The *host* has a different perspective, a larger, more comprehensive view because it is one motivated by a fundamentally different objective: to assure the success of the party, which is achieved by serving the interests and well-being of the guests. The host's mentality is informed by the question, "How can I best serve my guests' needs?" And this is not about appearances or pretense. There is no need to *appear* gracious or magnanimous or any other way for the true host. What others think of the host is more or less immaterial to her. Her focus is on the greater good, directed outward, on her guests.

The host, in effect, owns the outcome of the situation, whether it's a relationship, a social get-together, an educational meeting, a business gathering, a political event, or possibly even society at large. The host is the one who sets the immediate gratification of her needs aside in order to guarantee the well-being of her guests.

Let's say, for instance, that we're at a formal dinner party of about fifty people. It's the cocktail hour prior to the meal, and all the guests are mingling. You and I have not yet met (or otherwise identified) the people hosting the evening. But let's suppose we are able to discreetly step back and observe the proceedings, maybe from a staircase or a landing. Being the shrewd observers that we are, it is likely that after a relatively brief period of time we would be able to accurately guess who the hosts of the party are. Simply by watching how they are interacting with the other people in the room. Because their informing motivations are different than their guests, their ways of being are also noticeably different. In some instances their actions, too, are different.

In life the host is the adult, the true grown-up. Both personal transformation and powerful leadership require this type of adulthood. Indeed, this way of understanding adulthood has immediate and far-reaching implications for our engagement with the people we lead and the personal transformation we seek. I'll mince no words here: *Transformation at the most profound level and the power of transformative leadership make themselves available to those who would be and become true adults and* only *to those so willing.*

BUT IT'S WORTH THE TROUBLE

Until we are willing to take on the mantle of the host and experience what it means to live in this way, lasting transformation remains but a fleeting wish, a self-indulgence, an expression of the very narcissism for which our age is famous. Put another way, we cannot learn to truly lead our own lives, and we surely cannot become leaders of transformation in others and in the organization, until we learn to live our lives from the perspective of the host. But transformation's demand for adulthood is good news. Here's why.

First, our society is screaming for adults to step up, screaming for hosts, grown-ups, to show up at the party—crying out for true leaders, leaders who are genuinely committed to their followers, truly committed to the greater good. Leaders who have the courage to see what could and should be and are willing to take the risks necessary to see it realized. Managers who pretend to be leaders need not bother.

I'm not talking about the apparent adolescents in adult clothing who gummed up the world economy and pushed us to the brink of economic ruin four years ago—the guests who are still at the helm of many of our most important business (and political) institutions who even now seem hell-bent on serving their own selfish interests no matter the costs to everyone else. The social system as we know it in the West (the financial, business, and the political system) is broken. The true leaders that society needs today are unafraid to see and acknowledge this reality (and not simply spout platitudes about it). More important, they have the maturity and requisite will to do something about it. Adults wanted. Children need not apply.

The second reason that the demand for grown-ups is good news has to do with the experience of joy. Acting as the adult may bring some discomfort, but it is also a deeply pleasurable experience. Whether it's helping a neighbor repair a garage door or changing the lives of hundreds, perhaps thousands, of people in an organization, there is little that compares with the pure joy of seeing, connecting with, and serving someone else. If you've experienced it, you know precisely what I'm talking about and you know that in many ways the experience defies words—can be ineffably sublime.

The third reason may be the most inexplicable. When we display the maturity involved in getting past our own worries and needs and contribute to someone else in need, life just seems to work. Time and time again, during the past twenty-plus years I have had clients or students who were struggling with aspects of their lives come to me and describe how making a difference for someone seemed to get them out of the tailspin. By simply getting their own concerns and worries out of the way and truly giving to someone else, they were able to remember who they were and what they were about. And oddly enough, once again things started clicking right along.

It works, life works, that is, when we focus on contributing, *if* we are truly able to connect with, lose ourselves in sincere concern for and service of, the other person or persons. And yet, still we resist the power and joy of contribution. The question is *why*? Why do we fight it so?

IRRATIONAL FEAR AND LOATHING

Most of us already know instinctively that a rich and meaningful life is only possible via rich and meaningful relationships. Even without an awareness of the four higher needs, even without knowledge of the breakthroughs in neuroscience that tell us that we are wired for social connection at the deepest and most abiding levels, we already know we must connect with, love, and be loved by others if we are to experience life at its best. Intuitively we get it: We need each other; we've been created for social engagement; in fact, we cannot live without it. Even those who pretend otherwise know in their heart of hearts this is so.

Yet if this is so, why is it that when we look around what we increasingly see is a society that is more individualistic, more isolated, and more socially insulated than ever?[1] The answer is our *irrational fear of other people*. Really. Let me explain

Social engagement, even at a superficial level, entails risk. There is danger involved, even if we don't like to admit it, the danger of rejection, the danger of embarrassment, perhaps even the danger of shame. It's a reason theologian Paul Tillich says that the "courage to be"—the courage to embrace and own our individual existence in the face of life's uncertainty—must be balanced by the "courage to be *a part of*"—the courage to connect with and contribute to others.[2] It's courageous because it necessarily entails learning to *have* fear but not to be *run* by it. To make meaningful contact with others we must not allow the fear of rejection to determine how we live. It's risky business, indeed.

But what is at the root of this fear of rejection? What we are *actually* afraid of is almost entirely disconnected from reality, which is why it's said to be irrational. It's the result of a gift from our most distant ancestors, a function of one of the most primitive parts of our brains. For what we fear is, as we noted earlier, nothing less than death itself. No kidding.

Death by Public Speaking

Over the years numerous studies and an abundance of anecdotal evidence have reminded us that most normal human beings are dreadfully uncomfortable at the prospect of having to speak in public. It is telling that people will often declaim, "I would rather die than speak in public," for what they fear is not simply the possibility of public embarrassment. What they are unconsciously afraid of is death: "If I speak in public and fail, embarrass myself, I may be rejected and that may ultimately lead to my untimely death." Huh? Death? Yes, indeed.

Based on our hard-wired, primal programming, an instantaneous, automatic, and largely unconscious pattern of thought is activated at the mere prospect of being vulnerable in front of a crowd of listeners. The subliminal thinking goes something like this: "If in speaking before a group I flub up and make a fool of myself, I'll be publicly shamed. I may even be seen, and possibly ridiculed, as a fool. People will then discover that I am less desirable and valuable to the group than I pretend to be; they'll see that I'm insufficient, not enough. I'll then be ostracized, rejected by the members of the 'clan.'" At this point in the automatic process the deeply buried primeval wiring kicks into overdrive. "I will be pushed to the edge of the tribe or pushed out of the tribe altogether. Alone in the wilds I may be eaten by a saber-toothed cat, be killed by a rival tribe, or eventually just starve to death." Not a pleasant set of options. Embarrassment and shame at this primal unconscious level equal the potential for premature death.

Embarrassment and shame, of course, do not mean death. But as a function of residual, age-old synaptic patterns, the fear nonetheless exists at an almost immutable level. Many thousands of years ago it served us well. Today it is simply irrational, limiting, and in some instances debilitating.

Every time we put ourselves in a position for potential rejection we run the risk of triggering, in widely varying degrees, this basic, irrational fear. When we find ourselves in a new and different social setting—especially one that requires openness beyond the superficial norm—we make ourselves vulnerable to at least tacit rejection. Regardless of how foolish these fears may be to our rational minds, they still exercise considerable control over aspects of our behavior—hence the fear, terror in some instances, in which they wrap themselves. We may excuse it by saying "It's just the way I am" or "I'm just shy," but there are reasons for this shyness, reasons readily addressed and overcome. If we are going to learn to operate as adults, as hosts, if we are going to learn to live at the level of authentic contribution, we must be willing to address and grow past these unjustified fears.

It's the Reason We Lie: The Fear of Confrontation

I often work with clients to create better ways of challenging and supporting one another. It almost always entails teaching them how to more readily tell the truth and how to do so with less suffering. In this process I often hear clients say something like, "Well, you see, our culture here at XYZ corporation is averse to confrontation," as if that somehow makes this organization unique. That's a laugh. The fact is, the fear of confrontation is the norm, even for the most bellicose among us. The reason is simple: Telling someone something they may not want to hear may put our relationship with them at risk. What we tell ourselves to justify our aversion to confront is that our reticence issues from a concern for *their* well-being, that we don't want to hurt *them* or *their* feelings. It's because, we like to think, we are nice people and we don't want to cause them upset. But more times than not, this is all a rationalization. It's a lie. That's not to say we're not kind people, but that kindness is not why we're reluctant to confront when needed.

Most people who seek to avoid confrontation do so out of misguided self-interest, out of the fear of rejection. We fear we will be challenged or shunned or otherwise punished if we speak the unpleasant truth. We fear we won't be liked. The more we feel the need for acceptance, or worse, the need for approval, the more difficult the confrontation seems. If we tell a colleague that she is not handling her employees effectively or tell a friend that his attire is inappropriate or tell our neighbors that their children are out of control, she, he, they may not like us, which unconsciously triggers the fear that we may be rejected and pushed out of the tribe. Despite what we may tell ourselves in order to feel better about our cowardice, the discomfort is based largely on self-interest.

It's *misguided* self-interest because the outcome of well-intended confrontation is usually the opposite of what we fear. Though the recipient of the critical information may not like the message we deliver, more times than not, they respect and appreciate our willingness to tell the truth, at least in the long run, if not immediately. Of course there's always the legitimate risk that the person to whom we give the information may not be willing or ready to hear it all—they may deny, defend, and otherwise respond contentiously. But if our motives are genuine, if we have *their* interest truly at heart, the odds are they will be served, one way or another, and there is a better than even chance that the relationship will ultimately benefit.

Withholding the dicey information is the lie of omission. It assures that the relationship will remain at a largely superficial level, which is where the ordinary person wants it anyway. Moreover, it guarantees that the other person will not benefit from the information that we hold. But, doggone it, we'll be safe! Phew! No risky truth telling here. We're safe, comfortable, *and mediocre*. The prospect of having both parties benefit from honest, open communication is lost, simply because of self-indulgent self-interest.

Our larger point, then, has three aspects. First, it is out of fear of rejection, not because of our "niceness," that we avoid the difficult conversations. Second, frequently the avoidance of confrontation amounts to the withholding of information and thus amounts to a lie, the lie of omission—pretending that everything's fine when we know it is not fine—is lying every bit as much as knowingly communicating a falsehood is. Third, the fear that informs our avoidance of speaking the uncomfortable truths to others is a completely misplaced, irrational fear, the indirect fear of death.

AN ANTIDOTE TO PRIMAL ANGST

To live from a transforming state, and lead from such a place of power and purpose, we must embrace the mantle of the host. But to do that, we must find a way past our primitive, fear-based inclinations. *Courage* is the antidote to our primitive anxiety. Courage is a simple but powerful antitoxin—simple because it is a choice, powerful because it is an expression of consciousness. It isn't always easy to apply the courage nostrum, but it wouldn't be courageous if it were, now would it? Over time, however, as we retrain the brain, it can become second nature. Really. But first we must consider the meaning of courage a bit further..

The Greek philosopher Aristotle defined *courage* as the "middle way," what he called the "mean," between rash foolhardiness, on the one hand, and cowed timidity, or cowardice, on the other. In this middle way we are neither oblivious to the size of the danger we face and thus cavalier about it, nor are we intimidated by it and inclined to flee. We acknowledge the danger, the challenge, the perceived threat, and having already chosen our course, with our wits about us, we move forward in the face of fear, focused on who we would become and what we would get done. Courage, then, as we noted earlier, is not the absence of fear as much as the capacity to *have* fear, to *be with* fear, and still intentionally hold fast to the objective at hand. In effect, it is the ability to say, "Okay, I'm a bit scared, maybe even a lot scared. But it's just fear, and fear or no fear, this is the right thing to do. So I'm going over there. Let's go."

Thus, courage is not overcoming fear, for that implies muscling past or over the top of it, or possibly shoving the fear down with forced bravado. This sort of forceful response to fear leads to our senses becoming dulled—our emotions numbed, our vision constricted, and our thinking clouded. Powering through fear, denying fear, and struggling not to feel it, is not courage. It is the willful effort to control or subdue fear. Nor should we equate courage with fearlessness. More times than not, fearlessness is a reflection of stupidity—ignorance of the actual danger at hand, often the result of willful blindness or chosen numbness. It is fearlessness that leads to the rashness that Aristotle speaks about. It's the fearless leader who, rather than lead his people over the chasm to the other side, leads them off the cliff that he refused to fully see.

Far from being fearlessness, courage, remember, *requires* fear. We cannot have courage until we first experience fear. Courage represents the strength of character to allow fear to be present, to not fight it or be cowed by it, and to still remain resolute, clear, and committed. The otherwise daunting presence of fear now becomes a benchmark, one that underlines our commitment, possibly even reinforces it.

Taking it one step further, we might understand courage as the choice to *embrace* fear, using its anxious energy to fuel the fires of our intention, transforming fear into an ally. Fear has now become not only a benchmark for but also a *servant to* our larger, more compelling commitments. In welcoming fear we are in effect saying something like, "Yes, this anxiety tells me that I may be on to something good, something potentially new, something potentially big, possibly even beautiful. So it must be time to get busy." It is reminiscent of Campbell's assertion that the "goal of life is to live with god-like composure on the full rush of energy, like Dionysus riding the leopard, without being torn to pieces."[3] The "full rush" of anxiety now becomes a surge of exhilarating energy, possibly even a source of real power. As a result of embracing fear as an ally, fear has been transposed from a weakness into a strength, from a primitive, hard-wired, and unwarranted warning signal of looming danger into an opening for possibility, vitality, connection, and achievement.

When we choose to allow fear to be there while still moving forward or to embrace fear as an ally, fear is no longer an impediment in furthering our engagement with humankind. Fear has been transformed into courage. By virtue of this in-the-moment choice we empower ourselves to allow the natural impulse toward social engagement and human connection to be realized. The instinct to relate at increasing levels of meaning and power is no longer circumvented by the normal, fear-based tendency to avoid or even flee. And as a result we are more readily able to embrace the risk entailed in being the host, in seeking to contribute and in becoming more fully an adult.

TAKING ACTION: PLAYING TO WIN

There is one last facet of leading and living as an adult we need to consider: the relationship of the adult to authentic success.

The Host and the Will to Win

If the context of this commitment to radical growth, for both the individual leader and the organization, is established by way of the mind-set of the host, how does that mind-set translate to success, accomplishment, and the will to win? After all, the host is not focused on what she can get for herself but on what she can contribute to others. She sees and is committed to the possibility that exists for her guests. She operates from the highest and most comprehensive expression of contribution by owning the larger entity or event for which she is the host, whether it's a party, a relationship, a business enterprise, an educational experience, a social movement, or fund-raising for the United Way.

Yet the host, the true adult, does not play the game of life merely to play the game, to merely make sure that all the players are having fun. He's rejected the implications of the adage "It's not whether you win or lose, it's how you play the game." Of course he accepts the need for civility, ethics, and respect implied by the saying. But he takes exception with the suggestion that losing is an acceptable outcome. He understands that the only way he can serve himself and all those for whom he is host and leader is to win. And so that's how he plays: to win. He recognizes that going to the Super Bowl or reaching the World Cup finals is not the objective. *Winning it* is the objective. Indeed, as surprising as this may be to some, he *has* bought into another colloquialism, the one that declares, "Winning isn't everything. It's the only thing." But he understands this dictum in a way that Vince Lombardi, to whom the quote is attributed, probably never imagined.

The true adult, the host, who gets it about owning her life and truly embracing her causality in life, and gets it about the joy, power, and centrality of service, also understands the importance of being as big as she can possibly be in all arenas of life. That means winning, winning at the highest possible level, for her own sake and above all for the sake of the people she serves, that is, the people she leads. Where she differs from the traditional understanding is that she doesn't need to defeat others to win. That is, her focus is not on those who may stand between her and her success. Winning is not exclusively based on being better than those who compete with her in the game. Others may be playing with her or against her, but being better than them is not her focus. Her concern is with playing her absolute best, playing the game better than she played it yesterday or the day before that or the day before that.

Winning in the traditional sense remains one of her measures, certainly, but it is not the only one of her objectives, not even the primary one. She thrives on and takes unmitigated pleasure in being as big, wise, powerful, compassionate, inclusive, and generous as she can possibly be.

Moreover, the host does not pursue excellence from a sense that he is insufficient, that he is not enough. In other words, he's not subconsciously compensating for some old wound, some deeply buried sense of inadequacy by fighting to be better than the competition. Rather, he has arrived at an understanding that he must be perpetually and joyfully expanding his range, becoming the best he can possibly be . . . simply because it is possible. Indeed, he has understood and embraced still another maxim: "I must be what I can be." Meaning, "I must fulfill the potential I have within." It's a mind-set that says, that knows, "Who I am is fine, and because I have this innate promise, just because it's possible, I must realize it, do everything in my power to realize the joy and exhilaration, the goodness even, that is experienced in the process of becoming all that I still have it within me to be." To paraphrase the old U.S. Army jingle, it's about being all that he can be.

Pudding, Proof, and All That

For those who might think this interpretation of "playing to win" is naïve, perhaps even soft headed, consider once again UCLA basketball coaching legend John Wooden. His fierce, relentless coaching of his players was all about their improvement and growth, about their reach toward excellence, not about defeating their opponents. It was always about being as big and going as far as they could go, becoming what their potential allowed. "I never fixated on winning," Wooden says, "didn't even mention it. Rather, I did everything I could to make sure that all of our players gave everything they had to give, both in practice and in games."[4] And the "soft-headed" result? A record ten NCAA championships during his tenure at UCLA, that is, ten in twelve years (!), as well as endless other NCAA men's basketball records that most experts believe will never be broken.

His secret? An unswerving commitment to individual and team greatness, a commitment to the excellence of perpetually improving, perpetually getting better in all facets of the game and in all facets of life. At every possible moment both Wooden himself and his players were to climb higher, dig deeper, become better than they were last year, last month, last week, yesterday.

When Wooden died, a few days shy of his hundredth birthday, the tributes went on for days, into weeks. Though experts had long been eager to sing his praises (he had previously been hailed by ESPN, for instance, as "the greatest coach of the 20th century"), this time most of the praise came from former players, who seemed to line up to be counted as a product of the Wizard of Westwood, as he was fondly known. Most of these players still regarded him as their coach, many as the father they never had, the leader who had changed, transformed, so many of their lives. What they expressed was reverence and undying love. Wooden was recognized as one of the single greatest leaders in sports and organizational history. Indeed, Wooden was the quintessence of the host, the personification of the transforming leader.

Like Wooden, the host understands competition, achievement, excellence, and success at an entirely different level than the average A-type personality. He understands it at a much higher, far more powerful, and success-generating level. He understands that the game that's a true response to the deeper call of life comprehends excellence as a reward in and of itself; it's the challenging and fulfilling achievement of excellence for excellence's sake. And he grasps this not as an idea, not as some intellectual abstraction, but as an "of course," as a lived-out reality that he experiences firsthand. He understands that to truly elevate the life of those he hosts, those he leads and serves, he must likewise be perpetually elevating his own life, his own success, his own more powerful, more deeply enriched ways of being in life. *Of course*, he understands Wooden's success. He lives it every day in his own life.

SUMMARY

When the world economy collapsed in 2008 there was a groundswell of anger that claimed there were "no grown-ups in charge." The implication was that there weren't any leaders—any adults—who were looking out for the good of the whole. The further implication of the collective outrage was that most people understand that true leaders are concerned with more than their own good, more even than with the good of their tribes. Indeed, the biggest people, whether leaders or "civilians," realize that living a life of contribution to something greater than *me and mine* is not simply a high-minded ideal, a function of sterile obligation, but the only real basis for meaning and joy, strength and true success. They understand that there are two types of people in the world—the host and the guest—and they understand that the bigness they seek, the beauty, goodness, and authentic power they must express in their lives can only be realized as hosts.

What's more, those who answer the call of the transformative ethos know that the adult, the host, does not simply seek the pleasure of his or her guests. He seeks their success. His commitment is to seeing that they win in all aspects of their lives. He has understood that to be all that he can be, he must push himself and those he serves to experience all the richness and beauty that life affords. Excellence and achievement are virtues in and of themselves, and they are virtues because in attaining their summits we are forced to expand our existential range. We are forced to learn new and better ways of being and doing, better and more powerful ways of leading others and living life as we climb the mountain. In achieving excellence, even greatness, from a place of love and from a sense of our fundamental sufficiency and goodness, we serve and elevate all those in our immediate vicinity—our peers and those we lead, and surely those we love the most. The creative movement toward realizing the greater good and achieving extraordinary levels of excellence has a charisma all its own, a charisma that demands a response of integrity.

In chapter 17, we revisit the three-legged stool of transformation, and we take our understanding of adulthood and winning at the highest level and apply it within the larger principles of the transformative mind-set. The call is to act and act in this moment. We now consider, then, transformation in action.

CHAPTER 17

TRANSFORMATION IN ACTION: Power in Five Acts

> The discovery of the will in oneself, and even more the realization that the self and the will are intimately connected, may come as a real revelation which can change, often radically, a person's self-awareness and his whole attitude toward himself, other people, and the world. He perceives that he is a "living subject" endowed with the power to choose, to relate, to bring about changes in his own personality, in others.
>
> **—Roberto Assagioli**

The call of transformation is nothing if not a call to action. All this talk about transformation and responding to the deeper urgings of the life force within is of value only if we translate it into action. Just thinking about it won't do a damn thing. We must act and act now while the knowledge is fresh, while the fires are hot. Not tomorrow. Not next week, but now.

This final chapter of part II is a simple translation (and summarization) of the transformative principles—the three-legged stool—into vivid, concrete action. First we revisit the now-familiar stool. Then we briefly explore five essential *acts* of transformation.

THE TRANSFORMATIVE STOOL REVISITED

As we discussed in chapter 16, the all-encompassing context for personal transformation is the full embrace of true adulthood. The true adult is the individual who understands that he is the host and thus is committed to the welfare of his guests. Thus, the true adult is playing the game at the highest level, playing to win in the broadest and deepest sense. As a consequence he is unavoidably committed to assuring that all of his guests win. Such is the intellectual, emotional, and spiritual space in which transformation takes place.

With the host's sensibility as our context—someone committed to both the greater good of all and to the never-ending pursuit of excellence and achievement—let's briefly revisit our transformative stool (see Figure 17.1). Here the mind-set of the host represents the solid floor upon which the stool stands, its foundation.

Figure 17.1 The Transformative Stool Revisited

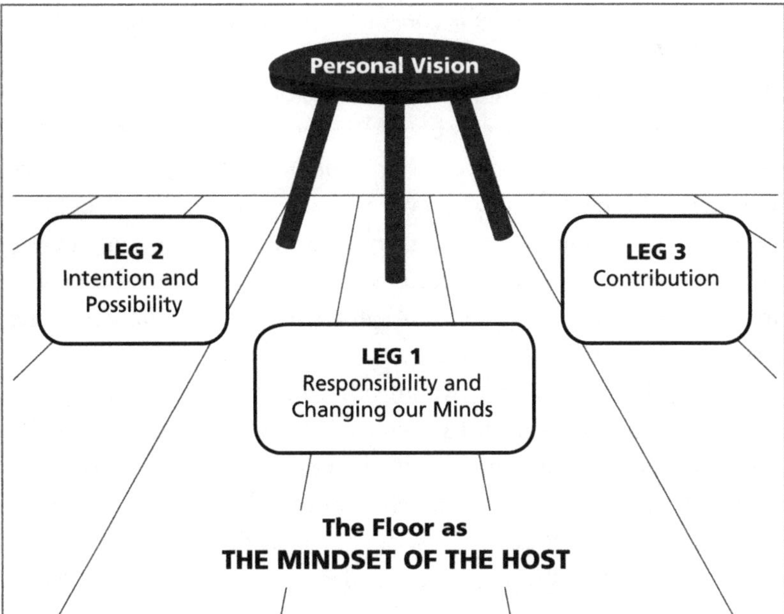

The seat represents the transformative personal vision, one that projects a life of contribution, meaningful and abiding relationships, accomplishment and success, joy and adventure, all of which expand who the person is in all facets of her life. The vision vividly speaks to the impact she has as a leader on the people and the organization that she leads—an impact that is, of course, transforming in nature.

Her embrace of her own transformation—of responsibility and changing her mind, Leg 1 of the stool—goes hand in glove with the context of the host. She owns her life in the same way that she owns the success of the body of people she leads: She's always at cause, always responsible. She embraces the opportunity to change her mind from the perspective that she *must* be what she can be.

As a host she understands that her essential mind-set is that of achievement, not to *try* but to *achieve* what she goes after. Thus, she knows at a cellular level what it means to operate from a place of true intentionality. Whatever she takes on as an intention is in some very real sense done from the moment she shifts to that intentional state. She thrills at living from the domain of possibility, thrills at the prospect of creating what has never before existed. Thus she realizes Leg 2, *intention and possibility*, of the transformative stool.

As a host, her very being is *contribution*, Leg 3. She knows that as a participant in life she must own not just *her* life, but to some extent life itself. She sees herself as a steward, as one in whom care for the planet, for society, and for its people has been entrusted. With sober-minded humility and awakened gratitude she quietly seeks to give herself to whomever and whatever is in front of her. She delights in the unexpected opportunity to transcend her ego and contribute—there's never any fanfare or pretense about it. She knows the deep, abiding joy of forgetting herself, of seeing and serving the other, whether she feels like it or not.

Indeed, she sees the sorrow and suffering in lives of so many, and she lives to see the gratuitous, unnecessary suffering eliminated. As one who has suffered a bit herself, she understands compassion (literally, "suffering with") and therefore knows that she is on the Earth to make a lasting difference. Yes, of course, as one who leads her life she lives for the adventure, the joy, the next challenge, the experience of life's abundance, accomplishment and success, but simultaneously she understands, paradoxically, that it's not about her, in a sense, it never has been. It is about those she can serve along the way, those to whom she, with her many gifts and talents, can contribute in such a way that their lives will be different, better, possibly even transformed. With every passing day she is more fully the host, more completely the adult. She gets it about, in fact she *is,* contribution. She understands the secret, the *real* secret to life.

TRANSFORMATION IN FIVE ACTS

The transformative process in five acts is a prescriptive summary, laying out the nuts-and-bolts actions of leadership and personal transformation. Each of the five acts is non-negotiable and requires immediate action. They assume a vivid and foundational commitment to life, to our lives, to being and becoming what we still have it within us to become and get done as leaders and as people. It's time to wake up, summon the necessary courage, and get busy.

In Act 1, *creating, recreating, clarifying the vision*, we recognize the untapped promise within and give it the richness and depth of a new picture of what's possible. It requires a willingness to see with new eyes, to remember, and to believe in our own capacity to have the life and leadership we truly desire. See chapter 4. If you haven't done the exercise, DO IT. If you have done it, now is the time to clarify and reinforce it.

In Act 2, *creating a fierce intention*, we establish our commitment to the full realization of that promise; until we are intentional about this promise, there is little transformative movement. Intention is the fuel that makes the vision possible. Without it, all of this is just a lot of blather. See chapter 13.

In Act 3, *identifying the paradigm, targeting the critical points*, we make the trusting descent within, uncovering our constricting, false perceptions, identifying the false, critical point beliefs to be reshaped in the transforming process. The vivid steps build in detail upon and add to the actions suggested in chapters 9 and 10. And remember, this piece takes a good deal of persistence—these unconscious beliefs of ours can be stubborn buggers. Get to it and stay with it!

Act 4, *creating a practice that changes our minds*, is the creation and use of a daily responsibility ritual, designed to do nothing less than reshape our brains by lighting up certain aspects of our critical point circuitry (while damping down others), thus liberating our authentic power and purpose. Based on the science of neuroplasticity, the daily practice is how we permanently change our minds, and as the name suggests, it requires daily use. Don't wait until you get your ritual perfect. Get something down on paper and then start doing it—you'll continuously refine it all through the journey. See chapters 11 and 12.

Act 5, *creating regular interruptions, asserting the truth,* is reinforcing the daily practice by regularly interrupting our old, faulty patterns of thought throughout the day. At well-chosen times we briefly interrupt our day (one to two minutes at the most) and assert (declare and *be*) our truest selves, the truth of who we are, what we are up to, and what we must get done with our leadership and our lives. It is simple and essential. It's only sixty seconds a couple of times a day, but when the statements are well chosen, done as a supplement to the

Figure 17.2 The Response to the Call of Transformation in Five Acts

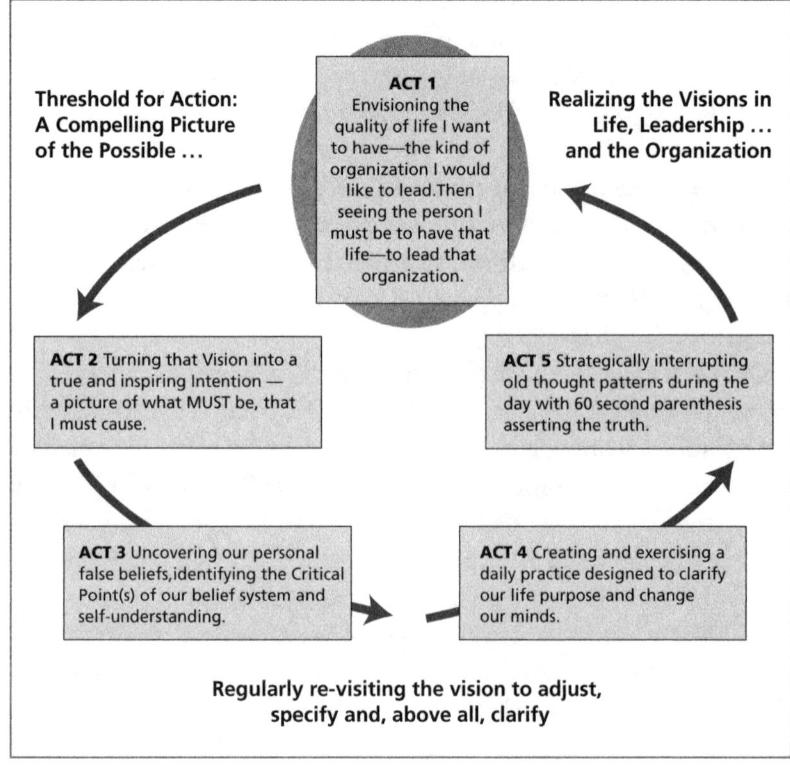

ritual, and done with commitment, they have a penetrating impact on who we are, how we lead, and what we achieve. Guaranteed. The five acts are illustrated in Figure 17.2.

SUMMARY

This transforming process in five acts is the means by which we move from managing to leading our lives, from adequately leading others to powerfully leading others. It's the means by which we put our metaphor, the transformative stool with three legs, into effect. Answering life's call means nothing less than calling forth the best we have within: imagining a better, braver, more powerful life and leadership (the seat); understanding and learning to live from true responsibility and doing the work of changing our minds (Leg 1); learning to operate from possibility and the highest level of commitment, intentionality (Leg 2); and stepping into authentic adulthood by living as the host, operating from ever-greater degrees of contribution (Leg 3).

As leaders we do this rigorous, transformative work so that we can better move others to meaningful action, so that we can more fruitfully and powerfully lead the organization. We do it so that we can become truly transformative in how we lead, accepting the "radical" assumption that holding people front and center—developing them, caring for them, and settling for nothing less than excellence *from* them—yields far greater returns than the conventional transactional model. It boldly promises anyone who'll listen that the extraordinary awaits the leader who is willing to embrace transformation's vivid but demanding ways. To a more comprehensive consideration of transformative leadership within the organization, then, we turn in part III.

Convention Turned on Its Ear:

Transformative Leadership and the Organization

CHAPTER 18

EXPERIMENTS IN RADICAL HONESTY: The World has Changed—So Must How We Lead

> People who shut their eyes to reality simply invite their own destruction, and anyone who insists on remaining in a state of innocence long after that innocence is dead turns himself into a monster.
>
> **—James Baldwin**

We must face up to the fact that the world has changed. And it ain't gonna un-change. The change didn't begin with the financial collapse of 2008, nor did it necessarily cause that collapse. But because of this change, putting the pieces back together in a post–Great Recession world will require a fundamentally different approach to how we understand leadership, business leadership in particular.

At least two distinct things have come together to cause this change. First, the social upheaval of the 1960s, with all of its political and moral discomfort, represents the start of a broader shift in our basic understanding of the nature of democracy and individual rights. Over the subsequent years many of the principles of the "subversive sixties" (good and bad) have become a part of mainstream thought in the contemporary world. The baby boomers, and more important, the children reared by the boomers (who increasingly constitute our workforce), thus, have a very different understanding of what could and should come from life in general and from their professional lives in particular. Their expectations for what a work experience should be invariably go far beyond those of their parents and grandparents. What they want and need from their leaders, therefore, is fundamentally, in some instances even radically, different from previous generations, particularly in terms of collaboration, contribution, and meaning.[1] And bemoaning the unique sensibility of Gens X and Y does little to address the leadership challenge they present.

The second aspect of the irrevocable change is more vividly and abundantly documented and more tangibly experienced every day: The technological explosion of the digital age (the information age) has fundamentally and permanently altered the nature and speed of communication (and the extent to which information is available) and given a whole new meaning to idea of networking (social media), and thus has created a situation where far greater transparency is unavoidable and rightly expected. Though these changes may not have caused our current economic/social malaise, they surely demand that how we address our mess be different, fundamentally different. We'll do well to keep them top of mind as we move forward.

THE NEEDED SEA CHANGE

As we survey the economic, social, and organizational landscape, what we see is a kind of wreckage that most of us have never before imagined. Slowly, it seems, we are coming to grips with the fact that we've missed the leadership boat. And while we may wring our hands in confusion about the nature of that missed departure—a debacle so vast that it has led to a near total collapse of our confidence in our leaders, especially our political and business leaders—this much should be obvious: The old transactional approach has failed and failed miserably. It's not the solution we need, especially in view of this changed and changing world. But stranded alone on the dock with no other ships in sight it's difficult to imagine how we will make our way across that churning sea.

Of course, this is the point at which transformative leadership, unapologetically (there's little time for false humility) steps into the leadership breach. TL soberly raises its hand and says, "You may want to look over here."

Transformative leadership understands some of the fundamental things that transactional leadership misses. At the most basic level it understands that what we are leading is an organization of *people*.

To which the ordinary leader, a bit annoyed, replies, "Okay, fine, whatever, I guess that much would seem obvious."

The transformative leader continues, saying that people are our *primary* responsibility.

"Whoa there, now," the transactional leader protests. "What does *that* mean? We ain't talking about charity here. Like the guy in *The Godfather* says, 'It's not personal, it's business.' Get it? Business is about, well, *business*. That means money, profits."

Actually, that's not entirely so, the transformative leader replies. That assumption does not comport with the larger reality, one that we have happily ignored, one that we ignore at our own continuing peril. The simple truth is that nothing should be of greater importance than the organization's people—not the stock price, not the market share, not even the bottom line. Nothing matters more than the people, because business, like it or not, is a *human* enterprise, a tough, demanding human enterprise but a human enterprise all the same. Business is to serve people, *all* of the people, not merely, not even primarily, the bottom line.

"Okay, that's it," the transactional leader says. "That's crossing the line. Are you completely nuts? That's the very soft-headed mush that'll lead us all to ruin, completely absurd," he warns, apparently unaware that we already stand at ruin's doorstep. "I thought we were talking about business," he firmly continues, "real-world, eat-or-be-eaten business. That's just goin' *way* too far."

Of course, from the transformative perspective the problem is that the transactional world of business simply does not go far enough. Not now when everything happens with that digitized speed and non-negotiable transparency we've spoken about—the Wikileaks phenomenon being but one extreme example of a reality that's not going away anytime soon. Not today when the twenty-, thirty- and forty-somethings expect so much more from their leaders and from organizational life.

Because of this forever-changed, new world, the flaws in some of our most basic assumptions about leading (in business and otherwise) have been exposed for all to see. And see them we must. We must have the raw courage to embrace that radical honesty we spoke of at the outset. We cannot afford to escape into the absurd denial that would suggest that all that is needed is a few thoughtful adjustments. Not when our honesty reveals that the extensive greed and corruption that led to our economic malaise are the nearly-inevitable consequences of the old transactional approach. In order not to become the monsters suggested by the James Baldwin quote at the beginning of the chapter, we must be willing to rethink some of those fundamental assumptions, rethink those assumptions about business and the organization, assumptions about leadership and life, and in so doing consider the bold, perhaps audacious alternative that transformative leadership represents.

The remaining chapters of the book guide us in doing precisely that.

THE TL BASICS REVISITED AND EXPANDED

The transformative method, you'll recall, asserts two primary principles or objectives that suggest two further objectives. The first is the growth and development of the people, and the second, the achievement of excellence at all levels as the result of this development. The achievement of these objectives requires a third element, the leader's commitment to his own growth, as a leader and as a human being. The fourth element, profits (and other objective results) are crucial to the success of the model but not as the primary end, not as the be-all to end all. Profits are understood as the quantifiable measure of the leader's effectiveness in growing and leading the people (and herself). In addition to keeping the machine running successfully, profit is seen as the byproduct of, and tool for measuring, the two higher ends, the people's development and excellence.

The four key elements of transformative leadership, then, are:

- a commitment to the growth of the people as a primary end
- a commitment to the realization of excellence via the people's growth and as a means to foster that very growth
- a commitment by the organization's leaders to develop themselves, both as people and as leaders
- the use of hard results (profits and beyond) as the measure of the leaders' success as leaders—in growing themselves, producing excellence, and above all in developing the organization's people

Beyond these four essential principles, and in addition to the five do-functions of transformative leaders discussed in chapter 2 (which are addressed further in the remaining chapters), there is one other underlying objective the transformative leader pursues to help realize the people's growth and the achievement of excellence (and the extraordinary).

Committed to Meeting the Four Higher Needs

Given that the TL organization is clear about its dual responsibilities of creating excellence (E) on the one hand and the growth (G) of its people on the other, it is conscious and intentional about addressing all four of the higher human needs within the workplace. Because, simply enough, addressing each one of the needs contributes, directly or indirectly, to the fulfillment of both primary responsibilities:

- Addressing the need to love and be loved, the first need, supports both primary TL objectives indirectly: When people are cared for and are encouraged to express caring, self-protective defenses are necessarily dropped and thus, talents and capacities are liberated (as addressed in detail in chapter 15). The result is we are expanding ourselves (G), and those liberated talents can be harnessed toward greater achievement well done (E).
- Addressing the need to grow, the second need, directly speaks to both responsibilities: Intentionally challenging and growing our people satisfies the need for growth (G), obviously, and growth is measured and supported by the stretch to achieve quantifiable accomplishment (goals/numbers), especially the accomplishment of excellence (E).
- Addressing the need to contribute, the third need, directly enhances growth and indirectly encourages excellence: The experience of authentic, consistent contribution to someone else almost invariably leads to greater collaboration and a sense of shared purpose, a sense of being part of something larger than self, which amounts to an expansion or deepening of personal identity (G), which in the transformative context can, and usually does, lend itself to achievement and excellence because becoming larger or more complex in one's self understanding

facilitates the release of otherwise inhibited talents (see chapter 15), and collaboration in a focused and directed environment typically supports high level accomplishment (E).

- Addressing the need for meaning, the fourth need, indirectly supports both objectives: When what we are doing is experienced and understood as meaningful and important, we are much more willing to invest ourselves to a degree that will afford high-level achievement (E), and the experience of meaning via a commitment to a larger purpose almost invariably demands greater development and growth to ensure its full realization—our talents and capacities are called upon, and we are thereby stretched or grown (G).

The correlation between speaking to all four needs within the organizational context and the growth and achievement of excellence of and by the employees assumes a larger transformative context, one that is driven by a vision, one that is unapologetic in its commitment to employee well-being, and one that is courageous and bold in its commitment to being and accomplishing the extraordinary. In other words, it's an approach with guts and some strong, sharp teeth. (The specifics of how the four needs are addressed is taken up in chapter 20—a case study of a TL organization, in chapter 21—on vision and on team, and in chapter 22—on the nature of TL teamness).

For all of its seeming radicalness, the transformative leadership approach, as we will see, also just makes good, basic sense. When people feel valuable and valued, are being challenged and are truly growing, are cared for and encouraged to care for others, and when they have a sense that what they are doing is meaningful, they show up fundamentally different than when these things are absent. As we've suggested, they are likely to go home at night feeling good about themselves and are likely to return the following day more purposeful, more committed, more creative and insightful, and more willing to go the extra step—without even being asked to do so. It only makes sense that these sorts of organizations would out-perform their transactional competition.

SUMMARY

Anyone who is willing to be honest knows that something is fundamentally broken with how we think about business and the organization. It doesn't require an expertise in economics to grasp this truth—merely a modicum of integrity. The solution to our brokenness is not going to be found in a tape and glue repair job, however cleverly we may apply the adhesives. The solution is found in, and begins with, an uncommon level of honesty, an honesty that in comparison with the old ways of doing things is radical. We must be honest about the fact that the old, transactional, exclusively for-profit model no longer seems to work. In fact, it represents the context that allowed for, even encouraged, the base behaviors that led the world economy off the cliff. Remember, the quid pro quo transactional model endorses an instrumentalist view of business leadership: the leader is the instrument of the people, used to get and keep a job (or get a promotion), et cetera), and the people are an instrument of the leader, used to create shareholder value; its what we can get for ourselves that matters and everyone is everyone else's tool, which readily devolves into the dehumanizing greed we have recently witnessed.

The solution, at least in part, begins with fundamentally rethinking the nature of the leadership model we employ and reimagining what we understand as the end game of leadership and business itself. And the best method for doing that, for reinventing ourselves as leaders and as organizations, is found in the transformative leadership model. The brave new world of this still-new millennium requires a bold and better understanding of what it means to lead. For those leaders who will create the twenty-first century, then, we now turn to the essentials of leading the transformative way, first by considering the qualities of the leader who emerges from the TL model.

CHAPTER 19

THE TRANSFORMATIVE LEADER IN PROFILE

Real beauty is my aim.

—Mohandas K. Gandhi

Let's not mince words. Transformative leadership says the entire context in which we've been holding business and organizational life is wrong—or at least is wrong for us today, wrong for the world we now live in. The transformative approach says that a new type of leadership and a new type of leader is called for. A new type of individual at the helm, a true grown-up in charge. Get the gist? Let's get on with it, then.

THE TRANSFORMATIVE LEADER IN PROFILE: AN IDEAL TYPE

The picture of the transformative leader that we are about to paint is a somewhat stylized picture of an "ideal type." But it is not created from whole cloth, nor does it necessarily reflect the characteristics of the perfect transformative leader. Rather, *ideal* here refers to the idea or concept of this type of leader. What we look at next, then, is an abstraction, a composite that nevertheless is made up of real characteristics from real people, primarily people I've worked with or observed over the course of my work with various kinds of leaders in various types of circumstances. In so doing we will examine seven of the essential character traits of such a leader.

Character Trait 1: Understands Self as a Work in Progress

The transformative leader is an individual who understands himself and his leadership as a work in progress. He has not been seduced—by his own fantasies and insecurities or by the perceived expectations of others—into the common folly of thinking that he should already know it all, that he should be complete as a leader. He realizes that leadership, *all* leadership, is on-the-job training. Always. And he has a strong enough sense of self as a person and as a leader to freely admit he has weaknesses that warrant attention.

As a consequence he understands that it is a strength to be able to acknowledge to his followers the areas of himself that he is developing further. He's smart enough to know that when done with integrity and discretion, revealing his vulnerabilities enhances rather than diminishes his authority and power. His recognized talents—courage, vision, compassion, relationship with results, et cetera—are all reasons he *is* a leader. But as a transformative leader his awareness and honesty about his need to *become*, to develop further as, a leader is a characteristic at least as important as any other trait. Because first, without it he is completely unable to expand his range, become better than he already is, as a leader and as a person. Second, it allows him to be human among the humans he leads. "He's our leader, yes," his followers think, "but he's still one of us."

Character Trait 2: Gauges Success by Impact on People

There are four essential ways by which the transformative leader measures success, three of which are based on her impact on people and the other is the consequence of that impact. She understands at a core level that her primary bosses are not the ones above her on the organizational chart. Those may be her formal and designated bosses, and in obvious and important ways they *are* her bosses, but in the larger scheme of things they are secondary.

The de facto reality is that her primary bosses are the people she leads. Because she has authority over them and because she more than anyone else influences their professional lives, though she may report to her designated bosses, she accounts to her followers. She accounts to them for how effective she is in leading them—for the quality of their work experience under her leadership and for the measurable success they achieve as a consequence. Her job is not to merely produce a quantifiable result, not even a spectacular quantifiable result. Her job is to produce spectacular results through, as a consequence of, those people, results that are a clear reflection of the degree to which she has fulfilled her primary obligations: affecting and developing the people she leads such that they attain a level of excellence that issues in exceptional, measurable results.

Thus, the first measure of her success is her effectiveness in growing her followers, and the second is in the quantifiable results (such as profits, market share, et cetera) that are an inevitable consequence of that growth. She gets that these two kinds of results (employee growth and results-oriented excellence) are complementary responsibilities and that success is not possible unless both are realized. She understands that her followers must have a tangible sense of growth and accomplishment, as well as the empirical result to prove it. Though this accountability in serving her followers is generally an unspoken, unwritten accountability (they have no authority over her and she never formally accounts to them in the manner a subordinate would), it is an accountability all the same.

As a consequence of her employees' success, she recognizes that she's in a unique position to influence her formally designated bosses, to lead her leaders and to do so in a way that elevates them even though she exercises no express authority over them. Thus, she looks for every opportunity to encourage, inspire, nudge, even confront and challenge her leaders so that they understand themselves, their leadership, their possibilities in richer, deeper, more meaningful and nuanced ways. The opportunity to elevate and develop her leaders, then, is the third measure of her success.

As a transformative leader she understands the interconnected nature of things. She accepts the reality of her indirect but powerful impact on the families of the people who work for her. She knows that how she is with her direct reports influences how they are with their direct reports, which further influences how *they* are with their direct reports, down through the organizational hierarchy, out onto the street and into the home. How she leads may have an immediate and material impact on whether or not a child of one of her employees goes to college, say, or whether a child is neglected or even abused.

Therefore she makes it a first-level priority in her job to ensure that her people go home at night better than when they came in that morning. And she knows that this doesn't mean they are to be coddled; in some instances it means they leave with a loving but firm "kick in the seat." Irrespective of how it is achieved, her employees are to be in the process of becoming better human beings who therefore have a more positive impact on their families. Thus, she has even created measurement devices to gauge the organization's effectiveness in serving the good of its employees' families. The improved well-being of the families she indirectly affects, then, is her fourth success measure.

As a host, a true adult, she holds and owns the entire scope of the organization's influence, measuring her leadership impact from top to bottom and on all parts in between. She thrives on the meaning this brings to her life. Such an understanding of her role as a leader is not a burden; it's an honor, both humbling and inspiring.

Character Trait 3: Has Vivid Relationship with Success

The intention of the transformative leader to care for, to develop his followers does not soften his commitment to winning at the highest level. Far from it. His commitment to his people's expansion as organizational players and as human beings demands that he teach his followers how to win in the biggest way possible. His natural competitive fire has been transmuted into a desire, a burning desire, to have all those who fall within the scope of his influence be successful. His competitive zeal has been transformed from a need to defeat others into a passion for creating success and abundance out to the very edges of his leadership reach.

He understands that he is not merely to have his followers try to achieve, try to accomplish, try to succeed. He understands that in the domain of results, to quote the great cinematic sage, Yoda, we simply "do or do not. . . . There is no try." His stand is to create powerful people, people who know how to succeed, all the way up and all the way down the organization. In the final analysis, he has developed an extraordinary, surprisingly supple, unassuming, and surely unattached relationship with results and success.

Another way of saying all of this is that the transformative leader lives a life that is empowered by the context of his achievements. He may have a multitude of accomplishments and an abundance of material wealth, yet those accomplishments and that wealth are nothing more than extensions of who he is as a human being. He is not lavish or showy, and he surely is not in the business of collecting trophies. Awards are of little interest (though he accepts them with humility and gratitude). Rather, he is in the business of expanding who he is as a leader, as a human being, for the sheer joy and satisfaction of self-expansion. The trophies, awards, and wealth are mere by-products of his commitment to becoming all that he can possibly be.

No, he is not concerned with gathering "things" around him. He never even thinks about it. The success with which he adorns his life is a natural reflection of his passion for excellence, for beauty, for goodness, a reflection of his understanding of life's abundance. In fact, he gives away as much as he has and still has more than he knows what to do with. His greatest achievement, as far as he is concerned, is his increasing capacity to lead others in learning to generate expansive success at this level. Ultimately, though, he knows that the achievements, the wealth, the abundance, and even the pleasure in leading others to achieve are all simply pieces of the larger whole that is the context of his life. And in that context he gives, he grows, he loves, he serves, he creates, he inspires, and yes, he achieves with an unaffected and sober-minded brilliance.

Character Trait 4: Committed (Fiercely) to Self-Development

The transformative leader understands that authentic growth and lasting development as a leader and as a person requires a lot of hard work. Thus she "takes herself on" with unwavering intention and thoughtful discipline. That she is the causal agent in her own life, that she is in fact responsible for her life as it is and as it shall be, is a given that she embraces with gusto. She understands that responsibility is not something that she can *take* for her life, because she already *is* responsible.

With this grasp of her causality, she further understands that in being human many important facets of her self-understanding and her understanding of the world remain out of conscious view. She recognizes that to truly grow she must do the rigorous work of changing her mind at this profound level. Finally, she understands that these old constrictive patterns of thought are resilient and selfish, that they die hard.

Consequently, she has made a commitment to doing the difficult, rigorous work of establishing a formal, daily practice, one that she guards jealously, assuring her faithfulness to her growth journey. She understands her practice must focus on things ranging from reminding herself of her deeper and higher commitments; to undoing her false limiting beliefs and creating new patterns around the truth of her bigness, goodness, and power; to calmly, meditatively perhaps, deepening her connection to and service of life. She also knows that her daily practice is a work in progress just as she is a work in progress. It's a living, dynamic experience. Therefore, she's always on the alert for ways to improve and update the practice as it unfolds in her life every day.

Her commitment to expanding her range as a leader and person is also manifest in her practice of regularly looking for opportunities to stretch herself (risk) professionally and in her understanding of what it means to contribute to others. She understands that remaining safely within the boundaries of her comfort zone does not lend itself to meaningful development. Thus, she regularly reaches out for support and challenge from her peers, her superiors, and her subordinates. She has learned to be *comfortable with discomfort*, learned that fear is just . . . fear. It's an emotion, one that she has made into an ally, into another opportunity for self-expansion.

Character Trait 5: Lives as a True Giver

Expanding the breadth and depth of who he is and how he shows up in life, the transformative leader knows, is tricky business. He understands that personal transformation cannot be easily codified. And since he also knows that "you teach best what you most need to learn," he aggressively seeks out others who are on a similarly committed path of leadership and life growth in order to push them, in order to challenge and support them, in order to invest himself in their leadership and personal growth. At the deepest level, he has come to recognize that sometimes the best thing he can do for his own growth and development is simply to give himself away. Forget about himself. Lose himself in someone else, in her life, in her journey, in her being and becoming.

He often remembers that one of the truly great joys in life is in selfless service of another. What some have called the very "secret to life" is all about getting past his puny self-absorption and seeing life from a larger perspective that is an ever-expanding sense of what the word "us" really means. With increasing regularity, therefore, he looks for the opportunity to serve, to contribute, to give of himself. To give to whoever may be in need. It's not so that he can get something for himself (that's the ironic key), not so that he "feels good" about himself. It's so he can give, connect, be a part of the greater whole from which he comes. It's so he can remember who and what he is as a leader, remember why he is leading in the first place.

The simple act of consciously choosing to give, to be available and present for his fellow human beings, has become a central part of how he understands himself. He has begun to understand why it is viewed as the *real* secret, the true key to creating a life of joy and meaning. He lives it out at every possible turn. "How can I contribute here?" has become his guiding question in life.

Character Trait 6: Gets the Centrality of Vision

The transformative leader vividly understands how misunderstood the whole vision thing really is, misunderstood in terms of what a vision is and misunderstood in terms of its central importance and essential power in genuine creation. She understands that a vision is a complex, compelling picture of what does not yet exist, an image rich in detail and texture, a mosaic of meaning and vitality that by its very presence in her mind calls forth her bigness. But above all, she realizes that the pulsating rhythms of a vision in a leader's imagination, in *her* imagination, are nothing less than a new world seeking to be born.

Thus she realizes that Albert Einstein's assertions about the importance of imagination are not merely the whimsical musings of an idiosyncratic genius. Not at all. She gets that the wise professor was, if anything, understating his case. She understands that the importance of an authentic, compelling, and clear vision cannot be overstated.

Consequently, the transformative leader puts considerable effort into constructing, refining, and periodically re-refining her own personal vision as a leader and as a human being, and she encourages her people to do the same. This personal vision is absolutely central in how she will shape her leadership and her life, in how she will expand her personal and professional range, in what she will bring into her life and what she will cause in the lives of others.

Moreover, she realizes that *not* having a vision is not humanly possible. She often tells her followers, "Every person alive has a vision"—by which she means a dominant and detailed expectation of what is possible and what is not possible for them and their lives. "Most don't know it though," she says, "don't realize that all that they've created in their lives is a direct consequence of the unnoticed vision they hold for themselves. By creating a new, more worthy vision and becoming intentional about it, you'll change your life." She knows. She's done it, is doing it. Virtually every dimension of her life is informed by that vivid picture of who she is becoming, what she is up to with her life, and what she must get done, and it's a picture that she *loves,* one that inspires her because it speaks to who she is at the very core of her being.

Of course she has also trained her powerful attention and energy on the vision of the organization she leads. Through dent of the hard work of imagining a different future than the reality that currently exists (and the one that existed in the past), she has inspired her senior executives to diligently cocreate, together to imagine and reimagine a future for the organization that is both detailed and compelling. It has not come easily, but it is a thing of beauty, something that elevates all who come in contact with it.

She has been diligent in assuring that all of the executives who are party to its creation are fully dedicated to its *full* realization, or as she likes to say, "committed out of their gourds to making it happen," regardless of the challenges they will have to overcome in the process. Thus, confident of the integrity of their commitment, she and her team have unveiled the vision to the larger organization, presented it in a "thousand different ways" until the people in the organization have begun to understand that this leadership body means it when they say, "With your help, we're gonna do whatever is necessary to make this thing a reality."

Character Trait 7: Is an Intention Wizard

The transformative leader is unafraid to accept the simple truth that every leader who has ever achieved anything worth doing has operated from an unswerving commitment to the what-must-be of it all. That is, he is willing to accept the fact that he and *only he* will be the reason his lofty proposition turns out and turns out as he deems it must. Of course, he enrolls his colleagues and his subordinates into sharing his intentionality. But he never shrinks from the fact that if it is to happen, it is up to him to lead with bold, clear, unswerving intention. He understands that the courage to truly be intentional is and has always been that state of mind that separates great leadership from leadership pretense.

He doesn't walk around talking about intention. And he never uses intention as a weapon—never glibly tells his followers that they're "just not being intentional enough." Rather, when he perceives insufficient commitment, he investigates and uncovers the reason for the blockage or resistance—whether it's fear (self-doubt), lack of understanding about the desired outcome, or anything else—and then seeks to enroll his followers (or himself) in the true possibility.

Furthermore, he is not careless or casual about intentionality. He knows that authentic intention requires considerable intellectual energy and sustained work and, of course, a fierce desire. Thus he is discrete in choosing what he will invest himself in, in deciding what he will become intentional about. He understands the importance of being clear about what is truly important, clear about what it means to be committed at the deepest level. But once he has chosen, once he becomes clear, everyone knows it, and few doubt it will be achieved.

As a result, he is known throughout the industry as the leader most likely to "get it done when it matters the most." He often makes it look distressingly easy. But he knows better, knows that it takes consistent focus, intellectual and emotional discipline, and a burning, well-thought-out desire. But once this is all in place, he makes it happen. Onlookers can think it's wizardry if they like, but he knows what it takes to be intentional. Indeed, as far as his followers are concerned, he *is* intention.

A NON-FINAL WORD ON TRANSFORMATIVE TRAITS

These seven traits are not the final word in our idea of a transformative leader. In fact, I can almost hear some of my clients protesting now: "It is inconceivable that you would leave out *courage* as a central characteristic." And I would have a hard time rebutting this challenge. After all, the transformative leader is committed to realizing the extraordinary, which invariably means overturning major aspects of the status quo, which further means experiencing "pushback," often violent, from those comfortable with and most deeply invested in the status quo. She's commonly the focus of attacks by those disinclined to seek greatness and usually resentful of those so inclined. Courage, therefore, is almost always a prerequisite. Indeed, courage is called for again and again in the TL approach.

The truth is there are many additional characteristics that are common, arguably essential, when embracing leadership as a response to the urge of transformation. In addition to courage, ways of being like openness and confidence—a strong sense of self or of one's abiding strengths—are high on the list. Therefore, it needs to be clear that our list of seven traits is not exhaustive but rather suggestive, intended to begin painting a picture of what a transformation-oriented leader looks like.

SUMMARY

After all is said and done, perhaps the best way of depicting the transformative leader is to say that he has a deeply felt sense that something profound, something far greater than him, something of lasting meaning and substance, seeks to be realized through his leadership. Whatever else that new emerging reality may turn out to be, he knows beyond any shadow of a doubt that it is to be a thing of exquisite beauty. He is, after all, compelled by the possibilities of life itself. Whether that power and beauty is expressed in a building designed by Frank Gehry, in a largely peaceful democracy movement in Egypt, or in an extraordinary business enterprise that is a revelation in its brilliant success, it is power and beauty all the same.

In chapter 20 we look more deeply at the expression of transformative leadership as it is manifest in the organization. We look at an organization that has embraced the transformative possibility and has the results to prove it.

CHAPTER 20

ADVENTURES IN AUDACITY I:
A Transformative, Visionary Organization—Cox Arizona

> We often take the limits of our vision for the limits of the world.
>
> **—Arthur Schopenhauer**

Not all leaders have the strength of character, the insight and imagination, the courage and the love to grasp the transformative approach. Fewer still have the staying power to see it through. But for those who do, I guarantee this: They will begin to experience organizational life as an adventure. They will have moments of unbridled joy and know a degree and quality of success that heretofore could scarcely be imagined. Guaranteed. But they must be prepared to pay the price, and that price is considerable: Arrows will surely fly, and they'll be directed at you and your key people; challenges to your leadership (and perhaps at times even your sanity) will be leveled, often by "well-meaning" people. The jealous will set upon you in surprising ways, overtly and covertly. You'll begin to discover in short order who your real friends are . . . and aren't.

Remember, by definition the transformative leader seeks nothing less than wholesale transformation, not a nudge here, a tweak there. *Transformation.* And at every level in the organization. By definition, they are committed to the extraordinary. And, remember, there's a damn good reason why the extraordinary doesn't happen every day. It's expensive. It's a pricey commodity, one for which few have the stomach (or guts, or any other anatomical metaphor for bravery you might like), one that few have the honesty and will, the strength and character to sustain. And very, *very* few have the staying power to achieve it alone. In fact, a case can be made for the assertion that *no one* has the capacity to achieve the truly extraordinary alone.

This much is clear: If we are to achieve the extraordinary in the organization—business, educational, nonprofit, military, governmental, or otherwise—two fundamental realities must be in place. First, a team, a *true* team, is required—not the functional, or semi-functional, groups that so often pass for teams in today's organizations. The sad fact is that most so-called organizational leaders don't have a clue what a team is. Frankly, most athletes and coaches who play on or lead "teams" don't know the first thing about true teamness. What is a true leadership team? Short answer: an authentically connected body of honest, talented, smart, committed-out-of-their-minds leaders who are willing to courageously and boldly go the distance for that team and even more important, go the distance for something far, far greater than themselves and the team.

This something that is greater than themselves is the second non-negotiable: It's a vision, a living, breathing, bold, compelling picture of the future that, in the minds of those who hold it, *must* be realized. It is not a glossy mission statement or a string of goals held together by flowery, multisyllabic words—though a mission and goals are often constituent parts of the vision. It is a picture, a painting, of richness and depth that tells a story of a world that does not yet exist, one that is in the process of being born, a three-dimensional world of detail and texture that each member of the organization can imagine him- or herself being a part of. But before we investigate either of these elements, a look at an organization that has manifested both realities and in fact is a transformative case in point seems in order.

A STUDY IN TL SUCCESS: COX ARIZONA

In 2000, the Arizona "system" of Cox Communications, Inc., (CCI) had not met a budget for three years, their P&L was in shambles, and overall morale was in the dump. Today, however, it's an entirely different story. The extensive Cox Arizona system is a model of organizational effectiveness, innovation, and productivity, and Arizona is the U.S.-based company's largest and most successful region. A $1.7-billion operation blanketing the state, it is the envy of cable systems industry wide. What caused this dramatic change, a change that represents a genuine transformation?

First, it took a new leader who had the courage to imagine and commit to a whole new array of outcomes. Second, it took a serious reassessment of the organization's entire leadership body by that leader. Third, it took a serious reorientation of their leadership approach, leading to the creation of a senior leadership team with a powerful vision, and then . . . transformation. And staggering profits followed.

J. Stephen (Steve) Rizley took over Cox Arizona at this pivotal point in time, in 2000. A deeply caring but tough-minded, naturally gifted leader, Steve immediately went to work focusing on the people in his organization. In his thoughtful and bold hands, a transformative approach to leadership yielded remarkable growth—like growing from $700 million to $1.3 billion in a little more than two years. So what specifically did Rizley and Cox Arizona do?

Rizley instinctively knew that for the organization to grow not only did he need the right leaders in place beside and beneath him but he also needed people who were themselves growing, professionally as well as personally. He understood that the growth of an organization mirrored the growth of its people, especially its leaders. Thus he set out looking for a leadership approach that was growth based. The model he settled on, as you may have guessed, was transforming integrative leadership. With the guidance of an outside consulting firm (Owl Sight Intentions, which in the interest of full disclosure, happens to be my firm), he began aggressively implementing the transformative method.

Having replaced all but one of the leaders he inherited, Rizley's first area of focus was forging this new collection of individual leaders into a real team. He accurately understood that changing an entire organizational culture must begin in earnest at the top. With his outside support, Rizley initiated the transformative process that in the first year alone entailed five two-day off-site TL workshops, held variously at resorts in Sedona, Tucson, and Scottsdale, Arizona.

The objective of each intensive two-day was not to get away and hang out together. It was, rather, in a sequestered and controlled environment, to confront, create, collaborate, and become:

1. to *confront* themselves and each other about what was important to them as leaders and individuals (personally), to *confront* their deeper reasons, their real reasons, for being leaders, and to *confront* their strengths and weaknesses as leaders
2. to *create* a radically honest and fearlessly caring team environment committed to calling forth the best that each individual and the team as a whole had to give
3. to *collaborate* in envisioning, owning, and causing the future that would be for Cox Arizona
4. to *become,* by way of these three endeavors, more powerful and complete individual leaders and an authentic *team* of leaders

Working within the framework of the four higher needs (the need to love, to grow, to contribute, and to find meaning, described in chapter 13), each of the two-day intensives *demanded* that each leader step well beyond his or her comfort zone in truth telling (honesty), caring for the team and the company (compassion and commitment), risk taking in the process (courage and boldness), and creative collaboration during the process and beyond (confidence, imagination, and intentional communication). And each leader was challenged to begin a systematic, ongoing process of personal and leadership growth.

The foundation of this growth process was the "power training" based on the growth principles enumerated in part II. It was not based on learning new or even conventional leadership techniques. In fact, initially it didn't focus on the "do" functions of leadership at all—instrumental skills such as how to motivate your reports, how to create a team, how to command more authority, or how to delegate effectively. Rather, the foundational focus was on growing and expanding leadership character traits or ways of being—such as courage, strength, imagination, confidence, passion, trust, compassion, boldness, honesty, integrity, authenticity, and so forth. The idea behind this "beingness" approach is simple: In living life, beingness always precedes doingness. That is, our state of mind or way of being dictates the authenticity, effectiveness, and power of what we do, whether we're aware of it or not.

This was the kind of leadership development process that Rizley and company embraced within the workshops and beyond. The ongoing growth program was specifically tailored to each individual leader's strengths and weaknesses, based on various types of real-time feedback that each leader received in the workshops and beyond, and based on the leader's self-assessment. Likewise, the development of the group of leaders into a true team, one committed to achieving the extraordinary, also happened both within the framework of the workshops and in the day-to-day affairs of creating an effective and powerful business organization. All participants were given the tools and support, often intentionally intrusive support, to achieve these growth objectives as individuals and as a team. It was a process that did not abide lightweights. Indeed, Rizley astutely surrounded himself with heavy hitters—smart, deeply caring people who were committed to success.

Rizley and team—who early on branded themselves "Rainmaker" rather than being known as something like "Cox Arizona Senior Leadership Team"—soon understood that true transformative growth was predicated on nothing less than consistent courage, radical honesty, and deep caring, for themselves and for each other. And they displayed all three of these qualities in abundance.

It Takes a Buddy and a Boss Who Plays

A mechanism used by the members of Rainmaker to achieve their compelling success was something known as the "buddy relationship." Each executive on the team was paired up with another member of the team to form a leadership growth partnership. Despite the lighthearted connotation of the word *buddy*, these buddy relationships were deadly serious. In short, the buddy's job was to ensure that his or her partner succeeded in *all* aspects of life—whatever that took. Though each respective leader's leadership success was often the most immediate and obvious focus of the relationship, all aspects of the leader's life were in play and subject to the focused attention of the "buddyship," including relationships with spouses and significant others, relationships with kids, personal financial concerns, other areas of personal growth and achievement, and concerns of intellectual, emotional, and spiritual growth.

The buddies understood that their commitment to their leadership partners' success was not an abstract idea but in fact a quantifiable, measurable reality, the success of which they were to guarantee, in a manner of speaking. Within Rainmaker, the buddy pairs became true partnerships. The buddies became intimately invested in each other's leadership and overall growth. The tenor of the buddy relationships within the larger context of the Rainmaker team was a conviction that failure was not an option for any one of the pairs. The caring and commitment that emerged within each buddy team thus became an important force in assuring the larger team's success.

More broadly, in the buddy, each leader had someone on whom he or she could rely for support and to whom he or she must account on a weekly basis—how they were serving and leading their followers, their leadership development, their personal growth, and how they were supporting and pushing Rainmaker itself. Finally, the buddy relationships became a microcosm of the team; if the buddy relationships were flourishing—confronting, caring, challenging, demanding, and producing results—then it was likely the team was doing the same.

Even Rizley, the most senior executive, participated in the buddy process, and does so to this day. In fact, he led the way in the entire transformative process, participating fully in all the nuances of the program. And by revealing his own strengths and weaknesses, fears and hopes along the way, he gained *more* respect, *more* power, and *more* leadership and moral authority—as both the leader of the eleven-person Rainmaker team (which is now thirteen people) and of the 3,000-person organization. In effect, he communicated something that all leaders communicate if and when they courageously make themselves selectively vulnerable to their followers: "I am confident enough in who I am as a man [or woman] and a leader to admit that I don't have it *all* figured out. Yes, of course, I have proven leadership talent and ability or I wouldn't be in the position I am in, but I'm also human. I have fears to be faced and blind spots to be overcome just like you. And like you, I still have a long way to go and grow on this journey of life and leadership."

Implicit in Rizley's gutsy and forthcoming participation in the process was a statement to his team and the larger organization: The days of the stoic, almost pathologically self-contained leader (as in the character of Don Draper in TV's *Mad Men*), or the

I've-got-it-all-figured-out leader, are over. Certainly at Cox Arizona, anyway. A new, more powerful, more open, more productive, and far healthier leader has emerged, one well suited to lead in the twenty-first century. With eloquence and authenticity, Rizley modeled and continues to model this new leader—for his team and the entire company.

That Whole Vision Thing

One of the most essential elements, indeed the heart and soul, of the Cox Arizona success has been Rainmaker's powerful, compelling vision for the organization. (See Box 20.1.) This was not merely a pastiche of financial goals and pretty words. It was a rich picture of an organization that, by definition, did not yet exist. It was a mosaic of sorts, a montage of meaning, depth, and texture that vividly expressed a possibility that the senior team—by wisely leading their people—would in fact realize. Over the course of several months of creative, courageous, sometimes confrontational conversation, under Rizley's guidance they fashioned a possibility that they all felt should become, *was* to be, a reality. It was a future that not only significantly expanded the bottom line but also boldly touched the lives of each employee (and his or her family), the local community, the national Cox business, and finally, the larger cable and communications industry, all in powerful and inspiring ways.

Box 20.1 Vision Declaration

Cox Arizona
September 2004

• The World of Cox Communications in Arizona •

Cox Communications Arizona is the leading media and telecommunications provider in the state—Cox is synonymous with Arizona as Coke is with Atlanta. Our television and telephone businesses are enormous, but our foundation is broadband. Customers no longer speak of dial-up

(continued on next page)

(continued from previous page)

or DSL; the tag is Cox Internet, like Kleenex or Jell-O. Few homes, businesses, schools, or institutions are without a live wire and wireless link through the trusted Cox name.

We are a multibillion-dollar business serving both metropolitan and rural Arizona. Our operations stretch from border to border, in large cities and small towns. We invest in the region and the specific communities we serve. Cox leadership in charitable giving, economic development, sponsorship, and education adds luster to our reputation as a (perhaps *THE*) leading business in Arizona. Cox's role in its Arizona communities is genuine. As heirs to a 100-year legacy of Cox-owned media informing, educating, entertaining, and connecting, we feel the urgent need to link to this noble heritage with a bright and optimistic future.

Cox is seen as the thought leader in public policy, a company whose input is essential in all business-related issues. Because of our preeminent position in residential and business customers' lives, we work hard to avoid reregulation efforts. The relationship with government evolves. State and cities cease to treat us primarily as a revenue source that tolerates unnecessary regulation; instead they engage us as partners. Our senior leadership members are friends and confidants of elected officials on the federal, state, and local levels.

We are deeply respected by our competitors (the smart, honest ones actually want to be like us), and we are sought after as a partner by local businesses. Vendors/partners regard us as tough but fair. Our brand and award-winning service stand supreme. People moving to Arizona will ask their realtor or neighbors who to call for communications needs, and the only answer will be Cox.

• The World of Cox Arizona within CCI [the national Cox business] •

Arizona seizes and retains CCI's financial and operational leadership role. Arizona becomes the model for the "way things are done" at Cox Communications. By the time Cox aligns all of its business units as statewide entities, Arizona becomes the gold standard for organization structure and results. New programs are tested there; promising managers are sent there to work for a season to improve their skills and résumés. Customer and employee satisfaction levels set the standard for CCI statewide alignment and productivity.

Arizona builds its reputation on audacious plans and execution. A new product rollout takes two-thirds the time in Arizona that it would require anywhere else. The company's entrance into the wireless industry is built on yet another bold and successful Arizona product launch.

Leadership structure, sales culture, packaging, new digital products, urban and rural solutions are born in Arizona and emulated throughout the company. The ranks of CCI General Managers and Atlanta leadership are populated with Arizona-bred leaders and the intentions and results of the ever-evolving Arizona region permeate the company. CCI's outstanding value is a reflection of the nimble, precise Arizona performance.

• The World of Cox Communications Arizona in the Industry •

Cox Arizona is the folklore of the communications industry. The legendary contributions of the Arizona system are revered in case studies and business journals. By 2010 its best-known story celebrated the advent of wireless in Cox Communications Arizona's product mix. In a follow-the-leader industry in which most other corporations would wear a Vienna sausage as an earring if they saw Comcast do so, the Arizona team convinced its Atlanta leaders to go another way, and moving out beyond the wire was the result. Cox Arizona was the first successful entrant in making its voice, data, and finally, its video products portable. The company anticipates trends ahead of the market and competitors. The extraordinary quality of Cox Arizona products and packaging cause our competitors to build their products in direct response to Cox excellence. Some large competitors choose not to enter the Arizona marketplace after evaluating the Cox market share and reputation. Competitors' employees constantly apply for employment to the winning Cox team, and our talent is widely sought after. By 2010 the name "cable" is a pleasant historical reminder of the company's roots, but is no longer descriptive of what Cox Communications Arizona does or the role it plays.

(continued on next page)

(continued from previous page)

• The World of Cox Arizona's Employees •

As the Cox Team traverses the digital frontier our employees take on a new significance. More than in any other form of societal endeavor, the movement into specialized, customized home and business digital media demands interpretation and assistance. In this milieu, Cox employees are tour guides, enabling the customer to move effortlessly from old communication technology to a more convenient and immediate reality, and explaining and celebrating this progress every step of the way. In surveys Cox customer respondents conjure a picture of workers who are more than just omni-competent; they find Cox people to be comforting, a flesh-and-bone assurance that someone is watching out for the Average Joe or Josephine as they move to progressively higher levels of digital communication. Though Cox employees come from every conceivable walk of life, there is a certain sameness to them. No matter what job or age or location, Cox people are upbeat, genuinely inquisitive, and obsessively focused on how to make customer experiences with Cox products predictable and successful. In training and employee communication, Cox leaders preach life balance, and the workforce heeds the call. Cox employees are far more likely than the general population to have well-adjusted and happy personal lives. The passion conveyed in the workplace translates into corresponding levels of engagement in community, charity, spiritual, and educational pursuits.

The preponderance of Cox leaders is homegrown and promoted from within. At early stages in their Cox careers the workers are made to feel that this is not just a job but rather a vehicle for career and personal betterment. As a result, the credibility and competitive advantage of the workforce is magnified as leaders connect more successfully with workers and reflect their needs and aspirations. By 2010 the workforce is still entirely union-free. As the workforce ages, an active and lively retiree association emerges, taking on a valuable role in mentoring and in celebrating Cox Arizona history. Employee churn is nearly nonexistent, and job openings at Cox Arizona are compared to acquiring season tickets to Chicago Bulls' games in the Michael Jordan era—watch the obituaries.

Hereby signing we give our sacred word, declaring without qualification that we will cause this vision to become a manifest reality:

Once this unapologetically grand vision was put into a document (of roughly 1,200 words), it was ratified—signed by each member of the team in a formal, private ratification ceremony. Then the team set it aside. They did not announce or even mention it, directly or indirectly, to anyone in the organization outside of the team itself. This document was not a wish or a hope or a prayer. It was a commitment. It was something that they had decided must, *must*, be realized. And so they waited until they were sure beyond any shadow of a doubt that all eleven members of the team were *in fact* truly committed to its realization, in word and deed.

With unanimous commitment apparent, some nine months later and well into year two of the transformative journey, they formally unveiled the vision to the larger organization. With understated but elegant fanfare (and a first-class video to boot), Rainmaker presented their dream of a Cox Arizona that was about to be created, making clear that this was not merely a new marketing angle or a facile attempt to elevate morale. This vision represented an unequivocal commitment, a true transforming, integrative intention, that would become reality. And they, the 3,000-plus employees, were now being invited to participate in, to help create, and to experience the results and rewards of this possible future.

The members of Rainmaker then began enacting a well-crafted strategy to enroll the entire employee population. They did not simply say, "Here's the vision. Isn't it swell," and leave it at that. Presenting the organizational strategy for achieving the vision was understood as insufficient. They set out—through various meetings, presentations, one-to-one interactions with midlevel leaders, and targeted new initiatives—to encourage, cajole, and otherwise inspire the employees, up and down the organization, to join them in their mission of transformation. It was an invitation rather than an order, a strongly encouraged invitation, but an invitation all the same. It was an ongoing process to engage the entire company, a process the members of Rainmaker embraced with passion and intentionality. To this day, nearly seven years later, this document, the "Cox Arizona Vision" (with the necessary updates, since it's a living document) informs virtually all major decisions and very nearly all minor decisions up and down the Arizona business.

Today, under Steve Rizley and his ever-dynamic team's leadership,

Cox Arizona is properly understood as a transformative organization. Though, like any company, they have their ups and downs, they continue to win, succeeding even through the recession and slow recovery. And they continue to amaze (even themselves at times), simply because they understand that the only alternative to their continuing evolution is stagnation, which amounts to little more than decay and death. They understand that "maintenance" is an illusion, an indulgence they can ill afford. To ever settle for anything less than intentional, ever-unfolding expansion is to risk, in fact to virtually guarantee, regression. And so, almost every day, they seek to become more engaged with the life and leadership journey itself. Such is the way of the transformative organization. And such is the way of extraordinary success.

SUMMARY

There is little doubt that embracing the transformative model is not for those who would dabble in powerful leadership. It is only for those who have the courage to make a powerful commitment and lead from that commitment, not from their feelings or fears. One of the most vivid examples of a TL organization in the American business arena is Cox Arizona. Under the passionate leadership of a man who understands his deepest commitments in life and who is unafraid to lay it on the line, they have shaken their industry and become the standard against which others are measured.

At the center of their success has been a vital, transforming vision, a picture of the possible that they have employed at every turn. Indeed, the heart and soul of every transformative organization is its vision. In chapter 21 we consider the nature of the TL vision in depth.

CHAPTER 21

ADVENTURES IN AUDACITY II: The Nature of the Transformative Vision

Without a vision the people perish. **—Proverbs 29:18a**

Nothing happens unless first a dream. **—Carl Sandburg**

One of the most common problems I run into as I consult with corporations is a misunderstanding regarding what constitutes a true vision. This isn't because corporate leaders are dim or lazy. It's because, like most of us, they are uncomfortable with genuine creation, particularly on a grand scale. And by *creation* I mean the act of bringing something new into existence, something of substance and meaning. It is this fear of creation and ignorance regarding the nature of vision that keeps us stuck in the ordinary. Indeed, the creation of a powerful, authentic vision is arguably the first and most important act in a process of exploding old worlds and bringing new and better ones into being. Without it, simply put, an organization cannot answer the transformative call of life.

The reason this whole vision thing is so uncomfortable is simple enough to understand. The creation of and commitment to an authentic vision is dangerous; it's a high-risk proposition. From the moment we assert what we believe to be possible and desirable, and then follow it up with a promise to make that possibility a reality, we have put ourselves at risk. The risk we run, of course, is the risk of failure, because if it hasn't been done or created before, there is no guarantee that we will succeed. In fact, for those who haven't yet understood the nature of intention, the odds are better than even that they *will* fail. And lurking just beneath the surface of the fear of failure is that perennial favorite we've already discussed: the sublimated, irrational fear of death—the ancient, hard-wired, instinctive fear that failure will lead to rejection, which means being pushed from the tribe, ultimately leading to death alone in the wild.

Yet, of course, this fear is many steps removed from our conscious awareness, and it contradicts the ego illusion to which we are so attached, the one that says we are rational, conscious, self-directed creatures. And so we look the other way, denying the fear's existence. But the fear is still manifest in our daily behavior in something called the "phantom needs": the need to be right, the need to look good, and the need to be liked (or worse, approved of). So rather than risking failure, and thus risking being wrong, looking bad, or being disliked—all the symbols for our fear of death—we play it safe and string together a collection of financial goals, wrapped in cleverly crafted sentences, and call this a vision. But it's not a vision. It's a collection of wordsmithed financial goals.

To be fair to ourselves about these pseudo-needs, as irrational as the deeper fear of death may be, the phantom needs and the behaviors they generate are deeply ingrained in our normal ways of operating in life. Think about it. We all want to be liked, or at least not be disliked. We all want to look good, or at least not look bad. We all (some more than others) have a desire to be right, or at least not be wrong. So the chance of falling on our faces in the mud by not delivering on a bold promise for the future of the organization is something we'd just as soon avoid. It's risky business. And at the very least, then, it's understandable that we would shy away from creating a powerful, compelling picture of what could be and what should be, a picture of what we are about to promise will be. It takes courage, and lots of it.

Thus, it is not without "reason" that the vast majority of organizational leaders consistently avoid the creation and implementation of authentic visions for their firms. Nevertheless, to create lasting, extraordinary success a vision is required. Indeed, for a transformative organization, a true vision is as central to success as air is to breathing.

WHAT IT IS AND WHY IT MATTERS

So what then is a vision? Transformative leadership contends that in the organizational world, an authentic vision is a living, shared picture of what is possible and, thus, of what does not yet exist in the empirical world. It is a compelling tapestry that inspires people to be and do what otherwise would be inconceivable. It inspires people to adopt new and more effective ways of being out of which they do and achieve what they would not otherwise do and achieve. A shared organizational vision is a painting rich in depth, color, and texture, or if you like, a narrative in which we are the heroes and heroines, telling a story of goodness and power that we have decided must be told. And initially this painting or narrative exists only in the collective consciousness of the body of people who have created it.

"Without a vision," says the biblical proverb, "the people perish." Without a vision, that is, people go into a process of decay, because without a vision we typically try merely to maintain. Maintenance is a logical impossibility masking the decay that's underway. A vision draws us forward, gives us something for which to prepare, something for which to hope, something for which to build. Even if we are not aware of it when it is happening, a strong vision calls us, causes us to develop ourselves, to better ourselves in anticipation of its arrival.

For instance, as a fervent snow skier—one of my great passions in life—imagining during the months of August and September layers of snow-swept mountains in January and February can inspire in me a drive toward fitness that the long, sundrenched days of summer never can do. Just seeing a ski magazine cover in a newsstand may trigger images of floating through waist-deep, virgin powder, or of rhythmically dancing through a field of moguls, or carving down the glistening face of a steep tree-lined run. And suddenly, the workouts that had been such drudgery are now infused with an energy and purpose that makes them almost fun; getting in six of 'em a week is now a breeze, whereas before, four would have been viewed as a success.

A powerful vision propels us forward, keeps us expanding, avoiding the degeneration that would set in were we not growing and anticipating. It keeps us moving "up and to the right," so to speak. Without it the process of perishing, the process of decay and death begins to take hold. A powerful vision keeps us out of the otherwise inevitable state of entropy.

A story of the bold possibility inspires us to *be* bold, to risk, to stand with conviction where we otherwise might back down in unjustified deference, demurely giving in and quietly slipping away without being noticed. And if it is a truly powerful vision, it is also a large vision, large in the sense that its achievement requires us to expand our range of being and doing. It requires that we develop our capacity for achieving and getting things done. In fact, if we are the leaders of that vision, we are necessarily called upon to become larger as people and as leaders—wiser, more confident, stronger, more courageous, bolder, more compassionate—in order to elicit the same from our followers. For if it is an integrative, transforming vision, it seeks to achieve what others would "reasonably" dismiss as undoable. It seeks to achieve the extraordinary, to put that dent in the universe. As a consequence, in the TL context the authentic vision elicits our greater development as men and women, as leaders and colleagues, as agents of change and guardians of our own future.

"Your vision is magnificent," I may tell my clients, if it *is*, of course. "It's beautiful, brave, and big, and you *will* achieve it, making a huge impact and creating considerable wealth in the process." At this point I usually pause for the sake of emphasis and then say something to this effect: "But what thrills me, what fires my jets about helping this body of leaders accomplish exactly what you have promised you will accomplish, here and now, is the leaders you must *become* to achieve it. What excites me is the degree to which you must necessarily stretch yourselves, thus becoming bigger, stronger, smarter, more courageous and confident in the process—wiser and better *leaders*, certainly, but also, necessarily, better mothers and fathers, husbands and wives, better friends and community members, better human beings, period."

Because when the vision is truly magnificent and when the leaders, each and every one of them, are genuinely committed to it, not only is the realization of the vision likely but their intellectual, emotional, psychological, and spiritual growth is all but guaranteed. And within the transformative context, all of this adds up to the development of *adult* leaders, leaders who know how to get it done and get it done wisely, at heretofore unimagined levels, from a truly comprehensive vantage point. It's that sort of leadership that operates as the host, from the broad perspective that says this extraordinary success must and will serve all parties, not just a few at the top. The TL vision demands adult leadership.

On the more immediately applicable side of the equation, one of the recommending features of a strong vision is its ability to facilitate and streamline the decision-making process. The vision in effect becomes a filter. It is after all the primary intent of the organization. A true vision has become the company's reason to be; it has become the corporation's fundamental organizing principle. It thus has also become a sifting device through which all new ideas, potential projects, plans, and initiatives must pass. If a new proposal does not serve the larger vision then it is dismissed or, at best, set aside for another day. If a proposal clearly and significantly furthers the vision's realization, then it becomes a matter of high priority.

Though it rarely makes leadership decisions black and white, the vision does create a potent context for weighing and understanding the various options and possibilities that may present themselves on any given day. We still have to think, in some instances think even harder, but it provides the basis for that thinking. The standard and objective has been set and as such it has become a tool that empowers the leaders in all decision-making processes, including the hiring process, especially in the leadership ranks.

Moreover, given that a powerful vision creates a clear and uncompromising purpose for the entire company, one that goes far beyond merely making money, it also satisfies one of the four essential human needs: the need for meaning and purpose. If it is a transformative vision, extraordinary financial success is a natural by-product of the excellence that the vision demands but a true TL vision sees a larger picture. In fact it is nothing less than a song of praise to the promise and power of life, for it explicitly addresses all aspects of the greater web of life that the organization touches, in which and from which the organization draws its institutional existence. That is, the TL vision understands that no organization exists in a vacuum. It addresses itself, therefore, not only to the business and the business world but also to society and the reciprocity that exists between business and society. It's not idealism. It's big-picture realism, or enlightened pragmatism, if you like.

And a TL vision is comprehensive internally as well. That means that every single employee, whether there are 50 or 50,000, can see her- or himself in the vision. From the chairman and CEO down to the part-time college kid working over the summer, the vision is real and the primary responsibilities each employee carries out, thus, have been imbued with a layer of genuine meaning that transcends but still includes the more elemental profit motive.

There is something special at play in the transformative organization informed by a true vision. It is something deeply human and meaningful, and it is the job of every single leader in the organization to make sure that all the employees, *all*, are systematically encouraged and challenged, are given a real and recurring opportunity to understand their place in that greater meaning, that greater purpose.

POWERFUL RESULTS INSPIRED, NOT MOTIVATED

Finally, one of the most obvious values of a potent vision is the facilitation of extraordinary results. Given the inspirational nature of the transformative vision, given the bold nature of the vision's expectations and standards for excellence, and given the demand for growth that the TL model exhibits, the achievement of results is assumed. But remember, within the scope of the transformative vision, traditional, transactional results take on a different meaning. They are seen as a reflection or demonstration of the extent to which the leaders have done their jobs in growing themselves and their people. As a measure of this type of success, traditional criteria like top and bottom line growth become far more compelling and therefore more inspiring. Transactional measures have become transformative indicators.

Consequently the natural, vigorous drive for excellence and achievement that inevitably emerges in the well-led TL organization is only further lubricated by this additional, transformative understanding of the hard, measurable results. In the conventional organization the annual goal of a certain percentage increase in profits, say, is able to motivate the achievement of results at only one level, the level of extrinsic reward or punishment: the hope for monetary gain or the fear of losing one's job, say. But the organization inspired by a TL vision does not seek to motivate toward the achievement of results or anything else. It doesn't seek to motivate at all. It seeks to inspire.

The word *motivate*, meaning "to provide with incentive; move to action; impel," from the Latin *movere*, "to move," connotes or tends to be associated with external or extrinsic rationales or incentives for behavior. To inspire someone, however, suggests something quite different. Originally the Middle English word *enpsire* meant "to influence, move or guide by divine or supernatural" force, from the Latin *inspirare*, "to breathe or blow into." The modern understanding is less explicitly theological but retains much of its earlier high-mindedness. *Merriam-Webster's Dictionary* says to *inspire* is "to exert an animating, enlivening, or exalting influence on." To be motivated is to be moved from without; to be inspired is to be moved from within, at a deeper, enlivening, even exalting level.

Thus, the transformative vision seeks "to exert an *animating* . . . influence on," to stir the life force, the soul, the *anima* (Latin for "life" or "soul"). The TL vision is one that animates (brings to life) the spirit of the leader and follower, and it does so in three related but distinct ways: (1) It inspires a result that is a consequence of the inherently rewarding quest for excellence and accomplishment; (2) it inspires a result that is the quantifiable reflection of the leader's success in growing and developing herself and her followers; and (3) it inspires a result that's driven by a desire to contribute to something larger than self, to someone other than self. All three represent enlivened efforts that are intrinsically rewarding, and though distinct, feed off of and complement one another. Combined, they have a self-perpetuating and results-magnifying effect.

The competitive drive for excellence has been united with deeper or higher drive to serve and contribute. In this instance, two more of the four universal human needs have been satisfied: the need for growth ("the noble battle for betterment") and the need to contribute ("it's who we are.").

TWO SIMPLE INGREDIENTS, WHETHER SHAKEN OR STIRRED

A sound transforming vision has two fundamental characteristics. The first is that it is exciting at a deeply resonant level. When the leader and his people think about the vision, they are moved by the prospect of having it realized and by being involved in its creation. When they read the vision document they are filled with a sense of meaning and purpose, a sense of being about something that truly matters. They are filled with a sense of the possible, and they recognize themselves in the promise of a joyful and compelling future that is to become reality. In short, the documented vision is inspiring through and through; it thus evokes passion and drive. It must make the constituents *want* to climb that mountain and then the next and the next, and the next after that.

The second essential quality is that it's a little bit scary. Almost as surely as it evokes passionate commitment, it must engender, yes, a bit of fear. Periodically, when the leader and her people consider the implications of the vision, their "stuff" comes to the surface, their otherwise buried self-doubts: "I don't really think I can handle all of this," or "This is just too big for me," or "I don't think I quite have what it takes to lead people at this level," or "What the hell was I thinking? Who am I kidding?" or "Someday I might be able to pull this off but not today. Holy crap!" Though these fears may remain unarticulated, they are there in all their anxious glory.

Are you kidding me? The transformative vision should make the leaders feel inadequate, you say?

Well, no. Not exactly.

Remember, the TL vision is, among other things, a tool intended to cause, demand, necessitate, or otherwise require the growth of the very people who created it and of all those who later embrace it. Thus, the vision must bring to the forefront our fears and doubts about ourselves and the doubts about our abilities to evoke the best from our followers. Without bringing that smaller sense of self to the surface, without making it apparent to us, no growth is required and the expansive development we seek to achieve will not be realized. When our historical, limiting beliefs are flushed up, we have to grow ourselves in order to rise to the occasion, we have to expand our sense of self, our sense of leadership self. We must now extend our range of leadership skills, expand our capacity to summon courage, confidence, imagination, commitment, passion, steadfastness, boldness, compassion, clarity, imagination, and so on. We also have to learn better some of the more basic skills in leading others, like communication and delegation, organization and implementation, as well as the capacity for urgency and demand balanced by understanding and patience.

Without both of these qualities—at once bold and compelling *and* a wee bit daunting—the vision will not work, and frankly, it's not a TL vision. A vision that does not fill us with a passion for the possible and inspire us to become larger as leaders will not get us past the inevitable challenges, personal and team-wise, that we will inevitably face. A vision that does not both enliven us and require us to step into greater degrees of power and potency, bigness and generosity, will eventually become as flavorless as an overcooked noodle—"Been there, done that."

In the final analysis, a truly transforming vision becomes the organization's mosaic of meaning. It becomes the primary animating force for the entire corporate body. It becomes the organization's reason for existence. Without it, in fact, the organization begins to perish. Though it may not show up immediately, for months or even years, decay and death have begun to set in, guaranteed.

In the academic world there's the familiar enjoinder, "Publish or perish," meaning if you aren't producing quality research and publications you won't achieve tenure or general academic success. In the organizational world it goes like this: "Dream or decay." The simple fact is that there is no other way.

SUMMARY

The central importance of a compelling vision for the thriving TL organization cannot be overstated. When properly created and implemented, it becomes the organizing and animating force in the organizational body from head to toe. Without it, the organization begins a slow but certain death march. But with it, the people and the leadership are infused with the vitality to play at ever-increasing levels of satisfaction and effectiveness and the courage to overcome the challenges and problems that will surely arise.

This organizational purpose, however, cannot be created and carried out without a powerful, engaged, and talented senior leadership team. True teamness must be present. In chapter 22 we dive right into the middle of what a true team of leaders is and how we go about creating one. No self-serving B.S. permitted.

CHAPTER 22

THE TRANSFORMATIVE TEAM AND THE END OF A MYTH: Beyond Laziness and Fear

> Give me a place to stand and I will move the world.
>
> **—Archimedes**

In the organizational world, few ideas have received more attention in recent years than the notions of team and team building. The word *team* has become so overused as to have lost nearly all meaning. And there are good and bad reasons for this sloppiness. One of the good reasons is that this overuse reflects our increasing awareness that great leadership never happens in a vacuum and rarely ever happens without great teams that help hold the leadership context. But this would seem a recent development, and it still fights an uphill battle.

In the West we have a deeply embedded need to believe in a solitary leadership figure of almost godlike proportions. It's the myth of the rugged individual, the one who, like a Clint Eastwood character in a Hollywood western, stoically rides into town and with a few bullets and even fewer words saves the day. Our mythology around leadership, especially this heroic type of leadership, far outstrips reality. According to Warren Bennis and Patricia

Ward Biederman, "Our contemporary views of leadership are intertwined with our notions of heroism, so much so that the distinction between 'leader' and 'hero' (or 'celebrity,' for that matter) often becomes blurred."[1]

Still, it would seem that the more thoroughgoing the study of leadership has become, the more aware we have become of the centrality of the team in creating leadership and organizational success. Thus, another one of the "good" reasons teamness has become such a popular idea is that this myth of the solitary, heroic leader does not hold us in its sway as it once did.

One of the "bad" reasons for the overuse of *team*, and one of the primary reasons the understanding of "team" has become so thin in the organizational imagination, is the human propensity for laziness. As Scott Peck points out in *The Road Less Traveled,* if there is such a thing as original sin, our laziness is it.[2] Our laziness regarding *team* shows up in both intellectual laziness, how we think about *team*, and in our physical laziness, how we act upon notions of *team*.

Though we may have some sense that *team* matters, we still are reluctant to invest meaningful thought into the importance and creation of the team. This tendency for intellectual laziness is only magnified when it comes to the group or collective of any kind, hence the well-documented danger of groupthink—the tendency of peer pressure and a culture of conformity to squash honest, open discussion and disagreement with the dominant point of view. Thinking is hard work, very hard work, but by avoiding thought about teams we fail to make some of the most basic distinctions between a true team and a functional group. In the place of substantive thought and action around teams, we have empty chatter about it.

WHEN PARTS DON'T MAKE THE WHOLE

A group of leaders who regularly meet together because their organizational responsibilities require it is no more a team than auto parts grouped together on the floor of a garage are a car. We can call the pile of parts a "car" till the fossil fuel runs out, but every time we walk into our garage all that we'll see is a heap of auto parts piled together on the floor. The various stacked-up pieces, by virtue of their existence together in one place at the same time, do not a car make. We can tell our friends we have a Maserati, say, and wax eloquent about the Maserati's legendary handling and power, but until we do the work of assembling the parts (or have a skilled Maserati mechanic assemble the parts for us), what we have in our garage is no more a Maserati than it is a tuna boat.

Similarly, bringing the parts of your leadership body (the individual leaders) together, even if you do it face to face, every week, in and of itself is not going to make them a team, any more than repeated references to *my team*, *the team*, *our team* does—nor does going out for drinks together, driving go-karts together, or doing the ever-popular ropes course together make you a team. Until you do the difficult work of *forging* the team, connecting the complex and nuanced human parts in the proper manner, all you have is a heap of team parts—possibly an extremely talented heap, but still just a heap of parts. You may even like and respect one another, which makes it easier to call it a team, but until you've done the work of forging a team—heating, pounding, shaping, cooling . . . and repeating this multiple times—it is not a team. Sorry. Sometimes this forging process can occur spontaneously, as the result of extreme adversity, for instance, but generally speaking it requires the conscious intent to heat, pound, shape, and cool.

This notion of forging a team brings us back to the truth about our laziness. It is here that our physical laziness becomes a problem. Because "teamwork," as a colleague of mine used to say, "is *hard* work"—it takes time and energy. And quite frankly, teamwork is unnatural. Here's why.

THE TWO UNIVERSAL FEARS THAT MUST BE OVERCOME

Coming together as a group, as a tribe, is a natural and normal function of human nature. Beyond our historical need for survival, it's a reflection of our intrinsic social nature. But becoming a true team is something altogether different. A *functional group*, often mistakenly called a team, is collection of people who get along, have a vague sense of a shared objective, occasionally unite around a specific initiative or tactic, but are still just a group of individuals

Figure 22.1 The Ascending Levels of Team

Great Team A good team that has sustained extraordinary success for an extended period of time, roughly two or more years (transitioning new players in without missing a beat) rarely happens, but when it does, the team's incomparable achievements are typically lauded internally and externally.

Good Team A team consistently producing extraordinary results in every domain of responsibility, soft and hard. Authentic power is the overriding constant, and people want to be in association with the team because of the compelling nature of the team's consistently expressed power, manifest in a fierce commitment to the organization's overriding purpose and to each other. Its occurrence is very uncommon.

Team A collective of players sharing a vivid purpose, to which all members are unequivocally committed. Producing good, often extraordinary results in most but not all domains of responsibility, they know how to win and do it the majority of the time. They are always a united front and consistently make each other better as individual players. They frequently experience synergy and accept it as a normal function of their commitment. Each member understands and regularly operates from intentionality. Real team is an uncommon occurrence and a praiseworthy accomplishment.

Functional Group A group of individuals who work reasonably well together when they need one another's assistance. As a rule they get along, at worst tolerating one another, at best having genuine affection for one another. They may produce good, on occasion exceptional results, but they do not necessarily enhance one another as individual players, and their success is typically contingent upon favorable circumstances. They are not consistently a united front. Though they try not to sabotage one another, saboteurs (often unconsciously) can exist in such a body. A functional group is a common occurrence in the organizational world.

Dysfunctional Group. A loose collection of people who come together only as required to do so by the senior leader. They do not function effectively together at any level, seeking to avoid one another, particularly in a group setting, as much as possible. Unhealthy individualism and competition is the norm. Jealousy and sabotage are accepted as inevitable, and disunity is the constant. A group of this type is relatively uncommon, but not as much as might be expected.

who are reasonably respectful with one other, trying not to overtly sabotage one another or the larger organizational objectives. Figure 21.1 places the functional group within the ascending levels of teams.

A *true team*, on the other hand, is a body of people who have come together around a vivid, compelling purpose, with each individual having declared that nothing but the full realization of that purpose is acceptable. A Team, especially a transformative team, requires a level of connectedness and commitment that is uncommon. It requires a level of thoughtful inter-relatedness and a degree of selfless, focused honesty that most of us find downright unnerving. The reason for the unnerving nature of such interrelatedness and connection is relatively basic.

On the flipside of the four higher needs described in chapter 15—to love and be loved, to grow, to contribute, and to have meaning—we find two universal fears, or more precisely two layers of one fear. And by *universal*, I mean, again, that they (or it) are found in every human being in every culture, probably in every epoch of human history. At its core it is a fear of not being loved or of losing love. Closer to the surface it manifests as a fear of being insufficient as a human being. While this fear may be buried more deeply in some of us than in others, we all have it in both expressions. Evidence seems to suggest, and simple logic supports, that the more effective we are in satisfying the four universal needs the less we are affected by this two-layered trepidation.

The Fear I Won't Be Loved

At the deepest level, the most essential fear most human beings have, beyond our explicit fear of dying, is this fear of not being loved. Given the importance our brains' hardwiring places on love and how central it is to survival, it is not difficult to see why the loss of love is such a fundamental fear. Much of what we do is done so that we will be loved. Indeed, one of the primary reasons we love (give love to others) is so that we will receive love in return. So much for pure altruism. The bottom line, however, is this: Lurking beneath the surface of our everyday conscious lives, to one degree or another, is the fear that if we are not careful we will lose whatever love we may have, a concern that suggests we'd better be careful or we might not be loved.

On the other end of the spectrum, of course, it is also true that the more love we experience in our daily lives, and the more that our deeper self-understanding assumes we warrant love, the more likely it is that we won't be adversely affected by this fear; there is less reason for its emergence. Nevertheless, the fear is still there in us. Dormant, perhaps, but there in waiting.

The way most of us guard against the danger of not being loved (or of having that love jerked away) is by being selective with whom we allow ourselves to be vulnerable. That is, we protect ourselves by not getting too close to too many people. The fewer the people who are able to hurt us by withdrawing their love, the safer we are, or so our primal inclinations tell us.

In the organizational world, then, if we have a reasonably high level of social intelligence, we may be polite, thoughtful, even cleverly gregarious, but not *too* open, not *too* vulnerable, not *too* emotionally risky. We develop acquaintances rather than genuine friends, though we may call them "friends" because it feels better. Most of our colleagues are merely professional acquaintances. We care but do so carefully and not too much. We show interest but only appropriate levels of interest and not too much. We allow others to get to know us a bit but only in socially acceptable doses and never, ever too much. In short, we are polite, and if we're astute, we may effectively pretend certain levels of closeness, but we still build that invisible public wall between ourselves and all but a few highly select people, those with whom we just seem to connect.

This self-protective behavior is more than understandable, even if on occasion it amounts to polite dishonesty. In fact, many of us, perhaps most of us, lie in this manner on a regular basis. When a coworker asserts a strong opinion, for instance, we may smile and politely nod, implying our assent. But what we're really thinking is, "What a silly idea; you've got to be kidding me! Do you really believe that crap?" So the nod of our head is a pretense, a lie.

But why? Why do we feel the need to pretend agreement, to pretend that we're right there with 'em when we're not?

Because it's much safer that way. It's much safer to slightly sacrifice our integrity than it is to challenge or disagree and risk being rejected or dismissed. It's the same reason most of us have an aversion to straight-up confrontation, why we don't much like delivering unpleasant information to a colleague or challenging that colleague or even challenging or confronting a direct subordinate. Rest assured, you're not alone on this one. The desire to avoid confrontation is almost as common as the need for water.

Then, adding insult to injury, most of the time, as we've already noted, we disingenuously tell ourselves that the reason we avoid confrontation is that we don't want to hurt the other person's feelings. It's not because of *our* discomfort, not because we're thinking about ourselves. We're thinking about *them*, or so we convince ourselves. This further lie makes us feel better about the first one, the pretense that we agree or that everything is fine. The truth, however, is not quite so pleasant. Our reluctance to confront someone, remember, is usually all about *us*, all about *our* feelings. We don't want to risk not being liked, and just beneath that surface anxiety lurks that deeper fear that we won't be loved, and if we're not loved we'll be pushed from the tribe, and . . . you know the rest by now.

The Fear I'm Not Enough

At a level much closer to the surface of our awareness, this fear of not being loved is manifest as a fear that we are *not enough*, a fear we touched upon in chapter 15. This expression of the fear has such an adverse affect (even if still largely unconscious) on so many of us, it warrants further consideration. The fear we're not enough assumes, remember, that there may be something inadequate about us, something that we must not to allow others to see. As noted, it's also referred to as the "imposter syndrome," a semi-conscious belief that we've apparently fooled everyone into thinking that we are the right person with the right qualifications (or that we simply are worthy) when deep down we're not so sure. This manifestation of the fear shows up in myriad ways, personally and professionally. And it is a uniquely influential fear because for most people it resides so close to our awareness.

Like the deeper, root fear (that we won't be loved), its strength comes, in part, from the fact that it is a direct response to our primitive, hardwired survival need to be accepted by the tribe. If the way in which we have portrayed ourselves to our followers, our peers, or our leaders proves to be less than accurate, if we prove not to be the person we may have said we are, adverse consequences may ensue; our followers may not follow properly, we may be demoted, fired, or otherwise rejected and thus pushed to the edge or out of the organizational tribe.

The irrationality of these ancient fears and their inapplicability to who we are in today's world is immaterial. Once the neurons get fired up, rationality be damned. Our more sensible understandings are overwhelmed and damped down, and their idiot cousins have grabbed the microphone. But hey, they're just doing their antiquated lounge act of a job, breathlessly screaming at us that we're about to be "found out," and that, of course, is not an option we can live with, something to be avoided at all costs. *All* costs. So dance faster, damn it. Dance!

These fraudulent beliefs about our fraudulence are a force to be reckoned with. But first we have to see their presence, or at the very least their instantaneous impact on our behavior.

And remember, this entire drama and the fears of insufficiency that inform it remain a step or two removed from our conscious understanding. We may feel their rumblings by way of mild discomfort, sometimes via full-blown anxiety, but just as often we don't even notice them at all—we just act, eagerly, desperately, even stupidly. But let's not kid ourselves. Not being directly aware of their activity does not keep them from running wild and, in fact, determining considerable amounts of how we show up as leaders and as people.

All it takes is the wrong look by the right person, or the uncomfortable challenge by a colleague, or any other number of everyday possibilities and instantly the wire is tripped and that danger signal begins to flash: "This is not good, you're vulnerable here, you'll be found out, *holy crap*! This is gonna get ugly and fast, take cover, *now*." And it all happens in a fraction of a fraction of a second. Our well-worn defense mechanisms automatically kick into gear; they're off and running. And *they* run *us*, not the other way around.

The list of not-enough behaviors is extensive. (You may want to revisit the examples given in chapter 15.) Indeed, most of us have several automatic not-enough behaviors. And remember, given their unconscious, preprogrammed nature, they run almost entirely unchecked by our rational, aware minds. But rest assured, they're there and they have a will of their own, until you begin to see them at work. Finally, we need to keep in mind that because the not-enough fear that triggers the automatic behavior is itself unconscious and automatic, typically the only evidence that the fear is in play are the feelings of discomfort (some of the time) and the automatic, well-honed behavior (all of the time).

Is it any wonder, then, that we are inclined to merely gather a collection of leaders together and *call* it a team? Too much closeness, too much connection, too much honesty, too much vulnerability, too much solicitation for help from a colleague, too much collaboration and—*bang!*—one or both levels of the fear kicks in: Our discomfort level spikes way up and our not-enough behavior takes over.

Because we would just as soon avoid the possible inflammation of such powerful insecurities, and we'd just as soon not uncover what lies beneath them, we seem to do one of two things. One, we tell ourselves that the importance of team is overrated and largely unnecessary. We dismiss the importance of teams out of hand: "Yeah, yeah, yeah," we say, "that's an HR, OD thing. Let 'em believe what they need to believe to feel important." Or two, we so dilute our understanding of what a team is that what we call a team is unrecognizable when it is compared to an authentic, powerful team, a team of leaders who actually lead. Then we work at convincing ourselves and others that our functional group of leaders is a team: "Yes, sir! Boy oh boy, do we ever have a great team. We like each other (more or less), we usually agree (face to face at least), and every year we spend two days together, in the mountains no less, working on strategy." Nice try.

SUMMARY

Despite our apparent and increasing awareness that teams and teamness are important, most leadership teams only vaguely resemble true teams. More times than not what we call a team is, at best, a functional group—not a bad thing but not a team in the most basic sense of the word. True teamness requires powerful and honest interrelatedness and a fiercely shared commitment to something larger than the individual self, and these things scare us.

Yet true teams *are* important, absolutely essential to organizational success, even in the transactional world. And in the transformative world of organizational achievement, nothing less than authentic, powerful, relentless teamness will do. Extraordinary success demands an extraordinary team. So here we come up against one more of those TL non-negotiables. To create astounding results, to generate a level of success that puts a dent in the universe, we must do the difficult and risky work of forging a true team of leaders. So what, then, does a true team, a transformative leadership team, look and feel like? What are its constituent pieces? In chapter 23 we answer to those questions.

CHAPTER 23

A LEADERSHIP TEAM THAT ACTUALLY LEADS: Rising Above the Reasonable

> The reasonable man adapts himself to the world; the unreasonable one persists in trying to adapt the world to himself. Therefore, all progress depends on the unreasonable man.
>
> **—George Bernard Shaw**

The unfortunate reality is that most leadership teams don't do much leading. Like the individual managers who constitute these "teams," the teams are content to manage and then call it leadership. It's sexy to be a leader and to be a member of a leadership team, but part of the reason it's so sexy is that it's risky, highly risky—both to lead *and* to be on a team of leaders. Managing has a much lower risk requirement. It's so much safer, and seemingly so much easier, to effectively maintain what already is and merely nudge it a few paces beyond what has come before—you know, increase the margins a bit, get those customer satisfaction numbers up some, and of course push the bottom line up and to the right a dash or two. Come on, for the management team that calls itself a leadership team, just forecasting wisely and hitting (or coming close to hitting) that budget is huge.

But that's not what a true leadership team, particularly a transformative leadership team, is after. Those sound management things get done, of course, but they get done as a by-product of the team's larger leadership objectives. They're a happy by-product, a natural outcome of the team's larger scope.

A true leadership team *leads*. It's a given that they must hit (and exceed) their numbers, and they realize that such is achieved as they pour themselves into establishing excellence on all levels of the organizations they lead. They understand that their job is to create, to bring into being things—new and better possibilities in all domains of the organization—that before were not present. In the process of creating functional and relational excellence they explore uncharted waters, map out unmapped territory, envision and disclose new worlds.

A transformative leadership team that (1) is constituted of true leaders and (2) is united around and committed to a bold, intelligent vision of the possible does not hesitate in the face of treacherous business conditions. Rather than being constrained by the challenges of circumstance, rather than hedging and sputtering, they're inspired by the challenge. Rather than contracting, they know how to consciously and intentionally expand, calmly staring a glowering adversity in the eyes as they do so. It boils down to this: They know how to seize the "opportunity of necessity." When they are faced with daunting challenges, they are forced, of necessity, to step out of their comfort zones and understand new and better possibilities. The greater the problem, the greater the need to respond with atypical imagination.

What to other so-called teams is a danger, to these leadership grown-ups is a possibility, frequently a delight—again, it's Campbell's "godlike composure" while riding the full rush of energy on the leopard's back . . . without being torn to bits. The transformative team understands this wild ride as the adventure, the audacious answer to the fear-driven response of the transactional leadership mind.

Sound a bit lofty? You bet, but it's not *too* lofty. In fact, it's mandatory—mandatory, that is, if what we're about is the extraordinary. At this stage of the twenty-first century the ordinary will no longer do. And even without such a need, remember, the nature of the transformative journey is the call to creation and expansion, to being and becoming our potential. It is the pursuit and realization of that which far exceeds the ordinary, what to others is unreasonable. The transformative leader shatters old conceptions and realizes new possibilities. Yes, of course, transformative leadership requires a willingness to fail along the way, to stumble and get scuffed up a bit. But that's one of the reasons we have a team, because a true team is a deep well of meaningful and reliable encouragement, not to mention resourcefulness. So we now turn to the nature and makeup of that team, a team that is comfortable with the notion of becoming legendary, a body of leaders compelled by the power and achievement, the beauty and goodness of the transformative promise itself.

THE SEVEN TRAITS OF TL TEAMNESS

When an authentic transformative team has been forged there are seven nearly palpable qualities that are present, all of which are based on the assumption that we have, or are getting, the right people in place:

1. There is a shared and unmistakable sense of *purpose*, one that is larger than any single member of the team, a purpose that will eventually lead to the creation of the organizational vision.
2. There is a vivid, exceptionally high level of *commitment* to the team and the team's purpose, held by every single leader on the team.
3. There is a profound quality of *connection* with and *caring* for the members of the team by all members of the team—readily recognized both within the team and outside of it, and above all, by others in the greater organization.
4. There is a pronounced degree of *respect* and ever-increasing *trust* among all members of the team, which shows up, first and foremost, in the form of radical honesty.
5. There is a uniformly powerful hunger for *excellence* and *achievement* found in all team members and manifest in their commitment to each other's growth, each other's personal achievement of excellence.
6. There is an abiding and ever-growing degree of *confidence* in this team, that it can and *will* achieve its mission, due in no small measure to its unfailing capacity for articulated intentionality.
7. Because of the existence of the previous six traits, there is that certain "it" quality to the team, a certain "magic" to

the leadership body. It is manifest (1) in the strange phenomenon sometimes called synergy and (2) in a level of individual achievement, a kind of über-achievement—individual leaders on the team all performing at far-and-away higher levels than at any other time in their professional lives, with their regular accomplishments (almost as an afterthought) usually far exceeding that of their counterparts in other organizations or industries.

Let's look at each of these traits individually.

Purpose

An authentic team becomes a team only when it has a higher, overriding sense of its mission. Remember, I'm not talking about a functional group here. I'm talking about a true team, and a true team requires the will and courage to do the hard work. Team for the sake of team is a losing proposition—true teamness is far too difficult to achieve without a considerable degree of inspiration. A powerful purpose takes us beyond mere motivation and speaks to the passionate need to be elevated out of the mundane and into the world of deeper meaning (which, if we are to be fully functioning people, is a *need*, remember, not just a groovy thing if we can get it).

Motivation, as we previously noted, tends to run close to the surface and usually is short lived; it can be positive or negative (for example, growth or fear); and it typically requires continual attention and work to keep it fresh. Inspiration, on the other hand, issues from a deeper, less transient, more soulful place; it evokes our spirit, appeals to our more noble, more powerful longings. It evokes true greatness. When we are inspired we are, in fact, *inspirited*—our spirits come alive.

The work of forging a team is expensive business, for in addition to regularly overcoming the considerable, often paralyzing, universal fears, there is an immense amount of time and energy required to create a team capable of greatness—and greatness is what we are after here. Thus a true team is always informed by a sense of meaningful mission, whether that mission is to win the World Series or the World Cup or to transform an organization and its people into something spectacular. A clear, relatively concise understanding of our team purpose—what we are up to, why we are going through what we are going through, and toward what meaningful end we are moving—is requisite number one. It must be big and compelling to all members of the team, simply because from time to time it will be called upon to encourage the team—to fill the team with renewed sense of courage for continuing on.

One further distinction needs to be made here. A purpose is not a vision. A *purpose* is the overriding, simple, crisp articulation that informs or is informed by the larger, detailed picture that is the vision. For the teams that report (directly or indirectly) up into the senior team that creates (or has created) the organizational vision, their team purpose statements, for obvious reasons, must accord with and further that vision.

Several examples of real-life team purpose statements are presented in Box 23.1.

Box 23.1 Examples of Team Purpose Statements

Note that all eight purpose statements begin with an assertion of the team's commitment, then an assertion of the ways all team members will need to be in order to achieve the intended outcome, and then the intended outcome. In creating these statements, each team was encouraged to begin from the desired outcome, from the new world they would disclose (the end game) and then work back to ways of being, and finally to the declaration of commitment.

"We, the BBB Leadership team, are committed to being Bold, Tenacious, and Imaginative as we Transform Ipso Facto, Inc., and the entire NOPQ Industry."

"SALT is committed to being intentional, courageous, and resourceful as we incubate ideas that grow local markets so that XYZ North America sets the standard for worldwide operation."

"We, Epoch, are committed to being bold, tenacious, entrepreneurial, and honest so that we create and live the model of sales excellence that revolutionizes the industry."

(continued on next page)

(continued from previous page)

"The Westchester Consulting Leadership Team is fierce in its commitment to being passionate, creative, and authentic so that we create an internationally recognizable brand synonymous with innovative, best-in-class, professional business services, an organization that impacts and enriches people's lives worldwide."

"The Central Asia Leadership Team stands committed to being creative, confident, and courageous and to leading our clients beyond their individual needs by looking inward, outward, and upward, so that all that we touch is a reflection of goodness."

"We, the EMEA Leadership Team, are passionately committed to being courageous, inspirational, and revolutionary, so that we lead a fundamental change in the way the XYZ industry serves its customers and are recognized as the industry leaders, the standard against which all others are measured."

"The TD MKDISQ Leadership is committed to being brave and bold by exhibiting supreme levels of integrity and discipline in creating the industry-leading organization sought by business partners, industry leaders, and the community."

"The Rosalyn & Associates Leadership is committed out of their minds to being courageous, visionary, and passionate so that we create a new legal environment and cause R & A to be understood as the measure of excellence for innovative legal services, exceptional client care, employee satisfaction, and community stewardship."

Commitment

There must be a willing and passionate commitment on the part of every member of the team to the team itself and to the team's larger purpose. Having a bold purpose declaration does not guarantee that everyone is sufficiently committed to it and to the larger team. While the level of passion for and commitment to the team and the purpose will vary from person to person, there must be a minimum level of commitment that every member accepts with integrity. The level of commitment in the transformative model is exacting, settling for nothing less than a drive to fully realize the team's objective and purpose. In a manner of speaking the TL purpose is a jealous creature, expecting, even demanding a quality of devotion that runs second to only a few other high-order commitments in life, like our spouses, primary relationships, families, faith, personal growth, et cetera.

Let's say that on a senior leadership team of nine people, seven are genuinely committed, heart and soul, to the team and its greater purpose, but two are merely pretending. The two who are pretending, conforming for the sake of protecting their jobs, perhaps, will inevitably become saboteurs. Whether consciously or not, they will seek to dilute the level of commitment of the other seven people. In fact, in being unwilling to throw in with the others who are dedicated to nothing less than excellence, they *must* connive and contrive to dilute and otherwise reduce the team's level of commitment to each other and to the purpose. In subtle and consistent ways, they must cleverly bring the level of passion, dedication, and desire down to their levels. For if they are unsuccessful in lowering the standard, they will eventually be ferreted out and be seen for what they are, a costly drag on the team and its success. So sabotage they must. And they will, guaranteed. It's a survival instinct as old as civilization itself.

Because there is such a pronounced tendency on the part of senior executives to look the other way when members of a potential team are pretending to be committed, I will be more brazen than normal in making the following point unmistakably clear: You are a fool, a liar, and a *coward* if you are unwilling to see and then rid yourself of the pretenders. It is far, *far* better to have a temporarily vacant seat or two on the team than it is to have faux commitment from a member of the would-be team. Promise.

A manager may be able to get away with such denial or self-deceit. But not a true leader. Certainly not one who is determined to create a team committed to making that dent. The simple fact is, a team of equally committed players can compensate for a temporary lack of a skill set (or two or even three) on the team, even a central skill set. A team, especially a transformative leadership team, however, *cannot* compensate for a lack of 100-percent-unified commitment. There is absolutely no way, *none*, that extraordinary success will happen without complete commitment to success, to being and becoming what is necessary to generate unmitigated excellence.

A case in point is the 2003–04 National Basketball Association Championship. The Detroit Pistons represented the Eastern Conference, while the West was represented by the Los Angeles Lakers, the heavy, nearly unanimous favorites. In fact the only "experts" picking the Pistons to win were from Detroit. It was perceived as such a lopsided, foreordained outcome that many prognosticators were saying the only question was whether Detroit would get "swept," losing four games in a row in the best-of-seven series, or whether they would be lucky enough to win one game—and for apparent good reason. Four of the Lakers' five starters (Shaquille O'Neal, Kobe Bryant, Karl Malone, and Gary Payton) were locks as future NBA Hall of Famers. Rarely before, argued some commentators, had an NBA team fielded a team of such strong individual talent in the starting five.

What the prognosticators failed to account for, however, was the committed teamness of the superstar-less Pistons. From the outset of the season, new Detroit coach Larry Brown's team had a clear and singular commitment. Speaking of Brown, backup center Mehmet Okur said, "We had one goal. He told us the first day [taking the NBA Championship] is going to start today." No doubt there was considerable talent on this Pistons team—Chauncey Billups, Rasheed Wallace, and Richard "Rip" Hamilton were no slouches. But the talent level was nothing compared to the Lakers. What was central to this group of athletes, however, was their commitment to each other and their fierce, unswerving quest for an NBA crown as a team. As series MVP Billups put it, "They [the Lakers] may have had better individual players, but we always felt we were a better team." In the end, their teamness trumped the Lakers' purportedly superior talent. *Demolished* is more like it. They thrashed the Lakers, four games to one, to become the champs.

Other things being more or less equal, authentic, shared commitment will always trump individual talent. Always. Therefore, a significant piece of each team member must be inextricably intertwined with the team and its purpose; that is, every player on the team must have a considerable amount of skin in the game. Full participation is mandatory. No observers allowed. No exceptions. Without an abiding commitment from each player, the extraordinary will not be achieved.

Connection and Caring

One of the most famous lines in American cinema is a line from the 1967 movie *Cool Hand Luke*: "What we've got here is [a] failure to communicate." No doubt one of the primary reasons it has so lodged itself in our collective consciousness is that it applies to so many pivotal relational, organizational, and social settings. When true team is present, however, this all-too-common failure begins to disappear. When a TL team begins to emerge from a collection of individual leaders, without fail, a powerful and meaningful level of communication has begun to emerge.

When genuine communication occurs, there is something else that is going on as well, usually at a deeper level. The presence of powerful communication means that there is a kind of communion taking place, not in any religious sense but in the sense that there is a deeply felt understanding and an accord, a kind of fellowship, occasioned by a common purpose. To commune with someone means to unite with, to become one with, that person.

To put the whole matter in more contemporary parlance, what is going on is a richly experienced level of human connection. People are beginning to recognize one another and as a consequence are better able to appreciate and value one another, and as a result, almost in spite of ourselves, we begin to care at an altogether different level. But this caring is not the adolescent hand-holding of a campfire sing-along. It's the sober-minded realization of a common cause, a shared and demanding challenge that cannot be achieved alone but *can* be realized together. A deep bond is being forged, through the collective struggle for a greater good—for the team and for the organization the team leads. Notice the implications of that word *forged*—as in hardened and strengthened like steel, out of the red-hot heat of the blacksmith's fire. This forging process does not lead to softness. It leads to toughness, strength, resilience, and endurance.

Perhaps the best example of the intense level of connection and caring that emerges on a transformative team is sometimes witnessed in the theatre of war. The TV miniseries *Band of Brothers* (based on the book by Stephen Ambrose) chronicles the experiences of the soldiers of E Company in World War II. The stories follow their efforts to help defeat the Third Reich and to simply keep each other alive. Through it all a bond of brotherhood begins to emerge, a level of connection, caring, and camaraderie that under ordinary circumstances would be unimaginable.

While it might seem exaggerated to equate a transformative leadership team with the young men of E Company, the reality is that when authentic teamness begins to emerge within the TL model, there is an extraordinary level of commitment to, connection with, and caring for one another. It is a toughened and tough level of compassion and interconnection.

Trust, Respect, and Radical Honesty

While nearly all of us may regard ourselves as sincere people, most of us on occasion are guilty of the "socially-sanctioned lie." It's a type of dishonesty usually used to conceal our personal beliefs and judgments and is perceived as no big deal by most people. It can be as benign as "No, Honey, you don't look heavy at all. You look great!" Or it can be as serious and potentially dangerous as telling our boss, "Yes, I absolutely support your decision to implement the new initiative," when in fact we harbor deep reservations about the decision's wisdom. Yet, while both of these forms of deceit may be socially acceptable, they are, of course, still dishonest. They are a form of lying. They are intended to deceive, to mask our honest perceptions or feelings. In polite society these sorts of self-protective deceptions may be acceptable, but in the TL team approach they are poison, a toxin that kills any hope of authentic and powerful teamness.

In the TL team process, the first rule is the rule of radical honesty. When the TL team begins to emerge, it has done so as a consequence of a willingness of each team member to be deeply honest with themselves and with each other. Each player has committed to tell the truth from A to Z.

The only important caveat is that this honesty *must* issue from a place of caring for oneself and for each team member. The reason for speaking up (or not speaking up) is at least as important as what is said (or not said). Simply put, using the truth as a weapon is unacceptable. That is, in the transformative approach we make a distinction between telling the truth in order to serve and telling the truth in order to harm (or serve a selfish, hidden agenda). Not using truth as a weapon does not mean withholding information because we believe it may be difficult for the recipient to hear. If we believe the other person will benefit by hearing it, because our focus is on their welfare, we make the truth known. And we do this despite our own discomfort. What not using the truth to harm *does* mean is that we are careful to assess our motives before we tell the difficult truth, ensuring that the reason we are sharing the opinion or information is out of concern for the other or for the greater good of the team or organization.

Radical honesty, founded in the caring and connection just noted, is the means for creating both trust and a deeper level of respect. The more we show ourselves as committed to honesty, to laying it on the line, the more we are understood as people of integrity, worthy of respect. The more we display honesty, the more likely it is that we'll be trusted. Distrust issues from a sense of being deceived, a sense that what a person says differs from what they believe or understand to be so. Trust is based on the assumption that what we say is what we believe, that our reasons are precisely what we say they are.

By not withholding or dissembling, by doing the risky work of telling it as we see and understand it, we are laying ourselves bare, ultimately saying, "This is me, take it or leave it, and this is the truth as I understand it." We are standing in a place of authenticity, a place that requires considerable existential courage. For we are saying, in effect, that it is more important that I be respected than it is that I be liked, saying that it is more important that I be accepted for who I am than it is that I be approved of because I have conformed to someone else's wishes.

Consider the distinction between approval and acceptance. Receiving approval from another person is contingent on a certain level of performance or on conformity to the wishes or tastes of that person. When we are seeking approval, we are not honoring who we are as unique and valuable expressions of life, and we're surely not honoring our distinct leadership potential. Rather, we are compromising ourselves for the sake of validation from someone else whose opinion we consider (in the moment, at least) to be more important than our own.

Genuine acceptance is an entirely different beast. We experience acceptance when someone else says, in effect, "I see who you are, warts and all; I 'get' you, and though I may or may not agree with or may or may not like this or that thing about you, I accept you. Period. As you are, here and now." When we stand in a place of absolute integrity, asserting, "This is who I am and this is the truth as I understand it," we are making ourselves available for authentic acceptance. Though some will not accept us, those who do will do so because they take us for who we are. No need to perform. No need to comply. We can simply *be* who we *are* and who we authentically aspire to become.

This very sort of honesty forms the basis for authentic personal power and is the only basis for TL teamness. For out of this radical honesty, trust and respect emerge. When in Shakespeare's *Hamlet* Polonius famously advises his son, "This above all: to thine own self be true," he is speaking, of course, to the heart of authenticity and what we are calling radical honesty. What we often forget, however, is the rest of Polonius's admonition. "And it must follow," he goes on, "as the night the day, / Thou canst not then be false to any man." Being true to oneself necessarily leads to telling the truth to others, and telling the truth to others necessarily leads to trust and respect.

Abiding trust and respect are earned over time, no doubt. But they are also a function of a decision in the moment, a choice to embrace and operate from radical honesty. Out of such a choice, in such an environment, trust and respect become a real possibility. The capacity for excellence and powerful teamwork is only possible when both of these qualities are present. And they both begin when a team context of radical honesty has been resolutely established.

A Passion for Excellence

Greatness is achieved only by those who settle for nothing less than greatness. Accomplishing the extraordinary is not done by settling for the ordinary done well. One of the single most compelling qualities of the transformative leadership team is its expectation and drive for excellence. It is understood, to a person, that this team expects nothing less than greatness. This team exists to leave their mark on the universe. Excellence for the sake of excellence is one of its permeating principles.

In keeping with their commitment to authenticity, moreover, the team does not pursue excellence for the sake of recognition. Recognition is fine and good. If it comes, great. If it doesn't, that's fine too. This team understands excellence as a reward in and of itself. Though not philosophers, the team members are aware that excellence has a certain innate beauty and that beauty, like goodness and achievement, are all goods unto themselves, rewards in and of themselves.

Further still, they grasp the sensible nature of playing the leadership game at the highest level, a sensibility summed up in a little rhyme I sometimes recite to my clients:

> There is no virtue in playing small.
> If you play, play *big* or not at all.

The TL team has accepted the simple fact that building a powerful team is always exceptionally hard work. There will be some difficulty, some required sacrifice, and significant amounts of courage. In building a team we are always dealing with those sometimes rational, sometimes wildly irrational animals, *Homo sapiens*. And because of our inescapable humanness, we are going to pay a price whether we simply seek mediocrity done well or we seek excellence and bigness. The ordinary done well requires that we maintain certain levels of socially acceptable inauthenticity—the phony smile, the socially sanctioned lie, and other forms of self-protection and defensive posturing—all of which are costly in terms of energy expended and anxiety experienced. But we're used to *this* sort of a price, we're familiar with such angst-riddled survival prices so we don't notice them to any great degree. Summoning the courage that playing big demands is equally expensive, but because it is out of the norm (beyond mere survival) we notice its emotional cost more readily.

Here's the point: We're going to pay a price either way. And since we will pay very nearly the same price whether we go for the gold or not, we might as well pay the price with a large accomplishment in mind, pay the price for something that's worth it. The lofty, then, becomes quite pragmatic. "We're gonna suffer some, regardless," transformative leaders agree, "so we might as well have that suffering be for the sake of something that's actually worth suffering for."

And playing big does not simply mean doing the grandiose. It means accomplishing something that is worthy of our best selves and doing it with excellence, a full embrace of excellence throughout the organization. Excellence, says Aristotle, is a function of habit. We cannot accurately say that we are excellent until we have made it part and parcel with who we are, until it becomes a central fiber in the fabric of our lives, until we demonstrate it again and again and again. When we don't need to discuss it much, when we don't even think about it much, when we just do it with an increasingly automatic "of course," then we have achieved the state of excellence, made it a part of who we are—as individual leaders, as a team, as an organization. It has become inextricably interwoven in our self-understanding and our understanding of what is worth doing.

Playing big means creating the extraordinary by virtue of living excellence, on our team and in our organization. It becomes the hallmark of the transformative leadership team and ultimately of the transformative organization. In every aspect of the team, in the lives of each team member, and in all facets of the organization that the team leads, excellence is pursued as the deed worth doing.

Confidence and Intentionality

Confidence is sometimes confused with arrogance, but arrogant it is not. Arrogance is a form of ignorance that, among other things, does not consciously recognize the remarkable degree of good fortune (grace) that typically accompanies achievement, even intentional achievement. Generally speaking arrogance is best understood as false confidence that must look down on someone or something else in order to unwittingly compensate for the deep self-doubt it seeks to quell. The arrogant individual displays a self-conscious sense of superiority, indeed has a need to feel superior because at a deeper level he feels inferior.

Genuine self-confidence, on the other hand, has no need for bravado, no need to persuade anyone or anything of its capability or worthiness. There is no need for such preening demonstrations of superiority because the belief in self is deeply founded and real. The word's etymology is telling. In the original Latin the prefix *con* means "together with," while *fidere*, from which we derive the root word, means "to trust" or have "faith in." Thus confidence can best be understood as faith or trust with or in someone or something. If I genuinely have confidence in myself (literally, faith with myself), in my abilities and my worth, I simply know who I am, what I am up to, and what I am capable of. Someone else's favorable (or unfavorable) opinion of me is irrelevant.

The person of abiding self-confidence does not know all the answers; indeed, he understands that knowing it all is unnecessary. The person of confidence simply has the ability to step back and with critical integrity say to himself, in effect, "I may not know how we are going to handle this or that situation, or how we are going to get there from here, but I'll get us there. I know who I am. I know where we're going, and I will figure it out, or find someone else who can." Because he knows and believes in himself, knowing all the facts or having all the experience is a luxury, not a requirement.

This same level of "faith with" can be applied to others, in our case, the team. In fact, the members of a TL team, to a person, have such faith in the team's capacity to achieve what they are after, to succeed in their audacious objectives. They don't shoot for the moon and settle for coming close. They shoot for the moon in order to hit it dead center because they know they can. They know they will. Of course, this faith is strengthened and solidified over time, but it's there early on as well, as they recognize the talent, character, and commitment of the individual team members, and consequently as they imagine what might be possible for such a collection of talent. They know that this body of leaders is talented as individuals but that together they are not merely talented, they are exceptional. Without pretense, there is a clear, quiet yet bold knowing that when this team gives its word, the deed is as good as done.

A primary reason for this supreme level of confidence is the team's collective capacity for true intentionality. As individuals and as a group they have learned to harness intention's sobering power. They understand that intention is not a wish or a mere desire. It's an unswerving commitment that is taken with considerable care. But once it is made, it's done. It's no longer a question of *if* but of *how.* The team has learned how to transmute a belief that a given outcome would be "really cool" into an understanding, embraced at a cellular level, that it "must be"—from "Wouldn't it be nice . . ." to "This must and shall be." Down to each woman and man, they know a carefully wrought intention is but a choice.

Thus, this team is characterized by an increasingly brilliant track record. That is, as they carefully weigh what is wanted and needed, what is truly worthy of standing for, they put their stake in the ground and stand without equivocation until it is realized. The net result is not a tendency for braggadocio or even cockiness. The net result is that quiet but fierce confidence. With every passing fiscal quarter, the team's belief in itself and its capacity to achieve the astonishing, intentional feat is fortified. They know and as a result they accomplish, over and over again.

A Strange Magic

The sum total of the previous six constituent pieces amounts to something that often defies description. In Hollywood, New York, London, Paris, and Milan they often speak of the current "it" girl (and on rare occasions the "it" guy). The woman who originally coined the term, Elinor Glyn, says in the beginning of her 1927 screenplay, simply entitled *It,* that "*It* is that quality possessed by someone which draws all others with its magnetic force. With *It* you win all men if you are a woman—and all women if you are a man. *It* can be a quality of the mind as well as a physical attraction." Whatever else "it" may be, it is something that is entirely compelling and often something that the transformative leadership team has in overflowing abundance. And while this whole "it" factor of the TL team may be something that defies explanation, we know what it looks like and why it is there.

The unadorned reality is that when all six traits—purpose, commitment, connection-caring, honesty-trust-respect, passion for excellence, and intention-based confidence—are consistently displayed, a kind of magic emerges. It is, in fact, a quality of charisma, an esprit de corps that elevates all who come in contact with the team. That is, people don't necessarily want to be a part of the team, as such, but do want to be *around* the team because in so doing their own bigness, their own possibility and promise are triggered; indeed, their very humanity is enriched. People are better just by being a part of the environment, the context created by the team.

Beyond the elevating effect it has on others, however, the magic factor of the TL team also produces something akin to synergy, within the team and beyond. *Synergy* is one of those business buzzwords that has been misunderstood and misused—surely overused—in the organizational world. But it is a real phenomenon, one that defies simple explanation. Synergy occurs when two or more people interact in such a cohesive and interconnected way that they generate a result greater than the sum of their combined parts—meaning one plus one somehow produces seven, for instance. It is a disarming reality but one that often happens when the right people unite at the right time around the right objective.

One of the best examples of synergy was the Beatles. As individuals, these four working-class lads from Liverpool were four talented musicians. John Lennon and Paul McCartney in their post-Beatles careers were like, say, Billy Joel and Elton John, or Norah Jones and Alicia Keys—gifted musicians who over the years have produced some fine music but not world-shakers. Subsequent to the breakup of the Beatles, individually Lennon and McCartney produced some good music, in several instances some extremely good music, but nothing close to what they created together.

As a band Lennon and McCartney, along with George Harrison and Ringo Starr, had synergy, a magic that had never been seen before and hasn't been seen since. They had a synergy that shook the world. They not only fundamentally shifted our understanding of popular music—how it's made and by whom, what it sounds like, and what it can and should say—they also altered, in some cases forever changed, culture around the world. They weren't merely a product of the radical 1960s; they played an instrumental role in shaping that iconic time. Together these four individuals had something they could never have had apart. They had magic. They had synergy: The results they produced far, far exceeded the sum of their combined parts, and we still feel those results a half century later.

The point here is that the magic "it" factor of the transformative leadership team does not issue in just a "groovy" feeling. They don't just make themselves and those around them feel better. Their magic issues in a qualitative and quantitative impact. They have synergy. As the team's results begin to come in, TL team members come to accept as an almost inevitable part of the transformative team process what to ordinary teams would be astonishing. They produce results that defy rational explanation and often do so with ease. Simple fact. And while it never becomes "ho-hum," it does become an accepted result of authentic teamness.

Beyond synergy, there is at least one other measurable result that this magic generates. The "it" factor seems to elevate the quality of performance of each member of the team. In a true team of transformative leaders there is a standard of excellence and achievement that in any other context would be both daunting and largely unachievable. Yet within the larger, growth-based approach of transforming, integrative leadership, it is not uncommon for every member of the team to consistently exceed their own expectations, typically performing at higher levels of effectiveness than at any other time in their careers.

This level of individual achievement is not entirely mysterious or inexplicable. In no small degree it's a direct function of the commitment of the team members as a whole to pushing and challenging one another within the larger team growth process. And certainly the buddy relationships described in chapter 20—with all of the hard, confrontational, sometimes grueling and time-intensive work that they entail—are central to the high level of individual accomplishment.

Nevertheless, the level of individual leadership success also seems to be a consequence of the larger context or cultural environment of the team itself. It is a result of the emergence of a "strong context," an intentionally created team culture that reflects an extremely potent collective consciousness. It seems to have an energetic reality of its own, elevating expectations of what is possible, what is acceptable, and what must be achieved. And it appears to be a central piece in the achievement of individual excellence.

What is clear is that when a team is formed of people who consistently exhibit all seven of these characteristics, the extraordinary follows. When the transformative leadership team has been created, not only do we see magic but, perhaps more important, we see hard, measurable results as well as human and organizational results. Lives are changed and whole organizations are transformed.

SUMMARY

Because they have learned to fearlessly take themselves on and to generously take each other on, because they understand what it means to be committed at a cellular level to something bigger than themselves, the true team knows that together there is little they cannot do. Together, as a band of brothers and sisters, they calmly, brilliantly stand. They stand with vision, compassion, and unapologetic boldness before the world and declare, "What we have disclosed, we will make a reality, circumstance be damned." To paraphrase the great scientist of antiquity, Archimedes, having learned to so stand, they have learned to move the earth. And they do so with regularity. Their leadership has become but an extension of who they are as individuals and, surely, as a team, the transformative team that audaciously says yes to the call, to the brave possibility of life's promise.

But what kind of an organization would a team like this create and lead? In chapter 24, we consider what such an organization would look like and what it means to lead a body of people in playing the big game and playing it to win.

CHAPTER 24

THE TRANSFORMATIVE ORGANIZATION: Playing the Big Game

"Your playing small does not serve the world. Who are you to not be great?"

—Nelson Mandela

A company is stronger if it is bound by love rather by than fear.

—Herb Kelleher, Cofounder of Southwest Airlines

There are two fundamental realities about the nature of life in the twenty-first century that today's organizational leaders must come to grips with if they are to be good leaders, understanding "good" both in terms of effectiveness *and* morality—and by the way, in the transformative model these two understandings of *good* are seen as inseparable.

The first reality reflects a macro point of view. Today, business is the most powerful institution in the world. For good or ill, whether we like it or not, business in effect rules the world. It shapes politics, education, entertainment, even religion. Today religion, especially in America, is marketed to the general public—witness the rise of mega-churches, which are shrewdly run *as* businesses, evangelical businesses that bring in millions of worldly dollars monthly to support their otherworldly mission. And in politics, the influence of business is even more palpable (if perhaps more insidious), reflected tellingly in the new nomenclature. Where do you suppose the notion of a Republican or Democratic *brand* actually came from? The language and thinking of the business world pervades and shapes all aspects of modern society.

Whether we like it or not, business is king. Thus, to over simplify a bit, if business as an institution proves to be good, human civilization by extension also stands a decent chance of being good. Human society may, then, continue to flourish, probably improving in areas where we still struggle as a society now. But surely the reverse is also true: If business is bad, effectively and morally, civilization will be all the worse for the wear and human society will likely decline (or *continue* to decline, depending on your perspective). Given the turn of events over the past several years in the world of business, from Enron to Bernie Madoff to the global finance scandals and beyond, recognizing this cause-and-effect relationship is not especially encouraging. Unpleasant though it may seem, it is a fact we must face and address.

The second point is more of a micro point. The average adult spends the majority of her quality waking hours in the workplace, focused on work-related issues, and not with the people she loves the most, focused on matters that are of greatest importance—family, friends, and other matters of personal life. Consequently work may influence her experience of the world as much or more than any other institutional aspect of her life. Work shapes how she understands herself and how she relates to the world—her family and friends, her coworkers and other professionals. Any way you slice it, today, work and the organization, and business in particular, shapes the world, our understanding of the world, and our understanding of our selves more than just about any other factor.

The implications are inescapable. To simply be honest leaders—transactional, transformational, or otherwise—and to truly be adult leaders, to be transformative leaders, that is, we must come to terms with the degree to which these two facts deepen our influence, extend our reach, and therefore expand our responsibility. As leaders in the organizational world, especially if that organization is a business, the effect of what we do reaches further into society, at a more profound level, than ever before. Denying this enlarged responsibility no more changes it than somehow believing that cigarettes are healthy makes them good for you. Denying it simply means we're liars and not the adult leaders we pretend to be. But denying it is not an option if we choose to lead from the transforming point of view. If so, the choice has been made for us: Stand up, face up, and lead as grown-ups by recognizing the scope of what is truly in front of us, like it or not. We're closer to that tipping point than we may realize.

THE TWO INFORMING PRINCIPLES

These two salient aspects of reality inform everything a leader must be up to in shaping the organizational culture. They also suggest the importance of the two most important underlying principles in the TL organization. The two require one another. The first is that *the organization must be designed to win, to play big, to achieve excellence at every level*. The second is *the organization must be founded in love rather than fear*. Yes, love.

Both of these larger principles must be present at all times. *Both* must be present. If, say, we have an organization that is exclusively committed to winning, then we end up with today's corrupted banking giants who callously led us into the Great Recession. Or if we are exclusively committed to the ethic of compassion, we can lose sight of the fact that the loving thing to do is to demand excellence and achievement. Thus we have mistaken rolling over for kindness. Because we are easily seduced into thinking that love is warm and fuzzy, excellence must be held up as a partner principle beside the ethic of love.

Our culture tends to reduce love to its affective dimension (love as a feeling rather than as a commitment and the source of true power). Thus, love loses its holistic reality as the very creative force of life that it is, and we lose sight of the fact that the transformative promise is one of the most sober-mindedly powerful expressions of love existent. As such it calls us to full self-expansion and to excellence as a function *of* that love, irrespective of how daunting the calling may be. Because of this reductive tendency (to reduce love to its by-product, the warm and fuzzy feeling), we must remind ourselves regularly that succeeding and playing big are aspects of the centerpiece of TL—in the context of the transformative model are, in fact, articulations of love.

THE LOOK AND SMELL OF SUCCESS

Based on years of research and more than two decades of hands-on work, I have identified what I see as the nine most salient characteristics of a transformative organization. These nine traits are surely not the final word, but they represent, I believe, a sound launching pad. A transformative organization may not necessarily be at full strength in each and every one of these qualities, but it will be strong in most and consciously developing in the areas of weakness.

1. *Inspired and inspiring people are the norm.* In the TL organization it is understood that an organization's most fundamental element is its people. As the term *corporation* suggests (the original Latin *corporare* means "to combine in one body"), the people—not the products (or services), not the policies or procedures, not the facilities, offices, or locations, not the marketing tag lines, the records, or the profits (or losses)—are the organization.

As *body* implies, we are talking about an organic entity. A corporation is not a machine, not a procedural mechanism for delivering product and profit. Rather, it is a living, breathing organism made up of people, *people* who create and sell products, *people* who implement policy, *people* who execute strategy. The people are the business. And in a cultural, political democracy where we are encouraged to believe that government is to be "of the people, by the people, and for the people," every day it becomes more and more difficult to pretend this is not so in business. Put another way, it is increasingly difficult to succeed when people are understood, consciously or not, as merely the *means* to the end of profits.

So the TL organization understands itself as an entity designed of, by, and for people, *inspired* people. When people have been inspired, literally "breathed into by spirit," they are fired up. The creative spark that exists in all human beings has been fanned into a full-blown flame. They have a sense of their own power and purpose, indeed their importance. It is not just the leaders who are inspired and inspiring. Employees from top to bottom are on fire. Their spirits have been called forth. They are excited about what they bring to the corporate equation. What they do matters, whether it's pushing a broom at 4 a.m. or presenting a new proposal to the board of directors at noon. The vision and rationale of the organization is shared by *all.*

And this shared sense of importance in achieving the larger organizational objective is not some manipulative fantasy used by the leadership to extract every last ounce of energy from employees. It is a fact, a consequence of a simple connecting of the organizational dots, done again and again and again, by the leadership on behalf of the employees, pointed out *to* the employees at every opportunity. And what is the underlying message of the connected dots? It is unapologetic and clear: Because who you are and what you do matters, we, the leaders, are here to serve you (gasp!) the united body, the corporation; we're not here to serve the bottom line (double gasp!). Your ideas matter. Your creative teamwork matters. Your efficient execution matters. Your growth matters. Your achievement of excellence matters. Your well-being and, by extension, your family's well-being matter.

It has often been said that leadership is a sacred trust. Wise leaders of every stripe understand the importance of this trust. Supporting this sacred trust is this sacred commitment: Our job as leaders is to inspire people, inspire them to recognize their importance, inspire them to contribute on a more meaningful level, inspire them to show up with enthusiasm, inspire them to serve each other, to serve the customer and the community, and to help us realize the vision.

I am increasingly convinced that this inspiration thing (which, remember, is not to be confused with motivation) is the single most difficult responsibility of the authentic leader. It requires perpetually renewed commitment, perpetually reasserted courage, perpetually reignited imagination, perpetually reestablished discipline. But here is the interesting thing about the value of legitimate inspiration: When the leaders have the guts to inspire and the people are thus inspired, the people themselves become inspiring—to the leaders and to each other. It becomes a self-sustaining cycle that reawakens the leaders' energy level, the leaders' hope and passion, and it reminds the leaders why they are leaders, if, that is, they are or are becoming transformative.

And make no mistake about it, this whole inspiration thing is a matter of leadership grit, intelligence, and substance (as opposed to mere cheerleading), a function of discipline and a determination to regularly rise to the challenge of keeping the fires stoked beneath the followers while holding the larger context for everything else. It is every bit as difficult as sustaining a powerful, effective team. *And it demands a vivid, compelling vision, without which this brave, enlightened level of inspiration is not sustainable.* But when a culture of inspiration is in place, when it is focused on and nurtured with consistency, nothing less than transformation and exponential growth occurs. Guaranteed.

2. *Teamness reigns.* The transformative organization is led by a team of leaders. But teamness is not exclusive to the top rung of the leadership ladder. It flows throughout the organization. The senior leadership team and the organizational vision are supported by the leadership teams in the sales organization, the finance group, the marketing people, the operations people, et cetera. Just as the CEO has her team, the senior VP of marketing, the CIO, the CFO, and so forth all have their respective teams, and each of the directors has her or his team, and each of the managers, on and on, down through the organization. With strong central leadership, this extension of a broad variety of teams does not create division. Far from creating silos, this extension of teamness creates greater unity. It breaks down silos, because when the teams are consciously constructed, each team's purpose statement is in alignment with the team to which they report, which is in alignment with the declared purpose of the team to which they report, ultimately all being in total alignment with the larger, stated organizational vision. This overall alignment is not remotely a stretch—it's an organic unfolding from a strong senior team with a powerful vision.

The integrative organizational vision that informs the leadership is one that transcends and includes all the various team purpose statements throughout the company. Beginning from the lower levels, each team is held by the greater team above it, which is held by the greater team above it, which is ultimately held by the senior leadership team at the very top. And the senior executive team is held by the larger organization itself, which includes the board of directors. Every team of leaders has its own purpose, and each purpose is in complete alignment with the larger purpose of the senior executive team, and all purposes serve the greater vision which informs every element of the corporation.[1]

This function of transcending and including is analogous to expanding concentric circles. The smallest circle is held by and within a slightly larger circle, and these two circles are held by a third, slightly larger circle, and this third circle is held by a fourth, and so on all the way out to the largest circle, which holds all of the circles. Figure 24.1 illustrates this encircled and unified nature of the transformative organization.

Teamness is not only central in the creation of unity; it also forms the basis for the individual growth that is the backbone of organizational excellence and expansion. It is in the team-building process that individuals are challenged to grow, to enhance their leadership and develop their work-related skills, all within the larger framework of achieving the declared corporate goals and objectives.

And it is in the team environment where accountability achieves its greatest hold, where individual leaders are held to account for their productivity and their other commitments in a forum of their peers.

Figure 24.1 The Concentric Circles of Teams

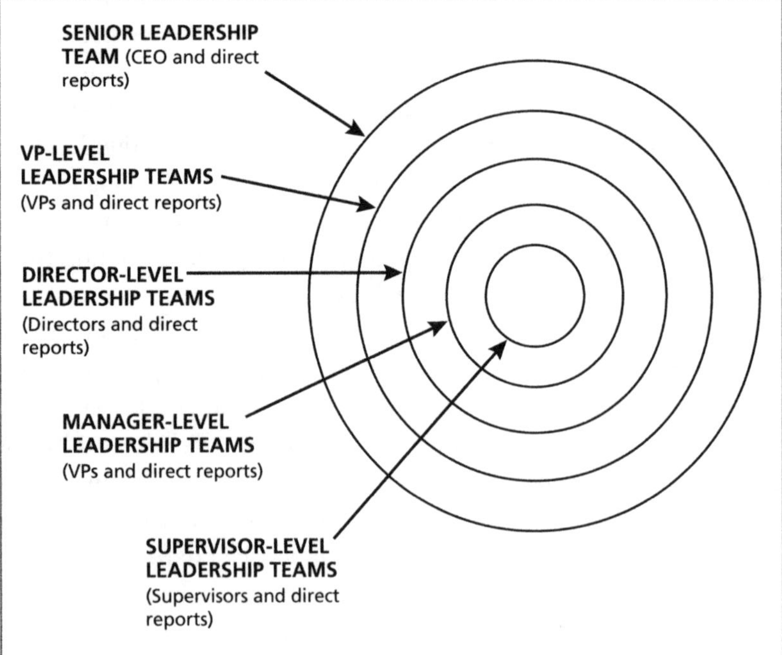

In a transformative organization the inner circle is not the elite. The inner circle is the field level teams which are held by all the rest of the leadership teams. The most outer level is the senior executive leadership team, which holds all the other teams and employees, understanding its primary purpose as serving those teams and employees.

It's in this environment where individual and team weakness are confronted and individual and team strengths are enhanced, where clarity of individual and collective purpose is achieved and regularly reinforced, where team and, by extension, organizational cohesion is established, and where the commitment to and capacity for honesty, contribution, excellence, and achievement is established, solidified, and reinforced. In fact, the team process forms the basis for all organizational growth and all organizational accomplishment. Both individual and organizational success issue from a tough and rich understanding and implementation of team.

3. ***Vision informs and guides through and through.*** The TL organization knows where it is headed. It is in the business of disclosing new worlds, of making real the vision that has been established by the corporate leadership. Everything that it does, from the creation of new sales initiatives, to the implementation of a reorganizational process, to accounting procedures, to all hiring and firing, to all community or marketing outreach strategies, is informed, directly and indirectly, by the vision. From top to bottom, people show up for work with an implicit or explicit understanding that the organization exists for the realization of the vision, for the disclosure of the world that the leadership has designed (with considerable employee input) and the entirety of the company embraces as their own. All goals, all awards and rewards, all promotions, all new hires (and dismissals), all possibilities and options are understood as contained within this larger, all-encompassing vision.

4. ***People are growing, learning at all levels.*** Inspired people are people who are growing, who are afforded the opportunity for genuine development as leaders, as employees, and as human beings. For at least two reasons, the TL organization has come to understand itself not merely as a business organization (or nonprofit, political, educational, or military organization) but also as an educational organization. The first reason for this more expansive role as educator is to facilitate growth. Remember that growth is one of the four higher needs described in chapter 15—fulfilled and empowered people must be growing, period. To have an excellence-based, productive workforce that is sustainable, you must have growing, developing people.

The second reason reflects the influence of business on society and culture. Transformative business leaders understand that they have a duty to consciously and intentionally choose how they influence their people. Business influences not just how we think about profit and loss but how we think about life. Since we spend most of our quality waking hours in the workplace, remember, we are being affected, even molded by that workplace. We become like those with whom we associate. There is no way to avoid it. It follows then that the business environment shapes the people (us) who then greatly contribute to the shape of adult culture. The honest, wise business leader accepts this shaping as one of her given responsibilities. As a leader she knows, like it or not, there's no opting out.

The transformative leader, in fact, embraces this responsibility with a passion. She not only sees it as an opportunity to affect people in the organization and simultaneously affect the organization's success, but she also relishes it as a chance to affect society and the world.

The form that this growth takes is based on two types of learning. First is the intellectual and emotional self-awareness training noted in chapter 20, which is fostered in the team environment and usually via the buddy system. Second, the more traditional type of organizational learning—technical job skills, management skills, sales training, organizational and business understanding—is systematically encouraged through a vital annual review methodology and through thoroughgoing, well-executed developmental plans for every employee, top to bottom. Thus, whether the organization is 40 or 40,000 people (or more), every individual is given the opportunity to "take himself on" as a human being, and every individual has an unfolding developmental plan to which and for which she must account.

5. *Accountability and expectation win the day.* The TL organization prides itself on its capacity to measure success and to hold individuals to account. It is only in honest and open assessment that there is opportunity for growth. It prides itself on the increasing levels of expectation and demand placed on its employees, because only in being challenged on a regular basis is the capacity for rising to the occasion learned. A shallow understanding of the TL model can misunderstand caring for and commitment to employee well-being as a form of "softness." But that misses the point of caring altogether.

When we truly care about the people we lead, while we meet them where they are initially, we do not ever regard them as incapable or weak, assuming they cannot rise to the organization's higher standards of working and living. Rather, we give them the necessary support and tools, the necessary opportunity and training, and then we firmly encourage them, aggressively challenge them, to step into more productive behaviors. In the transformative model that means that we push and demand, expect and hold to account at levels that far exceed even those of the best transactional organizations. In the transformative organizational world, people learn how to deliver on what they have promised (intentionality). In the TL universe, people learn how to honor their word (responsibility). Accountability in such an organization is itself a piece of the transforming tool kit, a way in which we grow and develop the best and the brightest.

Unswerving accountability standards and ever-increasing levels of expectation serve one other important purpose. Without both of these firmly in place, inspiration proves feckless. Unless people know that the goodness and greatness toward which, out of which they have been inspired is something that can be quantified, at least in part, unless they know that they will be held to account for their inspired commitments, after a few rounds of inspiring ideas and meetings the efforts to inspire greatness prove hollow—just more rah-rah presented by cheerleaders who call themselves business leaders. Inspiration without the productivity that accountability and expectation require soon proves entirely devoid of meaning and power.

6. *Creativity, courage, and risk taking are assumed.* Given that life seeks its own expansion, is compelled by the unquenchable urge for ever more life—seeks more complexity, more meaning, more beauty, and more power—organizational life at its best also exhibits these qualities in vivid detail. Perhaps the most vital quality of the life-giving ethic of transformation is creativity—bringing into existence the new and different, what before had not existed. In the TL organization creativity and its frequent companion, courage, are not only encouraged, they are rewarded throughout the organization. The transformative organization is always looking for new and better objectives and is perpetually in search of new and better ways of achieving its objectives. Thus it places the creative impulse in the pantheon of the highest leadership and organizational virtues.

The transformative organization, therefore, embraces well-chosen risks and smart risk taking. Further, it recognizes that to be able to legitimately encourage the creative capacities of its leaders and its employees, it must be tolerant of failure. It must accept and be comfortable with the simple reality that when creativity and risk are held at a premium there will be a good number of missteps and mistakes. In fact, in the TL organization, failure of a type—particularly the most creative and bold failures, those seen as the greatest expressions of courageous and smart risk taking—is seen as good and from time to time is itself rewarded.[2]

7. *Pride in belonging pervades.* The transformative organization, with its clear sense of direction and its compelling vision, its emphasis on teamness up and down the organization, and its unapologetic commitment to growing and serving its people, creates an environment where its employees know they are valued, where the people who constitute the corporation know they matter. As a result, the TL organization satisfies the fundamental urge that we all have to be a part of something larger than ourselves. The employees in such an entity not only go home in the evening knowing that what they do contributes and has meaning, but they also have a deeply satisfying understanding that they fit in, that they are welcomed, that they belong. It's not a stretch to suggest that the TL organization gives them a sense that they have a meaningful place in the world in addition to in their homes, families, and social or religious circles, a place that recognizes their worth and that truly adds meaning to their lives.

But the TL corporation to which they belong is not just any organization; it is an extraordinary organization, a cutting-edge organization dedicated to excellence, to achievement at the highest level, and it is dedicated to drawing out the best in its people, for the people themselves and for its customers. It has increasingly established a reputation that reflects all of these admirable qualities. It is no surprise then that the people who belong to this organization take considerable pride in their organization. They take great delight in telling their friends and family where they work and what makes the organization so unique, indeed so extraordinary. Yet they don't discuss their work life from a place of braggadocio. No, they speak about their organization from a place of gratitude, a place of deep appreciation for their good fortune, because they understand how it could be, how it was in the past at other, probably transactional, businesses and organizations. They know they have something special, know they have been blessed, and they speak about the organization with great respect.

8. *Exceptional and ever-improving talent is a given.* Like attracts like. What that means at the TL organization is that big people, and people who want to be big, are drawn to and want to work in the organization. It's not magic and it's not easy, but over time the quality and the standards of the leadership and the employees in general have risen to levels one would expect of an organization expressly committed to excellence, expansion, and the achievement of the extraordinary.

Those people who have embraced the opportunity for deep development have grown and begun to achieve new levels of accomplishment. And those people in leadership who have refused to "take themselves on," who have been unwilling to step up to the greater challenge that TL requires, have either self-opted out or have been encouraged to opt out, and have moved on.

An important feature of the transformative organization, however, is the fact that the individual is invited but not required to grow himself. For those not in leadership, the only requirement is productivity and a commitment not to hinder the growth of others. Solid individual contributors who carry their weight are respected and honored. Yet transformative leaders also understand that some of those unwilling or unable to engage at the higher standards of the TL model, over time, can become bitter, even toxic, and if left unchecked can do considerable damage to morale, intentionally or otherwise undermining the growth of others. The leadership is thus unflinching and unapologetic when it becomes necessary to sever ties with such people.

Finally, one of the more satisfying dimensions of the transforming organization is the degree to which its vision and proven commitment to bold accomplishment attracts talent. Quality people want to invest themselves with other people of quality, want to be a part of something worthy of their talent. Thus, the TL organization not only has strong and growing talent at all key positions, but they are regularly approached by rising and established stars in the industry who want to be a part of the unfolding in the TL adventure they've heard so much about. The talent level seems to grow by the day. It's an unavoidable, natural consequence of a soulful commitment to playing the big game.

9. *Extraordinary results are the norm.* At this point it should go without saying that an organization that possesses the eight traits we've discussed would be an organization that has become accustomed to generating stellar, quantifiable results. Talented, inspired, perpetually growing people, committed to a bold, brave vision of what could and what must be are inclined to be exceptionally productive and have remarkable results to show for their hard yet rewarding work.

What may not be as obvious is the fact that such people, the ones who embrace their causality and are led by leaders who understand intentionality at the deepest level, know how to produce extraordinary results irrespective of external circumstances, like the economy, for instance. Because they understand that their strength issues from within, because they understand life as fundamentally expansive, they know how to adapt and adjust to whatever life throws their way and still remain focused on the prize detailed in their vision. They are always innovating, imagining new and different products and services, and they have more ideas and possibilities to try out than they know what to do with. An economic downturn is a chance not to contract but to go bigger, get stronger, take bolder, braver risks—though still thoughtful and well-chosen—than ever before. The net result is that they remain at the forefront of those organizations who seem to continue right along while everyone else is falling to pieces. Extraordinary results are extraordinary results, regardless of which way the wind seems to blow. They expect and they produce nothing less.

SUMMARY

For some readers, this description may seem like "pie in the sky," more aspirational than doable. But I assure you, not only has it been achieved, not only is it being achieved, it is immanently achievable in any organization, in any industry.

Difficult, yes. Most things worth doing are. But the rewards that the TL model generates are incomparable and frequently life changing. And for the leaders who understand precisely how much is at stake, who are awake enough to recognize the precipice upon which we as a society stand, it is not only something that *can* be done, it is something that must be done. In the words of Starbucks founder, chairman, and CEO Howard Schultz, "There are moments in our lives when we must summon the courage to make choices that go against reason . . . but we lean forward nonetheless because, despite all the risks and rational argument, we believe that the path that we are choosing is the right and best thing to do. We refuse to be bystanders. . . ."[3]

We refuse to be bystanders because to do so would be to sacrifice our souls, to sacrifice all that we are and have the potential to be. We refuse because we know that deep within resides a leader who would do more than turn a profit, a leader who would do more than merely please "the Street." Deep within resides a leader of integrity and vision, of boldness and character, a leader who would stand and make a transforming difference in the lives of people yet unmet, a difference in a world that is broken and longing, a difference in a world yet to be, but one that must be, imagined.

In chapter 25 we return to that individual leader. We consider what it means to take ourselves on as leaders. We consider, in fact, what it means to refuse to be bystanders any longer.

CHAPTER 25

TAKING YOURSELF ON AS A LEADER: The Only Way Out Is Through the Middle

> There is a clinical difference between fending off threat or attack and positive triumph and achievement, between protecting, defending and preserving oneself and reaching out for fulfillment, for excitement and for enlargement.
>
> **—Abraham Maslow**

It seems safe to say that the majority of organizational leaders, particularly in the business world, are not in positions of leadership because of their deep commitment to contribute to the human condition, to grow themselves, or to achieve true excellence. They operate from a largely unexamined mind-set that typically sees achievement as besting their opponents. These are the defenders, consciously or not, of the status quo. They're not the game changers. At best they're champions of conformity. Conformity at high levels of financial success, perhaps, but conformity all the same—they seek to do the ordinary well, perhaps very well. But that's it.

It's not self-expansion or the realization of their latent capacities that matters. It's not the disclosure of new worlds, the creation of new and better possibilities, or the act of putting a dent in the universe that matters. Indeed, for many, it's as basic as defeating, preferably squashing, their competition. Their standard of measure depends on someone else. To them it's zero sum game, kill or be killed. To put it bluntly, this type of leader is a Neanderthal in a suit and tie—or a Chanel pants suit. And it's not courage that is required for these primitives who on the surface *appear* so twenty-first century. What's called for is cleverly applied force, sometimes brute force, with a dash of manufactured bravado thrown in. And if it's not survival they're driven by, then it's unexamined greed, which is merely survival magnified. Either way they are captives of fear, a fear-based, eat-or-be-eaten mind-set.

The new model represented by the transformative leader may not appear as machismo, but it requires far greater bravery and daring. Indeed it demands true courage, imagination, and *real* power. It calls for a quality of leadership that a world in upheaval, a world looking for a better way, desperately needs.

Curiously enough, the way in which this leadership courage is first manifest is in surrender. Surrender, you'll recall, does not mean giving in or giving up; it doesn't mean tossing in the towel in defeat. It is, rather, accepting the truth, seeing and accepting the reality that exists before us. What the transformative leader must surrender to is the simple but challenging fact that we must *take ourselves on* as leaders and as people if we are to play the transformative game. We must be willing to surrender to the fact that even though we may already be in esteemed positions of leadership, we still have a long way to go.

Even if we have demonstrated consistent leadership success, it doesn't matter who we are or what we've accomplished. We still have much to learn . . . about life, about being human, about leading others, about producing extraordinary results. No exceptions. Thus, the TL approach to leading others requires that we first accept and address this fact by challenging ourselves at the deepest level. To paraphrase the words of Gandhi, we must be the change we wish to lead.

Thus, to effectively lead others we must first and foremost lead ourselves. The only alternative, I'm afraid, is hypocrisy and, inevitably, failed leadership. Further, if we are to lead within the context of transformative leadership, we must be willing to break free from the pack of normalcy, the world of agreement (discussed in chapter 3), which at its best amounts to well-done mediocrity. We must break free from the strictures of what society says is and isn't possible and from what our own historically based patterns of thought, our well-worn personal programming, tell us is acceptable and possible. We must embrace the risky business of leading beyond our individual and organizational comfort.

And it always begins with us. You and I as individuals who would truly live life. And you and I as leaders of others, with a charge to move others to a better, brighter, and more enduring place of meaning and success. In the TL model it begins with the leader being willing to say to himself, "I must embrace my still only partially expressed power and learn to express it fully. Therefore, I must take myself on at every level. Now."

WAX ON, WAX OFF

So what, then, does it mean to "take yourself on"?

At the beginning of the film *The Karate Kid* (the original), the kid, Daniel, approaches Mr. Miyagi, the handyman/martial arts master, to teach him karate as protection against local bullies. Miyagi is at first reluctant. As a karate master he knows that his marshal art is indeed an *art* form and a way of life, not merely a type of fighting. To truly practice karate one must be willing to *take oneself on* from top to bottom, rethink everything, challenge nearly all aspects of oneself. It's a worldview, and it's a discipline in the strictest meaning of the word. Furthermore, from the point of view of the master, to truly teach karate, the teacher must be willing to *take on* his student, heart and soul, not merely teach him the physical moves of fighting. Given that Miyagi is unsure of Daniel's commitment, motivation, and worthiness, he is hesitant.

Yet as the kid persists, Miyagi relents—but only after testing him first. He summons Daniel to his home to begin his training, which Daniel is soon to learn initially amounts to painting fences, sanding decks, and washing and waxing his collection of antique cars—doing the tedious and repetitive work that indirectly relates to the art of karate and directly relates to the discipline involved in taking oneself on.

When Daniel shows up, Miyagi asks him, "You ready?"

The kid responds with a casual shrug of his shoulders, saying, "Guess so."

With a sigh of exasperation, Miyagi squats down to the ground, gently guiding Daniel down with him, and he then explains, "you walk on the road, walk right side—*safe*. Walk left side—*safe*. You walk middle—sooner or later get-a squished, just-a like-a grape."

Pausing and pointing to the ground, he continues, "Here, karate same thing. Either you karate do, *yes*. Or you karate do, *no*. You karate do, *guess so*, you just-a like-a grape." You play all-in or you do not play at all, he says. To play partially in and partially out at the same time, as in "guess so," is simply too dangerous. And Miyagi will have none of it.

Thus, he makes an agreement with Daniel, a "sacred pact," Miyagi calls it.

"I promise teach karate—I do my part," Miyagi says. "You promise learn. I *say*. You *do*. No questions—*that* your part. Deal?"

"Deal," Daniel agrees.

Then, placing a soaking sponge into his hand, Miyagi tells Daniel to get busy washing and waxing the cars. When Daniel begins to protest, Miyagi authoritatively stops him short with a fierce, staccato, "Heh!" and then soberly says, "Wax on, right hand. Wax off, left hand. Wax on. Wax off. Wax on. Wax off." Then with a more lighthearted tone, he says, "And remember to breathe. Breathing very important." With that Miyagi turns and walks away, in a few words having established both the intensity required and the commitment necessary if one is to be taken on by a master.

In our case we are both Mr. Miyagi *and* Daniel-san. Since we are taking *ourselves* on, we are both master and student. And we are challenging ourselves at many levels of who we are as leaders and as men and women. In the process of becoming transformative leaders, taking ourselves on means we must first lead our own transformation. We must lead the process by which we systematically call forth our promise, perhaps even our greatness. And we do that by saying "yes" all the way in. There is no "maybe." There is no "sort of," no "guess so." Only "yes" or "no."

And "no" *is* an acceptable answer, if it is honest and if it understands the consequences: In saying "no" to this growth process we are also saying "no" to the entire transformative leadership process. We cannot lead such an iterative process, a process in which we expect the leaders and followers we guide to take themselves on, unless we ourselves are doing the same. We must be willing to commit ourselves to the journey, to make promises to ourselves regarding our being and becoming, and *to keep those promises*. Unless we are willing to make that sacred pact with ourselves, we will be ineffective in wrapping ourselves in the mantle of transformative leadership. If we attempt to play *sort-of, kind-of, maybe*, if we try to walk in the middle of the road, we'll get flattened, "squished, just-a like-a grape."

WHAT IT LOOKS LIKE

Some of the best thinkers on leadership have long suggested that leadership is nothing less than a sacred trust between leader and follower, as we earlier noted. Indeed, the issue of trust seems more important today than, perhaps, at any other point in history. As leadership scholar Joanne Ciulla aptly puts it, "Gone are the bosses of the industrial era. Organizations have entered a new age where employees are partners, part of the team."[1] And without trust the words *partner* and *team* are little more than slogans. The best conventional leaders seem to have always implicitly understood the importance of this sacred trust and have tacitly agreed to something along these lines: "As your leader I will strive to be the best leader I can be; I'll guide you in a manner that has integrity and seeks to produce the best possible outcomes available for you, my followers, for all the stakeholders, and for myself." Or something to that effect. Not too bad, though it doesn't mean that the leader is going to *keep* this implied transactional agreement. It just means that the implied promise is there.

A Sacred Leadership Pact

In the world of the TL organization, the agreement is explicit and it goes much further. Indeed, it's a pact, and as Mr. Miyagi says, it's a "sacred pact." It's sacrosanct, never to be violated, to be honored perhaps above everything else in the leader–follower relationship and in the leader's relationship with her- or himself. It's a pact that has some teeth—big, sharp teeth. It's demanding, relentless, and therefore not to be agreed to lightly.

A formal transformative leadership pact has certain essential features, beginning with an assumption about the leader's talent: It's not an accident that you're a leader; we'll assume you've got the goods or you wouldn't be in your leadership position. But it also understands that no leader, regardless how accomplished or esteemed, has arrived. Not by a long shot. There's work to do. And for most of us, regardless of previous achievements, there's *a lot* of work to do. The first act of challenging ourselves to expand and deepen our leadership range is acknowledging our need to develop and then owning the process by which growth is accomplished. An example of the type of pact transformative leaders make with themselves appears in Box 25.1.

Box 25.1 A Leader's Sacred Pact

As a leader my first commitment is to challenge and grow myself in all areas of my life. While I acknowledge my leadership talents (and accomplishments), as a human being and as a leader I still have much to learn, much growing to do. Thus, my promise is to push, encourage, and otherwise move myself to growth—intellectually, emotionally, psychologically, and in any other way necessary to realize the full extent of my potential.

There are five reasons for this commitment: first, so that I'm better equipped to grow my followers—as individuals, as employees, and as leaders; second, so that I'm able to create and sustain a culture of excellence and achievement within the organization, one that generates nothing less than extraordinary results, and consistently so; third, so that as a result of this excellence and accomplishment the organization's employees positively affect their families, the larger community, and society; fourth, so that the organization enhances the value for all stakeholders, including shareholders; and fifth, so that I experience greater joy, meaning, and success in who I am, how I live and lead, and what I get done with my life.

One Large Step Beyond (and a Final Warning)

The transforming process described in part II of the book directly applies to the leader's commitment to taking himself on. Yet as a leader, indeed as a leader of transformation, there is now a higher calling. That is, for the transformative leader the larger call to a life lived to its fullest has a built-in rationale, one that says, "My leadership, by definition, demands that I leave my followers and my organization much better than the way I initially found them. My leadership is for something bigger than just me and my little tribe, however 'tribe' is defined. Yes, I and they matter, but that is just one small part of why I lead. I take myself on, I make this commitment *so that* I may cause something greater, more complex and meaningful that serves the good of all who are directly and indirectly touched by my leadership and by this organization."

Indeed, the commitment to take ourselves on has an entirely different and greater order of magnitude when it is made *as a leader* who intentionally responds to the urge of the transformative promise. The truth is, whether we like it or not, as transformative leaders everything we do is magnified. Not because we're special but because we have said yes to something that is committed to the possibility that would violate and transcend the world of agreement. Thus the implications of who we are and what we do will always be more extensive than may immediately meet the eye; we must surrender to and own this simple fact. In taking ourselves on as transformative leaders, by virtue of the declared intention, we are magnifying the impact of our successes and our failures. We are magnifying the consequences of our very lives, intending that magnification to be for the good of all those we touch, whether directly or several times removed. In taking ourselves on as leaders we are crossing the Rubicon. And once that river is crossed, it is difficult, perhaps impossible, to go back without significant, usually painful consequences. So choose wisely.

The Need for a Little Help from Our Friends

We don't do this thing called life alone. The more we wake up, the more we understand life and the human condition, the more we see how true it is that we need each other. It is only the idiot, in the truest sense of that word, who doesn't get this simple fact. The word *idiot* comes from the ancient Greek *idotes*, meaning private person, particularly someone who is ignorant because he lives almost exclusively in his own little world. Unless we want to follow the path of the idiot, we must come to grips with the simple fact that we truly are in this thing together—whether this "thing" is the improvement of our lives, or the success of our organization, or the survival of humanity. We don't do life alone, particularly not if we intend to do it successfully and powerfully. The same applies to our growth as leaders and as human beings. Significant individual growth requires a group, a team, or at the very least, a partnership.

A primary reason for this need is the simple fact that we don't see ourselves clearly. We cannot. We are subjective creatures, meaning we aren't able to observe ourselves with detached objectivity. We are unable to see the *subject*—us—clearly and without bias. We're not even close. At best we see ourselves only partially, *not* impartially. Our perspective on ourselves is unavoidably limited and, in fact, wrong much more of the time than we care to admit.

Consider, for example, the fact that you have never seen your own face. You have never directly looked at your sweet little mug. You've seen images of it, photos, perhaps drawings or paintings, and you've seen your reflection in the mirror an infinite number of times. But you've never looked upon your face directly. Simple fact. Think about it. Therefore, in one sense at least, you don't know what you look like. But your spouse or partner, your children or your friends do. They have seen your face and see it quite a lot. They see it all the time, in fact. Your colleagues, employees, friends, and neighbors have seen it. They all see it frequently. In both a literal and figurative sense, they see things about you that you simply can't, don't, and won't—like how you really look from behind (yikes!), how your posture and profile are, and more important, how you show up as a leader and a person.

The simple fact is the people with whom we surround ourselves understand aspects, good and bad, of who we are and how we affect others and the world around us that we simply do not and cannot understand about ourselves. It's impossible for it to be otherwise. It's the nature of the beast. To see where we are as leaders and as human beings, therefore, we must get outside input.

In a sense, we are all a bit like the majestic, flightless bird, the Emperor penguin. Standing three to four feet tall, this unusual bird molts annually, losing old feathers to be replaced by new ones. During this molting process, which can last as long as thirty-four days, the bird is in a fasting mode, in effect starving itself. It is genetically programmed to do nothing but molt. It will not, effectively *cannot*, eat until the molting is complete. The challenge for the bird is that frequently it must remove feathers that will not fall free on their own. Thus it must rely on other penguins to help remove the feathers on its backside, feathers that it can't reach by itself. Without this help the bird will starve to death. It must have other birds to assist it or it will remain in an increasing torpor until it falls over dead.

Though we won't die because of our unreachable, unseeable blind spots, we surely won't develop past those blind spots, those unnecessary limitations, without some help from our fellow penguins. To grow as leaders we need others who have perspectives we do not, who can see what we cannot about ourselves and our leadership. To pretend otherwise is to become mired in a kind of leadership torpor.

This is where the buddy relationship described in chapter 20 comes in. I frequently marvel at the power of buddyship. It is a growth and leadership application I've used for as long as I have done transformational work. When it is properly instituted—with people of good will, integrity, and commitment—it never fails. Never. And for numerous reasons.

First, we are innately social creatures, which means we necessarily have the need for the restorative touch of other people. The need for human contact and connection is built into our genetic code. We derive strength from people who are able to remind us of who we are, of our deepest commitments, and of where we are going. It amounts to nothing less than a need to be wisely and honestly affirmed. Even the strongest, most buoyant personality gets mired down in self-defeating perspectives and needs to be encouraged ("refilled with courage") from time to time by another's perspective. In the process of taking ourselves on, we frequently need this moral support to maintain our brave course of expansion and development. Whether with a swift kick in the pants or a warm, supportive arm around our shoulder, we all need to be reminded of our capability and purpose. The buddy is to play both the role of the relentless athletic coach who is tough because he cares and that of the wise, constant companion who sees our talents, believes in us deeply, and without fail reminds us that we can do it. The myth of the rugged individual is precisely that, a myth.

Second, we need someone we can turn to for perspective in the face of the day-to-day challenges of leading. Having an ally who is capable of offering an intelligent point of view on a daunting situation increases the chances we will act with wisdom in the face of the situation. It also increases the chances that we will better understand how and why we do (and are doing) what we do, increasing our self-awareness and our effectiveness as leaders. Powerful buddy relationships bring a broader, more objective point of view to who we are as leaders and how we are to better lead.

Third, the buddy relationship is a vivid means of contribution, one that expands our range and quality of influence. It's a mutual relationship—it works both ways. To effectively be served by our buddy, we must also serve our buddy. We must be pushing, nudging, encouraging, interfering with, and demanding from our buddy, exclusively for our buddy's sake. Ironically enough, there are few things more empowering and confidence building than standing strong and tall for *someone else* (and forgetting about yourself altogether). As we noted in our discussion on contribution, when we pour ourselves into someone else, for that person's own good, we are momentarily freed from our own irrational self-doubts, and we ourselves are emboldened. It has a liberating effect that virtually nothing else in life has. In stepping beyond ourselves we gain a larger frame of reference. In that moment we become bigger people; in that moment we move closer to true adulthood.

Fourth, the feedback we get in a healthy buddy relationship (both real time and after the fact, in formal or in informal feedback sessions) is invaluable in seeing our legitimate strengths and our often-ignored weaknesses. The opportunity to receive feedback dramatically enhances our ability to make wise course corrections in how we lead others and in how we develop ourselves. It helps us to see where we are on the leadership map, without which we have little chance of getting to where we want to be. Thus, the buddyship dramatically enhances our self-awareness and our capacity to grow, to become the leaders we now know we must be.

Getting On with It: Doing the Work

Actually getting down and dirty and doing the hard work of transforming ourselves as leaders amounts to summoning the courage to literally change our minds, and there is no way to do that without paying the price and doing the difficult work detailed in part II of this book. All that you do, and that includes *every* aspect of your leadership, is a direct function of how you think and how you relate to yourself. *You will not become the leader you have it in you to be, you will not seriously approach your potential,* until *you are willing to do this challenging work.* That's a promise. That's the simple reality, like it or not. There's no way to get around it, climb over it, or crawl under it. *The only way out is through the middle: uncovering the false limiting beliefs and doing the disciplined work of daily changing your mind.*

If you have not already begun to do the essential introspective work laid out in those chapters, it's time to get it in gear. Get to it, now. You may want to quickly review chapters 4 and 5 (paying close attention to Exercise 4.1), and then apply yourself with diligence and discipline to the rest (chapters 6–12), doing the work, the thought-actions suggested in each chapter. If you have a buddy (and/or a leadership coach) you will want to bring him or her in on what you are arriving at through this work: the limiting beliefs being confronted and how you are going about changing your mind. Your buddy or coach should, in fact, help you construct your transformational strategy. He is your support mechanism. He needs to know what's what.

SUMMARY

One of the central acts of transformative leadership is the act of taking ourselves on. Simply put, the model will not work unless the leaders seeking to implement it are willing to do the work with themselves. There are no short cuts, no easy ways out for those who would lead at the transformative level. Indeed the only way out of the ordinary, short-sighted leadership endemic to the transactional model is through the middle—through the middle of your life, of your leadership, of who you must be and become with what remains of your life.

To take yourself on is to embrace the disciplined, rigorous work outlined in this book, and it is not something that is best done alone—it takes support from others who can be trusted to care and to speak the truth. Finally, it requires a fierce commitment to live and love, to contribute and cause, and to stand for the good that is and for the greatness that may yet be because of people who, like you, understand that the only time we have is now. Not tomorrow. Not next year. Now. *Now*.

Indeed, for those of you who get the urgency and possibility of this remarkable moment, of *now*, I also make you this promise. If you are willing to do the challenging work with yourself, to truly take yourself on, and do the same with your team; if you are willing to create a vivid, compelling, and audacious direction for your organization by means of its vision; and if you are willing to commit to the promise of all of your people, then, in the words of Thoreau, "you will meet with a success unexpected in common hours." That is, you'll blow people away with the magnitude of what you accomplish and the integrity with which you achieve it. And we'll all be better because you did.

One final piece of wisdom to consider, advice given to a young American Indian at the moment of his initiation:

As you go the way of life,
you will see a great chasm.
Jump.
It is not as wide as you think.[1]

EPILOGUE

IS IT TOO MUCH TO ASK?

At the end of 2008 the world was in a state of alarm, leaning toward panic. The global economy was teetering on the edge of ruin. World financial markets were in near-total collapse, and we were staring into the very real possibility of a second Great Depression. We were well aware of the fact that somehow, somewhere along the way we had really screwed things up. There wasn't the time for deep reflection, however—we had to act fast to avert the unthinkable.

Today we have pulled back from the brink but not as far back as we might like to believe. The unsavory truth is we are still operating from some of the same greed-generated and fear-based ways of thinking that got us into this mess in the first place. Based on some of the current behaviors of our most powerful financial and judicial institutions, you might imagine that nothing of great import happened at all in the fall of 2008. Not one of the financial "masters of the universe" who in perpetrating fraud blew up the world economy is in prison. Not one. In fact the reality is quite to the contrary. These business executives who cavalierly destroyed tens of millions of livelihoods and hundreds of millions of dollars in 401(k)s in order to line their own pockets are some of the same people who got pats on the back and staggering bonuses at the end of 2008, 2009, and 2010. How is this even remotely possible in a representative democracy, a supposed nation of laws?

We must be careful in answering this question to avoid jumping to the obvious explanations, because it's not just that our political leaders are fearful and corrupt, and it's not just that our most influential business leaders are criminal manipulators of a weighted system. To boil it down in this manner is far too facile and misses the deeper issues that have made this kind of corruption and such bastardization of the world of commerce possible. The problem is our thinking. The problem is that our most rudimentary ways of understanding have caused us to completely misfire as a society. We have been poorly served by our understandings about what it means to be human and what it means to live and work together in a modern, free, capitalist society.

Our thinking about business and leadership, about work and living together, remains stuck in a worldview from a time long ago and far away. While over the past fifty years we have witnessed a rate of scientific and technological development that before only a Ray Bradbury might have imagined, our thinking about human nature and what it means to lead and be led is still infuriatingly mired in a mentality appropriate for the era of steam engines and petticoats.

Consider that when we began the new millennium we were riding high on unprecedented levels of economic prosperity and general optimism about progress and human promise. We were sure that with all that we knew and with the instantaneous access to information we had we would never allow the genocidal horrors that littered the twentieth century to happen in the twenty-first century. Not now. Not in this new era. Yet, of course, before the end of first decade of the new century we had witnessed firsthand, via the Internet and twenty-four-hour cable news cycle, the slaughter of hundreds of thousands of innocents in Darfur. Our promises about how this century would be different were already to no avail. Our old ways of thinking did not serve us especially well.

And here we are once again as we painfully survey the economic wreckage of the past several years, hoping that these same old ways of thinking about life and leadership, about working and succeeding together will somehow suffice. Even as we slog our way out of the mind-boggling economic hole we have created for ourselves, the best we seem to be able to imagine is reform.

Reform? That's it? A tweak here, a nudge there, and a new piece of legislation over yonder. Are you kidding me? We can't do better than that? Reform? Really? We were just run over by a convoy of runaway

Mack trucks and barely lived to talk about it, and all we can think about is modifying the way semi-truck bumpers are made? Huh?

Don't misunderstand me. I have great faith in reform, especially when it is *only* reform that is called for. After all, it was the Protestant *Reform*ation that led to the advent of individualism—which led to the modern understanding of individual rights, which further led to a blossoming of the democratic form of government, which has ultimately led to our unprecedented prosperity and freedom. But when we've just had a global, systemic, near-death economic experience and all we can come up with is reform, well, if we are not rendered speechless by this insipid response, then it must be we have lost our collective minds. A world gone mad indeed.

Reform alone is not what's called for. Rethinking is—a fundamental rethinking of what it means to be alive and to live together and a fundamental rethinking of what it means to work together and what it means to be a leader.

Is it far-fetched to imagine that our thinking about organizational life and the leadership of those organizations might catch up to our astonishing progress in science and technology? Or is this just too much to ask of ourselves?

Is it not possible that we might bravely and honestly examine how we got to where we are without falling into hackneyed, twentieth-century (or nineteenth-century, even!) ways of thinking? Is it too much to believe that there might be new and better ways of living and leading, of working and succeeding together? Is it too much to ask?

What we need is a more vivid and accurate way of understanding the human circumstance, and we need to have that understanding inform our approach to organizational life. What we need is a smarter and more robust way of understanding capitalism itself. What we need is a willingness to step way back for a moment and gain some perspective as to where we are as a society and where we ought to be going.

Finally, what we need are a few strong, smart, courageous leaders who are willing to commit themselves to the possibility that there might be a better way—a more sustainable way of making a profit (huge profits, at that), a more meaningful and productive way of working together, a better way of leading others and leading our own lives. It doesn't have to be *my* way, the one I've outlined in this book—though I'm partial to the transformative way of leading and living. It simply must be a way that emerges from a pragmatic, non-ideological, growth-oriented understanding of human promise, of organizational life, and of leadership. And then a thoughtful consideration of how all three of these elements might work together to shape twenty-first-century society. The lightning speed with which technological change occurs today and the resulting breakneck rate at which information is created and disseminated seem to demand nothing less than this kind of intellectual courage.

Perhaps I'm wrong here, but it seems to me we are still in the midst of a crisis that we have not yet honestly addressed, a crisis of leadership character in the political, financial, and business worlds, a crisis of clarity and understanding of where we are as a species and how we must proceed. Maybe all we need are a few tweaks here, a minor adjustment there. But I don't think so, and my suspicion is you don't think so either.

We must remember that a crisis is not by itself an opportunity, despite what some of the more recent business literature suggests. It is a painful inflection point at which decisions must be made, decisions that can lead to further and deeper despair if we choose wrongly, or decisions that can avert the disaster if we choose well—*if* we have the courage to see the problem and learn from it. If we do avert the disaster, then, and only then, there might be an opening that can become beneficial, that is, that might become an opportunity.

Only in this last sense can a crisis be seen as good or leading to good, and this good only comes as we endure the pain of looking at and seeing the reality that is before us—whether in our personal lives, our professional lives, or our leadership or business models. It all depends on how we respond to the perilous moment. If we slip too easily into denial, if we fail to see the dangerous precipice on which we stand, then the looming danger may become a reality. If we simply forestall the problem by reverting to old solutions, we may delay the danger. But we must not kid ourselves. The danger remains like a perched vulture, implacably peering at us, waiting for the inevitable to run its course.

If we have the courage, however, to look and see with integrity and intelligence and to respond with the proper measures, then indeed goodness may emerge and a legitimate opportunity may present itself—if we have the character to recognize and address the fundamental questions that our circumstances raise.

We as a people, as a society in which business has become the most powerful institution, are at a point of decision. We can throw the switch one way, making a few reforms but by and large doing business as usual, the business as usual that got us into this mess. Or we can throw the switch the other way by rethinking the purpose of our individual lives and the objective of our business and organizational lives. One—reform—is relatively easy. The other, a fundamental reexamination of who we are and what we are up to as individuals, as leaders, as a society, requires a significant amount of moral courage.

But if we have the guts, we may yet turn our crisis into an opportunity, we may yet seize the day, seize the transformative moment. It is a moment that with our good-faith efforts may turn out to be replete with possibility for the new, for the better, for the good of all. *If*, that is, we have the courage to surrender to what is and still imagine what could be. For if we do demonstrate such character, the change we seek as individuals, the change we need in our most important institutions and in how we lead them, the transformation we long for as a society may all be within our reach—but only if we are able to summon that will and strength of character. It's a lot to ask, but in view of what may await us otherwise, I don't believe it is anywhere near too much to ask.

My deepest hope is that you are one of the few who have the moral courage to take yourself on, the imagination to truly lead, the openness to discover a better way to more lasting success. My suspicion is that you are one of those with the integrity and sense of purpose to answer this call, the very call of the transformative ethic.

You have heard the call many times before. You've felt the breeze of possibility caressing your face. You remember. I know you do. You've heard the whisper of beauty, reminding you of what ought, what could, what might yet be. You recall. You've even experienced the stunning flash that thrills with exquisite clarity, revealing in an instant all that is still available. You've known all along—you've known all the way down to the incandescent core of your being. And what you've known is this: It all depends on you—you and others like you.

A world that longingly awaits disclosure depends on you, depends on your loving and brave answer to the call of transformation. The rest of humanity and the future itself eagerly await your reply.

It doesn't seem too much to ask.

APPENDIX

FROM TRANSACTIONAL TO TRANSFORMATIVE: Getting It All Started

> Powerful people stand for something and have their stand alter reality.
>
> **—Unknown**

For a senior leader—CEO, president, general manager, managing director, or any other leader in a position to determine the organization's direction, structure, and culture—there are a number of things to consider before initiating the transformative process in the organization. Foremost among them is the extent to which you are willing to commit to such a formidable path. There are no shortcuts to creating a transformative organization. The rewards are incomparable, but the prices are steep. If you are still merely considering the transformative path, still trying to make up your mind, then keep considering until you are sure. You can only implement this process with both feet in the game.

If, however, you have decided to play all in, irrespective of the difficulty that may ensue, there are a few other things to consider and then keep in mind as you get the process underway.

• • •

IT'S A PROCESS

First, remember that the process *is* a process. That is, the initial stages that move an organization from the conventional into the transformative unfold over the course of time, usually a relatively long period of time, anywhere from 12 to 36 months or more. That it takes time is not surprising given that for most of us the TL approach represents a fundamental change in our understanding of what it means to lead and what the organization is meant to accomplish. For most people change of this order of magnitude is not easily achieved. The requirement, then, is urgency balanced with considerable patience and persistence. Becoming a transformative company is a bold process and involves maneuvering unexpected curves and the occasional hole in the road. It requires a long-term view and the capacity to see things through to the end, despite the difficulties that will ensue.

ENROLLMENT IS ESSENTIAL

Second, even though you may have complete authority to implement these dramatic changes, you must learn the art and skill of enrollment to its full extent. While many of the leaders who report to you may "get" the TL process quickly, almost invariably there will be others who struggle with and resist the whole idea of growth—growing themselves, growing each other, and growing their followers—as a leadership function. And yet, getting their full buy-in, getting the entire team's buy-in, is essential, a non-negotiable. That's where enrollment comes in.

Enrollment is a process whereby you, the enroller, seek to gain this buy-in from your key people, the ones to be enrolled. Enrollment amounts to helping others see the power and possibility of the transformative process (or of anything for which you seek buy-in) but seeing it *for themselves* (how it applies to them) and seeing those possibilities so clearly that they are ready and willing to, and actually do, take the action—in our case the necessary action to see TL implemented. Said another way, enrolling your followers is inspiring them so that they embrace the new method heart and soul. Your job is to help them connect the dots, to see the value for themselves and their direct reports.

The nature of the transformative model demands leaders who truly want to play at this rarefied level. Until they can see the value for themselves, until they can actually see themselves in the transformative proposition—seeing how they and those they lead and care about will benefit from it—they are unlikely to embrace it in the necessary manner.

COMPASSION IS THE FOUNDATION

The last point to keep in mind is that the transformative process expects you to care at an exceptionally high level, a level that affords you the toughness necessary to handle the uncertain and the unexpected—and helps you to live with the discomfort that such surprises often bring. Leading people to higher and better ways of being and doing can be a bit messy—it often involves dealing with the difficult emotional dimensions of the human mind and heart. Remember, as part II intimates, in delving into the hopes, fears, and desires of the human psyche we are never sure what we'll discover. Just beneath the surface there are great treasures, as well as the occasional land mine. Be prepared to handle both.

In ways that are hard to imagine from a transactional perspective, the transformative leader must care enough to *be* with her people—to be present and supportive as they go through the often-trying experiences involved in genuine leadership growth and personal development. Put more simply, you must be willing to operate from a place of authentic compassion—which, recall, literally means to suffer with someone. You must have the strength of character (the intellectual and emotional toughness) to firmly stand beside them as they confront some of the deeper obstacles that would impair their effectiveness as leaders, employees, and people.

As we've noted, for many reasons the transformative approach requires a bigness of character, a willingness to summon our greatness of spirit, a greatness we may not even know we have inside. But we do have it, and to create and lead a transformative organization it must be summoned.

A NOTE ON OUTSIDE HELP

The basic steps that follow are, as a rule, best taken with the help of an outside expert who is familiar with the underlying principles of the transformative model—this is particularly true when it comes to creating a transformative team. Retaining such an expert is not absolutely essential, but with the right collaborative consultant, the chances of your transformative quest being highly successful (and happening with greater ease and speed) are dramatically improved. Simply enough, the proper support affords greater objectivity and the results that come with a greater degree of honesty. However, it must be the right consultant, someone who clearly grasps the non-negotiable principles of TL: of growing the people, first; of having that growth lead directly to excellence; of using results (like profits) as a mechanism for growth and expansion and as a measurement of leadership effectiveness; and of having an unswerving commitment to creating the extraordinary in all domains of the organization.

If you cannot find the right person, it is better to guide the process yourself without any outside support—having the wrong person is typically far worse than having no outside support. And if you decide to use someone from within the organization to facilitate (from the organizational development or human resources area, for instance), be certain he or she has a personality strong enough to handle the ego-strength of you and your direct reports, and be certain this individual is given total permission for honesty, *absolute* honesty, with you and those on your team. Without this unswerving, non-negotiable commitment to truth telling, the process invariably gets bogged down in the typical lightweight, disingenuous bullshit that goes on in everyday social and organizational interaction—no room for transformation there, to be sure.

THE MOST ESSENTIAL STEPS

With these points in mind, then, we turn to the essential first steps of transforming a transactional organization into a transformative organization. Three of the four steps that follow (take yourself on, create a true team and team context, and create a true vision) are elaborated in other areas of the book. Revisiting those specific chapters will be helpful as you begin taking the suggested actions. The other step (enrolling your senior leaders) is explained in more depth, following.

Step 1: Take Yourself On

Hypocrisy is alive and well in the twenty-first century, and while we can get away with it in some professional domains, it does not work in the transformative model, based as it is in authenticity. To lead others in the TL process you must be doing the work yourself. This doesn't mean you're to wait until you've "transformed" yourself. It means that you're to be in a real process of growing yourself as a leader at the same time you are taking on your reports and challenging them to take themselves (and each other) on.

Since we've already spent the entire previous chapter covering this matter we won't dwell on it further here. An important point we've not yet addressed, however, is the fact that, typically, your people will be willing to go only as far as you're willing to go—there's no tolerance for do-as-I-say-not-as-I-do nonsense. If you want them to grow themselves, to push and nudge each other on to bigger, smarter, more powerful leadership capacities, then you must start doing the work with yourself and do so with the intent of taking yourself as far as you can possibly go. What's more, in effect, you'll be informally starting the entire transformative process for your organization by initiating your own transformative journey. Step 1, then, is to begin the process of taking yourself on.

Recommendations

1. Spend a full day alone—that means you alone with you—just considering the areas in your life (leadership and personal) where you may want or need to develop. It may have to do with your self-confidence (or your courage, creativity, passion, vision, consistency of commitment, et cetera). It may have to do with your effectiveness in your personal or professional relationships. It may have to do with your communication skills (one-on-one or in front of a group). It may have to do with your health, weight, fitness, and so on. Or it may have to do with creating

more vivid standards for work-life/home-life balance (working to live and not the other way around) and beyond.

2. Document these observations extensively (think on paper) in your journal and document how you might address each one of the areas you note—as systematically as possible.

3. After you've completed the day alone, enlist support—from a buddy (see "It Takes a Buddy and a Boss Who Plays" in chapter 20), friends, and/or colleagues, as well as, from experts, perhaps, (coaches, consultants, et cetera). We don't do these things called life, growth, and success alone. That is not how the game is designed.

4. After reviewing what you've written, think through and then write out your own leadership declaration (sacred leadership pact) as suggested in chapter 25. Use the example there as a model.

5. Reread the short section from chapter 25 entitled "Getting on With It: Doin' the Work," and then get it in gear! That is, do the work explained in part II.

Step 2: Enroll Your Key Leaders

Assuming that you have begun your own personal TL journey, the second step is to *enroll your team of direct reports*. If you wish to first make it clear (declare) to your followers that you and they will be going in this new direction, that is fine (you're not asking for their permission, after all). But simply telling them that the organization is embracing transformative leadership is not enough. For most individual leaders, getting them to buy in completely to a proposition is not achieved by a directive from on high. And without their full engagement, becoming a transformative organization simply won't happen. Each member of your team must be on board (or in the active process of getting on board). Every last one. What that means is pretty simple. Long before you formally initiate the transformative process in the organization (which *formally* begins with the senior team process, following), you must be working on and with your reports one-on-one, getting them to embrace the new model *for their own reasons* before it's ever formally initiated.

To enroll someone into anything is to inspire that person to see new and better possibilities for himself such that he willingly takes decisive action toward that new possibility. Thus, enrolling someone requires you, above all, to listen and thereby understand what the person being enrolled wants and needs and how your proposition (whatever it may be) will satisfy those wants and needs. It means asking your direct reports the right questions and from the insights that emerge understanding how they might be inspired or supported by or otherwise benefit from the transformative process and the creation of a transformative organization. The final step, then, would be helping them make the connection between what they want and need and how the new transformative process meets that need.

For instance, why is your direct report a leader in the first place? What is of greatest importance to her as a person (outside of work, perhaps) and as a leader (in the workplace and beyond)? What is her deepest passion when it comes to the organization and to the people being led? What are the biggest difficulties she has in her own leadership style—what are her greatest leadership liabilities that need to be addressed and greatest talents to be enhanced? And does she want, is she willing to address them? What is her secret hope for herself as a leader, for the organization, and for its people? Understanding the answer to these and other fundamental questions will allow you to help your direct reports become sincerely invested in the process.

Finally, you must be clear about *your* commitment to the TL process so that you'll more easily handle whatever fears and resistance you may encounter from them, so you'll be able to lift your followers up to where you stand, to see some of what you see. Your singular job, then, is to find a way to inspire them to play and win the big game that leadership at this level makes possible.

Recommendations

1. Begin with having a list of questions (in your head or on paper) that will help you determine the needs and wants of your team members so that you can better help them legitimately associate TL with the solution (see the example questions in the preceding

paragraphs). Remember, this act of helping the enrollee make the connection is the heart of enrollment.

2. Carefully choose the order in which you will approach each of the leaders on your team. Do not select the toughest nut first. As tempting (for some) as it is to immediately go after the chronic resisters, this is not the wisest tack. Rather, first approach those whom you suspect will be likely to "get" and embrace the transformative possibility. These more open leaders are likely to serve you and the enrollment process in at least two different ways. First, their support and enthusiasm will fortify your confidence in making the TL leap—and don't kid yourself, every true leader, irrespective of displayed independence, needs this kind of support. *Every* leader needs it. Second, the leaders who are more inclined to get the TL model may well supply you with additional reasons for making this change at this time—reasons you may have not thought of that would be of support in enrolling the resisters.

3. Formally schedule enrollment one-to-ones with each of your reports and give extra time (usually double the norm) for each of these sessions. If a typical one-to-one would be forty five minutes long, set this enrollment one-to-one for ninety. You may not need that much time, which is fine. But you may need longer than the standard forty five minutes. If you do need more time because, say, of the depth of the conversation, you don't want to have to cut the meeting unnecessarily short—there is too much at stake.

4. Go covert. Use those leaders on your team who grasp and are enthusiastic about this new model as agents, your "enrollment agents," to help you get the stragglers and late-comers on board. Two (or more) heads usually *are* better than one, especially when they're all committed to the same greater cause. Employing these differing personalities (from a careful strategic mind-set to better achieve buy-in) is just the better part of wisdom.

Step 3: Create a True Team and Establish an Organizational Team Context

Given the considerable space that has been dedicated to the transformative team (a portion of chapter 20 and all of chapters 22 and 23) what we say here will be brief but important.

Taking your team on means making sure that you truly have a *team,* rather than a functional group or worse (see The Ascending Levels of teams Figure 22.1 in chapter 22). The challenge here is not being seduced by the flaccid standards of teamness that the transactional world typically uses. A true team consists of a body of people, all of whom are fiercely committed to (*committed to*, not attracted to) the team, to its explicit purpose, to the organization's emerging vision and success, and to each other. This means each team member vividly understands why the team exists—its rationale for being a team and what it seeks to get done as a team. And it means that all the players are committed enough to one another and to the organization's victory that they consistently tell the unvarnished truth to each other out of their commitment to the common good.

Beginning the team-building process, the creation of authentic teamness at the senior executive team level, represents the formal beginning of the transformative leadership process within the larger organization. Everything that unfolds within the transformative process issues directly or indirectly from that.

Recommendations

1. If possible, employ carefully chosen outside assistance from the outset of the team development process, as noted above. There is an abundance of progressive, cutting edge consulting firms offering systematic leadership and team development help. An internet search should render numerous legitimate options. Just keep in mind the transformative principles that are essential as you begin the search process and be willing to invest the necessary time to find the right fit.

2. New books are being published almost daily on the creation of authentic teams, many of which provide suggestions for activities and workshops that lend themselves to the transformative

leadership journey. With the assistance of either your in-house OD expert or your well-chosen outside consultant, do some research and together begin the process of building the off-site workshop content and context. As you are in the midst of this creative undertaking it will serve you to revisit the process followed by Cox Arizona (chapter 20) and to reread the chapters 22 and 23 with *your* team in mind, noting the things that stand out for you and how the series of workshops you are designing might address this or that issue, personality, or situation. And then make sure that individual leadership development and transformative growth are a central piece of the team-building process you and your consultant/OD leader are designing. Finally, commit to doing at least four off-sites (one each quarter) in the coming year and schedule them accordingly. It may seem difficult to justify this time "away" from the business, but like any investment worth making, the TL process comes at price. If you are truly committed to this process (and you'd be a *fool* to attempt something on this scale without such a commitment) it will quickly begin producing dividends.

3. Demand, and I do mean *demand*, that your subordinates, all of them, aggressively commit to taking themselves and each other on in the team process (and beyond it). This expectation may begin as a request or an invitation, but over the course of time (weeks, not months) it should evolve into a given for each of your team members. After all, if you're doin' it, you've got every right to expect that they do so as well. Regardless, the TL process requires that all senior leadership team players be fully invested, all the way in. So make the demand of each of them. No exceptions.

4. There is one caveat we should consider: Given that in the beginning of the process people may struggle a bit to get their minds around what it means to grow oneself at the transformative level, some patience is in order. But even at this initial stage each member, at the very least, must be legitimately open to the possibility of their own transformative promise. Those fundamentally resistant to doing the deeper developmental work with themselves (or to even considering it) either have not been

sufficiently enrolled in your emerging vision or, to put it a bit bluntly, should not be in their position of leadership to begin with—if, that is, your intent is transformative.

5. After the TL team-building process has been successfully launched (that is, shortly after the senior team's first off-site session), begin driving TL teamness down through the entire organization (as a principle, as a vehicle for individual leadership growth, and as a means of team effectiveness and accountability). Each of your direct reports should use the same process used by the senior team (modified as appropriate) with their direct reports and begin it immediately—preferably with the same facilitator you used with your team. Your CFO or your senior VP of marketing, for instance, would be expected to do the very same work with his team of leaders, following the exact same level of commitment and expectation. This is then carried down to the next level (VP or senior director) and beyond. Synchronizing, or at least assuring there is no conflict with, the purpose declarations (each team having its own working purpose statement) within the larger array of teams (see The Concentric Circle of Teams, noted in chapter 23) is essential and is not as difficult as it might at first seem; assuring alignment should be carried out by either your OD expert or your team development consultant.

Step 4: Create the Transformative Vision

Outside of creating true teamness, there is nothing within the TL organizational hierarchy that equals the importance of the transformative vision. Its significance in the larger success of the TL model cannot be overstated.

The vision creation process is best begun at the second senior team off-site workshop. Once the vision's language and expansive commitments have been agreed upon by all members of the senior team, it is to be ratified by each member. That is, during a formal process at the leadership workshop immediately following the vision document's completion (typically the third or fourth off-site workshop), each leader on the team is to sign an official copy for himself and for every other team member—meaning that if there are nine leaders on the senior team, there should be nine copies to be signed at the ratifying process. In signing the document the leaders are declaring that they are *unequivocally committed* to the full realization of the vision. They are giving their sacred word, promising that they will do whatever they must to see the vision come to fruition. Revisit chapters 20 and 21 for the specific essentials and rationale of the TL vision.

Recommendations

1. In the second off-site workshop (probably on the second day) work on the vision document is divvied up by way of small groups that correspond to the areas the vision will be addressing, with one small group focusing on employees, for instance, and another focusing on the industry, and so on (again, see chapters 20 and 21). This workshop drafting exercise represents just the initial stage of the process, and the vision work should be carried on beyond the workshop room, subsequent to the offsite, via these small groups.

2. A part of the senior leader's job is to assure that the leaders of each small group are driven by excellence and the extraordinary but do not get bogged down in the process. The recommended time for completion and ratification should not exceed four months (which is not as long a period of time as it may seem when you consider the bigness and importance of the task).

3. Keep in mind that the vision process, the process of imagining something bold and compelling, something that has not before existed, is exceptionally difficult. So be aggressive and generous in supporting the team members who have been tasked with carrying the process forward beyond the confines and safety of the workshop room. Inspire them, perhaps by reminding them of your own commitment to the grand venture and reinforcing the central importance of the vision and the opportunity they are being given, one that will likely positively influence untold numbers of lives, within the organization and beyond. Do not let them become daunted by the heft of the task they have undertaken. Inspire, inspire, inspire!

4. Remain aware (and keep your team members aware) of the fact that this vision is something you and they intend to achieve in full. It is not something that you will merely shoot for. As big as it may be (and it must be big enough to inspire the entire organization), it is something you and they will attain together. Thus it's something that will likely force all team members to grow as leaders and as human beings in the drive to achieve it in full. Remember, that is part of the reason for its grandeur: to force your own necessary growth—all of you.

5. During the creation process, remind your team regularly that this vision represents the grand "what"—the endgame, the larger organizational objective, the intention—not the "how"—the means, method, or mechanism for realizing the intention. It's the intention that matters, the picture of what must (and shall) be—for within every true intention, remember, is an endless array of mechanisms. For now, and during the course of this entire creative process, they are to remain completely focused on the "what" or the what-must-be of the vision. The "how" will come later after the vision has been established.

6. Regardless of whether it seems to be something that will be easily achieved or something beyond the organization's current means altogether, what is to guide the creation process is the leaders' deepest yearnings for the organization and its people, what is passionately desired, the what-*MUST*-be of it all. If the picture being painted is sufficiently beautiful, truly compelling, vividly meaningful then it can become a true intention and, therefore, a brave new reality in the three-dimensional world. As a result our world (business and beyond) will be better, and untold numbers of lives will be dramatically improved. Your job, then, at the moment at least, is to keep the leaders focused on boldly conceiving what could, what should, what must, and what shall be.

CONCLUSION

These four initial steps do not cover everything, of course. Nevertheless, if you execute the four essential steps *fully and consistently*, a very strange thing will begin to happen: You will realize that many of the necessary leadership actions that must be taken to assure a successful transition from transactional to transformative leading (and to assure extraordinary organizational success) will become very nearly obvious—because, among other reasons, teamness and commitment will be on the rise at all levels, leadership capacity and confidence will be increasing dramatically, and it will all be happening within a vision-inspired context that lends itself to rational, informed decision making.

This is not to suggest that things will suddenly become easy or that all major problems will magically disappear. To the contrary, as your success increases so will the size of your problems. The difference will be that your capacity to *rationally* address these problems and not be tormented by them as you do so (that is, your capacity to have peace of mind as you deal with them) will be increased exponentially. Moreover, let's not forget that the transformative model is perhaps the single most challenging model of leadership available today. The early stages are often fraught with challenge and discomfort, but as it unfolds it is increasingly infused with joy, meaning, power, and a level of accomplishment that no other model can promise.

NOTES

Introduction: The Modern Mess and Why It Calls for the Best in Us

1. Economist Daniel Kaufmann, for instance, writing for Forbes, addresses what he describes as a culture of "subtle" corruption, noting the "various forms of corruption underlying the current global financial crisis that started in the U.S." He refers to the "legal corruption" that is found in the capacity of private interests to "influence the nation's regulation, policy and laws." Daniel Kaufmann, "Corruption and the Financial Crisis," Forbes.com, January 27, 2009.
2. In speaking about the apparent fraud at the heart of the housing bubble and the foreclosure crisis, Matt Taibbi writes that underneath the "inability" of many of the world's largest banks to keep accurate mortgage records "lies a fraud so gigantic that it literally cannot be contemplated by our leaders, for fear of admitting that our entire financial system is corrupted to the core—with our great banks and even our government coffers backed not by real wealth but by vast landfills of deceptively generated and essentially worthless mortgage-backed assets." Matt Taibbi, "Invasion of the Home Snatchers—How the Courts Are Helping Bankers Screw over Homeowners and Get Away with Fraud," Rolling Stone, November 25, 2010. Whether or not it is beyond the contemplative grasp of our leaders, few dare argue with the assertion that it was greed-inspired criminality that played a major role in the financial meltdown of 2008.
3. The $550 million (plus additional millions in legal fees) that Goldman agreed to pay was the largest penalty ever paid to the SEC (though that only amounts to roughly 3.4 percent of the company's 2009 bonus pool) and

came with a public agreement to "reform its business practices," according to the SEC's press release on the settlement.

4. As cited in Cleve W. Stevens, "Transformation as a Way of Life—and Doing Business," in *M World* (American Management Association). Fall 2010, ??? (Original quotation from article for the Huffington Post, Spring 2010).
5. As cited in Andrew Cave, "Milton Friedman Got It Wrong on Profit Being the Only Aim, HSBC Chief Green Argues," *Telegraph*, http://www.telegraph.co.uk/finance/economics/7878097/Milton-Friedman-got-it-wrong-on-profit-being-the-only-aim-HSBC-chief-Green-argues.html. July 7, 2010.
6. John Wooden and Steve Jamison, *Wooden on Leadership: How to Create a Winning Organization*, McGraw Hill, 2005, 10.

Chapter 2. An Entirely Different Game: The Emergence (and Basics) of Transformative Leadership

1. James MacGregor Burns, *Leadership*, Harper & Row, 1978.
2. Thomas Wren, "James Madison and the Ethics of Transformational Leadership," in Joanne B. Ciulla, ed., *Ethics: The Heart of Leadership*, Praeger, 1998, p. 146.
3. Peter Senge, C. Otto Scharmer, Joseph Jaworski, and Betty Sue Flowers, *Presence, Human Purpose and the Field of the Future*, Doubleday, 2004, 230.
4. Burns, *Leadership*, 4.
5. There are at least two distinct ways in which transformative leadership goes further than transformational leadership. First, generally speaking, in the sort of organization rightly called transformational, employees are much more likely to be seen as subjects (rather than objects) and as ends (rather than means to the end) than would be the case if they were in a transactional organization. Even so, typically in the transformational organization profit still remains the highest end. The people's growth and improvement are still tied to, achieved for the sake of, the bottom line. The emphasis on people's growth and importance is a vast improvement over transactional approaches, but in the end people, to a significant extent, are still the means. In the transformative model, conversely, profits matter but primarily as a tool to grow the people and as a measure of the leader's success in doing so. People are resolutely the reason for the organization's existence—profits are to be prized but only as the servant of and means to that higher end, the people's (leaders' and followers') expansion.

   The second way the transformative approach goes beyond the transformational is the extent and nature of, and the systematic approach to, the growth of the leaders and followers within that transformative structure. Unlike the transformational method (which focuses largely on changing or developing external behavior and conscious thinking and does so almost exclusively in terms of professional effectiveness), the transformative model seeks to systematically plumb the depths of the leader's person, getting the leader past conscious and unconscious, limiting false beliefs, which not only serves the leader's effectiveness in the professional domain but also serves every bit as much the leader's effectiveness in life. People are the reason for the business, and thus all aspects of the individual's life are in play.

6. Burns, *Leadership*, 20.
7. For some of the research and rationale that confirms the efficacy of transformative leadership's predecessor, transformational leadership, see Bernard M. Bass and Ronald E. Riggio, *Transformational Leadership*, 2nd ed., Psychology Press, 2006.

Chapter 3. Dispatches from the Gates of Hell: Disclosing New Worlds (and Upending the Old Ones)

1. Farhad Manjoo, "Apple Nation," *Fast Company*, July/August 2010, 70.
2. Ibid.
3. Steve Jobs, Stanford commencement address, June 12, 2005, http://news.stanford.edu/news/2005/june15/jobs-061505.html.
4. Derek Thompson, "The World's Most Valuable and Fastest Growing Brands," *The Atlantic*, May 11, 2011. theatlantic.com/business/archive/2011/05/the-worlds-most-valuable-and-fastest-growing-brands/238697/.
5. Friedrich Nietzsche, *Beyond Good and Evil*, Penguin Books, 1990, 102.

Chapter 4. Getting the Picture: A View from the Top

1. Ernest Becker, *The Denial of Death*, Free Press, 1973, 82.
2. C. G. Jung, *Memories, Dreams, Reflections*, Random House, 1961, 325. The larger context of the quotation reads as follows: "If we understand and feel that here in this life we already have a link with the infinite, desires and attitudes change. In the final analysis, we count for something only because of the essential we embody, and if we do not embody that, life is wasted. In our relationships to other men, too, the crucial question is whether an element of boundlessness is expressed in the relationship."
3. Becker, Denial of Death, 82.
4. James Robert Brown and Yiftach Fehige, "Thought Experiments," *The Stanford Encyclopedia of Philosophy (Fall 2011 Edition)*, Edward N. Zalta (ed.), last modified July 29, 2001, http://plato.stanford.edu/archives/fall2011/entries/thought-experiment/.

Chapter 6. Acknowledgment: Facing Up to Our Unconscious Condition

1. Timothy D. Wilson, *Strangers to Ourselves: Discovering the Adaptive Unconscious*, Harvard University Press, 2002.
2. The *U.S. News & World Report* article "Mysteries of the Mind: Your Unconscious Is Making Your Everyday Decisions" is a vivid articulation of

this understanding. The article cites leading neuroscientists and says, simply enough, that "our decisions, actions, emotions and behavior depends on 95 percent of our brain activity that goes on beyond our conscious awareness." Marianne Szegedy-Maszak, February 28, 2005, 52.

3. Wilson, *Strangers to Ourselves*, 6.
4. Award-winning Danish science writer, Tor Norretranders, points out that the last decade of the twentieth century was something of a watershed period as it relates to our understanding of consciousness. The 1990s, he writes, was a decade of "breakthroughs in the scientific acknowledgement that man is not transparent to himself." At the heart of this breakthrough in our understanding was the "knowledge that has been apparent for the last thirty years: that the ratio of what we sense [with the unconscious] to what we perceive [consciousness] is 1,000,000 to 1." Tor Norretranders, *The User Illusion: Cutting Consciousness Down to Size*, Penguin , 1998, 161.
5. Norretranders says that what "we actually experience [with our conscious minds] has acquired meaning before we become conscious of it." Norretranders, *The User Illusion*, 187. That is to say, long before we ever perceive an experience of fear, joy, doubt, love, anxiety, et cetera, our unconscious mind has already determined our reaction, our emotional response, even our intellectual understanding and interpretation of it.

Chapter 9. Recognition: Seeing Our Personal Paradigms

1. Thomas S. Kuhn, *The Structure of Scientific Revolutions*, University of Chicago Press, 1962.

Chapter 11. Changing Our Minds to Change Our Brains: The Beginnings of a Practice

1. Sharon Begley, *Train Your Mind, Change Your Brain: How a New Science Reveals Our Extraordinary Potential to Transform Ourselves*, Ballantine Books, 2007, 6. Sharon Begley has been the senior science writer at *Newsweek* and currently writes regular science columns for *The Wall Street Journal*, *Newsweek*, and other publications.
2. Ibid., 8.
3. Ibid.
4. M. M. Merzenich and R.C. deCharms, "Neural Representations, Experiences, and Change," in *The Mind-Brain Continuum*, Rodolfo Llinas and Patricia S. Churchland, eds., MIT, 1996, 61-81.
5. Norman Doidge, *The Brain That Changes Itself: Stories of Personal Triumph from the Frontiers of Brain Science*, Penguin Books, 2007, 116.
6. Merzenich and deCharms, "Neural Representations, Expriences, and Change," in *The Mind-Brain Continuum*, Rodolfo Llinas and Patricia S. Churchland, eds., MIT, 1996, 61-81.

Chapter 12. Changing Our Brains to Change Our Minds: Rewiring Our Circuits

1. See Michael S. Gazzaniga, *Human: The Science Behind What Makes Us Unique*, HarperCollins, 2008, 9.
2. Norman Doidge, *The Brain That Changes Itself: Stories of Personal Triumph from the Frontiers of Brain Science*, Penguin, 2007, 117–18.
3. David Hawkins, *Power Versus Force: The Hidden Determinants of Human Behavior*, Veritas, 1995, 45.
4. M. M. Merzenich and R.C. deCharms, "Neural Representations, Experiences, and Change," in *The Mind-Brain Continuum*, Rodolfo Llinas and Patricia S. Churchland, eds., MIT Press, 1996, 67.

Leg 2: Intention and Possibility

1. As cited in Walter Isaacson, *Einstein: His Life and Universe*, Simon & Schuster, 2007, 548.

Chapter 13. Intention: The Heart of Power

1. As cited by Evan Carmichael, "Herb Kelleher Quotes," accessed (date), http://www.evancarmichael.com/Famous-Entrepreneurs/1972/Herb-Kelleher-Quotes.html
2. John F. Kennedy, "Special Message to the Congress on Urgent National Needs, May 25, 1961," John F. Kennedy Presidential Library and Museum, http://www.jfklibrary.org/Research/Ready-Reference/JFK-Speeches/Special-Message-to-the-Congress-on-Urgent-National-Needs-May-25-1961.aspx
3. John F. Kennedy, "John F. Kennedy Moon Speech—Rice Stadium," September 12, 1962, The Multimedia Space Educators' Handbook, NASA, last modified July 21, 2011, http://er.jsc.nasa.gov/seh/ricetalk.htm
4. While the three requirements for true intentionality would seem self-evident in their simplicity and logic, I first encountered them in the philosophical, scientific, spiritual writings of Deepak Chopra. See especially *The Spontaneous Fulfillment of Desire: Harnessing the Infinite Power of Coincidence*, Three Rivers Press, 2003.
5. Albert Einstein, letter of 1950, as quoted in the *New York Times*, March 29, 1972.

Chapter 15. Contribution: The Soul of Power

1. *William James: Writings 1902-1910: The Varieties of Religious Experience / Pragmatism / A Pluralistic Universe / The Meaning of Truth / Some Problems of Philosophy / Essays*, Library of America, 537.
2. Thomas Lewis, Fari Amini, and Richard Lannon, *A General Theory of Love*, Vintage, 2000, 153.

3. "Commencement Address by Dr. Paul Zak," *SPE Newswatch* 2, no. 1 (2003): 5.
4. Lewis et al., *General Theory of Love*, 157.
5. Ibid., 87.
6. As cited in *A Joseph Campbell Companion: Reflections on the Art of Living*, Diane K. Osbon, Harper Collins, 1991, 37.
7. Viktor Frankl, *Man's Search for Meaning: An Introduction to Logotherapy*, 4th ed., Beacon Press, 1992.

Chapter 16. In Search of Adulthood: Fear and Loathing in Guestville and Playing to Win

1. As Harvard's Robert Putnam points out in *Bowling Alone*, today more than ever we see the disintegration of what he calls "social capital," the breakdown of "the very fabric of our social connections," from which we draw our sustenance as human beings. Robert Putnam, *Bowling Alone: The Collapse and Revival of American Community*, Simon & Schuster, 2000.
2. Paul Tillich, *The Courage to Be*, Yale University Press, 1952.
3. As cited in *A Joseph Campbell Companion*, 297.
4. John Wooden and Steve Jamison, *Wooden on Leadership*, McGraw-Hill, 2005, 10.

Chapter 18. Experiments in Radical Honesty: The World has Forever Changed—So Must How We Lead

1. See Lynne C. Lancaster and David Stillman, *The M-factor: How the Millennial Generation is Rocking the Workplace*, Harper Collins, 2010.

Chapter 22. The Transformative Team and the End of a Myth: Beyond Laziness and Fear

1. Warren G. Bennis and Patricia Ward Biederman, *Organizing Genius: The Secret of Creative Collaboration*, Perseus, 1997, 1.
2. M. Scott Peck, *The Road Less Traveled: A New Psychology of Love, Traditional Values and Spiritual Growth*, Simon & Schuster, 1978.

Chapter 23. A Leadership Team that Actually Leads: Rising Above the Reasonable

1. As cited in *A Joseph Campbell Companion*, 297.

Chapter 24. The Transformative Organization: Playing the Big Game

1. Nested teamness, where all teams are ultimately held by the senior team, draws loosely from the integral philosophy of Ken Wilber and his notions of "transcending and including" and the larger web of being.

2. All failures are not created equal. There are good and bad failures. Well-led TL organizations know the difference: a "good failure" is a well-chosen risk—imaginative, thoroughly examined with sufficient input, and then executed with discretion and strength; a bad failure results from inadequate forethought or poor execution, or simply wasn't worth trying in the first place—insufficiently imaginative or bold, say, or not potentially rewarding enough to warrant the risk. That is, the smart transformative leader can distinguish between the courageous and the foolhardy risk.
3. Howard Schultz and Joanne Gordon, *Onward: How Starbucks Fought for Its Life Without Losing Its Soul*, Rodale, 2011, 9.

Chapter 25. Taking Yourself On as a Leader: The Only Way Out Is Through the Middle

1. Joanne B. Ciulla, "Leadership and the Problem of Bogus Empowerment," in Joanne B. Ciulla, ed., *Ethics: The Heart of Leadership*, Praeger, 1998, 63.

Chapter 26. From Transactional to Transformative: Getting It All Started

1. As cited in *A Joseph Campbell Companion*, 298.

ANNOTATED BIBLIOGRAPHY

Readers who seek more information on some of the topics discussed in the text can consult the following works.

Mind and Consciousness

ERNEST BECKER, *The Denial of Death,* Free Press, 1973. In this Pulitzer Prize–winning book, the well-regarded American scholar considers the modern predicament. In an intellectually and emotionally challenging manner he asks the reader to consider what it means to live life from a greater degree of existential honesty—by accepting our mortality with a "heroic" determination to live for something larger than ourselves. It's a complex book that should be read carefully, but it is worth the effort that it requires, especially for those who are committed to faceing the deeper riddles of existence and life. Highly recommended.

JOSEPH CAMPBELL, *The Hero with a Thousand Faces*, 3rd ed., Pantheon Books, 2008, and *A Joseph Campbell Companion: Reflections on the Art of Living*. Edited by Diane K. Osbon. Harper Collins, 1991. *The Hero with a Thousand Faces* may be the renowned mythologist's most influential work. In it he shows, in myths that transcend time and place, how the archetypal hero must descend into the place of great peril and darkness, but being supported by supernatural forces the hero is able to win a great and decisive victory and return to society with a boon that if received will bring great good to the world of men and women. From the perspective of the transforming leader, it amounts to nothing less than the transformative act of taking oneself on—descending deeply into the nether reaches of the artificial self (into the unconscious) and winning a victory of an emerging, authentic self, then returning to serve the greater good of society by way of the organization and leading as an act of contribution. *A Joseph Campbell Companion* is a collection of excerpts of Campbell's lectures and writings collected by one of his students, Diane Osbon. It provides an overview of the sweep of his work and thought, including what he means by his famous (and famously misconstrued) phrase, "Follow your bliss."

VICTOR FRANKL, *Man's Search for Meaning: An Introduction to Logotherapy,* 4th ed., Beacon Press, 1992. In this classic, a philosophical and psychological tour de force, the famed psychoanalyst, professor, and Holocaust survivor reveals what it means to live with courage, power, and love. Frankl convincingly argues that the most basic human motivation is the will to meaning: "For success, like happiness cannot be pursued; it must ensue, and it only does so as the unintended side-effect of one's dedication to a cause greater than oneself or as a byproduct of one's surrender to a person other than oneself." From the transformative point of view, this brilliant memoir is mandatory reading.

DAVID HAWKINS, *Power Versus Force: The Hidden Determinants of Human Behavior,* Veritas, 1995. Hawkins is a psychiatrist who in recent years has become more of a spiritual teacher than a conventional psychological thinker. Though some of his methods are questionable (for example, calibration via kinesiology), his overall philosophical message in *Power Versus Force* is commendable, an understanding that aligns with the "perennial philosophy" (see Aldous Huxley, following). It is founded on the notion that the lower-level emotions or states of mind (shame, anger, and sadness, say) are based in fear and amount to a forceful way of being, while the higher states (courage, confidence, compassion, and so on) are based in love and amount to authentic power.

ALDOUS HUXLEY, *The Perennial Philosophy,* Harper & Row, 1945. Known more for his novels (including *A Brave New World* and *After Many a Summer*), short stories, and essays, Huxley wrote this philosophical and metaphysical treatise as a popularization of the much older belief that all of the world's great religions possess or emerge from a universal truth manifest in the higher virtues and ethical standards that transcend cultural and historical context and are based in the one true ground of all being, the divine "Reality." The philosophy offers a rationale for, among other things, the need for meaning and the importance of selfless service of another—love and contribution.

ABRAHAM H. MASLOW, *Toward a Psychology of Being,* 3rd ed., John Wiley & Sons, 1999; *The Farther Reaches of Human Nature,* Penguin Books, 1971; and *Religion, Values, and Peak-Experiences,* Viking Penguin, 1970. The president of the American Psychological Association in 1968 and the founder of humanistic psychology, Maslow is most famous for his hierarchy of needs schema and his assertion of the importance of self-actualization via the realization of B-values (beingness values). One of the most influential psychologists of the twentieth century, his determination not merely to study mental illness but also to understand the healthy mind led to a more serious study of human potential and served as a backdrop for the human potential movement of the late twentieth century. A superficial reading of Maslow can lead to a misunderstanding of his view of human nature that is overly sanguine. Maslow's brilliance and contribution, however, is best understood in his ability to balance the fatalism often present in the interpretation of psychology by his predecessors with his well-founded sense of the emergent possibility of humankind and human society.

ROLLO MAY, *Freedom and Destiny,* Dell, 1981. May was an existential psychologist, an esteemed psychoanalyst who was a friend and student of the theologian Paul Tillich. May united the philosophy of existentialism with humanist psychology to form a unique understanding of the human condition, reflected in his numerous works (including *Love and Will,* Norton, 1969, and *The Courage to Create,* Norton, 1975). In *Freedom and Destiny* he addresses the tension between seeming polar opposites: destiny, "the patterns of limits and talents that constitutes the givens in life," and freedom, the capacity in the face of these givens to choose who and how we will be and what we will do. His understanding of destiny and how a healthy person can choose in the face of it has extensive implications for authentic personal and leadership development.

TOR NORRETRANDERS, *The User Illusion: Cutting Consciousness Down to Size,* Penguin Books, 1998. Norretranders is Denmark's leading science writer. The author of numerous books, his interest has primarily been on the interactions between science and society. In *The User Illusion*, he makes a compelling, if at times troubling, case for the extent to which we are not the conscious masters of our destiny that we would like to believe we are—because the conscious mind processes far less information at a vastly slower speed than does the unconscious part of our minds. An understanding of our true condition of consciousness, however, is not a fatalistic proposition. Properly understood, it liberates us to an embrace of the sublime, of the possibilities of beauty, joy, love, and pleasure that await those who disabuse themselves of the user illusion.

PAUL TILLICH, *The Courage to Be,* Yale University Press, 1952. One of the most powerful public intellectual voices of the mid-twentieth century, Tillich addresses the anxiety of the modern person and does so in a way that is both readable and challenging. As poignant and applicable today as when it was first written sixty years ago, *The Courage to Be* incisively frames the courage to be an individual (not unlike the courage required for self-expansion) within the balancing context of the courage to be a part of larger society (not unlike the courage to truly lead others). The intelligent leader must comprehend both expressions of courage.

TIMOTHY WILSON, *Strangers to Ourselves: Discovering the Adaptive Unconscious,* Harvard University Press, 2002. Wilson is the Sherrell J. Aston Professor of Psychology at the University of Virginia and a respected scholar and researcher of self-knowledge. His research suggests the difficulty in the domain of self-knowledge, due in no small measure to the extent to which our perceiving apparatus remains out of conscious view. *Strangers to Ourselves* is a smart, readable explanation of the nature of the unconscious domain that places our current understanding of mind within its larger historical context.

Neuroscience

SHARON BEGLEY, *Train Your Mind, Change Your Brain: How a New Science Reveals Our Extraordinary Potential to Transform Ourselves,* Ballantine Books, 2007. Begley is one of the preeminent science writers in the United States and was the science editor and a science columnist for *Newsweek* and a science columnist for *The Wall Street Journal.* She has received numerous awards for her writing and for her contribution to the general public's understanding of important scientific issues. In *Train Your Mind, Change Your Brain,* she skillfully weds recent breakthroughs in neuroscience and neuroplasticity with the discipline of focused meditation of Buddhism to suggest the remarkable capacity we have to change the way we understand and experience life.

NORMAN DOIDGE, M.D., *The Brain That Changes Itself: Stories of Personal Triumph from the Frontiers of Brain Science,* Penguin Books, 2007. A Canadian-born psychiatrist, psychoanalyst, and researcher, Doidge currently serves on the faculty of both the Columbia University Center for Psychoanalytic Training and Research and the University of Toronto's department of psychiatry. His best-selling book, *The Brain That Changes Itself,* introduces the profound breakthroughs emerging in the study of neuroplasticity and how it is transforming the lives of ordinary people around the world. A compelling, if startling, read.

MICHAEL S. GAZZANIGA, *Human: The Science Behind What Makes Us Unique,* Harper Collins, 2008. Gazzaniga is the director of the University of California, Santa Barbara's SAGE Center for the Study of Mind and is one of the world's top researchers in the field of cognitive neuroscience. *Human* is a smart consideration of the questions of what makes us human, what separates us from other life forms, and what all of that means for our understanding of consciousness and social interaction.

THOMAS LEWIS, M.D., FARI AMINI, M.D., and **RICHARD LANNON, M.D.,** *A General Theory of Love,* Vintage, 2000. Drs. Lewis, Amini, and Lannon are professors of psychiatry at University of California, San Francisco School of Medicine, and in *A General Theory of Love* they apply recent understandings in neuroscience to demonstrate the extent to which love and its rhythms are essential in the formation and healthy functioning of the brain and in the realization of emotional stability and life effectiveness.

BRUCE LIPTON, *The Biology of Belief: Unleashing the Power of Consciousness, Matter and Miracles,* Elite Books, 2005. *The Biology of Belief* represents Lipton's fascinating, somewhat controversial argument employing breakthroughs in neuroscience and cellular biology to contend that our thoughts and general brain functioning affect all aspects of our bodily functions. A developmental biologist holding a PhD from the University of Virginia, Lipton energetically and persuasively contends that epigenetics offers an understanding of the connection between mind and matter.

M. M. MERZENICH and **R.C. DECHARMS,** "Neural Representations, Experiences, and Change," in *The Mind-Brain Continuum,* Rodolfo Llinas and Patricia S. Churchland, eds., MIT Press, 1996. One of the foremost experts in the world on brain plasticity, Merzenich is a pioneer in the study and application of brain enhancement and a professor emeritus of neuroscience at the University of California, San Francisco. A student and colleague of Merzenich, Christopher deCharms is a neuroscientist, entrepreneur, and inventor and has published multiple peer-reviewed articles.

ANDREW NEWBERG and **MARK ROBERT WALDMAN,** *Why We Believe What We Believe: Uncovering Our Biological Need for Meaning, Spirituality, and Truth,* Free Press, 2006. Newberg and Waldman explore the neurobiological basis for some of life's most enduring questions and why we have the unavoidable need to have them answered. It's a thoughtful exploration of crucial ideas.

JEFFERY M. SCHWARZ, M.D., and **SHARON BEGLEY,** *The Mind and the Brain: Neuroplasticity and the Power of Mental Force,* Harper Collins, 2002. Schwarz is a research professor of psychiatry at the

UCLA School of Medicine. *The Mind and the Brain* is an intriguing look at both the implications of advances in neuroplasticity and their impact on the philosophical debate regarding the distinction between (or conflation of) the mind, on the one hand, and the brain, on the other.

PAUL J. ZAK, ed., *Moral Markets: The Critical Role of Values in the Economy*, Princeton University Press, 2008. Zak is one of the founders and leading voices of the new science of neuroeconomics, a multidisciplinary field that seeks to better understand and inform human decision making based on, among other things, recent breakthroughs in neurobiology. Zak, a professor at Claremont Graduate University in Southern California, earned his PhD in economics from the University of Pennsylvania and completed a fellowship in brain imaging at Massachusetts General Hospital. He is the author of numerous scholarly articles, including, with Robert Kurzban and William T. Matzner, "The Neurobiology of Trust," *Annals of the New York Academy of Sciences 1032* (2004): 224–227.

Leadership, Business, and Society

BERNARD M. BASS and **RONALD E. RIGGIO,** *Transformational Leadership,* 2nd ed., Psychology Press, 2006. According to James MacGregor Burns and Georgia Sorenson, "The study of leadership has many mothers, but it was Bernie Bass who became its driving force." Bass is the scholar who formalized the measurement of transformational leaders and their impact on the motivation and performance of their followers. Over the course of his illustrious career he published more than 400 scholarly articles and 26 books. In *Transformational Leadership*, co-written with colleague Ronald Riggio of Claremont McKenna College, he articulates a comprehensive review of the theory and empirical research behind the transformational leadership methodology.

WARREN G. BENNIS, *On Becoming a Leader,* Addison Wesley, 1989; *An Invented Life: Reflections on Leadership and Change*, Addison Wesley, 1993; and with co-writer Patricia Ward Biederman, *Organizing Genius: The Secret of Creative Collaboration*, Perseus, 1997. The *Financial Times* said that Bennis was "the professor who established leadership as a respectable academic field," and *Forbes* once referred to him as the "dean of the leadership gurus." The most recent of his 30 books (written or edited) was published in 2010, but the classic *On Becoming a Leader* was a bestseller and a finalist for a Pulitzer Prize. A gifted writer and shrewd social observer, he remains one of the towering figures in leadership studies. He is the founding chairman of University of Southern California's Leadership Institute, is a distinguished professor of business administration at the USC Marshal School of Business, and chairs the advisory board of the Center for Public Leadership at Harvard University's Kennedy School of Government.

JAMES MACGREGOR BURNS, *Leadership,* Harper & Row, 1978. Pulitzer Prize–winning author, groundbreaking scholar of leadership, and world-class historian, Burns is the professor of government who first popularized the distinction between transforming leadership and transactional leadership. In his seminal work, *Leadership,* Burns draws out the distinction, placing emphasis on the power and efficacy of the moral leadership of the "extraordinary leader"—the transforming leader—who makes the being and becoming of his followers his primary focus of attention. The authority of Burns's elegant voice is but one of the reasons he is viewed not only as one of America's preeminent political scientists but also one of its compelling social philosophers. Any serious study of leadership requires at its beginning a careful consideration of Burns's *Leadership.*

JOANNE B. CIULLA, ed., *Ethics: The Heart of Leadership,* Praeger, 1998; and *The Working Life: The Promise and Betrayal of Modern Work,* Three Rivers Press, 2000. Ciulla holds the Coston Family Chair in Leadership and Ethics at the Jepson School of Leadership Studies at the University of Richmond and is one of the leading academic voices on the interplay between moral decision making and leadership.

DANIEL GOLEMAN, *Social Intelligence: The New Science of Human Relationship,* Bantam Dell, 2006. The psychologist and author who redefined what we mean by intelligence and made "emotional intelligence" an everyday term, Goleman (who earned his PhD from

Harvard) brilliantly argues for our ineluctably social nature by artfully combining the latest research in biology and neuroscience. *Social Intelligence* is a fascinating read for anyone who would better understand the implications of our sociability for better living life and leading others.

CHRIS HEDGES, *Empire of Illusion: The End of Literacy and the Triumph of Spectacle*, Nation Books, 2009. Hedges is a trenchant social observer and Pulitzer Prize–winning journalist and has taught at Columbia University, New York University, and Princeton University. He holds a master's of divinity degree from Harvard University. In *Empire of Illusion*, Hedges makes a disturbing yet compelling case for his contention that our society has embraced a culture of illusion. We have blithely diverted our attention from environmental, political, economic, and moral decay, and thus, he argues, are in the process of dying. While unsettling, this book is important for anyone committed to leading societal change.

THOMAS S. KUHN, *The Structure of Scientific Revolutions*, University of Chicago Press, 1962. The publication of Kuhn's most important work was a watershed moment in the history and philosophy of science. Kuhn forced us to come to terms with the subjective nature of knowledge and scientific knowledge in particular, pointing out that progress occurs as a result of the upset of "normal science"—the realization that the prevailing theories may not be able to account for a new array of data and that better theoretical constructs might provide a more compelling yet simpler explanation of the world. A paradigm shift, he says is the result of sociological functions, enthusiasm, and intellectual promise. *The Structure of Scientific Revolutions* is not an easy read but provides an understanding of the larger implications of subjectivity and radical cultural change.

ROBERT D. PUTNAM, *Bowling Alone: The Collapse and Renewal of American Community*, Simon & Schuster, 2000. In an age of social media and Internet "friends," the social change called for must address the decline of what Putnam labels "social capital," or true civic life. *Bowling Alone* is important on many levels and especially so for the leader who would understand the challenges, responsibilities, and opportunities faced by the modern organization in light of this decline in communal activity. Putnam is the Peter and Isabel Malkin Professor of Public Policy at Harvard University.

PETER M. SENGE, *The Fifth Discipline: The Art and Practice of the Learning Organization,* Doubleday, 1990; and, with C. Otto Scharmer, Joseph Jaworski, and Betty Sue Flowers, *Presence: Human Purpose and the Field of the Future,* Doubleday, 2004. Senge is the director of the Center for Organizational Learning at MIT Sloan School of Management and was named by the *Journal of Business Strategy* as the "Strategist of the Century" for the twentieth century. A remarkably original thinker, Senge represents a progressive sensibility of atypical breadth and depth. *Presence* is an imaginative, important, and underestimated work that considers the human predicament and can be read as a meditation on change and possibility.

JOHN WOODEN and **STEVE JAMISON,** *Wooden on Leadership: How to Create a Winning Organization,* McGraw-Hill, 2005. The legendary men's college basketball coach here displays his unconventional transformative leadership principles for all to see. Though his guiding ideals are simply and clearly articulated, it takes a keen eye to grasp the depth and meaning of this unpretentious Midwestern sage.

J. THOMAS WREN, ed., *The Leader's Companion: Insights on Leadership through the Ages,* Free Press, 1995. Wren is professor of leadership studies at the Jepson School of Leadership Studies at the University of Richmond. *The Leader's Companion* is a compendium of some our best historical and contemporary leadership thought.

INDEX

R

LIST OF BOXES, EXERCISES, FIGURES, AND TABLES

CHAPTER 11

CHAPTER 12

CHAPTER 17

CHAPTER 20

CHAPTER 22

CHAPTER 23

CHAPTER 24

CHAPTER 25

ABOUT THE AUTHOR

CLEVE STEVENS has worked in the field of leadership development for twenty-five years, working with corporate executives in Asia, Europe, and North America. He holds a BA from the University of California at Irvine, a Master of Divinity degree from Princeton Theological Seminary, and a PhD in social ethics from the University of Southern California. Cleve has taught at the graduate and undergraduate level at USC, Beijing University, and North Eastern University (China), has published numerous articles on leadership and the psychology of leadership, and was recently featured in the *Sunday Times* of London.

Dr. Stevens is the founder and president of the Los Angeles based leadership consulting firm, Owl Sight Intentions, Inc. When not on the road with clients, he is either at home in Southern California or, in the winter months, pursuing his first love, snow skiing anywhere there's good snow.